Books by W. S. Merwin

POEMS

Selected Poems 1988
The Rain in the Trees 1988
Opening the Hand 1983
Finding the Islands 1982
The Compass Flower 1977
The First Four Books of Poems 1975
(INCLUDING THE COMPLETE TEXTS OF
*A Mask for Janus, The Dancing Bears,
Green with Beasts* AND *The Drunk in the Furnace*)
Writings to an Unfinished Accompaniment 1973
The Carrier of Ladders 1970
The Lice 1967
The Moving Target 1963
The Drunk in the Furnace 1960
Green with Beasts 1956
The Dancing Bears 1954
A Mask for Janus 1952

PROSE

The Lost Upland 1992
Unframed Originals 1982
Houses and Travellers 1977
The Miner's Pale Children 1970

TRANSLATIONS

From the Spanish Morning 1985
Four French Plays 1985
Selected Translations 1968–1978 1979
Osip Mandelstam, Selected Poems
(WITH CLARENCE BROWN) 1974
Asian Figures 1973
Transparence of the World (Poems by Jean Follain) 1969
Voices (Poems by Antonio Porchia) 1969, 1988
*Products of the Perfected Civilization
(Selected Writings of Chamfort)* 1969
*Twenty Love Poems and a Song of Despair
(Poems by Pablo Neruda)* 1969
Selected Translations 1948–1968 1968
The Song of Roland 1963
Lazarillo de Tormes 1962
Spanish Ballads 1961
The Satires of Persius 1960
The Poem of the Cid 1959

W. S. Merwin

THE
LOST
UPLAND

"Là-bas il n'y a que des pierres. C'est le causse perdu."

Henry Holt and Company   New York

Henry Holt and Company, Inc.
Publishers since 1866
115 West 18th Street
New York, New York 10011

Henry Holt® is a registered trademark
of Henry Holt and Company, Inc.

Copyright © 1992 by W. S. Merwin
All rights reserved.

Published in Canada by Fitzhenry and Whiteside Ltd.,
91 Granton Drive, Richmond Hill, Ontario L4B 2N5.

Library of Congress Cataloging-in-Publication Data

Merwin, W. S. (William Stanley).
The lost upland : stories of southwest France / W. S. Merwin. —
1st Owl book ed.
p.   cm.
Contents: Foie gras — Shepherds — Blackbird's summer.
1. Country life — France, Southwest — Fiction.   2. France,
Southwest — Fiction.   I. Title.
[PS3563.E75L67   1993]
813'.54 — dc20   93-12162
                                                                              CIP

ISBN 0-8050-2593-6

First published in hardcover by Alfred A. Knopf in 1992.

First Owl Book Edition — 1993

Printed in the United States of America
All first editions are printed on acid-free paper. ∞
1   3   5   7   9   10   8   6   4   2

"Foie Gras" was originally published in *The New Yorker*.
"Shepherds" was originally published in *The Paris Review*.

For JANNAH *and* SERGE ARNOUX

Contents

The Lost Upland

Foie Gras

A S HIS paunch extended and late middle age tightened around him, Fatty the Count came to rely more and more heavily upon M. Bruyère's pharmacy to furnish him with pâté de foie gras. An unlikely source, on the face of it, even in a region where a carpenter, a blacksmith, or a wool merchant might be a reputable supplier of illegal liqueurs, and where the local creosote factory, to the despair of young planners in the prefecture, all but closed every summer at the height of the strawberry season, while the workers stayed home to pick and market their strawberries. And where a nearby market town full of noble towers had fallen into dilapidation as the eventual result of a mysterious abundance of truffles in the woods, which had increased unpredictably and lasted just long enough for everyone in the neighborhood to forget any form of gainful employment except truffle hunting and professional discussion of the subject in the over-flowing cafés opened and kept by speculators with accents. A region where, when the rumors of mushrooms began to race in the autumn, a priest could be pointed out who had raised a cudgel in defense of a patch of chestnut forest in which Divine Providence annually re-vealed the prized boletus exclusively for him.

M. Bruyère's pharmacy certainly did not give public notice of of-fering pâté de foie gras, or any comestible more substantial than herbal teas, black currant throat pastilles, or an expensive line of translucent dietary crackers prescribed for diabetics, for sale across the counter. Probably it never had. No one from the small town of Sérignac itself

3

would have been likely to ask aloud for such a product in the store, among the carefully polished antique jars, the high racks of the latest high-quality toothbrushes, the venerable tiers of black and gold tin medicine boxes, the arrays of luxury soap, the fine, righteous, clinical smells, and in the summer the life-size cardboard young woman in a bikini, recommending suntan lotion. If there had ever been such a request—from a tourist, say, in August (for some foreigners apparently imagined that a pharmacy was obliged to supply everything)—and it had been addressed to one of the serious young women clerks in pastel smocks, she would have said plainly and definitely, "No." If it had been M. Bruyère, the son, who had been asked, he would have managed not to hear the question once or twice—a tactic acquired, but acquired without style of any kind, from his father. Failing that, he would have ignored the question, busying himself in a search on an upper shelf, rearranging small boxes in the recesses of the stockroom. But if reminded at last, he would have shaken his head, with a brusqueness, a distinctness, that might have surprised anyone who had been watching him while waiting.

M. Bruyère, the son, spoke little at any time, and he resembled his father so little, in feature and manner, that no one who did not know the relation would have suspected it, and their dissimilarity provoked, for years, the inevitable mocking speculations, which settled into patterns in no way modified by considerations of Mme. Bruyère, the mother: her ghostly reticence, her frail health, her colorless piety, her cold, shadowy air, her whine, and the prevailing mute lumpishness that characterized her family, which had nevertheless provided her with a large dowry and the ancient house on the back road along the valley, where she and her husband had spent much of their married life, and where M. Bruyère's family pâtés were made.

The son, in his late forties, wore his hair cut short like grass above his pale square face set upon a square white shirt that billowed slightly around the thick waist. His motions were at once jerky and lumbering, hurried and regretful. It was a surprise to hear him speak at all, and his toneless words left the impression that there had been some mistake, even when what he said was exactly to the point. He seemed to be anxious to get things over with. He had been like that in every respect, even as a schoolboy.

As for M. Bruyère, A. (for Albin), the father, it would have been hard to envisage an ordinary customer asking him to sell them something just to eat, and if anyone had done so it would have been apparent immediately that the notion was misdirected. With increasing years the elder M. Bruyère came to spend less and less time in the pharmacy itself, and to care for his own health and leisure at home in the country house where his wife's family had been born. But he continued to come in to the shop on most afternoons during the tourist season, and on the days, twice a month, when there were market fairs and the broad square in front of the pharmacy was filled with the trestles of itinerant vendors of dry goods and hardware, shoes and dolls, and the edges of the awnings above them shaded the antique jars and the elegant botanical posters in the wide pharmacy window. And when he was in the store, in his later years, he almost never donned one of the white smocks that he had worn there for half a century. He spent only part of his time behind the counter, and devoted the rest of it to standing or passing to and fro, in his impeccable suit, among the customers, seeing to the displays, and presiding like an official at a revel. An appropriate request would be received and entertained: he would stand very still, and the motionless ivory parchment of his face would tilt upward, the long polished hairless skull would tip slowly like a searchlight exploring the ceiling, the reflections in the gold-rimmed pince-nez would slide off, and an answer would come at last, so papery and hushed, and from so far away, that it seemed to be conveying a confidence of remarkable gravity, when in all probability M. Bruyère, Albin, was simply being judicious and preparing to refer the whole matter to one of his employees. Which he came to do in most cases involving ordinary commerce. Yet there was no question of his turning into a figurehead, a mere symbol of the place. He retained an astonishingly encyclopedic acquaintance with the current stock in the pharmacy, including the latest medicines and the most fashionable health nostrums and cosmetics, and he continued to discriminate without hesitation or reticence between what was valueless, however it may have been advertised, and what was of real quality; between what was merely novel and showy, and what represented a genuine advance and deserved to be included in any self-respecting pharmacy with a policy of remaining abreast of the times. This distinction was important to the reputation of his establishment, and had something to do with the fact that most of the doctors of the region referred their patients, as a matter of preference, to M. Bruyère's pharmacy—a bit more expensive, perhaps, but you could rest assured.

It was a snobbism, and no doubt it had always been a snobbism, and had perpetuated itself as such, as a kind of unspoken conspiracy in which the building was a participant.

From the beginning the pharmacy had been housed in one corner of a *palais* of indeterminate age; probably it had been built, or restored, not long after the Wars of Religion, in the late sixteenth century. The two square towers with their pointed slate roofs, joined by a Renaissance balustrade across the façade in which the slate-blue shutters appeared to be permanently closed, had come to be no more than the background to the commercial premises occupying what had once been its inner courtyard: the pharmacy was flanked, along the square, by one of the oldest cafés in town, an enterprise with a tradition of its own. Outside the tourist season it was a meeting place for the older members of the professions. There the papers, bought at the tobacco and stationery shop next door, were opened and read; excellent meals could be ordered, though the fact was not publicized and there was no menu; tickets could be bought for sporting events and for the buses, which stopped to unload there; and in the autumn, mushrooms, fresh and bottled, were for sale in the back room next to the kitchen. In the winter, students crossed the square and sat around the marble tables, in the yellow light, still wrapped in their scarves, and conferred until suppertime. Besides the café, and the stationer's, which grew more gaudy each summer with postcards and magazines for tourists, there was a grocery store on the other side of the pharmacy, around the corner from the square, in the Rue de la France. None of them had been there, of course, when the Bruyère family had acquired the building, at the time of the Revolution—a fact to which Fatty, le Comte d'Allers, had made allusion regularly, over the years, in conversations with M. Bruyère: public conversations, for they had had few others.

No one could be entirely certain of the earlier history of the *palais*. During the Revolution many records had been lost. In local—and vague—tradition the building had been the urban seat of a family of minor nobility whose name had died out before or after the building had changed hands. Even they, as the Count was content to remind listeners, had been *noblesse de la robe* and not *noblesse d'épée*. There was a possibility that the towers had passed into bourgeois possession well before the Revolution, and by the time of Louis XV had become the pride of functionaries, financiers, or lawyers. They were plain, and without any grace except their height and their age, and yet Fatty spoke as though their acquisition by a family with no title at all was a personal affront, one that he was accustomed to overlooking, in the present hopelessly vulgarized state of the world, but one of the many that he could not be expected to forget.

His allusions to the Bruyères' status as arrivistes in the noble pile facing the square were seldom more than passing slurs when he was speaking to M. Bruyère in person. In conversations outside the pharmacy he referred more openly, and more habitually, to M. Bruyère as a venerable nobody. The Bruyère family had been magistrates before the Revolution. Their sympathies during that period appear to have allowed them to survive and prosper. They had provided the town with solid citizens in each generation thereafter, and with no historic scandals. The pharmacy had been a family business for over a century. M. Bruyère, Albin, himself had twice been mayor of the town.

It must be said that M. le Comte's easy scorn did not single out the courtly withered pharmacist for unique attention. Indeed he accorded M. Bruyère almost no particular notice, and his disdain was quite as prompt in reference to the other recent mayors of the municipality. The office had been passed back and forth, or so it appeared, for several decades, among three of its most substantial burghers. Most recently it had been the charge of M. Gentiane, Henri, a wholesale wine and liquor merchant, third successor in the business, a man who lived alone, as a widower, in an ugly new house, one of the few modern buildings in the town, a stucco villa in the tiny *banlieu* behind the seventeenth-century school. M. Gentiane prided himself on the open and progressive nature of his conservatism, on his military record in the '14 war, and on his subsequent erudition in local history, a subject of which he had a more thorough and better-documented, if drier and remoter, knowledge than M. le Comte himself. He had disputed, openly, some of M. le Comte's boasts about his family's role in the region, and Fatty, whose proper name was Pierre, seldom referred to him at all, and his contempt when he did so bore more personal animus than usual.

Far more, for instance, than he displayed toward old M. Belpech, Auguste, the private banker who had been the mayor before M. Gentiane and after M. Bruyère's second term. M. Belpech, *père*, was a scion of a family of bankers that could trace its line back at least to the Wars of Religion. They had occupied, even in that period, the same massive, stately gray house along a stream that had been arched over, covered, and paved as a street only in the present century. Their small private park, with its high stone walls, survived, on the side of the house nearer the town, and M. le Comte could recall pleasant summer evenings stretching back for many years, when the guests had retired there after many sauces and many wines, to gossip and digest and nod, for a while, by lantern light, under an ancient lime tree.

M. le Comte's scorn of M. Belpech was relatively gentle and good-natured: the banker was absentminded and giggled; he scratched everywhere, and most often where it was least seemly; and bit his nails, and heard only half of what was said to him, but smiled. M. le Comte, who was called Pierre in the Belpech household, would not have given, as a further reason for his scorn, the fact that M. Belpech, who had been mayor at the time when the Germans entered the region to occupy it, during the Second World War, had walked, flat feet and all, at the head of a small deputation of the municipality's wealthier citizens, to meet the approaching troops on the road and formally welcome them to the town, presenting them the key to the *mairie* with his own hand. There were unattractive rumors about M. le Comte's own politics at that time, though all that was known was that he had held a modest post in Vichy during part of the occupation. He made fun of old M. Belpech more or less in the way that almost everyone did, but the meals in the Belpech house were good, and the family bank kept his account open, and gave him credit, for years, when there was no money in it.

His particular disdain for each of the three mayors returned tire-lessly to the desecrations of the ancient town for which each of them as individual administrators had been responsible, and some of which they remained proud of. M. Gentiane numbered among his own most estimable accomplishments the fact that he had paved over the long open square that ran from the pharmacy to the small park several blocks away, cutting down all the old lime trees and sycamores around one end of it and turning the whole area into a parking lot. M. Belpech, at the suggestion of several of the town's Rotarians whose goodwill he especially valued, had built a truck weighing station at one side of it, where there had been a small park with shaded benches, and a balustrade, along one of the town's still uncovered streams. M. Bruyère had been guilty, during his first term in office, of allowing many of the shopkeepers along the Rue de la France to destroy their sections of the ancient and elegant arcades that had stretched unbroken from one end of that street to the other, and replace them with large, rectangular, ordinary display windows set in artificial stone which looked like plastic. He had modernized the pharmacy in the same way—but to his credit, he at least, as Pierre allowed, had had the taste and decency to realize that he had made a mistake, and to regret it.

In speaking to foreigners, Pierre, M. le Comte, Fatty, might contrast the administrations of the barbarous burghers of Sérignac to his own term, during the war, as mayor of the village of Saint-Val, several miles outside town, where he lived in the small château that was all that remained of the family fortune. If he did, he would dwell upon the care and economy with which he had applied the scant municipal funds to the restoration and preservation of the ancient buildings which should indeed have been the pride of the village—including, as a matter of fact, the roof and certain essential structural work on his own house, which after all was registered as a national historic treasure, open to the public from ten until two, three days a week, for a modest entrance fee that certainly could not be expected to pay for keeping the roof repaired. He had also undertaken to house, at his own expense, and in his own château, all the village archives from the mayor's office, including documents relating to all the property in the village, some of them dating back to well before the Revolution. He would note that the papers, when they had come into his charge, in the mayor's office, had been in utter chaos, and that he had devoted many hours—gratis, and generally unappreciated—to putting them into order, a contribution that had been forgotten later, when his successor, and the village council, had asked to have the papers returned to the village office. Where, Pierre had warned them, the archives would merely be neglected once more, and left to the mercy of the rats and the damp. Whereas, while in his keeping, he had made good use of them in pursuing his researches into the history of the locality. He had even offered to serve as custodian for the papers, lodging them rent-free, and taking care of them for a token consideration if any, but of course the council was made up of small-time elected officials, know-nothings with the souls of petty functionaries, and they had insisted until at last he had returned their precious wastepaper to them.

The issue had left him embittered toward several citizens of the village, in particular toward one youngish carpenter with political ambitions—but what could you expect of someone who covered the ancient masonry of his house with gray cement, replaced the stone window frames with factory-made metal horrors, tore down the old walls along the road and put up pipe fences, and adorned his cement gateposts with large plastic dice standing on their corners, of the sort that one had come to expect outside the houses of wholesale butchers. The same person continued to circulate a rumor that the village archives had included old engravings and valuable tomes that had found their way into the antique shop which Pierre ran in one room of his château, or had simply been shown to visitors and sold. Pierre dismissed the rumor and its source. Such a person, he declared, had never had any idea of what was in the archives. He was suffering from common envy and pique at the thought that he might have missed a chance to steal something of value and sell it himself, when in fact he would not have known an engraving from the label on a bottle of cure-all, and was beneath understanding anyone who might have been concerned to rescue objects of beauty from neglect and certain destruction and to help them find their way into the hands of those who could appreciate them and would preserve them. This, he said, he had come to realize was part of his mission in life. He had helped to nurture taste in some of the bourgeois of the region whom he had supplied, from time to time, with articles of worth. Some of them remembered it. He had even helped some of them to decorate their houses when they had the sense to be aware that they did not know how to do it themselves. As for the charge that some of the engravings on their walls had been cut from old volumes by Pierre himself, with a razor blade, he scoffed at it. Half the framed engravings in France, he said, had once slept between the covers of books, where nobody saw them. Everyone knew that. Why assume that Pierre had personally cut out those that happened to pass through his hands? The subject was not worth pursuing.

His markedly different view of a mayor's role was not the only thing that kept Pierre from setting foot inside the café next to the pharmacy on Saturdays, or on days coinciding with events on the municipal calendar, when the mayors of Sérignac, past and present, tended to gather there. Their other companions at such meetings were usually the Rotarians of the town, owners of hardware stores and hotels, vendors of clothing, food, and building materials, young notaries, a young doctor or two living in a modern stucco house, a veterinarian with aspirations. They referred to Pierre, to his face and behind his back, as le Comte d'Allers. They would have described their political outlook as "evolved." It was acquisitive and cautious. Their conversation circled around money, gossip, and sports. Gossip, for Pierre, was a relentless passion, and he would have listened to anybody, but he would not have joined in, with those people. He did not concern himself with sports. When a fat woman in a large car had pulled up alongside his rusted wreck at a country intersection in midsummer, and shouted out of her window, in a thick Mediterranean accent, "My radio has broken. What is happening in the Tour de France?" Pierre had answered, "In the what?" "The Tour de France, the Tour de *France!*" she had insisted. "I'm not interested in the Tour de France," Pierre had said, and turned away with his eyes closed. "You're not interested in the Tour de *France?*" she shrieked, eyes wide, unable to believe her ears. "What *are* you interested in?" "The First Crusade and the private life of Louis XV," Pierre had replied at once, and had driven on, as he preferred to do after such exchanges through the car window, as dramatically as his battered car would manage. As for money, it was a subject that he would not have discussed among the company in the café, partly because he owed some to almost everyone there.

The same subjects, come to that, were staples of the talk in the gatherings next door, in M. Bruyère's pharmacy; and some of the same rounded fronts and faces appeared in both. But the subjects were treated differently and the protagonists occupied different roles in the neighboring establishments. Some of the habitués of the assemblies in the café always seemed to arrive as though they were attending a board meeting and were anxious not to be late. They checked the company to see who was there. They took the local soccer leagues seriously, and business ventures occupied them more often than private affairs. When M. Belpech, *père*, and his son, Jean-Paul, turned up at the café gatherings, the father stood at the edge of the group, in his dark suit, smiling his slightly embarrassed smile, looking off at nothing, and pivoting slowly back and forth on one foot while chewing on a fingernail. His son took part in the tumbling conversation, good-humored yet a little distant, as though he were there with the fondest of intentions, but between travels, in his banker's suit. And M. Bruyère himself stood silent on the margin, like M. Belpech, as the Pernods and coffees went round, and looked even more ghostly and desiccated, more like a white empty chrysalis, in the sallow fluorescent light, than he did next door in the pharmacy, with its atmosphere of a church vestibule.

There was nothing businesslike about the private gatherings in the pharmacy. The few who talked of soccer there did so with an air of indulging a taste that was no less personal for being popular. Most of those there who professed any interest in sport meant, by the word, partridge, hare, and rabbit shooting, or joining in a rare *battue* for foxes or wild boar, or even badgers, in the fall. Money, when spoken of, involved bank rates and known fortunes, the fluctuations of estates both as wealth and as land and buildings. It was spoken of gravely, deliberately, and out of earshot of the customers in the pharmacy, as though it were a family matter. And gossip—there was the tabloid chatter about people whom the speakers knew slightly, or knew about, in the region: open theft, buildings burned for the insurance, roofs collapsing, enormous fish caught, car accidents, priests, nuns, servants, lecherous veterinarians, new doctors, newborn babies found on village dumps, idiots, illnesses. And then there was the real family fare, installments of stories involving the lives and kin of the pharmacy habitués themselves. Not all of their lives and kin, of course. Most of them were staid, predictable, tight-lipped, lacking in feature. They seemed to have no stories apart from parish-register matters: marriages, births, deaths. Ailments and mishaps and losses. Anyway, it was part of their general faith in their own decorum to maintain the assumption that they were not, in fact, gossiping, but keeping abreast of the events of their time, among their peers. A responsible activity. The assumption contributed to the earnestness with which they dropped their voices and conferred about the latest developments in the private life of Bertrand Defelle, one of the stalwarts of their group, when he was not present. The way they did so, that is, once his existence became disastrous and interesting.

No one would have expected such a thing to happen, at least not until he married that woman. Bertrand, everyone agreed, was a decent, honorable, steady sort, with a small castle—really a walled country house—in a village twenty miles south of Sérignac, in which his family had lived for generations, producing notables and characters, but few scandals. His grandfather had been a freethinker and had been buried in his own grounds with an acorn in his mouth. The oak tree reminded his descendants of something or other which they might claim but could not know. There was land but not much money. Bertrand grew up in that house, went to the village school, and in his forties, a broad stocky man who drank Pernods in the village café with lifelong cronies, and *fines* after dinner with friends of his own station, he still played soccer with the village team, and tramped through the October leaves with neighbors and their dogs and guns. He had expanded the estate he had inherited, and he farmed it in a moderate, traditional manner, reforesting old abandoned farmland, planting poplars along the stream, repairing the neglected buildings. He was bluff, matter-of-fact, good-natured, and the only irregularity that could be attached to his account was the fact that he was related to Pierre, the Count d'Allers—but related to him "on the left hand," as Pierre carefully and infallibly pointed out. The mésalliance had taken place sometime before the Revolution. One of the principals had strayed from a line of local worthies with doughy faces, ponderous noses, and small, pouchy, unlit eyes, as the portraits in the old house testified. An ancient family distinguished by the name of Poulichon, and apparently by little else. Pierre pretended to know the details of the liaison and its progeny, and of the castles from his own patrimony that had drifted out of his legitimate inheritance as a result, but Bertrand merely shrugged and laughed at any allusion to the matter. By his time the ancient transgression was no longer even an anecdote; a flourish in his remoter history; a joke.

He himself had married late, and that woman, Titi—from Brigitte—was years younger than he. He was said to have found her somewhere in Marseilles or Nice or some such place, where her parents had been divorced, and it was said that at one time she had modeled clothes. Maybe she had, maybe she hadn't. Her hair had never been that color naturally—a bright rust—and she was very clever at dyeing it, but she had been known to make mistakes. Anyone could tell what magazines she paid attention to. And her figure. There was no denying that she had a pretty figure. But it was very thin. And she was obsessed with being still thinner. She starved herself until she made herself sick, of course. She followed every fad diet and some others of her own devising, and she took pills to lose weight, and they too made her sick, of course, and contributed, furthermore, to exaggerating her tempo, which was, at the best of times, that of a film run uncontrollably fast. Her voice seldom descended from a modulated shriek, and she entered every conversation before she entered the room, her high heels detonating on the polished tiles and the waxed walnut floors. She spoke of herself as a racehorse and as an Amazon, and in obedience to her Bertrand acquired blooded horses and a groom, and she took riding lessons for a while until she fell and sprained her wrist and grew bored with the routine and with the riding instructor. Sometimes she stayed in bed for days, with the curtains drawn. In fact, she made no friends. But she prided herself on her fantasy. She had the old rooms redecorated with pink and blue and yellow wallpapers covered with butterfly motifs—her signature. And Pierre laughed at her taste, but she deferred to his and bought things from his antique shop, which may or may not have persuaded him that she was amusing. He laughed to see the blue paper butterflies that she had stuck to the noses of the family portraits of Bertrand's Poulichon ancestors. He said she was original. She trilled and waved and he chattered and let fall unrepeatable asides not all of which she heard, and they waltzed from room to room to the sound of their voices.

He continued to talk of the butterflies and her originality after she started an affair that before long was a matter of common knowledge, with a veterinarian from a neighboring market town, a person of regular features and few words whom the neighbors described as scarcely more than a boy, and who everyone agreed was as vacant as a human being could be without blowing away. His father was a local politician who had been publicly accused of large-scale corruption, and was known to be implicated in at least one scandalous dispersal of public funds intended for public works. Titi went riding with the young man and brought him back to the château and locked herself in with him. She had the cook prepare meals on trays, and went and fetched them herself. It would go on like that for a day or so, and be repeated a few days later. Nobody knew what Bertrand said to her. Once he knocked her down and gave her a black eye. Some of his friends made it plain that they would no longer receive Titi in their houses. Two different priests came to talk to her about her way of life. Between episodes with her visitor she had bouts of sickness: ulcers, heart murmurs, sinister pains and blackouts. Doctors came and went, and the skyline of drugs on her night table grew more elaborate. But she paid no attention to anyone's warnings. She talked. She talked without pause, without regard for who else might be present, her voice like a steam whistle, and when she stopped talking she locked herself into her room. One afternoon Bertrand came home to find that she had left on a trip with her young companion. They went to Provence for almost a month and nobody was certain whether they would come back at all, but most who knew Titi predicted that she would be back for financial reasons if no other, even though Bertrand wired her money all the time she was away.

The pair turned up again without announcement and resumed life as before, and Bertrand took an apartment in town and spent more and more time there. Titi virtually moved her young veterinarian into the château, keeping all the shutters closed night and day. No one in the village would speak to him when they saw him. Bertrand took a job for a while as a representative for a firm that installed irrigation systems, and said he found it interesting. He refused to take action for divorce until Titi demanded that he make over the château to her. Then when he began preparations for divorce she defied him to make her leave the château. She tore the butterflies off the Poulichon portraits and ripped holes in several of the paintings. Soon after that her health collapsed altogether. She could not leave her bed. She was taken to the hospital. Multiple ulcers, a rare metabolic imbalance, and a related blood disease; a limping heart; permanent damage wrought by years of drugs and diet pills. It was said that she was dying, and she was allowed to return home. There was no question of her seeing the young veterinarian, and he was forgotten. Bertrand had two nurses move into the château, and he came nearly every day to see her, but he kept his apartment in town and slept there most nights. She went back to the hospital, was allowed to go home again, began to swell up until she was unrecognizable, her limbs the texture of a pudding. That went on all through a hot summer, and in the autumn she began to lose her sight, and by winter she was blind. She died in the coldest part of the year, in February, and was buried in the frozen ground with only a few figures around the grave.

Pierre was one of them. Throughout the whole story he had called at the château every few weeks, usually without warning—the telephone was little used in the region. While Titi's affair was in full swing he had managed to remain in possession of fresh details which he relayed, as warm as possible, expressing concern and admiration for Bertrand, and anxiety—mingled with a certain envy—for Titi, and what would become of her. He took a keyhole interest in every turn of her adventure, and he alone, in the neighborhood, pronounced the young man imbecile but attractive. He came in for an occasional unscheduled meal at the château, alone with Titi, or with Titi and her silent partner, while that lasted, or even with Titi and Bertrand, and at different times he managed to borrow money for gasoline from each of them. He declared himself to be an amoralist "except about things that mattered," and to reward his sympathy Titi sometimes remembered his weakness for foie gras—which she would not dream of eating herself, and which she said was bad for Bertrand—and slipped him a jar or two from the château kitchen as he was leaving.

Usually his calls were made in the middle of the day, and afterward he would proceed, with the latest news, to some other noble building in the region, some château or ancient manor whose owners he knew or wished to know, and favoring them with his confidences he would cement old acquaintances or form new ones. Châteaus and old houses of the region, year by year, were passing into the hands of outsiders —French from Paris or farther north, Greek, Spanish, English, American, some of them rich—whom Pierre did not know, and who did not know Pierre. "I am the Comte d'Allers," he began. He prided himself, he said, on remaining broad-minded.

His trips and visits were turned to account: usually he had an old framed engraving, mirror, or ancestral painting wrapped in a rug, or a few pieces of faience or Sèvres, scarcely chipped, picked up from somewhere or other, in the trunk of his weathered car, and would manage to bring the conversation around very quickly to the subject and fetch them in to be admired; and remarkably often he was able to persuade his hosts that he had had them in mind in choosing the objects before them, that the pieces corresponded with their own tastes and the needs of their houses, and that the price he was asking was more than fair. As he said, "a price of friendship."

And when Titi began her final decline he continued to call at the château, to learn how she was, to sit at her bedside and amuse her, perhaps. In the neighborhood they said that M. le Comte was a kind man "after all." Several of the local tradespeople whom he kept informed about the state of her health allowed him to buy cheese, coffee (for his wife), chocolate, sausage, pâté, on credit, and he was generous with his praise. He brought Titi small presents, and sometimes she told him to take this or that object when he left. Among them were things which Bertrand, later, said had come from his family and had been there for generations, but never mind, what difference did it make? There were long stretches during the story when Bertrand did not come to Sérignac—it was not his own shopping town—and the pharmacy at all; and in those times none of the cadre which gathered there after mass on Sundays had any recent tidings concerning him or that woman he had married unless Pierre happened to come in. They did not swallow his account uncritically, they assured each other, but they swallowed it provisionally. None of them went to Titi's funeral, and Bertrand left the region immediately after it, but Pierre still called at the château when he was in that part of the country, on his rounds. She had left him some odds and ends in her will. By then he knew the servants, and they gave him their news. In any case there was the ancient kinship, such as it was, and the château, like many of the more imposing ancient buildings in the region, was one which Pierre was used to pointing out to strangers as having figured at one time among the local holdings of his family. Occasionally he left the shuttered building with some book or piece of china under his arm which Titi had wanted him to have. Pierre remained for some time the chief source of information about the château and about Bertrand himself. When Bertrand came back at last he was welcomed with more warmth and sympathy than ever, but his story—what was told about him—was all but over.

Even at the height of it Pierre himself, in that group and in many others in the region, was the abiding center of gossip. He did not visit the pharmacy regularly on Sundays until his later years, when his financial affairs, which had long been dubious, became messy. For years before that, the latest rumors about him were added continually to the body of legend that everyone in the circle knew, some of it half forgotten, as in any family. When he did turn up, on a Sunday morning, someone would have seen him at church and spread the word, and someone would see him before he arrived, in the course of his shopping: the short, pudgy figure sailing along with tiny steps on tiny fat feet, nose in the air and belly far in advance of the rest of him. They awaited him—they braced themselves for his arrival—with a weary and only partly acknowledged pleasure. He could be counted on to enliven their morning, but some of them would have to pay for it, in vexation or in substance, or both.

He would step inside the glass door and stand on the black and white tiles, holding his shopping bag, turning slowly like a small pouter pigeon, greeting them. His face was fat, egg-smooth, and pale, and he lisped. His clothes were as undistinguished on Sundays as on every other day: baggy pants, short-sleeved pea-soup-colored shirt, an old gray cardigan or grubby gabardine. He dressed like any retired shopkeeper, only much worse. His clothes were never clean, and they smelled, and so did he, body and breath, an unhesitating fetor. He puffed, and they returned his greeting as though they had been caught at something. If someone asked about his health he would explain how he suffered with it: his headaches, palpitations, liver—and M. Bruyère might be called upon to refill a prescription, and put it on the bill.

The older and more courtly of the group might inquire as well about his family, starting—and usually ending—with Madame, his mother, while she was alive, for she spent the last fifteen years of her life bedridden. Apart from the banker's son, and Bertrand, no one in the circle had been out to Pierre's château for many years, but they all knew everyone in the family, and most of them could remember Mme. la Comtesse when Pierre had been a youth white as a frog's belly, and his mother a dark, determined, imperious woman, stocky and prone to gesture, who dressed in shiny blacks and many plumes when she whirled into town in a carriage with a coachman, a footman, and more plumes in the horses' silver-buckled harness. In those days she was already a widow. Some of the elders of the circle still referred to her as Mme. la Générale: Pierre's father had been a general in the colonies, and had died when Pierre was a child. Pierre, in some company, claimed that his father's death had been heroic and tragic. In others, he admitted, more prosaically, that M. le Comte, his father, had succumbed to an outbreak of cholera or some tropical disease. But it was certain that the elder M. le Comte's foot, which had been amputated after the Battle of Tonkin, had been preserved in some darkening fluid and was still to be seen in a jar, at the château. To be seen? It was displayed: taken down ceremoniously from the top shelf in a linen cupboard and thrust in front of those visitors who seemed deserving of special attentions. One unfeeling foreigner had referred to it as Pierre's pedigree.

After his mother took to her bed, visitors—particularly foreigners, if they were of interest—were led in to see her, and when she was feeling up to it, as she usually was, she would hold court. Pierre would go in first and plump up the pillows and pull her into a sitting position and hold a mirror so that she could powder her face with its two or three remaining front teeth and push her hair back under the lace nightcap that covered her head, and perhaps help her into a clean nightgown. And she would receive, holding out her twisted arthritic fingers, offering her cheek to be kissed, urging her guests to be seated and tell her about themselves, sending Pierre for a tray and glasses so that she could press them to ratafia or walnut liqueur or—if they were unlucky—wine from the château vineyard. And sugar cookies out of a tin. She would ask them about where they came from and what they had seen, and if the conversation grew lively—which it often did, for she managed, at her age, to see everything as a rather preposterous comedy—she might venture an anecdote or two from the history of the region. Something, in every case, that seemed to her appropriately odd. "Indeed," she would begin repeatedly, with a slow, graceful, sidelong wave of a bony hand whiter than the ivory lace from which it emerged.

Her allusions to the local past often assumed a familiarity with its characters and customs, or an ease with French, that were beyond her guests, and if their response remained hesitant and their smiles tight she might—depending on her mood—offer her hand to be kissed, and dismiss them, or move on to a few samples from her vast fund of Marseillais jokes about Fanny, Marius, Olive. She contrived to roll out the Marseillais accent around her last teeth without relinquishing the manner elaborated in the drawing rooms of another century, and at Pierre's prompting she might end with a story that was distinctly off-color, and then, relishing her guests' astonishment, bid everyone goodbye, with some laughing remark about the season, the flowers, the world out of doors, or the news in the morning paper. She might point to her window, and the view of the small, exquisite manor next door, a building much older and more beautiful than her own château, so that visitors looking for the château often made the mistake of going instead to the manor, which was not open to the public. "How lucky I am," she sometimes said, "to live here and have that lovely building to look at." A pause. "Instead of living over there and having to look at our house. Besides, there has been no one of interest living over there for at least three hundred years."

Once the guests had been led out into the adjoining room and the door closed, Pierre was likely to try to continue the entertainment that his mother had provided for their guests, fishing up more Marseillais stories, progressively less savory, and passing on to others wholly uncommendable. He was said to be a good son. His enthusiasm grew as that of his guests sank away. He put out his tongue as he laughed. Finally, when he noticed that a story had utterly failed to delight his audience, he would very possibly remark that it was his wife's favorite joke—especially if they had met his wife, Mathilde: tall, graceful, elegant, charming, gentle, someone whom everyone seemed to like. It was almost never said that he was a good husband.

If he felt particularly expansive and confidential, Pierre might show his guests rotogravures of his mother in her youth, and of himself "when I was young and handsome." She looked, certainly, intrepid and solid, for all her parasols and jet fringes and huge brims, as she leaned against one heavy balustrade after another, or prepared to mount into a carriage. And Pierre's features, as they had come to be—the face he liked to characterize as "Neronesque," turning his profile and posing beside a small relief of that emperor so that his guests might compare the receding brow, aquiline nose, fleshy cheeks and lips, and pendulous throat of the imperial and current models— they could all be made out, in embryo, in the pallid, plump ephebe over whose studio photograph he lingered with nostalgia. If he got as far as the pictures it was only a step to their setting: to his childhood in Indochina, memories of earthquakes, ghosts, Oriental servants, and always of standing, small and alone, in the great shadowy dining room, at the hour in the afternoon when everyone was asleep, and looking at a bowl of eggs on a table, and a large rat emerging from the wainscot, followed by another. The rats made their way, with professional as-surance, to the bowl of eggs. One rat embraced an egg with all four legs and the other seized it by the tail and dragged it off, egg and all, back to the wainscot and out of sight. To reappear in a moment and repeat the performance. And the child stood watching as egg after egg departed.

Pierre believed he had seen it. It was at least as vivid to him as the memory of being taken to see Bernhardt, the Divine Sarah, already overblown for the role, but undaunted, in scenes from *L'Aiglon*, first, and then discovered seated in a balcony, with an open book in her lap, from which she proceeded to read, with great expression, poems by Ronsard. The light on her page and on the wall and on her person was intense, perhaps simulating a Mediterranean noon, and the child had been fascinated to see, in its glare, that the elaborate cosmetic structure sustaining the white throat from which the sounds were coming was not equal to the strain. A seam began to part below the famous ear, and as the jaw continued to move and the verses to swell, it widened and peeled away, and a pink sack of skin began to force its way through, "like a testicle," growing until the poem ended and the curtain, without lingering, fell. After the performance the child, with another, had been led backstage to meet the great actress and had heard roars of rage filling the corridor; the admirers were kept waiting for some time. Finally they were beckoned forward and led into the presence. She was reclining on a chaise longue, completely restored, and in seraphic tones she called, "Come, come, my children. I *adore* children." Pierre was sure he had seen all that, too, and that during the same audience she had confided to them that what she prized above all was simplicity. "Simplicity," Pierre repeated, raising his chins and pausing piously. "It is my own guiding principle."

                                    .   .   .

It was hard to see the figures in the pictures of Pierre and his
mother as having been more attractive than their later appearances.
Neither of them looked young, but neither of them looked quite real.
Considering the wry, gnarled style of the lace-trimmed white figure
in the bed, her wit and lightness, it seemed that she must have un-
dergone a complete transformation from the bustling, impervious per-
sonage, arrogant with neighbors, heedless of bills, servants, and the
preferences and comforts of others, who persisted, half memory
and half legend, but utterly distinct, in the minds of M. Bruyère
and his contemporaries. And certainly she had changed remarkably,
and fortunately—but not, of course, completely. She still ran the
house, through Pierre. She treated her daughter-in-law, who came
from a grander and older family than her own, as a servant enjoying
special privileges. Few decisions concerning the family could be made
without reference to her—her comfort, her health, her tastes, her
entertainment—and no one in the house supposed that it should or
could be otherwise as long as she lived: not Pierre himself, nor Mathilde his wife, nor any of their four children, with whom she conspired
constantly, advancing and withdrawing her favor, hoarding confidences. Some evenings all six of them took their dinners in to sit
around Mme. la Générale's bed, and even when they ate, as they
otherwise did, in the smaller downstairs dining room, if all the children
were at home, or in the improvised upstairs kitchen, once the elder
children had gone, they all trooped into her bedroom after dinner and
sat with her for an hour or so, and talked with her, and read the paper
with her, listened to her opinions about the news of the village, the
country, and the world.

In the summer Pierre set up trestles and boards in the room, and
worked in there by the foot of the bed at reupholstering senile chairs
in cheap fabrics, awning materials, ends of lines which he fetched
away on credit from one dim old shop or another on some back street.
The industry was conceived of, at least, as part of the redecorating
services which he placed at the disposition of discerning owners of
large houses in the region. It was a pursuit—the upholstery—for which
he kept declaring that he had a natural gift, though that was not
immediately apparent. And as the mismatched stripes, crooked seams,
chewed bindings and bludgeoned nails were fixed into places from
which only further mutilation could remove them, he repeated that

he was teaching himself this art as he went along. Sometimes the patterns of curtain brocades, as he hacked at them, reminded him of costumes in a private performance, at a château, one summer in his youth, in which he had played Hamlet, all in black. His small hands, plump even then, and his face had been spectacularly white. Others had been wearing brocades. He had been very moving. He had delivered the great soliloquies—however they began. De dum de dum de dum. Or sometimes the fabrics evoked the opera. Once, as a young man, before he had married, he and a few cousins and their wives had taken a windup Victrola to the top of the waterfall at the head of the valley and played Wagner, in the shadow of the cliffs. The Ride of the Valkyrie. And Pierre had stood up, his fist on his breast, like Chateaubriand, and had declared, to the surrounding white crags, "Ah, it's too beautiful, *too* beautiful. I can bear no more." And jumped over the edge. Knowing, as the others did not, that there was a broad grassy terrace some four feet below. And the party had screamed, obligingly, and one cousin, a very dull man, had threatened to hit him. Some members of the family had no wit.

Mme. la Générale could drop off to sleep to the sound of Pierre's upholsterer's hammer knocking and crunching, and flies would circle the foot of the bed, and he would settle back, himself, in a Louis XIV wing chair on which he had spent some time learning but which had not yet been quite right for anyone's decor, and begin to snore. She would snore, he would snore.

Once he dreamed of that same waterfall flowing close by again, and again heard shrieks, and laughed, looking up at the faces appearing in the sky above him. But there was only one face, and it was Mathilde's, and she was shouting to him, with her gold fillings flashing, about water in the house, and he jumped up, and tripped over a stool, and ran out remembering the duck bread, the duck bread! The huge round loaves, too stale for anyone to buy to eat, that he had acquired by recent agreement with the village baker, and had the garden boy bring home in a wheelbarrow. They had been harder than ever when they arrived, enormous millstones, gray and powdered, and he had lugged them upstairs to the bathroom and stacked them in the cavernous ancient straight-sided zinc bathtub, where Mathilde kept the gladiolus bulbs all winter, and turned on the water. One of those summer days when there was almost no water in the pipes. The château drew its own supply from the stream that continued below the waterfall, down the valley between the cliffs. It had been a dry summer. The stream had narrowed, and splashed languidly from rock to rock. There were runnels here and there that led to gardens in the village, and when their sluice gates were opened still less water ran in the stream, and in the château the faucets in the cellar ran feebly, those on the ground floor scarcely trickled, while on the floor above, where the bathroom was, a mere thread dribbled and bubbled and stopped and resumed ridiculously, from the brass tap, accompanied by a continuous faint wheezing. So that, for example, the box for the toilet flush, high on the stone wall, would not have filled at all, even back in the days when it had been in working order. And if you wanted to wash your hands it was more practical to take the large empty tin pitcher that stood beside the old commode and go down the stone stairs and fill it from the trickle in the main kitchen. Or forget the whole thing. At the rate the faucet in the tub was dripping, that afternoon, there would have been no point in waiting for the tub to fill in order to soak the loaves to feed the ducks, and Pierre had gone back to his languishing furniture and his sumptuous daydreams, the stones of the hall echoing his footsteps, the village silent, smells of hay and honeysuckle drifting in around the white curtains at the window of his mother's room.

He rushed out, feeling that he must still be dreaming, and the hall seemed dark. He splashed into the water before he saw it. The whole hall was an inch under the surface and the water was streaming happily down the stone staircase. It had soaked the carpet on the landing, spilled off the sides, and leaked down along the wall behind a full-length portrait of an ancestor in a red eighteenth-century uniform, and elsewhere had flowed into a piece of sagging, dark, unrecognizable tapestry and was dripping from the unraveling threads along its lower edge. There was enough current so that some of the smaller loaves had already bumped their way over the rim of the tub and out of the bathroom and along to the head of the stairs and had rolled down all the way to the landing, and others were following as fast as they could. Pierre floundered past the whole mess, wanting to call out something and not knowing what to call, and turned off the faucet and slewed around, in water up to his insteps, to survey the damage.

Besides the bathroom there was a *chaise percée* in his mother's room, and an outhouse in the vegetable garden. But the bathroom was essential, Pierre remarked from time to time, for entertaining, particularly for entertaining foreigners, in whom Pierre increasingly rested his hopes of revenue. Even so, as a bathroom it remained for years more symbolic than functional, and the tin enameled pitcher that was supposed to stand beside the commode moved around the room, usually empty, or wandered into another part of the house on some errand or other. When the upstairs auxiliary kitchen was rigged up at the end of the hall, past Mme. la Générale's room, with two tabletop burners, an oak and zinc icebox from the time of her own youth was disinterred from the cellar, white with mildew, and maneuvered up the stone staircase to the broad hall. There was no room for it in the new kitchen, so it was walked into the bathroom and jammed into the corner behind the door. Which meant that it was a long walk from the kitchen, at the opposite end of the hall that ran around two sides of the stairwell, and was too inconvenient to use as an icebox except on special occasions.

Such as the celebrated dinner party which Pierre and Mathilde gave toward the end of one summer, the guests, many of them foreigners, drawn from châteaus and old houses of the region. It was one of Pierre's later attempts to ingratiate fortune, and he had planned it far in advance, taking all summer to assure himself of who was coming. He planned to use the main dining room, which had become no more than a gallery through which tourists were led, ticket in hand, and shown the portraits and the collection of porcelain on the walls, the looming armoire and sideboards, the long table, about which Pierre recounted noble histories, and so forth. Even small groups, passing through, could feel the floor shudder as they stepped, hear clinking in the sideboards, note the plates wiggling on the walls, and wonder whether the armoire should really be leaning so far into the room and opening its doors as they passed. The dining-room carpet was almost thirty feet above the bottom of the wine cellar, an unlit crypt whose floor, in wet weather, was an echoing puddle. Huge gray vats hulked in the darkness. In one or more of them the thin sour wine from the vineyard across the narrow valley blackened.

When Pierre had proudly shown the place to one foreigner who was himself refurbishing a château in the region, someone whom Pierre was particularly anxious to cultivate, the man had shone a flashlight up into the cobwebs overhead, noted the sagging beams, and declared on the spot that he would be afraid to walk again through the dining room. Only a few of the beams, Pierre insisted, were really unsound. But he realized that before filling the room with a large dinner party the floor would have to be shored up, and he managed to entice a carpenter from a neighboring village to raise and multiply a system of underpinnings, using old beams that had survived the collapse of a shed down by the duck house to supplement new ones. There was a whole scaffolding woven around and over the vats before the job was finished. And to finance the construction and the dinner, Picrre had left in midsummer on one of his periodic trips to Vichy, from which he was known to return, usually, with funds for a while. No one knew where they came from or how they were acquired, and there were inevitable imputations touching upon the war years and the occupation, and who knew what about whom, and there were those who leapt to conclusions, but in general Pierre's acquaintances found it preferable to have him solvent, more or less, and shoulders were shrugged and no one pressed the speculations very far.

Pierre managed to pay for the propping up of the dining-room floor, or at least to lay out enough to get the work to where the armoire stopped leaning forward and its doors swinging open when someone walked past it, and to where the plates hung almost still on the walls, and it was possible to walk through the room without feeling unexpectedly afloat. Wine was ordered through the wife of one of the invited guests who came from a family of wine merchants. One of the courses was duck. Mathilde managed to borrow silver and glasses from a neighboring château, as she had done before in recent years. Both Pierre and Mathilde were renowned cooks, and they had help from the village for the day. The bathroom pitcher was filled and put in its place by the commode, that morning, and the younger children were instructed to keep it full. But there was a great deal going on in the household, and guests who made their way to the bathroom during the dinner found the pitcher empty, and the top of the icebox laden with the waiting desserts: bowls of fruit, peaches in liqueur, a hazelnut mousse, and Mathilde's renowned chocolate almond cake.

There was usually an element of the makeshift and the prudently mysterious in Pierre's financial plans, major or minor. But the past was equally unclear: that is, just how he and Mathilde had arrived at such straits, and how far their fortunes had fallen. She had come to the marriage with a dowry that included a château and estate in the mountains two hundred kilometers to the east. It was no longer theirs. Her own family was known to be rich, and their name and titles allowed them to speak of Pierre as though he were an arriviste who had dragged their Mathilde into the mud. He referred to them, and to Mathilde's elder brother in particular, as a stuffy, stingy, boring set of snobs, the very sort of people whom he never could endure, and he insisted that they had always been like that. But it seemed that there must have been some more definite episode, some rupture that neither he nor Mathilde ever recounted. And it was known that there had been differences over money. Which surprised no one. On Pierre's side there must have been money in his youth, the days of his mother's jet beads and carriages with footmen, even though she had been famous for ignoring her bills for everything from feather boas to hardware, and it was easy to see where Pierre had found the example for his own cavalier disregard of such things. She may indeed have acted, as he did later, as though such neglect were a personal taste, with niceties—perhaps a whole aesthetic—of its own.

Pierre watched eagerly when new grocery stores opened in towns within his range, and would turn up soon after an opening to introduce himself, with his title, and some allusion to private lives of an earlier generation in the vicinity, and to begin his patronage with a generous selection of samples, trying their Roqueforts, their sausage, their macédoines, wines, and foie gras, on his newly opened account. When his credit had been long exhausted in most of the less imaginative shops of the region, he had been known, after a day of convivial sightseeing with some foreign family, to invite his companions home for supper, remembering only after the invitation had been accepted that the cupboard at home was bare, and that he had forgotten to bring shopping money. Even after his guests had agreed to supply the provisions he would not hear of patronizing just any establishment that happened to be convenient. Some would not have been acceptable under any circumstances. "I detest purveyors," he said, "who present their bills twice."

His demeanor was intended to remind his hearers, whatever their station and aptitude, of an age when the honor of supplying—of divining—the wants of his family had been universally acknowledged, a time before the tasteless considerations of commerce had insinuated themselves everywhere. The actual decline of his family's material position was never recounted. Pierre and Mathilde both referred to losses during the war, and still more crippling losses in the shifts and devaluations that followed it. And before the war there had been disastrous reverses—forced sales and ruinous surprises during the twenties, which had swallowed up Mme. la Générale's carriages and footmen, her box at the opera and her house in Provence. But before any of those obvious and more or less explicable misfortunes within living memory, Pierre mourned remoter cataclysms, vaster and more vague, that had swept away whole eras and domains, and in his daily assumptions he relinquished none of his titles to those lost expanses. There was scarcely a history of the great families of France, picked up in some junk shop or garret, gilt-edged, bound in red cloth, with engravings worth rescuing, in which he could not find traces of his own genealogy: quarterings, names of persons or places or houses.

He was also able to say, in most cases, how a particular estate had passed out of the keeping of his family, who had acquired it, and all too often how it had been abused by later owners. Depending on what he knew of the proprietors, or they of him, he might actually lead his guests onto the grounds as though the property were legally his, conducting them through gates and into courtyards, pointing up at the elegance or desecrations of windows, eaves, dormers, doorways, and recounting scandals that had taken place on the tower stairs. A chatelaine who had received visits from the village carpenter. A duel in a hallway. Sometimes he actually called on the present owners, his usual effrontery supplemented with the clear implication that they were there as the result of some combination of sufferance, oversight, and miscarriage of justice. Tenants at best, and tenants of a family of whom he was—however lightly he might carry the role, however cruelly he might have been deprived of its joys—the rightful heir.

There was the château of Lise, for instance: spacious, square, noble, on a gentle rise, beside an oak forest; it had been built originally around four sides of a long flagged courtyard, in cream-colored limestone, the fourth side housing a great arched portal carved with rows of flowers. Under Napoleon the wing along one side of the courtyard had been converted into a stable. But even that had been done with some taste: the openings were constructed of stone and formed an arcade. In the present century the whole entrance wing, the portal and the pair of towers that flanked it, had been dynamited and removed to allow cattle trucks into the courtyard, and the open maws at the ends had been sealed up with cement blocks. Both sides of the courtyard, by then, were in use as barns, the one for cattle, the other to pen sheep and pigs. Pierre led his guests through the manure to the wide stone steps and the terrace at the far end, and the main door, whose arch had repeated that of the demolished entrance, and knocked on the parched wood—the door knocker had long since been removed. A door farther along the terrace opened and a man in high rubber boots stood looking out, waited, and beckoned them all into what had been a dining room but had become a kitchen: it was dark; the windows had been boarded over. Several men were sitting on a bench at a long table. A stove stood in the fireplace, and smoke had all but obliterated the painted ceiling. Pierre led his guests away without lingering, and on to other relics.

If the owners did not know him he used his full name and title and a description of his château by way of introduction. If they did know him he was more likely to emphasize and embellish the distinctions of his foreign companions. And his tours were not limited, after all, to the estates that he claimed as shards of his lost patrimony. He never pretended to the ruins of the Blackbird Tower, in the mountains, on its pinnacle almost surrounded by a rushing stream, nor to the roofless abbey fortress of Taillefer on its cliff commanding miles of broad valley, nor to Aynac with its friezes studded with symbols of ancient artillery. He loved the region, loved showing it to strangers, chattering incessantly as he went. He knew the bends of the road from which one had the best views of rivers and rolling country and towers on hills, and knew the way to Romanesque chapels hidden in ivy, and to deserted villages built like fortresses, under enormous trees. He had lived there since his youth, and could guide his guests past the games of children into the hall of an immense château, waving away the protestations of furious schoolteachers, saying, "Yes, yes, madame, I know perfectly well that it's forbidden. I used to play in this room before you were ever conceived." And proceeding to point out details of decoration—carvings, paintings in the ceiling—which the teachers themselves had never noticed there, and to describe the children's parties, the governesses, the cakes, the games, that had existed once, there where the children were playing.

He had always been convivial and curious, and loved outings and picnics and talking and meeting new people. His excursions with visitors to the region, or with new residents if he found them inter-esting, were a natural development once he obtained a license to open his château to the public and charge admission. He began to set up signs at crossroads advertising it as a tourist attraction, and to ask strangers with whom he fell into conversation whether they were ac-quainted with his house. Visitors to whom he enjoyed talking, who excited his curiosity, whom he found attractive, in one respect or another, as he showed them the gilt sofas, the ancestral portraits, the pieces of Sèvres, the carved armoires, might be invited to picnic by the duck pond on the stone benches in the shade, and from there it was a step to proposing an expedition somewhere, in the visitors' automobile, because at the time when the château was first opened to the public, and for some years thereafter, Pierre did not have a car himself. The only vehicle in the household, apart from the old wheelbarrow, was a bicycle belonging to his younger son, an object far from new when acquired, years before, and afflicted with a perceptible bend in its front wheel. In those days almost any visitor, passing through the region, might be good for a ride into town to do some shopping. Visitors might have room for more than one: Pierre, and one of the silent children to help carry the groceries. Or Pierre might propose an expedition at once, and if accepted, guide the party, on the way, to a grocery, a butcher shop, a charcuterie, in some village at a distance.

If he was being driven, he preferred to sit back "like the British queen mother," as he liked to say. And if it was an open car "like a bathtub" he would fasten an olive-green necktie around his forehead, with the tails hanging down behind him, to keep his gray hair from blowing around his face, and would sit back with his nose in the air, glancing down the slopes to either side. He insisted, rather arbitrarily, that the headband emphasized his resemblance to Nero. Certainly its eccentricity did not diminish his usual effrontery, the manner in which he turned from admiring a sunset over mountains to chat with a woman shutting up her hens in the hen house for the night. He asked her whether she had any eggs for sale, and when she told him she had none, asked her whether her hens were stuck, and they both laughed as he sailed on. Or the countenance with which he addressed two women of his own age, in black straw hats and churchgoing clothes, standing by the road in a village to which he had directed his companions in order to show them a small beautiful fortified church of a remarkable shape, a building dating from the Knights Templars, its one squat massive tower incorporating the entire nave and transept. He had told the driver to stop, on the narrow road through the village, opposite the door, so that he could point out the crossbow slits in the tower, the Gothic doorway with its lintel two steps down from the road, the eagle's talons carved in the stone over the portal, and the two women watched him and the foreign car without braking their talk.

Although it was summer they were wearing coats: long black coats, in keeping with their purses and their hats. Across the road from them was the high crumbling stone garden wall of a half-dilapidated stone house, perhaps the presbytery, shaded by a walnut tree. Just beyond it was a small square almost filled with the old tile roof of a marketplace, supported on round columns of white limestone. Beyond that, an oval stone pool for washing clothes. On the other side of the road, beyond the two women, was an ancient village green; in the middle of it a stone fountain, like a square monument, bearing a date from the sixteenth century. The village was hushed in its midsummer, midday, midcentury, midcontinent sleep.

The old house next to the church, and directly behind the two women, had been done over recently. The windows had been reconstructed. From the graceful proportions traditional in the region they had been, apparently, widened and shortened until they were square. Their stone settings had been replaced with poured cement. The stone doorway had been altered in the same way, and fitted, overhead, with a protruding brim of frosted glass. A pipe fence ran along the front of the house a few feet from the façade whose stones had been cemented over and the cement painted a pistachio green, against which the darker green of the door, the shutters, and the pipe fence stood out distinctly. It looked as though the paint had just dried.

Pierre was aghast. "It has all happened *this summer*!" he said. "That house," he said, "was *of the period*!" And look! Unpardonable anywhere. Hideous. But next to that church, virtually *touching* that masterpiece—a desecration. A *des-e-cra-tion*! It should never have been permitted. Where were the gentlemen of the Beaux Arts when this was going on, I would like to know. What good does it do to preserve a unique marvel such as this church and allow the retired sausage makers of the place to perform an outrage like that right beside it? The commissioners are hopelessly inadequate, as everyone knows, but there is *no* excuse for this."

Raising his voice, and pointing to the house, he asked the nearer of the two women, "Madame, if you please, to whom does this building belong?" "To this lady," she answered, with obvious satisfaction, indicating her companion with a sweep of her hand and the air of someone who appreciated the recent transformation. As she spoke she stepped back to allow Pierre a better view of the shade of green and of its owner. "Ah, madame," Pierre said, turning to the other, "it is an atrocity! It is hideous. Bad enough to have ruined a beautiful old house anywhere, but to have had the brutal vulgarity to deface the house standing beside that lovely church—it is an outrage! It is like a pustule on a beautiful face. If your own taste did not forbid it, it should have been prevented by law. Drive on before I forget myself."

As he swept on he continued to enlarge upon his theme: the neglect and defacement of the buildings and works of art of the region, an ancient place famous for its architecture and furnishings. He led the way, on foot, puffing and wheezing, up a steep road through a chestnut forest, to a half-ruined château, "pure Victor Hugo," whose owner had pushed a dozen of the crenellations off the top of the keep to make benches for himself at the base of the tower, beside the clothes-line hung with his socks and underwear. That was what things had come to, Pierre announced. He stood catching his breath, then walked with tiny steps around the cropped grass that had once been a great courtyard. He peered into an uncurtained window. A bare kitchen table, a bare light bulb, a few battered chairs, clothes on the backs of them, dishes in a sink, a calendar on a wall the color of wrapping paper. The present owner, Pierre said, was a retired customs inspector from up north, a widower who had been looking for a villa, at the end of the war, and had bought the castle because it was cheaper.

The walls rose from the top of a steep hill, two gnawed rings of fortifications, the massive keep, the remains of a portcullis gate, and inside the enclosure, across the green studded with pieces of masonry, an enormous barn. To one side of the green was a roofless banquet hall with shell vaulted fireplaces in each corner and a stone minstrel gallery high on the wall. Sheep clattered among the fallen stones fluted and carved with flowers and vines, inside the building, and fled through the far end. Chaffinches, blackbirds, black-capped warblers, and a nightingale in full daylight sang in the chestnut woods on the hillside below the thirteen encircling watch towers. Pierre remarked on the family chapel that they had passed on the climb up the hill, and the crest above the door: a shield bearing the device of a stone fist holding a stone dagger from which a stone drop was falling. He said the motto of the family had been "I make bleed," and that the history of the place had been as Gothic as the buildings.

Back at the beginning, as he told it, the owners had been famous for their iron-fisted heartlessness. They had become involved in a feud with another household along the valley, which went on for several generations and brought about the deaths of heirs and retainers and the burning of villages on both sides. At last both families had agreed to end the feud. Gifts were exchanged, and the eldest daughter of the other family was betrothed to the heir of this one, and a wedding party arrived to celebrate the nuptials. As they rode into the courtyard the gate was dropped behind them and they were butchered on the spot, every one of them.

Later, he said, during the Wars of Religion, one army had locked up some fifty prisoners in the dungeon under the tower, which was still entered through a tiny door not four feet high, set below ground level. The prisoners had been abandoned there without food or water, in the dark. Weeks later someone had opened the door and found the few survivors eating the bodies of the dead. Some time after that, a scion of the family had been distinguished as an ambassador for Mary Queen of Scots. But Pierre relished murkier accounts. The last heir of the line, he confided, had been known in the neighborhood, early in the century, as a miser. He had never married, and finally had shut himself up in a room at the top of the tower, its only entrance a trapdoor in the floor, which could be reached by climbing a long ladder set on a platform at the head of a final narrow flight of stairs. Once up there he had pulled the ladder up after him, and had drawn up his meals daily in a basket on a rope. His sanitary arrangements had consisted of the medieval stone perch jutting out from the castle wall. For years he had lived that way, not exchanging a word with anyone. Finally, when the trapdoor had not opened for days, the remaining servants had been too frightened of him to climb up and investigate, and had waited and waited. When at last some brave soul set up another ladder and broke through the trapdoor the heir had been found dead on his mattress, half eaten by rats, and the mattress full of gold pieces. It was Pierre's stories, after all, that were pure Victor Hugo. There was even a tawny owl that flew out of the ivy under the battlements at an appropriate moment, startled at the sound of his voice.

A nearby village was famous for its goat cheeses, *cabicous*, half an inch thick and no bigger than slices of potato, set out on beds of straw, or bundled together in rolls of half a dozen, creamy and bland for a day or so, if kept in the cool darkness of a cellar; then growing soft and pungent, melting and yellowing. Or else, depending on the temperature, harder and chalkier. Finally becoming dry and peppery, the color of parchment, with a wrinkled skin. Or wrapped in vine leaves soaked in goat urine or white plum brandy, tied in bundles with straw, stored in a crock for weeks or months until they bit back when tasted, and brought sweat to the face on a winter evening.

Pierre led his innocent charges to a minute general store in that village, a door with a frosted glass pane set in a plain façade beside the road. The one room, scarcely larger than a vestibule, was lined with shelves sagging under felt slippers, rope-soled slippers, canned goods, garden seeds, wooden shoes, hats, flour, rat traps, socks, flypaper, aprons, spools of thread, bottled oil, flashlights. A counter crossed it, with a scale on one side. Through the open door beyond the counter the dim kitchen was visible, scrubbed and still, and on the far side of the kitchen a door standing open into a garden full of hollyhocks and dahlias; and beyond them the farmyard, ducks, hens, the darkness of an open shed. When a pale woman had set out the *cabicous* on the counter, and Pierre had encouraged his companions to sample them, and had also gathered together a little pile of other staples from the shelves—fly-spotted cans of ham and of chestnut puree, a package of sugar cookies, another of coffee, butter from the farm—he began the ceremony of having forgotten his wallet. His gray subsiding features expressed surprise, distracted concern, vexation. He patted pocket after pocket, murmuring, "My wallet, my wallet." Rapidly and authoritatively he informed, or reminded, the woman of his name, his title, his château, and either she gave him credit or his companions saved the day.

It was a ceremony that grew familiar to those who saw much of him. When he had been showing tourists through his château for several years, suddenly he owned a car, a vehicle that came to seem as much a part of him as his gold-rimmed spectacles, his fat fingers, or his lisp. Nobody knew just how he had acquired it or the money for it, and so there were the usual speculations about deals, promises, swaps, and the legendary source in Vichy. It was a veteran machine, a Citroën—a *traction*—from well before the war, black like the horses that spirited the family carriages into town in the high days of his youth, though the paint was chipped and the body scratched and dented and rusty. The right front fender was despondent and came to rely on wires, which had to be replaced frequently. The tires were bald to begin with, but Pierre managed to acquire others, slightly less so, through farsighted trading and timely promises. Only half the door handles and a quarter of the window cranks worked, and there were permanant clouds in the windows and the windshield—that windshield that Pierre invoked to describe the cold winter in the uplands, the freezing fogs of the long nights early in the year.

His example was a night when he and Mathilde and "the Princess," who stayed with them occasionally, had set out to dine at a restaurant in a remote village on the uplands, a small yellow-lit room, the kitchen behind it known locally for its goose preserves and its omelettes filled with the slippery boletus prized in the region. The decor had been enlivened, that same year, with checked tablecloths, cuckoo clocks, and lampshades bedight with pictures of red coaches pulling up at tavern doors. The Princess was short, short-haired, and gruff; wore a cape indoors and out, and was never without her Pekinese under her arm, even at table. She smoked cigars one after the other, and argued endlessly about everything, with everyone—shopkeepers, garage owners, the police who dared object to her driving through stop signs, Mathilde, Pierre's mother, and above all and through all, Pierre. On the way back across the uplands that night, Pierre said, the air was so cold that the narrow roads were covered with ice, and the fog closed in. They could see so poorly that Mathilde got out and walked a few steps ahead of the car, to show the way. Then ice formed on the windshield. There was no defroster, of course. The windshield wiper was useless, and it did no good rubbing with papers, rags, hands. Pierre declared, with relish (clearly this was the point of his tale), that the only way he had managed to defrost the windshield was to climb onto the front of the car and water the glass "personally" several times before they were safely home.

From the start Pierre favored certain gas stations, as he favored certain grocery stores, with his demanding custom. Places whose proprietors gave him credit, deferred to his title and the allusions to his château, laughed at his jokes, and periodically nursed his ailing car. For at least a year his loyalty clung and his praises warmed to a gas station at one end of a village across the river from his château, an establishment with pumps on both sides of the road and a garage in which two cars could be worked on at once. After Pierre had his own car he insisted upon using it for most excursions with foreign companions, and on driving himself as well as commenting on the route as he went. Approaching the gas station, he spoke with admiration of the young couple who had taken it over quite recently, of the wonders they had wrought. It was they who had put the new pumps and the second tile-and-glass office on the other side of the road, which was so practical. He lingered over their seriousness, courtesy, and charm, their reliability and modest prices, the promptness and excellence of the repairs that the husband performed, his willingness to travel for miles with his tow truck, how well their three small daughters were doing in school. And the young couple were so good-looking, he added.

As his turtling black car stopped by one of the pumps he was greeted by the wife, whom he referred to as Zizi, though it was not her name. A slender woman in her thirties, with red ringlets, wearing a tight semitransparent polka-dot blouse with a low drawstring neck, very short white shorts and high wedge heels. She flirted and laughed with him, and as she set the nozzle of the hose into the opening of the gas tank, Pierre remarked on her pretty thighs, and then upon the legs—her husband's—emerging from under the front of a car across the road in the garage, clad in grease-blackened blue working pants, and ending in greasy ankle-high laced boots. The soles rocked to a broken rhythm, and the legs seemed to belong to a body that was twitching and writhing back and forth in agony. Pierre said again that the man was as good-looking as his wife, and lowering his voice to a whisper, he said that she had confided to him that they took siestas in the summer and that her husband was never in a hurry. The man emerged from under the car as Pierre was talking: medium height, thin, dark, sharp-featured. He waved and went into the office. Pierre watched him and said that he was a man of few words, but that assuredly he would be successful. And he went on to say that their house, above the garage, was simple, but very clean: modern, full of Formica, plastic, and curtains, and that Zizi, on occasion, had invited him up for a *goûter* of pâté and Pernod. And for dinner, too. Lowering his lids and raising his right hand, he declared that Zizi was a very fine cook.

Rather than strain his credit, Pierre would usually reach into his pocket, when the cover had been put back onto the gas tank, the oil topped up, the tires inflated and the radiator filled, and would discover that he had forgotten his wallet, and his guests would remember the reasons that he had put forward for taking his own car—with its stuck white windows, its exhaust leak through the floor, its devastated upholstery, and the dump into which the passengers willy-nilly inserted their feet—instead of their own.

Once he actually did lose his wallet, perhaps because of the unfamiliarity of having it on his person. He took it to the annual fair in Sérignac, on a night in autumn that had turned unseasonably cold. It was in the days when he and Mathilde had resorted to having what they called *des paying guests*: young people of either sex, but usually girls, usually foreign, shy, pale, and hoping to add something to their all but nonexistent French. Most of them were recruited through friends working in travel bureaus in Paris, and came from moderately wealthy, hopeful, ill-informed parents anxious for their children to spend time in the real Europe, in a family setting that would be at once cultural and safe. Tall thin redheads from Texas; blond, shapeless, silent siblings from Amsterdam; eager, energetic, gingham-gowned students from Manchester—they had never seen plumbing or grandmothers, or eaten meals like that. Pierre let them help the garden boy, and plied them with the château wine at meals, to educate them. Mathilde let them help with the ducks, and tried—largely with prayer—to keep them from getting into trouble in the village, or on their long walks, for instance, in the afternoon.

Several of them were taken to the fair, that year—a valedictory outing before they went home for the autumn. They had not expected such weather, and had not brought enough warm clothes. They wandered around, with old borrowed sweaters and scarves over their summer things, blowing on their hands, stamping their feet, saying "Hoooo," and laughing, like everyone else, stopping to throw balls at wooden clowns, trying to win a doll, or to bang a machine with a sledgehammer, or staring at Yama, a woman sitting in a cage, in a bathing suit, blue with cold, playing with large slow snakes said to be pythons, while peasants in their winter corduroys stood watching, scratching under their berets and telling each other that the snakes were drugged.

Pierre took all his young charges for a ride on the Caterpillar, a miniature green roller coaster over which a green hood closed, once the cars were in motion, so that the sickening ride proceeded in green semidarkness. He did it chiefly to get warm, but he disliked the ride, and got off afterward covered in a cold sweat, feeling shaky and nauseated, as though he were about to come down with some ailment. A number of his acquaintances were standing watching the contraption as he shuffled off, and as he spoke with them and discouraged them from making his mistake he patted his pocket and froze, and then whirled and clutched the air behind him, saying that he had lost his wallet. It was a moment before some of those who knew him believed that what he was saying might actually be true. But Mathilde took him seriously, and reminded him, and everyone, that he had just paid for the tickets, out of his own wallet, before the ride. The Caterpillar was whizzing and screaming around its track again, by then, but as soon as it stopped, the children, who had learned what had happened, and had no reason to doubt it, disappeared under the tracks and trestles. The ticket taker shouted after them, but they were gone, on hands and knees. Pierre rushed to the ticket taker, explained rapidly, breathlessly, with stirring gestures and trembling glasses, the awfulness of the crisis, and disappeared under the tracks himself, on all fours, a revolving hump in an old gabardine. The ticket taker cursed, and then laughed and watched, as the crowd grew around his concession. In a remarkably short time, in the chaotic shadows, Pierre found the wallet himself, and emerged with it, shaking but restored. It was not the money, he said—making sure that each bill was still there—that had concerned him, but his personal papers, his credentials, and the pictures of Mathilde as a young woman and of his mother. He bought the children a bag of hard candy and crammed them into the car again, on each other's laps, and took them home.

The century was moving on; young couples were in fact becoming successful; children were outgrowing their clothes; Pierre's credit with gas stations and with grocery stores ran low, and the quest for new sources of supply impelled him, like an empire, in widening circles. When he drove foreign visitors or friends on excursions in the region it became increasingly difficult to tell whether the route was directed toward visits to buildings or to purveyors who had never heard of him, Pierre, le Comte d'Allers, or to whom he was no more than a vaguely noble name. But he had a passion for uninhabited buildings of all sizes, from shepherds' shelters set in stone walls, facing east or west across pastures, to shuttered castles or disused churches. He was interested in the history, the legends, the ancestry, and the scandals associated with the owners; in the details of architecture, the ruin, the restorations. He was interested, also, in the produce—eggs, cheese, wine, sausages, preserves, pâtés—and the cooking of the farmers who were tenants or caretakers or neighbors of the closed houses. He was interested—practically, as it turned out—in the furnishings, the decorations, the odds and ends. He was delighted to find that a foreigner whose company he liked was looking for a house in the region. It provided him with a fresh impulse for sequences of conversations linked like treasure hunts, with peasants, retired railroad conductors, gatekeepers of estates and railroad crossings, housekeepers of vacant presbyteries. Encounters that began as requests for information led to explorations, discoveries, anecdotes, gossip, and often would end with food. They added to his own never appeased craving for something in the region itself, to his uneasy claim upon it on grounds in danger of being forgotten even by himself. They allowed him to speak with authority as the intimate of the place: not its vendor but its son.

In the châteaus Pierre frequently alluded to old acquaintances with the owners, divulging little matters that—if they were true—the protagonists might have preferred to keep quiet. He was familiar, in one way or another, with the caretakers. Left at large in the shadowy rooms, he would lament the neglect, the evident unconcern for the contents, speak of their historic and aesthetic value, their rarity, their elegance, their associations. Paintings were propped against damp walls. Chairs and tables sheltered yellow hills of beetle dust. Tapestries hung in gray shocks. Curtains were laced with cobwebs. Footstools lay on their backs on mounds of ashes in cold chimneys. Pierre expressed regret that the owners were unable to be there, to take care of what was theirs. He spoke with assurance of their concerns, their tastes, their wishes. They would have wanted him to have this little bench to remind him of other days, to save it, rather than leave it here unappreciated, to be broken, or stolen. They would certainly have wanted him to take away this rolled engraving, already stained from the leak in the wall, yellowed, full of dust, and mildewed along one margin, to prize and preserve it. It had virtually no commercial value in any case, in its present state, after the way it had been simply flung there and left for heaven knew how long. It might be beyond saving, but someone should realize what it was, and make the effort. He entered each room with a sound half exclamation and half sigh in the tall doorway; a syllable that announced amazement, excitement, and sympathy for the unattended relics.

The region was full of empty houses. It had been inhabited by humans as far back as the Magdalenian Age, and had been beloved of the Cadurcii in the days before Vercingetorix defended it against Caesar. The open uplands with their radiant hours were still marked with roads and divided by walls set there by the Romans. The architecture, from pigsty to abbey dome, and the character of the inhabitants, had attained their distinctive forms during the Middle Ages. The Moors and the First Crusade had passed along the valleys. The Black Prince had found the shapes of the roofs and the manners of the people much as they were when the Archduke Franz Ferdinand was assassinated at Sarajevo. But an exodus, from the uplands in particular, had begun in the first half of the nineteenth century, a gradual ebbing, quickened into torrents by a series of disasters. The one that still reverberated with the most vivid accumulation of feeling was the phylloxera, a word that seemed to gather up the terrors and miseries of all the plagues of Egypt. It must have been heard by children as it was pronounced by their grandparents, who remembered what it referred to. It seemed characteristic of the region that the disaster that had become its symbol of devastation, its Great Flood, the mark set between its ancient and its later days, should have been a calamity that ravaged its vineyards—when in fact its wines were never famous, and were raised almost exclusively for home consumption. The phylloxera, destroying the vines, had shattered a way of believing in the world.

In the eyes of the survivors' descendants and of later visitors it would appear that the peasant principles of family and village self-sufficiency and of union with a place they saw as their own must seldom have been so happily realized as it had been between the Revolution and the coming of the phylloxera. There had been devastations and horrors before, of course. One of the flat-topped buttes in the wide valley was Uxellodunum, where Vercingetorix had finally capitulated to Caesar, and where Caesar—subsequently admired by scions of empires, definers of civilization, and smooth administrators — had cut off the right arms of the defeated, numbering, according to his own self-justifying account, some sixty thousand. The Black Prince had destroyed many goodly towns, to say nothing of the villages. At the end of the Wars of Religion the main market town of one of the broad uplands had nine surviving inhabitants and wolves lived in the cellars. But after these scourges the human life on the land had always returned; the ways, the buildings and ceremonies had been restored. When the phylloxera struck the Industrial Revolution had begun. The destruction of the vines brought a new poverty and a new despair: the land, like anything considered as a possession, was worth only the value that was ascribed to it, and suddenly the land that had always been the source of returning hope was no longer to be trusted. A virtue had gone from it. It was said to be of no value. The alternatives were the growing cities, even the colonies. After the phylloxera each of the disasters was spoken of as something final, a disappearance over the edge or a stage of an irrevocable loss.

The event that had sealed the fate of that ancient world, silenced the work songs, and the anvils, and the looms of the weavers, and left the fields and the pastures to the briers and the barns to burn or collapse, had been the First World War, the Marne, the Somme, Verdun, the trenches, from which the men did not return to the villages except as names on the pedestals of the monuments. Yet the customs, and the local language, older than French, survived. In another generation, and by the time of the Second World War and a few years beyond it, it came to seem again almost as though things had always been just as they then were, with most peasant families possessed of several houses, with manors and towers and whole houses of many rooms used for drying tobacco, storing grain and wool, old furniture, chicken and rabbits and goats. Richelieu's determination to destroy every castle in France that could be defended against him had been interrupted by his death before he had managed to force his edicts on that part of the country, and there were castles and ruins of castles and walled farms and abbeys every few miles along the valleys and on the ridges and cliffs and hills. A number of those still inhabited earned a small revenue as tourist displays. Many of the empty ones had been stripped bare, at the time of the Revolution or later, the roofs had fallen in, and the high-walled enclosures lay open under the clouds and birds.

But it was the domestic architecture of the region that was an apparently unlimited treasure. There were sharp, clear divisions between the *ségalas*, or chestnut forests, on their steep hills clothed in acid soil, where ferns and mushrooms and birches grew happily, and the *causses*, or limestone uplands, with their rounded barrens, their scattered isolated hills dark with oaks, their green hollows called *limargues*, their walled fields lined with old walnut trees. The different terrains had been settled by different tribes. The *ségalas* had attracted a paler blue-eyed race, laconic and reserved. The *causses* had been settled by a dark-eyed people known for their smiling nature. And the styles of building were as different as everything else. The houses of the villages on the steep slopes of the chestnut forests were built of a dark gray stone flecked with mica, and were roofed with slate. They huddled into their hills; small windows, and the barns often half sunk in the earth. On the uplands the oldest roofs had been built of slabs of limestone and were pitched high because of the weight and the angle at which the stones lay. Later they had been roofed with flat tiles hooked to lathes of split chestnut, but the lower rows along the eaves were often still formed of the original stone, and creatures, welcome and unwelcome, and mosses, nestled among them. The marvels of the Napoleonic Code, which excite the piety of French lawyers, include inheritance laws that contributed to the neglect of many of the house and farm buildings and their contents. In most villages there were houses that stood uninhabited, complete with all their furniture, linens, and china, until they fell, because an owner had died and the property, as provided by law, had been left to a complex progeny who could not agree among themselves about who should have what, what could be sold, and what must stay.

Often the doors were not even locked. It had not been the custom to lock them, in that part of the country. Or, if people did lock them when they went out, it was common for them to leave the key in the door, so that a visitor might be able to wait inside until the owners came home. Or a shutter would be loose, a window open or without glass. If a neighbor was in charge and kept the place locked, the key might be on the ledge over the door.

Pierre would open it, letting light into the room smelling of rats, must, wet wood, cold limestone, dead ashes. Past the stone sill, beds with high wooden ends, around the walls of the central room, the kitchen. Candlewick bedspreads trailing from them to the floor, in rags, stained with rat urine, and the woolen mattresses torn open and half gutted by rats, the stuffing strewn around the beds, and piles of gnawed walnut shells on the beds and floorboards. A long farmhouse table, blackened with damp to the color of a car tire, under a green tin lampshade hanging from a beam. A few bowls still on it, in which some liquid had dried black. A carved armoire against one wall, half full of linen, some of it already chewed and tunneled with rats' nests. Another armoire, full of linens and dishes. Chests full of dishes. More beds and armoires in the next room. A bedside cupboard full of dusty medicine bottles. A white porcelain dish shaped like a goose, for pouring medicine into the mouth of an invalid. A sprig of box tacked to the scaling plaster wall under a crucifix.

Pierre would lead the way, showing the place to his friends whether or not he knew it was for sale. They tiptoed in, at first, as though they might be overheard, or as though they were unsealing a tomb, and after a moment Pierre would begin to explain the house to them, even though he might never have seen it before. One of them would open a shutter and the cool sweet air would come in from the plum trees by the window and the grass below. A view of wide uplands, or river valley. They would lean out as though they lived in that house. The silence outside was a surprise after even a few moments of the silence inside. They felt like children. All around them was the sound of age, unfamiliar but unmistakable, awesome, beautiful, chill, enticing. Often there were children along. The foreigners brought theirs, Pierre brought his, they had planned a picnic somewhere. The children picked up this or that—bottle, old coin, bird's nest, bent spoon, chamber pot—and would ask whether they could keep it, and the answer would be hesitant. Pierre himself, if he knew the owner, might be prompted by the same prescience that guided him in certain of the châteaus, and recognize objects that deceased friends would have wanted him to have, or things that the present owners had overlooked and would have wanted removed to safety. Some things he might simply pick up and take, mumbling something, perhaps, about arranging matters with the owners later. He might say that, whether or not he knew who the owners were. And if he did not know them, and the house, for some reason, was undesirable, he might simply rescue some of the contents—linen from the rats, china and glass from breakage, pewter from loss, pictures, mirrors, furniture, from the leaks in the roof. From a pile of books moldering at the foot of a rotted cupboard he might hand a Molière or a Bossuet to one of his companions, and a stained but ironed tablecloth to another, saying, "I make you a present of it. Say nothing of it." Some of his foreign friends, after all, had houses of their own to furnish, and were not above helping him save some of the neglected objects from certain destruction. Through a mixture of curiosity and solicitude the luggage compartment of the car, even the back seat, might be congested before they drove away.

Pierre cleaned up and painted one of the ground-floor rooms of his château as a permanent antique shop, and offered more things for sale than he had displayed in the past, yet the poverty of his household did not seem to improve, and if he called on friends in the neighborhood, as he often did, near mealtime, he might inquire what they were having to eat, and then say that at the château, that evening, he and his family were having *café au lait*, "to save money." That way he saved more, usually, by accepting invitations to stay and dine, which he would repay with gossip and a succession of his dirty jokes, and then move to an armchair and snore and belch for most of an hour, which he said was essential at his age. Maybe the next time he would turn up bearing a small chipped china vase, or an old oil jar lacking a handle, or a rusted lantern with no glass, as a present. And he would try to lure his friends out with accounts of houses heard of or discovered, householders with attics full of things for sale, fallen roofs, treasures standing naked to the elements. It was true that owners were found, and sometimes salvaged objects were paid for. Not often. Usually it would have been complicated and imprudent to raise the subject. And Pierre's reputation was his own affair, but his foreign companions, one by one, declined to set out on further expeditions with him. Particularly after he had revealed the more unbridled forms of his salvage operations. The outing, for instance, on which he had preferred to be driven in the closed van belonging to certain of his friends: he had asked them to wait for him in a village to which he had directed them, and had returned, a few moments later, puffing with the weight of a long bundle wrapped in his own old gabardine, which he shoveled into the back of the van. He climbed in after it, sweating and trembling, and said, "We can go." The bundle, it turned out, contained two bas-reliefs of angels which he had rescued from the leaking wall of an abandoned church. He had come equipped with a big screwdriver.

That evening he repeated, in impassioned detail, his disappointments with the shortcomings of the priesthood, in this day and age. As he saw it, they were shamefully ignorant, the priests; they knew nothing about art. They were not even honest. They sold off the contents of their sacristies, anything, anything at all that was left in their charge, if they knew the things had any commercial value. They allowed the rain to leak in onto frescoed walls, ruining irreplaceable masterpieces. They appreciated nothing. They did not even understand the services they recited. He imitated, as he loved to do, the lugubrious liturgical wail of the village priest, and told once again of the funeral service for a member of his family at which the priest had moaned and whined and gabbled faster and faster, sounding as though he were about to burst into tears, and circling the coffin three times, at the end of the service, almost at a run. After the service, when Pierre had reprimanded the priest for crude and unfeeling haste in the performance of the divine office, the priest had answered, in the same woeful whine, "Oh, monsieur, my bladder, my bladder, I had to go, I had to go!"

Pierre also repeated the story, which he kept as the seal of justification for his own operations, of the priest whom he and Mathilde had met years before, on their honeymoon in Provence, a dirty and unlettered old person whose beautiful small church in the mountains was full of ugly modern statues. The original wooden ones had been piled in a corner somewhere in the sacristy. Pierre had thought of asking, at the time, whether it would be possible to buy any of them. But he and Mathilde were just beginning their trip, and the priest had been churlish and unwelcoming. Pierre had hesitated to ask about

buying anything. He had brooded about the old statues after they
drove away, and weeks later, on their way back, they had stopped
again at the church, intending to try to buy some of the old pieces,
most of which must have dated from the Middle Ages. And when
they had asked, the priest had told them that he had burned the whole
pile in the stove during an unexpected summer cold spell, when he
ran low on wood, and that they had been so old and dry that they had
burned up beautifully. Pierre said that such outrages should be prevented by law. There ought to be—it was an idea that made more
sense to him with every year that passed—there ought to be a Commission of Sacred Art set up for the protection of objects of artistic
and antiquarian merit, and to such an organization he would be willing
to dedicate his own services and his support.

He would not have wanted anyone to suppose, either, that he was
untouched by the religious nature of these works of art, even though
he might speak lightly of the Church itself from time to time. It was
the kind of liberty that might be taken within one's own family. He
had been—he might remind his foreign and perhaps Protestant or
unbelieving hearers—a Catholic from the moment of his baptism, and
it was a faith that was with one all one's life. He felt a particular
devotion to the Virgin, an intimacy, a confidence. She understood him,
when others did not. She watched over him. As his affairs grew worse,
and the circle of his debts widened, and the world grew colder, his
eyes would fill with tears as he told of the moment in the winter when
the Virgin had saved him from mortal sin. The weather had been cold
and foggy. There had been no money at all, and no prospect of any.
Sometimes, Pierre said, he thought with longing of walking down to
the river, leaving his clothes on the bank, where someone would find
them later. But he would be gone. Free at last. He would leave what
he could for his wife and his children, and he would hope that a few
of his friends would miss him. But it was too much. His head ached
more and more often. He had begun to have flutters and pains in his
heart. One knew what that meant. Was there any reason for prolonging
it? His children had brought him worry and despair. How many real
friends were left? He believed, he said, that he would go to a Valhalla
of Wit—he and Oscar Wilde. It was an old vision of his, and it consoled
him, but only momentarily.

Just when the world seemed lightless and his sufferings insuperable
he had dreamed one night—when at last he had fallen asleep after
hours of insomnia—of the Virgin. She had shown him a small church

down on the river plain, disused for years, and all but abandoned. He had seen it long before, and entirely forgotten it. In it there were statues ... In the morning, at first light, he had gotten into the car and driven to the church, standing isolated in the fields. He had managed to open the door with no trouble, and there, scarcely attached to their settings, were two superb baroque saints, half life size. It was a miracle that they had not been ruined already by the damp, and so forth. Within minutes he had them loaded into the back of his car, wrapped in blankets which he traveled with for such contingencies, and he had driven straight to Paris, where he knew someone who had been looking for statues of that exact description. And he had sold them—he named the impressive price—before the end of the day. It had saved his life. He had gone at once to the nearest church and put a whole bill in the offering box, to thank Her.

Probably his forgotten wallets and other sleights of hand with money, and his relentless and worsening jokes, did as much to alienate his old acquaintances and bring them to calling him Fatty, behind his back, as anything they knew or suspected about his rustlings in churches or elsewhere. And all his actions grew more frantic as his own circumstances gnawed at him. He kept settling his roofless and flustered hopes on his four children, one child after another, with inadequate observation of their desires, their abilities, or, of course, their characters.

His eldest, Henri, who for years—the early years—he described as his heir, was a dark, lean, sharp-featured, hard-bitten young man, cold, unsmiling and laconic, discourteous to both his parents and scarcely less so to his grandmother. He did not finish school, but as an adolescent found means of support which he discussed with no one, though they were suspected, on good grounds, to include small objects belonging to his parents and their guests. Pierre and Mathilde were relieved enough to sound pleased when Henri, using his family name and his mother's relatives, landed a job with a used-car dealer in Marseilles. But it was no more than a few months before Henri was arrested for siphoning off remarkable sums from his employer's account, or as the peasants in the village put it, getting "caught with his paw in the drawer." Everyone in the family told different stories about what happened after that, but the young man was convicted and sent to jail. From there he managed to get himself into the Foreign Legion. After that there were vague references to the eccentric but essentially noble form in which Henri had chosen to discharge his military service: "our son in the Foreign Legion." His grandfather, after all, had been at the Battle of Tonkin. Henri reemerged, after some years, leaner, more than ever like a ferret, his manner smooth, his eyes and hands never at rest, preferring to stand, murmuring softly of the Legion, alluding to things he had seen which were better not discussed, expressing a fondness for weapons, and within six months he was in trouble again, and Pierre was paying, or promising to pay, someone in Saint-Etienne so much a month, to keep his son out of jail.

And then Catherine: a tall, intelligent young woman with sensuous, heavy features, a lofty air, and a gift for languages. An old friend of the family got her a job in a tourist office, first in a provincial city and then in Paris, where she kept her own small apartment and lived her own life, coming home as seldom as possible but providing her parents with a place to stay when they went to the capital. Pierre thought the arrangement was all very well for a short time, to allow her to feel that she was grown up and could manage on her own, but he began to fret about her wasting her life. He fussed about her living alone. "It's not that I'm a prude," he said. "Far from that. She's a modern young woman. What she does is her own business." But he thought she might consider her family and its needs, of which he reminded her when there was an opportunity. And what he meant was marriage. A good marriage. One, in fact, which he had worked hard to arrange. Through a mixture of luck, exploitation of connections of several kinds, and of family ties, he formed an acquaintance with the Marquis de Brille, still young though no longer in his first youth, extremely rich, with estates in the Berry and the Vendée, and a man of culture. And he arranged for the Marquis and Catherine to meet. He was delighted with the result. He said that they seemed to speak the same language at once, as though there were no difference of age whatever. That they obviously found each other's company very pleasant, and that Catherine got along wonderfully not only with the Marquis but with his friends, including the Marquis's closest friend, a very original young man, half Chinese, a boxer, who made dollhouses which Pierre thought so charming that he brought several of them home to sell, on commission, in his antique shop. Catherine was soon spending many of her weekends and her vacations at one of the Marquis's estates, where the Marquis, Pierre reminded his hearers, lived quietly, receiving only a very few close friends. The wedding had been mentioned, he said; it had been discussed. The plans were not yet definite, but perhaps within the year. They were getting to know each other. Then one day Pierre was shattered to learn, from his daughter herself, that she had moved the Marquis's friend, the boxer, into her apartment in Paris, and that they were living together. Even then, Pierre said, the Marquis was prepared to forgive them both and have her back, but she would not hear of it. She even talked of marrying the Chinese instead of the Marquis, a possibility which filled her father with despair. "Of course," he said, "she says this young man is very good for *all that*. Morning, noon, and night, apparently. And so on. And why not, if she likes that. She takes after her father. But marriage! She could marry the Marquis and still have her friend, after all. And how often is there an opportunity for marriage like that one? The Marquis is a man of intelligence. He is not narrow-minded. It's true that he's not much physically, but those things are not what's important in a marriage. And one knows they don't last. Maybe the marriage wouldn't last either. But look at the difference! It's not that I'm a snob, far from that. But after two years, say, the thing breaks up with the Chinese. Where is she? Who is she? Perhaps after two years she divorces the Marquis. *Then* who is she? The Marquise de Brille. That counts for something." Catherine evidently made it clear that she did not welcome his advice, and went on living as she pleased. Pierre said that he did not look forward to staying with them both, in her apartment, on his visits to Paris.

The younger son, Albert, had inherited his father's egg-white skin and soft contours, but not his cultural leanings. He played with the village boys when he was growing up, but without grace or gift, and with a tendency to cheat or to cry if things went badly for him. He made few friends. He made a slingshot and stalked under the big trees around the duck pond shooting at small birds and occasionally killing one, which pleased him. His grandmother, and his parents, ventured to hope that he might be destined for a military career, in the tradition of his grandfather, whose foot was up there in its bottle. But as he approached adolescence his interests and his energy both dwindled away until he seemed to care about nothing but lying on his bed reading schoolboy adventure novels full of escapades that may have been attractive precisely because they were impossible. At least those were what he read when the door was open. His father kept having to tell him to leave his door open. It was important, Pierre felt, to get the boy away to school, so that he could meet young people of his own age, of good backgrounds, who would widen his interests and provide opportunities for him to develop his natural abilities. Pierre had in mind a school in the north where the children of certain diplomats, foreign movie stars, and other international celebrities from the tabloids were regularly parked. It was not easy to procure admission to such an establishment for a boy with no visible intellectual, athletic, or social aptitude, from a family with no money. Fortunately it was a place which continued to foster a respect for traditions, the true values, and Pierre's family name counted for something. Mathilde's family name must have counted for more, particularly as it was combined with the influence, personal and financial, of Mathilde's brother, whose efforts—after three years—bore fruit. Albert, puffing and shrugging, was bundled off to the gates, lawns, and terraces of the academy for the children of the rich and limelit. He almost never wrote home. The headmaster told Mathilde's brother that of course the boy liked it there. But his record was so undistinguished that continued contributions from Mathilde's family were required to per-suade the school authorities that there was any point in trying to educate Albert at all.

The younger daughter, Madeleine, was also pallid and retiring, but though she almost never spoke, her interest in the opposite sex was plainly developed even when she was still a child. She was pretty, like a doll, and whatever she wore looked like doll's clothing. She went to the girls' boarding school in a nearby town, where the daughters of notaries and of rich aspiring peasants were sent, and she was ex-pected to follow the provincial curriculum after that, and marry and raise a family. Instead she came home and, her parents said, ran around. Went to the fairs, in the summer, with the young people of the region and the fast summer crowd. And in the winter became the friend of a retired professional man in town, whom she visited almost daily and who, she said, was kind to her and gave her presents. Pierre said that his children, he sometimes felt, had no consideration for their family at all.

With the other *antiquaires* of the region Pierre's name increasingly counted for knavery. Depending on the character of the dealer and the circumstances that had been endured, a reference to the Comte d'Allers would elicit amusement, or raised eyebrows, dropped eyelids, or dark looks and tales of outrage and fast talk, misrepresentation, and broken vows. Old Boujou, who occupied a run-down palace on a corner in Sérignac, the whole building stuffed with decades of undistinguished but enticing clutter—damaged Empire armoires, Art Nouveau mirrors flanked by cast-bronze nymphs in ball gowns, mildewed engravings, burst armchairs, standing clocks that had not run in the present century, old orthopedic appliances, medical examination tables—was as forbearing toward the Count as any of his colleagues. But M. Boujou himself was a man who took things more or less as they came, was only half serious and, as he said, half honest about his trade; who had married a whore out of a brothel, the first time round, and been happy with her, and after her death had married a woman from Sérignac who was commendable and dull, and whom he described as "good, but heavy going." He spent as much time as he could by the river, with his dog, fishing. It was he who described le Comte d'Allers as "a fox." But one who made him laugh. He knew the stories, and had suffered the loss of a few objects taken on consignment, a few engravings carried away on one pretext or another. But he shrugged them off. The other *antiquaires* were less charitable. Their indignation at the mention of the Count was often in direct proportion to their own pretensions, the amount they had spent on building authentic towers for their shops, having wrought-iron grilles, imitated from châteaus, specially forged for their windows, fitting up their front rooms as castle halls, with cut-stone fireplaces brought from considerable distances, baronial firedogs, and assorted noble props.

And yet the name, the name—their own tortured euphemisms and elevated little fingers were subscriptions to rules which forbade them to call him anything but M. le Comte, and allowed him to maintain a distance from them that he surely preferred. The peasants, too, referred to him always as M. le Comte, and with a certain admiration, most of them, even if he had talked them out of their old furniture, whose value they had not suspected, or had borrowed money, or taken home carved stones or fruit, or preserves or pâtés which he had never come back to pay for. Some of them—vicarious anarchists—plainly rejoiced in his impudence and his outlawry. But the roster of those who did not grew with the years like a stain. He kept moving his theater of operations. He renewed old acquaintances with rich widows. For a time he sheltered in the company of a Vicomtesse in a town some miles away who owned a well-known canning factory: canned truffles, *cèpes*, goose livers. Her name was Hortense; she was generous and hospitable, respectable, shrewd at business, aging. And her escort,

Bubu, was a man of the world. Which is to say that "this lad," as she and several other wealthy chatelaines of the region referred to this tall balding man approaching sixty, had spent several years in jail as the result of some misunderstanding about money. There the ladies vied at ministering to him with baskets of delicacies on every visiting day. He was the cue for the dropping of voices at social gatherings, and a great deal of whispering behind hands. And he exploited in every way he could imagine, including several face lifts, a resemblance, both fancied and real, to Noël Coward.

Pierre imagined that Hortense's circle and Bubu's connection, Hortense's respectability and Bubu's unscrupulousness, might all be turned to his own advantage. But in fact once Bubu had managed to meet those among Pierre's friends who interested him, he made fun of Pierre behind his back, turning up his nose at the jokes, the taste, the figure, the clothes, the snoring at table, the petty crookedness— it was clearly the magnitude rather than the thievery that he scorned. Pierre was made to feel ridiculous and unwelcome at Hortense's, and at the houses of her friends. Bubu was ahead of him with stories of Pierre's selling a hideous false Chinese lamp to a young woman in a nearby château, overcharging her, and when he came to deliver it falling backwards over the cord, breaking the lamp, without ever interrupting his monologue on the decoration of the château.

With old acquaintances, when he found them at home, Pierre— Fatty by then—spent more and more time recounting his own conversations, his sallies of wit, asking, "Wasn't that a fine thing to say?" He talked more insistently than before of his health, his cardiogram, his medicines, his headaches. He referred frequently and theatrically to his temptation to leave his clothes on the riverbank and be gone to Valhalla. He began an affair with the garden boy. Passersby heard them giggling, in the afternoons, at siesta time. On daytime visits to friends he might ask for a needle and thread and take off his pants to sew on a button, uttering little shrieks as he lowered his white hams onto a stone terrace wall

His mother was dying, of cancer of the rectum, among other things—an ailment which she considered hilarious, and which led her to remember or invent a whole new line of salacious stories, narrated from under her lace nightcap with all her regal gestures of hand and wrist. At M. Bruyère's, on Sundays, the pâté Pierre asked for was for Madame, his mother, a treat he could not bear to deny her. Everyone knew that it had been decades since she had been able to digest

anything so rich, and no one was surprised to hear that Pierre had
been seen repeatedly in his car, by the side of the road, stuffing himself
with fresh bread and foie gras on his way home.

But that source of pâté too was becoming increasingly grudging.
And then the Bargues opened their emporium one block away. They
were an enterprising, industrious couple. Twenty years earlier M.
Bargues had been a rag merchant on a back street. He still owned
and operated his ragpicking shed, to which he and a son and a hired
boy, every week, brought wagonloads of rags, gathered in the town,
and sorted them, and pressed them into bales to be sold to a paper
mill. From the proceeds, and his wife's dowry, they had been able to
open a children's clothing store, one of a chain, on the same street,
and after a few years the company had enabled them to modernize
the old building, which had fronted onto one of the original canals of
the town, inserting huge plate-glass windows into the stone façade
and covering the rest with yellow Formica. They continued to run
that establishment as well, after another chain made it possible for
them to convert a handsome ancient building on the square into the
first supermarket in town, the first that most of the inhabitants had
ever seen.

Over the garage door of the rag shed nothing was written. On the
door it said PRIVATE PROPERTY DO NOT PARK. Over the windows of
the children's clothing store, large red letters spelled plain BARGUES.
Over the shining windows of the new store on the square, red letters
of the same size and shape read SUPERMARCHÉ BARGUES.

Opinions were divided as to whether a supermarket would be a
good thing or not, and about the Bargueses. What was a supermarket?
One more chain store, but more modern. The food would come from
longer distances and be older. Everything would be refrigerated or
frozen. All the trucks were freezer trucks. Everything would come out
of freezers. Things would be cheaper but worse, and they would be
more expensive and no one would have any choice. The wine would
all be bad. The vegetables, my God! They even had bread in packages.
It was the planners in Paris who planned everything. The Bargueses
were sly ones, but they worked hard. They would do anything for a
sou. You couldn't stop progress.

The square itself where the *supermarché* was evolving had been
classified by the Fine Arts Commission and was protected—too late
to save it from M. Gentiane's tree fellings and asphalt and M. Belpech's truck weighing station. But it was not possible for the Bargueses

to modernize the old building at pleasure, without the approval of the Commission, which may have been just as well. In fact, the prospect of the new business and the preparation for it had a visible effect on the Bargueses, Madame in particular. M. Bargues, in keeping with the position he felt was enjoined upon him by the new venture, left his old rag cart behind the shed, to the rain, sold his ageing horse to the butcher, and bought a used delivery van from the chain that was his new sponsor, a corrugated-aluminum box with a sliding side door. His old linty dark gray clothes and his sidelong manner remained the same, and he had always smiled to himself. But Mme. Bargues wore her smock indoors, and her black coat and round black straw hat outdoors, with a new distinction. An aura of triumph lit her blank tight features, the pallid cheeks and flat brow, the small shallow eyes. She said she was anxious for the transformation of the building to be done in good taste.

The renovations tore out the severe classical doorway, near the corner, removed as much of the ground-floor façade as was structurally feasible and replaced it with sheets of glass, gutted the interior completely, covered the walls and the floor with bright, hard synthetic materials, filled it with fluorescent lights and islands of shelves, and lined the sides with refrigerated cases and freezers with glass doors. At the corner a double glass door allowed customers to enter and walk to the small gleaming turnstile that admitted them to the neatly stacked and brightly lit wares, but would not allow them out again. The exit was past the long Formica counter and the modern cash register at which Mme. Bargues sat, tirelessly ringing up the purchases, greeting her customers one by one with the same chill smile.

Pierre reviled the new descrations of the square. He scorned the Bargueses, the sort of people who were always behind such operations. Even as a ragpicker M. Bargues had grown haughty. In the old days Pierre had occasionally dropped by the shed on rag-sorting days. He had persuaded M. Bargues to set aside old printed military handkerchiefs or crocheted bedspreads or ancient linens, and Pierre would gather them up for next to nothing and take them home for his shop. Now the prices! Bargues, who cared nothing for such things except what they might fetch, was saving them for himself.

On the other hand, a new grocery was not something to be dismissed, however vulgar and regrettable its appearance. Pierre began to give some of his custom to the new emporium. He would go in to try the coffee, the spaghetti, the olive oil, the cheese, the sausage. To compete with the long-established and renowned charcuterie on the side street there was an array of local pâtés, including an imposing selection of foie gras. After the third or fourth visit, when he had forgotten his wallet, Mme. Bargues even advanced him credit, with an indulgent expression, raising her finger, as to a child, as she said, "Until next time." Pierre would stop by the pharmacy after mass and borrow what he needed, he said, for the Sunday dinner at home. Most often it was Bertrand from whom he exacted tribute. Until Bertrand would see him coming and reach into his pocket, saying, "Oh well, it might as well be me. I'm more or less one of the family." And Pierre would invoke his mother's need for foie gras, pocket the money, and waddle across the *place* to the supermarché Bargues. He said that he admired the way everything was set out in the light, so that one could examine it. And he liked the little wire baskets, he told Mme. Bargues, and the cleanness of everything. He praised the brand of noodles they sold, and the Saint-Nectaire. He let her know that he was becoming one of her more loyal customers.

Then, late that spring, his mother died. She had reached a great age and had come to seem all but transparent, and she went peacefully. She had been fading, and the old priest had come and given her extreme unction. After that she rallied and lasted several days. One afternoon Mathilde came into her mother-in-law's room to find Pierre asleep in the chair at the foot of the bed, and when she turned to the bed she realized at once that his mother was not sleeping, as usual, but dead. The nuns came and laid her out on the same bed, and arranged a bowl of water and a sprig of box on the table beside it, and twined a rosary in her gnarled white fingers. The two aged unmarried sisters, the Demoiselles de Courtille, who lived in the village, a few houses away, were notified. They would come as friends and be in the house all night, and help Mathilde; and the one would play the organ and both of them would sing at the funeral service. Pierre could, and often did, give a spirited imitation of each of them, with special attention to the facial expressions and the high notes.

The church no longer had a funeral carriage, and the most suitable vehicle that could be obtained for the occasion was the village mason's gray Peugeot truck with its canvas cover stretched on hoops like a prairie schooner's. The coffin was carried down the stone stairs inside the château and across the courtyard and up the steep cobbled lane to the square, where the truck was waiting, emptied of trowels and troughs and shovels and sacks of lime, hosed out, and lined with flowers. The procession formed behind it and moved slowly the short distance to the church, where the elder Demoiselle de Courtille was already fumbling through an arrangement of Gounod on the wheezing organ, and the priest with the flimsy bladder wailed through the service, pausing to allow the Demoiselles to raise their dogged voices in song. When the coffin had been loaded back into the truck, the procession started again down the hill to the cemetery below the village. But the mason was in the middle of a job a few miles away. The proprietor he was working for was paying well and was impatient. One of the assistants had come, during the funeral service, to say that the mason was urgently needed on the job, and the procession down the hill moved forward without the dignity of its beginning. The truck rolled ahead too fast for the mourners, on foot, to keep up with it. For a while they trudged disconsolately after it, but by the time they left the village the hopelessness of the contest came home to them one by one, and they walked along in gloomy silence with nothing to follow, feeling naked. The first haying had begun, and the sweet smell filled the valley that spread out just below the village. The truck was waiting, with the tailgate down, when the mourners arrived at the open gate of the cemetery.

Along the cemetery wall was a stone ledge where, in the old days when Pierre and Mathilde had first been married, people from the village would come and sit in the summer evenings, and talk until after dark. The late hay wagons, drawn by cows leaning shoulder to shoulder on the incline, would lumber toward the village. Once an asp had flicked its head out of the hay and bitten someone standing there by the gate as the warmth of the load passed. The mourners filed in to stand by their family graves, with heads bowed, and as soon as the coffin had been lifted out to be carried up the path to its tomb, and the flowers had been handed out after it, the truck was on its way again, at an unseemly clip.

Pierre was furious, and a few days later when he went to pay the mason he told him that if that was the way he fulfilled his part of the bargain at a time of bereavement, if that was the best he could do by way of respect for the dead, he should be ashamed to accept the sum they had agreed upon. And after all the years the mason had known Pierre's mother, besides, and her goodness to his family. In fact, Pierre's mother had never had anything to do with the mason's family, apart from employing the mason's father once, years before—and that had ended unfortunately. The mason grumbled something about

Pierre's concern for honoring his own agreements, and they parted on bad terms.

Pierre's vexations proved to be heralds of a gloom that deepened upon him once his mother was gone. The loss of her pension did not improve the family finances. He tried harder than ever to fill the house with *des paying guests* for the summer, but he ignored the ones who came, and left them to the care of Mathilde, and to whatever entertainments Albert and Madeleine might dream up. In company he was capable of regaling persons whom he had just met with stories that they found quite revolting. He slept with difficulty, except after meals, and he complained more than ever about his heart and his headaches, and went nowhere without his boxes of pills. He locked himself up more often than before with the garden boy, until every ambulatory villager had heard their giggles and his shrieks, and the boy's mother came and threatened him with arrest for corruption of minors, and could only be quieted by Pierre's hiring her as a laundress, at outrageous wages, one day a week, *with* her noonday meal. She was dirty and ill-humored and light-fingered and lost clothes, and if he mentioned her shortcomings she threatened to take him to court. Mathilde said nothing, apart from an occasional "Ah" of exasperation, raising her eyes and showing her gold teeth. More and more, in the village, she was praised for her patience, which was linked to the general belief that she was extremely devout. Some said she was a saint.

Pierre, in his melancholy, was putting on even more weight. He ate at random, wherever the opportunity offered, stuffing his mouth hastily, failing to wipe crumbs from his chin or egg from his shirt. He always made a shopping trip to town on Sunday, for foie gras, whatever the weather, but he could no longer invoke his mother's appetite in his pleas. One Sunday, that rainy cool autumn, he came up to Mme. Bargues's counter in his old gabardine, with nothing in his wire basket but two packages of noodles and another of bouillon cubes. She nodded, and rang them up, and waited before ringing up the total, looking up at him. Finally she said, "And the foie gras?"

"What foie gras?" he asked, raising his head and looking down his nose at her.

"M. le Comte," she said.

"I don't know what you mean," he insisted.

"The foie gras in that pocket," she said, pointing to his gabardine.

Fatty's pale face trembled. M. Bargues had emerged from one of the side aisles and was watching. "And the foie gras in *that* pocket," M. Bargues said, pointing to the other side of the coat.

"You are quite mistaken," Pierre said, drawing himself up. "You may keep your noodles. I will not endure such impertinence." He turned and took a step toward the door.

"Just a moment, please, M. le Comte," M. Bargues said. By that time everyone in the store was watching. "I am sorry to bother you, but I watched you take foie gras from the shelf last Sunday, and the Sunday before, and leave without paying for it. If you will pay for it this week—and be more careful in the future—we will say no more about it."

"I am not used to being insulted in this way," Pierre said, "and I will not permit it."

"*That* is the foie gras I am talking about, M. le Comte," M. Bargues said, tapping a can in Pierre's coat. The sound was clearly audible throughout the store, and Pierre's demeanor collapsed.

"I beg your pardon," he mumbled. "It was thoughtless of me. I don't know what I was thinking of. I completely forgot. It's the first time that has ever happened."

"If it had been the first time, M. le Comte, I could have overlooked it," M. Bargues said. "It might have been a mistake. But as I say, it happened—"

"How much?" Pierre asked. M. Bargues told him, and Pierre, with shaking hands, counted out the notes, leaving very few to put back into his wallet. He left the store without a word.

That afternoon the first of his friends learned of his death. He had gone home and complained of a headache and indigestion and had shut himself in the large state bedroom on the ground floor, which the family called the Renaissance room, with its huge ornate stone fireplace and its red-canopied bed. It was almost never used except as a showplace for tourists, but he said that the children made too much noise on the upper floor where he and Mathilde normally slept, and he said he needed to rest, and told the children not to open the room for tourists. Mathilde said he did not look well when he came home, and that his hands were cold. She found him, later in the afternoon, still warm but unconscious. The doctor was sent for, but when he arrived Pierre was already dead. An empty container of one of his remedies, with a warning saying that an overdose could be fatal, was found by his bed. It was not entirely certain whether he had died of the drug or of heart failure, but the latter cause was written into the record.

He lay in state in the same room, under the red canopy. He looked as though he was acting out some joke and was about to laugh, with his tongue out. The Demoiselles sat by the bed with Mathilde, who seemed to be in a dream, utterly stunned. The mason was working on some job miles away, and no one wanted to ask him whether his truck could be used for the funeral. In the end the best thing they could get was the baker's delivery van, with its corrugated-aluminum body and sliding side door, through which the large coffin could be maneuvered only by tipping it on its side. It was autumn. The Demoiselles stripped their garden of flowers for the church. Their voices rose more falteringly than ever. The door of the baker's van opened with a roar and shut with a crash, and the old priest snuffled and puffed and wailed. At the cemetery they had difficulty again getting the coffin out of the van, but it was as nothing to the trouble that awaited them at the square stone opening of the tomb. The grave was below it, and the aperture was too small for the coffin to be lowered through it decorously. The bearers did what they could, but a mason would have been needed to lengthen the entrance to the vault. Finally they had to tip the black box on its side and then upend it so that it could descend into the earth like a sinking ship, bumping sonorously as it went down and settling at last with a hollow clump. There was some doubt among the spectators, for a while, as to whether it was really in place. Then, hesitantly, timidly, they began to file past, for their farewells, and up to Mathilde, to kiss her on both cheeks as she stared ahead through her black veil. "Some of them probably came just for that," her daughter Catherine murmured. "It's not often they get a chance to kiss a Countess."

The villagers wandered out through the gate in black coats and corduroys and black suits and stood talking in the road about Pierre and about other deaths and about sickness in other families and their cows and money and the walnut crop. One peasant from the next village up the hill, who had known Pierre since they were both children, and whom Pierre had cheated out of furniture on more than one occasion, stood by the gate for a moment while the others passed, with his beret off, smiling and slowly shaking his head.

Shepherds

FOR A FEW YEARS I had a garden in a ruined village. I worked through the long summer afternoons on a limestone upland full of the sound of cicadas, in a place that I had found.

The garden was a long triangle surrounded by gray limestone walls worn at the tops like old mountains. When I first came to it there was no garden to be seen. Only one wall was visible. The highest one, chin level. No doubt the oldest. The wall ran along the lane, with long streamers of blackberry canes flowering over it into the bleached rubble and thin grass, the wild marjoram and red herb robin scribbled along the lane. It faced south and saw the whole day. The other side of the wall was deep in a rough sea of wild blackberry bushes. They crowded the undefined corner west of the ruined one-roomed house with its roofless stones, its whole west wall the back of a chimney.

I looked over from the lane onto the storm of blackberry bushes. Beyond that there were three walnut trees standing in broken stones, and then a grove of small oaks, dark and still, with their feet in their own leaves and shadow. M. Vert said they were truffle oaks, and that was a truffle grove. But he added, though he wanted to sell the land, that no one had found a truffle there for a very long time. It was also true that anyone who knew where truffles grew would deny the fact, to keep it secret.

M. Vert pointed to splashes of shiny black balls spilled in the lane. Fresh sheep droppings. "The neighbor," he said, with contempt. He meant, as I realized in a moment, the neighbor's sheep. The neighbor, he explained, pushing up his lower lip hard against the rest of his face, the neighbor permitted his sheep to go anywhere. As though the whole place belonged to him. The neighbor took his sheep in there too, he said, jutting his chin toward the ruin and the enclosure around it.

He showed me where the neighbor had deliberately let his sheep in to that bit of stony upland. The old entrance from the lane, with its stone gateposts, had been destroyed at some time in the past. The huge rough stones that had once been there had been removed. M. Vert told me that he had dragged them away himself, on the trailer behind his tractor. The frayed ends of the wall had collapsed into the long grass and blackberry tangles. A barrier of dead sloe branches, laid across the opening, had been pushed aside. Behind the wall, in the shadow of the bushes, the soft, thick grass of spring, sicklewort, agrimony, horsemint, had been broken and trampled here and there, in thin lines. M. Vert indicated more sheep droppings, pale and old. I would do well, he said, to tell the neighbor he had no business in there, and keep him out.

They were no good in that family, any of them, M. Vert told me, shaking his head as slowly as a bull's, all the way from one side to the other, with his lower lip crumpled up again. They were good for nothing. "They have nothing," he said, as though he were saying everything.

He had stopped under the mossy walnut tree just inside the barrier, to make his point, jabbing the stumps of two lost fingers of his right hand in my direction, twisting one side of his face and closing one eye as he peered up at me. The father was like that, he said to me, and the grandfather. The old woman is just the same. "They do nothing," he said. "They do nothing."

Some land they sold for debts, he told me, and he looked to see whether I knew what "debts" meant. In the pause I realized that he had dropped his voice, and that the oaks were utterly still. The grandfather drank, he continued, still more quietly. They sold some land for that. He touched his forehead and shook his head. "Look," he said, stepping aside, covering his mouth with his hand. "The father. He drank too. He and the sons went hunting. They were always going hunting. They loved to hunt. They had time for that. Doing nothing."

"One day they were going out hunting. They had the dogs. They were just along from the green across from the house, there. Already—" M. Vert held an invisible bottle up to his face, with the

stumps of his fingers, and tossed back his head. "And it was the
morning. They were climbing over the wall, and the father caught his
leg in a bush and the shotgun went off. They got him home but nobody
would go for the doctor, and he died. The sons were drunk at the
funeral."

"You mustn't let them in here," M. Vert said. "They're not to be
trusted. Things have been known to disappear. One knows what one
knows. The neighbor can't work for anybody around here. He doesn't
do anything anyway. He takes out the sheep. The old woman isn't
any better. She's always out looking for something. She has her pension, you understand, and as long as they have that, that's what they
have. They're crazy."

It was an old walnut tree, over us, but it had stayed small in that
thin soil. Three others of the same age followed the wall along the
lane, shading an overgrown inner enclosure. M. Vert was standing
outside the gray wreck of the stone house. A shepherd's house. The
stones of its front door, like the entrance stones along the lane, had
been extracted. M. Vert said that he had pulled them out at the same
time that he had taken the tiles off the roof, and the stones framing
the nearer of the two windows. The stones of the other window were
already cracked from the frost, at the time, he explained, and so he
had left those. That was years ago.

The single room of the ruin was full of whitened rubble from the
walls, pieces of stone clinking underfoot, moss and nettles and blackberry bushes clouding the corners. And yet the walls appeared to be
intact except for the jagged spaces laced with blackberry canes where
the door and front window had been. They still bore, along their
steep-pitched upper edges, the shallow staircases of flat stones, lapped
to keep the rain out. And there were the sockets for the ends of the
oak beams. M. Vert had "pulled" those too, he said, and the rafters.
They were good. He had used them. One heavy beam that was the
mantelpiece of the fireplace was still there at eye level, running most
of the way across the western end of the room into a notch in the
upright slab of rough limestone that made, all by itself, the chimney
corner. Between that stone and the wall, M. Vert explained, they had
piled firewood to keep it dry. It was one of the few things, I thought,
that we knew about them. In the back of the fireplace the small hollow
left by their fires was disappearing under the wiry tangle of small
bushes but it was there, washed white again.

The south wall, where the door and one window had been, and the north wall, with the other window embrasure across from the door, were the lower walls, on which the eaves had rested. The stones inside had been covered, up to the height of the beams, with an uneven coat of sandy cement in which, at a later date, on the east wall, a cross had been scratched, and a few illegible initials, something that looked like a date, over near the north window. The east wall rose higher, to take the end of the rooftree. Above the level where the loft floor had lain on the beams the stones were not cemented or mortared. There was a small stone window hole up there facing out into the walnut leaves and the blue sky. The east wall was already leaning outward. It was, M. Vert said, merely the stones. He turned, and it was clear that he was referring to the whole building.

For some reason, when he had torn out everything he had wanted, he had left the shallow stone sink in the base of the south window, where the dishes had been washed. Outside the window, hens had followed us in from the lane. The neighbor's, M. Vert said. From the trees, voices of chaffinches and black-capped warblers circled us. The walls held the light like a prism, framing a piece of sky in which a few clouds slipped southward so that when I looked up the ruin seemed to be rolling silently toward the shadowy oak trees. It smelled as though the roof were still on and the house had been standing closed.

"I saw it inhabited," M. Vert said. "The old woman here," he said, speaking of the last person who had lived in the house, "grew good potatoes in the garden there."

The inner wall of the garden, on the side away from the lane toward the oaks, ran along under bushes to a low building at the end, round as the houses of the Gauls and roofed with stone slabs of limestone broad as tabletops, piled up in the shape of a straw beehive. An oven. A stone shelf crossed the front of it at waist level: a sill, plain, elegant, and practical. Neglect had roughened it. But inside, the vaulted brick ceiling had never moved. The rusted oven door was still leaning against the dark arch of the opening, held in place by blackberry vines, and the dust on the square bricks of the oven floor was still gray with the ashes of brambles. The gray dust hung in the cobwebs and the few hair roots that had found their way down through the stone roof into the still cave. Field mice lived along the sill. In time I pulled the brambles from the cracks outside, and replanted irises and shepherd's thyme where they had grown before, around the edge of the oven roof and along the tops of the garden walls as they emerged.

The back of the oven occupied one corner of the garden, a small

Romanesque apse, a formal cave in the open, floating through the centuries like an ark on a river. The stones had been as beautifully cut and fitted as they were in the masonry of the churches of the region, and the stone eaves, at waist level if one were standing in the garden, sat on the walls in perfect shallow tiers, like the rings on the cap of a mushroom.

As the brambles were drawn away from the back of the oven their shadows came with them, dark green shadows, and the stone appeared, pale to the sunlight and also facing south, but in a curve, looking onto the south of the world, the southern stars, the south wind with its lashing rain.

By the time I had got to there I had indeed found the garden. I wanted to see where she had grown her potatoes. I wanted to grow some there again.

I had brought a sickle and an old pitchfork with a handle made of a hazelnut sapling, for clearing the brambles. I had watched the people of the region cutting blackberry bushes, the branches that moved in as you turned your back, and made the old men welcome the new machines not as means of profit but as weapons of vengeance upon the brambles that had beaten them from the fields. The machines vindicated them, avenged them, routed the enemy. But even with machines appearing here and there, the old continued to cut the brambles with sickle and pitchfork, at the edges of fields, along the crumbling walls. It was good for them, they said, clearing under the walnut trees before the walnuts fell, and under the plum trees before the plums ripened. And before the plums, here and there the cherries, if they bothered with cherries. Sometimes they cleared the brambles from around the roses at the edges of manure piles, the Autumn Flowering Damasks, the Roses of Four Seasons, as they called them.

The *cantonniers* used a sickle and a pitchfork. They kept their murky bottles tucked under piles of freshly cut green grass in the shade of the sloe bushes as they worked their way along the blowsy verges of the back roads, clearing and leaving a trail of neat piles to vouch for them. They knew where the springs were in the shade. They paused to roll cigarettes, which they smoked soaking wet. They sharpened their sickles carefully, patiently, endlessly. The sweat of a *cantonnier*, according to a local saying, is very bad. The saying was repeated like a chorus, as the *cantonniers* sharpened their sickles in the shade. Some of them were rotund and red and had worked at other things at one time. They kept their hair cut short up the backs of their necks, and they glared and puffed and sweated. Some were languid, silent, fair-haired. It was surprising to learn that they had wives and children. It was also surprising to see how much they had cleared in a day, and where they piled the brambles, keeping them separate from the grass. At one time the young canes of blackberry bushes were used for wrapping the rye straw and then stitching the long rolls into beehives. And the dried bramble cuttings were piled up to burn in the ovens, to bake the big loaves of bread for the week. For cutting thick brush, sometimes the people of the region used a heavy crescent-shaped sickle at the end of a long handle—a billhook, a *serpette*—but I was never very adept with one of those. With the ordinary sickle I could watch what I was doing, catch sight of what was growing under the brambles before I swung the blade, cutting the years.

The hens followed me through the barrier and scratched among the oak leaves. There were so few people on that upland that there were almost no words in the day. To the left of the place where the entrance from the lane had once stood framed in stone the bushes were thick and dense, the soil under them black. Some kind of out-building must have stood there, with its back to the beautifully built wall that formed the narrow end of the garden. That section of wall, I saw as the brambles were drawn back, still bore its top course of flat stones lapped vertically. All of the walls that were built to last, it was said—which meant all of the walls until the present century—were built like that. The vertical stones held the tops of the walls together, and the sheep, and even the goats, did not like to run on them. The entrance to the garden was at the narrow, eastern end, just at the corner near the house. There was a stone sill at the opening, for a gate, one step up. A garden of blackberries, nettles, and wild marjoram. I wondered why I should change it, but I did.

In the fair afternoons of spring, with the light still downy, the air sweet from the ground, I came day after day to slip through the newly reopened garden entrance and cut another patch of brambles. I carried off the thrashing, snatching, scratching tangles of vines on the end of the pitchfork, out of the old garden, to stack them along the low places in the walls, where the hens came over. The narrow end of the garden was not much more than a dozen feet across. West of there, the garden ran for some sixty feet or more. The far wall, hidden in brambles, seemed buried in the remote future. Here and there through gaps in the brambles I could see that it too had most of its vertical course of stones along the top. One morning while the air was still cool I found, in the dark damp shadow of the brambles, the white translucent skin of a large harmless snake. In two pieces.

When I had laid bare a little of the inside of the wall along the lane, M. Vert came by one afternoon with a load of sheep manure and forked it over the wall, where I found it later in the day. A present. He had told me that he liked my efforts to revive the garden, and when I saw him and spoke of the manure he said that he had been taking it out to the fields anyway, and had just brought me a load in passing.

By then I had begun, with an old digging fork, to turn over a little of the area I had cleared, working the tines down into the heavy red clay and the mass of roots that had become the possessors of the place. I laid bare the hard brown knots of ancient blackberry kingdoms, the wiry arteries leading down between stones, mats of finer roots full of the dark soil that they had helped to make. The limestone base of the garden was seldom more than a foot below the surface, and I came to learn, a few inches at a time, clefts and fissures that led down through the porous shield of the upland with its endless galleries and caverns and underground streams far below me out of the sun. The place itself was a memory that I was recovering. Some few of the living, perhaps, and many of the dead, one by one, had known it this way, inch by inch, root by root. They had carried many fields in their minds, like this, and had spoken from that knowledge and had died with it. It was not something you could tell, apart from particular details, now and then. Every day it was strange to me to realize that I was letting the light in, and that as I did so the colors emerged without hesitation from where they had always been.

The first time the soil was turned over was devoted chiefly to the roots, levering them, tracing them, working them loose from their lives in the dark, hauling them into the sunlight. But even in that first disturbance of the contented ground I found signals of other lives to which I was wholly unforeseen. The shafts of worms. The iridescent tracks of snails. The crumbled litter of field mice and their children in the walls. The moles that had tunnels under the walls down into the cracks of the rock. One hot day as I went on interfering I lifted a stone and surprised a viper under it, who flexed, watching me, and waited. I let the stone back down carefully and never saw him afterward. The same encounter had happened years before, miles from there, and I began to expect it to come round again.

The heavy soil was full of stones, fragments of the bedrock, pieces shattered by the frost or fallen from the hands of the builders of walls, or from the walls themselves. There were fossils: extinct mollusks as large as lemons, etchings of sections of ferns. Small square nails made by hand. The iron sole from a wooden shoe. A bone button. A small coin from the last century, which someone had missed. Shards of crockery with pictures of flowers. The day I broke the second tine of the digging fork in a cleft of the rock I found an older digging fork in the ground next to the wall, the handle rotted out and all of its tines broken at different lengths. Even with short teeth, M. Vert explained to me later, the old forks were still good for digging potatoes. The day I reached the back of the oven, in my clearing, and pulled the brambles back from the masonry, I found, tucked among the flat stones of the eaves, part of the curved blade of a sickle.

By the time M. Vert had brought his load of manure I was ready to start layering some of it into the compost pile of weeds and grass roots that I had started in the corner, and digging some in where I thought to put in the first seeds, along the inner wall. Radishes, to have something soon from that garden to encourage me. There was a variety that promised radishes in eighteen days, and it was true. Less than three weeks after I had sowed them I took some up the lane for my supper, and some to Mme. Vert for theirs. She gave me a handful of lettuce plants from her garden, wrapped in a piece of wet newspaper. And I set in the first furrow of beans. Broad beans. It was still early enough in the year for them, and they grew well in the heavy lime soil of the region. They could even be sowed there in the fall, like St. Catherine peas. You wanted to get them in late, so that they would scarcely have begun to make leaves before the real frosts, otherwise the tender shoots would be bitten back by the winter. But if you caught the right moment in late October or early November, and the moon and the rain were right, and it was a mild winter, they would start off early in the spring while the ground was dark. A late hard frost could kill them then too, if it was severe enough, but you had a good chance of having young broad beans and St. Catherine peas weeks early, and if you lost them you could dig them under as soon as it was dry enough, and start again.

The wide trench for planting broad beans always looked like part of an archaeological survey. Any roots that were still left after the soil had been dug and dug and manured and dug again trailed in from the sides like hair and could be lifted out and tossed to the pile in the corner. I had one of the wide heavy mattocks of the region, bought at a fair without a handle—the handle came later. It seemed to do the job by itself, lifting out the soil a few inches deep, along the stretched white string.

The flat beans went in with the brown eye facing upward. An old woman in her walled garden in the village three miles away explained that the reason for that is that the sprout comes out of the eye and grows upward. If you have the bean on its side or with the eye downward the sprout has to grow farther. It may have to grow all the way around the bean to get to the surface, and it takes several days for it to do that. It will be behind the shoots that started the right way up. In heavy rains, she said, the bean planted wrong way up may even rot before its shoot reaches the surface.

I never knew beans of that kind when I was a child. They were unheard of where I grew up, in Pennsylvania, unless they were grown by some of those "foreigners" whose gardens my parents and their friends made fun of because instead of having patches of dazed shorn grass known as lawns, and nameless unnoticed bushes around their houses in the approved fashion, they "crowded every inch with vegetables." It may still be important in some neighborhoods to show that you are above the need to do anything of the kind for yourself. It seems to me that I saw, outside Pisanelli's Italian grocery store, on the steep curve of Lower Taylor Street, leading down into town, tall wicker baskets full of beans of that kind, lying on their sides, a pinkish or greenish tan, thicker than lima beans, longer and not so round, shaped more like a human ear or fetus. There were other baskets nearby filled with snails. If I was with my mother she remarked each time that foreigners ate those things. Everything about the place drew me as it was not supposed to: the sharp, troubling smells, the cheeses, sausages and hams hanging in string halters, the bundles of herbs, the gold of the cans. My mother shook her head at the flies and hurried us along home. When I was older and alone I walked past more slowly, a little anxious, listening to the strange language coming out of the darkness inside: the foreign-language station on the radio, which I learned to find in my room at home and play quietly, in secret. I suppose the beans in those baskets had been imported. I remember now the light sound they made when someone, thinking of buying some, picked up a handful and let them run out between fingers and fall back into the basket like the dripping of eaves. Dried like that, they are smooth as foreheads, and it was a pleasure, those years later, to set each one back into the ground.

Always when they were planted it was cool. And each time I put them in I saw again the first field of them that I had come upon, long before I ever grew any myself. That was in Spain, in Mallorca, at the middle of the century. The north coast of the island. In the first weeks of the year when the days were sunny I climbed the stone paths and the steps built into the faces of the olive terraces far above the sea, toward the oak woods where the pigs ran, toward the huts of the charcoal burners, and the cliffs looming above me. The almond trees were in flower and the peaches in bud. The spring wildflowers on the terraces changed from one day to the next: anemones, lilies, cyclamens. The air was heavy with the smell of flowers, and as I climbed the fragrance grew still more intense. I heard a man singing a few long phrases, then talking, then singing again. I climbed a terrace wall and beyond two rows of olive trees there was a small open field, a surprise on the steep mountainside. The air was cooler up there, and there were wisps of cloud drifting from the cliff down across the field, and the strongest and sweetest smell was coming with them. The field was full of grayish-green broad-leaved plants, less than two feet tall, covered with flowers like white-and-black butterflies. A young man in black was walking away between the rows behind a mule that was pulling a small cultivator. He was talking to the mule, and singing. Then he came to the end of the row and turned and started back, and saw me. He stopped singing, and he talked to the mule in a lower voice. When he came near and I greeted him he scarcely answered. He wanted me to go, and I knew it, but I asked him what the plants were that he was growing. Not believing me—how could anybody not know that?—he told me that they were beans, and I left. But it was not until I grew broad beans myself, years later, and the oval leaves unfurled and the white-and-black flowers opened and the scent was there again, that I knew what kind of beans those were with the chill mist flowing through them.

The beans came up along the inner wall facing south, and I set some young plants of savory, that I had grown in pots, at the ends of the rows, thinking already of picking savory sprigs to steam with the beans when they were ready. The limestone upland, the *causse*, was fragrant too, in whatever season, and its scents changed through the hours as the shadows moved, and the cool patches in the air, the damp currents from under the trees. Beyond the west wall of the garden, in the spring, three big bird cherry trees silently exploded in white flowers, their thick sweetness laced with a rank bitterness like that of almonds. The bees hovered for hours in the sunlight reflected from the clouds of translucent petals among the small, waxy, pale green leaves. The smells of wet leaves and moss wandered along the walls under the oaks and walnuts. In the middle of the day the sun brought out the subtle smell of the upland itself, made up of scents of thyme and marjoram, of the baked stones and leaves and earth, the acrid notes of box and ivy. They turned through the day, undefinable but clear, and out in the garden on the *causse*, among the network of overgrown walls, they came to be a kind of sundial. From the scent of the air I could tell what part of the day it was.

And the *causse* was not silent. Bending toward the soil I would hear the sounds of the upland rise in my ears like water, though a moment before I might not have noticed that they were there. The leaves and the grass rustling. Cicadas, as the days grew warm. Crows off in the woods, half echo. Finches. The tsip of titmice. The occasional distant clonk of a sheep bell. The pensive hens cawing to themselves up the lane, reminding me of someone. There were few voices, and few sounds that broke the low continuo. Sometimes on the breeze I would hear M. Vert herding his half dozen red cows down another lane beyond the broad green, taking them to pasture in the morning, usually on foot. "Veng, veng, veng," he would be calling. He was away out of sight of the garden, but I knew that he was walking along rapidly in his black rubber boots crusted from the barn, a man short as a dwarf in a fairy tale, with his rod over his shoulder, looking back from time to time at the lead cow, whose clear bell was singing behind him. If it was raining he walked more slowly under his big black umbrella.

Some days he came with his daughter Jacinthe, taller and more robust than he, and the black dog Montagne, who barked along behind them. Sometimes she came by herself, calling "Veng, veng, veng," more melodically than her father, more like the bell. Or one of them drove after the cows in their Citroën 2CV *fourgonette* that could take two sheep in the back and you could squeeze their lambs in after them. If the cows were brought down to one of M. Vert's pastures in the morning after milking, they would be fetched home at milking time in the evening, and when I heard him or Jacinthe talking them up the lane, and the bell steadily receding, it was time to start putting the garden tools away in the oven and—once the garden had begun to supply me with things to eat—to start picking something for supper.

But I did not hear that every day. M. Vert had several pastures and moved the cows around for reasons having to do with the weather, the grass, or where he happened to be working. There were other sounds that told of the progress of the day, that it was growing late. There were the birds. And there was that other herding voice, the neighbor's, coming from the direction opposite to M. Vert's—from the east, from out of sight too, when the neighbor was bringing his flock of thirty-seven sheep home along the lane where it dipped through dark oak woods, widened as it descended across a slope of naked rock, still between walls, then wound through a green hollow with glowing young grass in meadows on either side and more woods beyond them, and passed beside the spring under overhanging rocks that had been the water source for the ruined shepherd's house. An arch of rusted iron and the crumbling lace of a pulley were reflected against the sky in the surface below.

I could hear the neighbor coming from as far as the oak woods, shouting at his sheep, "*Meh! Meh! Veux tu?*" Scolding at their tails, while their heads were poked through wooden gates into the tempting green. He was pretending to drive them past the rich grass that was not his, but he waited until they had a chance to get a bit of grazing first. A voice thick rather than deep. Rapid and crabbed, belligerent and anxious.

The sheep pattered through the mud and wet grass below the spring and scattered on the green space where the walls fell aside unevenly at the site of an intersection of lanes, some of which had long been abandoned, one of them leading down into the thickets and shadows of a hollow of oaks and sloe bushes. Two that were still used parted on the slope and continued to climb in diverging directions. From the spring the neighbor could take his sheep home along either of them. He could bear to the right and go up the bank to the paved road that had buried the lane for some distance, and follow the road to the left, under the railroad bridge, and then pick up the lane again—his and mine—on the other side, and clamber over the big rocks, like steps, on the slope, toward the garden. But he never came that way, although M. Vert said it was the way he was supposed to come. I could see why the neighbor would not want to take his sheep on the paved road, the long way around, under the railroad bridge. Instead he came the way he was not supposed to, turning left on the track made by his own sheep, up the railroad embankment and across the track, and on up through the no-man's-land of rocks and scrub on the other side, to pick up the old lane there.

They crossed at a spot where a small maintenance hut stood by the tracks on a bed of crushed stone that looked alien, like the rest of the embankment, even though the actual stone had come from nearby. There was a grilled opening under the wooden eaves of the shed, and the door was seldom locked. The neighbor always paused to peer in through the grille, and sometimes opened the door to look inside, as though he were checking. And then he shut it carefully, quietly, and turned to his loud reminding of the sheep. He knew, of course, the hours when the trains came by, but even so he hurried them off the right-of-way, the single track, and onto the rough hillside beyond it where they knew the way up the slope and along to the left, to the walls that led under the walnut trees before the garden. Once the sheep were well away from the track his scolding lost some of its urgency. His voice dropped and became more absentminded, even confidential, shooing them home, the few old bells bonking their dull notes, the lambs baaing, the ewes' guttural answers. They were still hidden from my sight, around the curve of the lane, behind the ruin of the shepherd's house and the overgrown enclosure under the walnut trees, when I began to hear their hooves coming like a rain squall on the bare rock of the lane, and then the sound of their jaws tearing at the grass at the foot of the walls. Then if I straightened up in the garden I would see them nosing in at the entrance. When they saw me they always startled and panicked and rushed a few steps backward, falling over each other, and usually about then the neighbor would appear around the bend, from the left.

He was stocky and short. Somewhere in his late thirties. He dressed like no one else on the *causse*. A tight sleeveless tank top, of a bright color, usually red. Satin athletic shorts, usually red. Sneakers. (In the summer.) His arms and legs were thick and tanned, and he wore no hat—a fact that, for M. Vert, was the ultimate mark of depravity. But M. Vert regarded the entire costume, which obviously had been im- itated from pictures in the sports sections of the papers, as evidence of insanity, and a deliberate affront to the world as it should be. "He doesn't wear a hat," he said, shrugging his shoulders to sum it all up. "He'll kill himself." M. Vert washed his hands of the whole bad business, and deliberately talked of other things for a minute or two.

M. Vert had a well of calumny about the neighbor into which he dipped whenever I saw him. He would inquire about the neighbor and leer confidentially and then produce the next morsel of innuendo. Things missing from empty houses in the village across the upland. Things missing from another empty house among the pastures. Nobody else around there would have taken anything, M. Vert repeated. Then a few years before when a nice young foreigner camped by the green the neighbor had come and hung over the wall and made remarks. He had made remarks, Mr. Vert repeated. "Reflections, even," he added by way of elucidation, but he raised his face with an expression indicating that he would carry the nature of those reflections in silence to the grave. The reflections had got worse, if possible, when the young foreigner was joined by a young woman and they both slept in the same tent and sometimes took naps in the hot afternoons. The neighbor leaned over the wall and watched them, and tried unsuccessfully to start conversations. He called in at them when they were in the tent in the afternoons. On the Sundays when his brother the roofer came from town to visit, bringing his fiancée in her tight bright clothes who stood and watched while the brother dismantled his car outside the house, on the green, she and the neighbor and the brother played the car radio as loud as they could and made the car engine roar, vroom, vroom, vroom, just to keep the foreigner and his girlfriend awake. And the neighbor had leaned over the wall and shouted, "Shouldn't sleep in the daytime," over and over. He and his brother went and sat on the roof of the hen house, where they could look down into the grass around the tent, and from there they threw nutshells, twigs, and little stones at the tent. The neighbor's two dogs never stopped barking at the foreigners. When the foreigner had guests once or twice, who went home after dark, the neighbor jumped out from behind a bush, in the lane, to frighten them. M. Vert ended every installment of his detraction by saying, "He's crazy. They're all crazy," and often with an insistence that it had always been so.

I wondered, in fact, how the legend surrounding the excluded family had grown up, and how it had started, and whether it had been part of the neighbor's life from the beginning. I did not want to ask M. Vert, but I was not surprised one day to hear him mention as a further detail of his scorn for his neighbor, "He can't read. The old woman either." The neighbor had been the youngest child, M. Vert told me, and had scarely gone to school at all.

M. Vert's scorn included the neighbor's dogs, Tikou and Finou.

"Somebody gave them to him," M. Vert said. It was the usual way of acquiring dogs in the country, but M. Vert's tone implied that in this case it had been a way of disposing of animals nobody would have wanted. Many farms had two dogs at least. One would be the working dog, the herd dog, the dog in charge of the place, the watchdog, who on some farms was shut in with the cows or the sheep at night. The other, which was needed as a sign of gentlemanly leisure, was the hunting dog, who did nothing most of the year but eat soup and wander under the brambles sniffing, until hunting season.

The neighbor's hunting dog had been a trial to the young foreigners too, M. Vert informed me. And they were perfectly correct, the young people, he insisted indignantly. But the neighbor's dog had got in there more than once and stolen their food and left his dirt. When they emerged from their camp the dog barked at them, running in circles around them. That was the older dog, a rather large, dirty, white-and-black fox terrier, more or less. Tikou. When he had run around the green barking for an hour or so Tikou was capable of picking up some scent or other, down a lane, or over a rock pile, and then he would be gone for hours, not returning until late, and there had been complaints from the village across the *causse* of visits from Tikou. Stray dogs might be shot in the country, and the owners, M. Vert said, were liable for any damage they caused. The neighbor took to locking Tikou into his kennel, an ancient stone pigsty roofed with slabs of stone in the ruins behind the house, from which Tikou's muffled barking might rise, as from the grave, at any hour, and go on and on.

The other dog, Finou, was a dark smooth-haired bitch of no recognizable ancestry who had arrived skinny and half grown, and had learned all she knew from Tikou: how to run around the green and bark, how to duck around corners and bark, how to find things and slink off with them. She was the working dog. But she spent most of her time nosing around the green or tied up to the doghouse inside the chain-link fence that enclosed a few square feet of ground in front of the neighbor's house. The brother the roofer had built it like the pictures, with a tile roof, and Finou would jump onto the roof and bark for a while and then slither down into the doghouse below. Finou obviously was not much help with the sheep, ignoring them, rushing off in one direction or another, having to be shouted back, and the neighbor seldom took her with him. If she was along he could be heard coming from farther away, roaring at her to come back, "Finou!

Ici!" much louder than he bawled at his sheep. And because they were coming home she was likely to be well ahead of the sheep, coming around the bend in the lane. Then she would catch sight of me over the wall, and though she knew perfectly well who I was she would stop as though she had been caught in a robbery, and start to bark, and back up, and run back, colliding with the sheep, and hide behind the neighbor, peering around his legs and growling.

At first the neighbor looked at me that way himself, when he saw me in the garden straightening up beside a pile of cut brambles. The dog was not with him, and he was surprised and glowered and clearly was not disposed to answer my greeting with anything more than the unavoidable monosyllables. Yet day by day, evening by evening, the solemnities lengthened. They were warmed by mutual curiosity. The neighbor passed with the wall at his chin level, and he glanced over. But he said nothing and shooed the sheep homeward, sounding like rain going ahead of him. The hens and ducks had gathered in the lane and were waiting for his mother to get back with her load of firewood, to feed them outside the disused stone barn with holes in the roof that she used as a hen house. "It doesn't belong to them," M. Vert said. "It belongs to a cousin who bought it from the family. But they use it as though it were their own. Someday he's going to want it." It was part of a whole farm, with a yard in front of it full of brambles, and several huge walnut and oak trees. In the middle of the courtyard the stone lid of a cistern full of water, and a stone drinking trough awash with dead leaves. As he got to the entrance to that courtyard the neighbor always turned to look back.

It went from "Good evening" to "Good evening. How are you?" "Very well. And you?" "Very well. Thank you. Lovely evening." "Oh yes. So you're making a garden." "Seeing what I can do." "The old woman" (he had a slight stammer), he said, "who used to live here raised good potatoes." "What did she use for manure?" "Oh, I think it was sheep." Before each sentence his eyelids leaped up drawing the eyes wide and his mouth opened into a small *o* through which he inhaled. "I don't know whether she had rabbits." A revelation came to him. "She had her goats," he said. "And her sheep. Yes. That's what she used. I'm sure of it. That's what she used."

We became friends.

One evening as I was going up the lane toward the west, after leaving the garden for the night, with my vegetables and some of the tools in the wheelbarrow, I saw him watching me over the wall in back of his house, to my right. The wall was beautifully built up to shoulder level, and above that a few sticks propped up a couple of feet of chicken wire. The chicken-wire gate hung open. The neighbor was standing inside, in weeds up to his chest.

"This," he said, "is my mother's garden."

"Oh, is it?"

"She has lettuces," he said. He reached down and pulled up a beautiful broad head of lettuce and handed it to me. "Here," he said. "And here's another." I protested. "That's pure manure," he said. "She puts chicken, too. From those," he added, pointing to the red fowls waiting with the draggled white ducks in the lane. "She grows vegetables," he said—and words failed him for a moment. Then he raised one finger and shut his eyes and said, "Extra."

As I thanked him I said I imagined the soil must be very good in there. "Oh yes," he said. I asked whether they suffered from moles. "Oh—" He shook his head as at a proof of immorality. "It's disgusting."

"What do you do?" I asked. But he told me instead what you could do, and we went down the list, hoping that that would keep the problem at bay for the night. You could put a piece of bramble down the mole tunnel, the "gallery," leaving the thorns on, and then the mole would run into it in the dark and hurt its nose and go away. Some said that if you put onions into the galleries the moles went somewhere else, but the neighbor said he believed those sly beasts only made other tunnels around the onions, right away. He was sure of it. And they could do it faster than you could move. "They're sly, those sly beasts," he said. Then there was the plant. The mole plant. The neighbor's uncle had a mole plant and he never had a mole on his place. I said I had the plant and the moles had come up under it and uprooted it.

"You can trap them," he said. "At one time they trapped them. With traps. In the tunnels. Everyone set them. That's the best. You can be sure that way. You can go with that."

I asked him whether he could do that.

"What?"

"Trap moles."

"Oh yes," he said, not believing it himself. And then there was poison. I asked whether they used poison. "Oh no," he said.

"There's gas," he remembered. He had heard that some used that, but he was not sure how they did it. "And rockets." Rockets appealed to him. "Say," he said, "it's like this. You take the rocket. You put the match to the end. Sssss! You put it in the tunnel. You stamp the ground down on top of it so it can't get out. Ssssss! Phoooo! It goes everywhere. Like a rocket. You see smoke coming up out of the ground over here, over there, over there."

"Have you seen it?"

"Oh yes. At my brother-in-law's. I saw it in the strawberries. My God."

"And is that what you use?"

"Oh no."

I stopped asking what they used. The chicken wire held up a few pea vines loaded with peas. He told me they grew by themselves. "We haven't put anything in here this year," he said. "I should do some work here. If I had time. Leeks," he said. "There are leeks." He pointed down through the long spring grass where I could make out rows of leeks fattening.

"Sometimes I work here," he said. "Sometimes my mother. She likes flowers." Several clumps of thick weed complete with soil and root flew through the gate into the lane, where the hens began to worry them. Tikou's ghostly barking beat at us steadily but without hope.

"Would you like some radishes?" I asked the neighbor, holding out a bunch.

"Oh, how beautiful they are," he said.

"Take them," I said.

"Oh no. One doesn't need them," he said, his eyebrows making a wild leap. "One doesn't need anything."

"You gave me those beautiful lettuces for my supper."

"That was a present. That doesn't count."

"It's a small return. It would be my pleasure."

"Well, after all—" But he didn't move.

"Do you eat radishes?"

"Oh yes," he said, firmly dispelling any notion that they might not eat radishes. But he looked doubtful. I held them out to him again. "It's very kind," he said, "but there was no need."

The hens broke and moved back down the lane to intercept the neighbor's mother, who was arriving slowly dragging a small dead tree. We turned and watched.

"It's my mother," he said. "She's bringing some wood. For the fire." After a moment he asked, "Do you eat soup?"

I assured him that I did. His mother came up to where we were and stopped. She appeared to be in her seventies, thin, with a hand-some narrow aquiline face, leathery, but hatched with deep white lines. Her head was constantly tilted backward, so that she looked out along her nose from under narrowed lids. She was wearing a faded cotton dress that reached almost to her ankles, with an apron bleached to pale gray over it, and frayed sneakers without socks. Her gray hair was pulled back into a bun.

"It's my mother," he said to me again.

"Good evening, madame," I said. We had already spoken when I had seen her passing in the lane. But she had never gone beyond returning my greeting. "Good evening," she said, as always, distantly, as though she were looking past me and might be greeting anyone at all.

"Look at that. What he has given us," the neighbor said, holding up the radishes.

"And your son gave me these beautiful lettuces of yours," I said to her.

"Oh yes, I gave him some lettuces."

"Oh yes," she said, her voice trailing off. "Good."

"One has too many," he said to us both, and to the world. I thought it the moment for formalities, and told her my name.

She nodded, narrowing her eyes further, and wiped her hand on her apron before shaking mine. Her hand was cold, like a chicken's legs. I turned to shake the neighbor's warmer substantial hand.

"I'm called Michel," he said to me.

"Good evening," she said again, faintly, behind me, and started off, dragging the dead tree on to the corner of the building, the sound of scratching branches and of hens clucking after her suddenly cut off as she disappeared.

"She's going to make soup," Michel said. I said I must do the same.

"You make soup?" he asked. It seemed hard for him to believe.

"I eat what I've got," I said, pointing to the first peas beside the lettuces and radishes in the wheelbarrow.

"That's very good," he said, to say something, and I thanked him again and picked up the handles of the wheelbarrow, to be going.

"After all, we're neighbors," Michel said. "If you need anything."

"Thank you," I said. "And the same to you." And we nodded to each other and I took the same route his mother had taken, along the wall of the low building. It was set at an angle to the corner and formed one side of a kind of gateway into the open green. From the back it looked incongruous: a beautifully made wall built of dressed dry stone, with huge slabs for eaves not six feet above the ground, and a course or two of flat stones above those, giving way to an elaborate patchwork of overlapping pieces of rusty tin, old signs, lengths of sheathing and of stamped-metal paneling, carefully laid, and held in place with rocks.

But the end wall, rising to a blunt peak, and topped all the way up with lapped flat stones, appeared to be perfect, and the façade, around the corner, made it plain that the building was very ancient, its real age beyond determining and its structure exemplifying a tradition that went back to the architecture of the Gauls.

Everything was built of stone. The eaves, at eye level, as on the other side of the building, were covered with similar slabs of flat stone, and the stones continued to the top of the roof, as on a pyramid. The façade was utterly simple: one door in the middle, a step below ground level. The ceiling inside, as I learned, was a stone vault. The building was what the family referred to as their cellar.

On the *causse*, in many places, it was all but impossible to dig cellars in the solid limestone that underlay most of the upland. If the houses were built out on the relatively level pastures an adjoining building was set a few feet into the ground to hold the coolness of the earth, for a cellar. In many places the cellar was much older than the present house, and had seen several houses come and go with their owners and clothes and languages.

In the cellar they stored potatoes and hung carcasses, kept eggs and wine, cheese in flat baskets, sausages hanging from hooks. Each cellar had an intimacy of its own, like that of the family bedrooms. Only the family went there. Only the family knew what was in there. In the daily course of existence people did not pry into each other's cellars, and did not go along if their hosts went to fill a bottle. It was not altogether polite to stare into a cellar, any more than it would have been to stare at a bedroom window. This was particularly true of the neighbor's family. The cellar was full of what they needed.

Attics were another matter. Unless someone was ashamed of something in the past, attics simply represented storage of what was no longer needed. The owners could recognize it and laugh about it. The things people used to wear. The family knew what was in the cellar. They had forgotten what was in the attic, except perhaps for a cleared area where walnuts were dried, or grapes left to shrivel, to be made into liqueurs. In some houses the attic was simply a disused room on the ground floor, full of piled-up furniture. No one from outside the family had seen into the cellar at the neighbor's house. But no one outside the family had seen the attic either, and few had stepped inside the front door. There was an invisible wall halfway between the chain-link front gate, set between columns of cemented *causse* limestone, and the doorway, which stood open in good weather if anyone was home. On summer evenings Michel could be seen sitting inside there at the table in the main room, which was called the kitchen. He was eating, or simply sitting. He waved. But if he wanted to talk he came out to the gate.

The house was much more recent than the cellar. Perhaps a couple of hundred years old, but it was hard to tell because it had been covered with makeup. The brother the roofer had replaced its dark mossed red tiles with bright red, modern, pressed, "mechanical" tiles. From the pitch of the roof it was plain that the house was not of an age to have been built, originally, with a roof entirely of stone. Thatch to begin with, perhaps, or the flat tiles—in either case with a few layers of flat stones along the eaves, at the base.

"It's more convenient," the brother the roofer, whose name was Robert, told me one Sunday, referring to the bright "mechanical" tiles. We were standing outside the strip of chain-link fence in front of the neighbor's house, on the green, with the ducks and sheep clattering among the stones behind us, nosing the curled grass and clover and calamint out from under the scrub sloe bushes and long gray velvet leaves of mullein. "It's more convenient. You can go with it." He leaned back in satisfaction against the wall of the stone oven, and looked at the roof. The stone eaves had gone, and the lips of the lowest tiles hung over the edge of the roof, above a new metal rain gutter.

"It doesn't fear the frost as much as the old kind," he said. "The old ones are good, though, if you put them on right," he added, slightly patronizing, straightening the visor of his peaked cap made of brown suiting material. The jacket of his brown suit was draped through the open window of his worn pale green car, in which the radio was playing softly. He was wearing a white shirt and his vest. He was not planning to tune up the car that Sunday.

He had brought out a few bottles of store wine from town. Michel was still picking pieces of chicken from between his teeth with his fingers. Robert's pale fiancée (as she was always called; her name was Martine), in a tight blouse, an aquamarine cardigan drawn around her shoulders, was standing with her arms folded, looking out at nothing over the green. It did not seem likely that they would be staying long. But meanwhile Robert gazed with approval at his handiwork on the front of the family house. A simple façade: a solid door in the middle, one window to either side, the woodwork painted brown. A fly curtain of strips of red and yellow plastic drawn back in the doorway. "The mother's" two pairs of white fantail pigeons came and went from a pigeon box tacked up under the eaves by the door. The massive flat polished stone set in the ground in front of the door was safely embedded in cement, which extended under the wooden threshold and some way into the room before the board floor started. And in front of the house where the old wall had been, only the stone foundation remained; above that the chain-link fence now enclosed Finou's tile-roofed doghouse, the pigeons' cement drinking dish surrounded by duck droppings, and a patch of "the mother's" hollyhocks, dahlias, and marigolds.

Robert shrugged. "As for the pitch, the roof didn't need to be so steep for the mechanicals," he said. "That was the way they built it for the old ones. But to change it? All the rafters? My faith! For that? And besides, one needs the attic." He sucked his teeth. "It's a good chimney," he said. "Doesn't smoke much. Oh, maybe when it blows from the south, like everywhere. But I don't like that roof the way it is around in the back there," he said, tipping his head toward the cellar. "It needs some work. It's old. My faith. The stones froze. With time. The cats live up there. It's better. For the rats. It was full of little bones up there."

"What kind of bones?"

"Every kind of bones. The cats took them, you know. New bones, old bones."

"That one," Michel said, pointing to a very small, stringy, whitish cat with thin fur, slipping out of the house and dashing along the wall toward the lane. "My God she's good for the rats. Oh! One has no rats, that's all. That's how it is."

"The females are the best," Robert said.

"You mustn't nourish them too much," Michel said. "Just enough."

I asked Robert what he would use to repair the cellar roof.

"Tin is cheapest," he said. "The undulated galvanized. I can even get it wholesale secondhand."

"Yes," Michel said. "That's the cheapest."

"But it's not worth it, to put it up there," Robert said. "By the time you put up something to nail it to. You might just as well put up rafters and lath and do it in tiles. Old tiles. Even channel tiles. The pitch is better for channel tiles. But one doesn't pick them up so easily. Tiles are expensive now."

"Oh, they're expensive now," Michel said. "One has some saved," he added, with a sly, conspiratorial look. "There," he pointed to a walnut tree beyond the house. The brambles were head high underneath it and among the brambles I could make out the square bulk of a mossy stack of tiles.

"One keeps them," Michel said. "And one has more." And he remembered, "Have to stack them the right way. Or they freeze." He chopped the air with his hand. "Zero."

"They're falling all the time," I said, pointing across the green to the west, to another ruined shepherd's house like the one at the garden down the lane. It had stood there empty for as long as I had known the green and the parallel walls of its lanes trailing off in three directions over the limestone. Off to the east, to the ruin where I had the garden. To the north, all the way to the paved road, passing on the way another empty farmhouse under big lime trees, and then the home fields of M. Vert's farm, and to M. Vert's farmhouse, and beyond the farm and the road, on up the hill through the woods, past ruins, ruins. And to the west past the great half-ruined, half-restored farmhouse where I was living, and on out between pastures to another empty house among massive rocks, and more oak woods.

Every year I watched the shepherd's house on the green move farther into decay. When I first saw it one could peer through a crack in a shutter on the south and through another on the west, and see that it was full of furniture. There, emerging from the night of the room, were the ends of machine-made nineteenth-century high beds with headboards, footboards, lathed wooden globes on square columns at the corners, the old wood varnished, the varnish blackened. White lace bedspread. White opaline glass kerosene lamp hanging from a beam. I thought it would be wonderful to be inside, to see it. But I saw it through the shutter. There was one room. I saw the end of a table, part of a shelf over the fireplace.

The house sat back inside its wall, which ran along the green and turned a corner. The sheep barn that had accompanied the house had dissolved into a pile of stones on which the hound's-tongue and stonecrops grew in the spring, and the neighbor's sheep rattled and browsed in the first evenings of summer. The walnut trees that had stood near the house had died. A few cherry trees still lingered, with dead branches and yellow leaves. A small stone outbuilding at the entrance, perhaps a cart shed or goat shed or hen house once, was no longer anything but an enclosure, the roof long since gone. The owners had taken its tiles to repair the house roof, which in turn was falling. On nights of storm and wind I could hear tiles slide down the roof and smash on the ground, and the rain would come down harder afterward. At times on still nights a tile would let go and grate its hoarse way down the roof and crash like splashing water, leaving the green startled and dark.

On the stone above the door the date 1819 had been chiseled, with a heart upside down above it. A date meant nothing. It could have been put on at a later time. Or the stone could have been brought from an earlier building. But that looked to be about the date of the house. Talleyrand's Europe. The local pieties of the time. Some of the same bells are still ringing.

"Too bad they don't fix that," I said.

"It's the family," Michel said. "Can't do anything."

"All that furniture," I said.

"I don't know," Michel said. He accompanied his sheep in there around the house almost daily, as though it were a home pasture, to M. Vert's disgust. The grass was cropped short among the fallen stones and tiles, right up to the walls.

"They can't reach an agreement," Robert said. "There are four or five heirs. The children. They're old. Some are in Tulle, I believe. Some are in Limoges. They never got along. They came here once a few years ago to reach some decision about the property. They couldn't. They argued. The wives argued and the husbands argued. One of them said that if the others reached an agreement he wouldn't. So they left it. And now he's in an asylum." He turned to look at the house. "They'll die."

"But the house will fall down."

"That may be," Robert agreed, with a resigned sigh.

The empty house along the lane to the north was also the property of aged heirs who lived elsewhere.

"The old man," Robert said, "is in a home. He doesn't know anything. And the sisters can't do anything. They've tried. He won't let them do anything. It's the law. They don't want to live here, I don't think. But they can't do anything with the place."

"The roof is still good," Michel said. Robert rocked his head from side to side, expressing doubt.

"Oh yes, it's good, it's good," Michel insisted.

"The cistern is good," Robert allowed.

"It's clean," Robert said. The sheep did not go in there, much. The grass was thin in the shade of the big lime trees which on spring nights scented the lane and the green and the fields around. Along the boundary wall between that property and the neighbor's was an arbor built of long split chestnut vine stakes, with grapes trained along the top—a rare sight on the *causse*, where relatively few grapes were cultivated and arbors were almost never used. Another arbor had been built on the neighbor's side of the wall, and the vines had grown together.

"It gives good grapes," Michel said.

"They're sour," Robert said. His fiancée made a face and laughed and turned away.

"For wine," Michel said. "One can make wine. But one doesn't need it. One has made it," he persisted. "Eh?" he asked Robert.

"Oh yes," Robert agreed.

"It was good," Michel said. "Last year it wasn't good. It rained too much. Not good. But I don't need that. I drink water, I. Cistern water. It's better for the health." He patted his solid middle.

I asked whether they had any idea of the age of the lime trees.

"They're old," Michel said.

"My mother always saw them," Robert said. "And my father. My grandparents. They were always there. They always gathered the flowers and dried them, for tea."

"But we have our own," Michel said. "Lime trees. We have several, if we need them. At the other house." He made a sweeping gesture toward the east, referring to the ruin that was my other neighbor, when I was in the garden. It stood a hundred yards or so beyond the narrow end of the garden, there on the next hill, which had been part of the same ridge until the railroad cut had been carved through the upland a century before. There was still the carcass of a much larger farmhouse than the one Michel and his mother were living in. The sun rose beside it out of the line of dark oaks on the shelving *causse*, and the moon hung above it and its tall thinning lime trees. I knew better than to ask about it directly. One day when we were standing at the bend of the lane, looking at it across the slot of the railroad cut, Michel confirmed what M. Vert had already told me.

"It was burned down," he said. "And the barn. Everything."

M. Vert had said that one of the children had burned it down, when left alone in the house for a minute. "What could you expect?" he said.

"Does anyone know how it happened?" I asked Michel.

Michel shrugged. "Matches," he said. "An accident." He paused, looking at it. "It was before I was born. They say it was my other older brother, the one who died. My sister was looking after him, but when she wasn't looking—what do I know? That's what they say." He added darkly, "Other ways it could have happened too. There were people who would have been glad to have it burn down."

In one ruin I had found a pressed pewter plaque embossed with the figure of a crowing rooster and the name of a fire insurance company, and I inquired vaguely about insurance, more or less as a formality, feeling I knew the answer.

"Oh no," Michel said, rejecting the very idea. "It was not insured. There was no insurance in those times. It burned, that's all.

"And," he added, "there were no firemen. Firemen? Ha! My faith. What was there? The spring, there, at the bottom of the hill. That's all. It burned."

He said it without passion, finally. A fact. A bit of history that he knew.

"One has thought of rebuilding it," he said. "Yes. Fix it up. New. The walls are solid in spite of everything. But for the moment one doesn't need it."

He stood looking at it across the cut.

"It's a terrible place for lightning," he said, with a gesture as though he were shaking water from his hand. "Ho! You see that lime tree? All dead the one side? That big lime tree? That's the lightning. I heard that myself, in the night, the storm. I came down the next morning and saw it like that, half of it gone. And that one there, almost dead all one side? That's the fire, still. Look at that. My God. If there is one place in the whole corner where the lightning strikes, it's there. If it's going to fall anywhere that's where it falls, that's where. It had its own cistern too."

As we stood looking at it, to the east, the tracks out of sight below us began to ring faintly in our ears, and then the train appeared around a rise in the *causse* that did not look like anything at all but clearly the rest of the world was back there. The train was traveling fast, westward, on its way, ultimately, to the river and the north. Only two cars, yellow. The sky full of the luminous clarity after sunset, all the glare gone. The train approached, snaking along, rushing, clicking, clacketing.

We stood watching the house across the cut while the roofs rushed past below us and were gone, and the bushes blown by the wind it raised were still again.

That was another of the sounds of evening. There was a train that went east and south late in the afternoon. I scarcely heard it coming through the cut, when I was in the garden, until it emerged with a sudden loud burst and raced for the dip around the far corner. From the garden, or the bend in the lane, or anywhere on the lane, only a small section of track could be seen. The train had to appear, to show where the tracks ran. The inhabitants of the *causse* knew the times of the trains as they knew the days of the week, or the seasons.

Living on the upland with its long swells and hollows and deep abrupt ravines and its caves leading to underground streams and caverns, another tracery of thoroughfares gradually emerged from beneath the railroad and the one paved road. Many of the lanes were overgrown or partly overgrown, or had been amputated here and there to open the way for some use of machinery. But they resumed their routes farther on, winding through country that had become secret. The green had once been an intersection, with its three branches. The lane from the south had come in below the bend, at the spring, and had gone on to the north from there and joined the northern lane from the green, up on the hill that now looked back on M. Vert's farm. The lane that led past my garden and its ruined shepherd's house, and circled the hill to the east, and around past the spring and out across the *causse* through the woods, was a bit of the old Roman road, built by the legions after the defeat of Vercingetorix on a hill overlooking the valley, less than ten miles away. It was the Gauls from these uplands, woods, valleys, mountains, the Cadurcii and Arvernii, who had been rounded up after the battle and had their right arms cut off by Caesar's orders, in the name of civilization. After destroying the language and culture, the Romans too had crumbled, leaving a legacy of admired abstractions. Their presence was more remote than that of the far older hunters from the days of the painted caverns under the *causse*, some of them still unlisted on any map or registry. There were a number of entrances to that dark dripping world within a mile or so of the garden.

When I worked in that garden I was living in the one other house on the green apart from Michel's and his mother's, and the empty 1819 house full of furniture, from which the tiles slid through the nights.

The first time I had come to the green, years before, I had walked alone up the lane from the east, past the ruin and the storm of brambles that would be my garden, and had picked my way past the fallen stone buildings until the wide grassy space opened suddenly in front of me like a hidden valley, but level, running out to its written lines of walls and the black clouds of trees. I did not see the big house to the south of the green at first, behind its huge walnut tree. That first time no dogs barked, and I was accompanied onto the green by silence, and was almost halfway across before I saw the tower to my left, the massive square shape climbing past the walnut limbs.

Years later when I saw it next, M. Vert led the way down the lane from his own farm. It was a building he wanted to show me, he said. He hadn't decided what to do with it. Coming to the green from the north, down the narrow lane with walls four or five feet high on both sides, the tower beside its walnut tree was the first thing one saw. The tower roof had dark holes in it, and two ominous cracks forked like roots down the walls. Part of the house roof behind the tower had begun to sink. Some of the rafters had gone. West of the tower the high wall that was one end of the house faced directly onto the green, with no windows. It narrowed at the top to a broad stone chimney.

M. Vert walked and talked with the same rapid flapping motion, like a rooster running, and he looked up as he spoke, and twitched his right cheek for emphasis and exclamation. He led the way to the entrance, a five-bar chestnut gate held in iron rings that in turn were set in the big stones of the opening in the high wall along the south side of the green which was shaped like a bow. The gate was beginning to show signs of rot and frailty. He opened it with difficulty, lifting the wooden bar out of a hole in the stone and carrying the gate inward onto the tall mixture of grass and meadow flowers. The big walnut tree stood in a raised enclosure, a walled platform, to our right, as though it were rising from a stage. And on the other side, to our left, in a grove of lacquer trees, rose a slope of broken stone, a dry glacier flowing around the stone doorways of several collapsed barnyard cubicles. A stone hill, with a flat top edged with vertical stones. He told me it was the threshing floor. It was one of those things that one is told and hears but does not attend to at the time, and only later notices and remembers.

He repeated to me that this was the house where his mother had been born. The courtyard sloped down from the gate. We walked in through the chest-high flowers. To our right the house ran along,

south from the tower. All of the side of the roof facing us had begun
to subside, a slow lurch. Beside the tower a long stone porch, a *bolet*,
embraced the house, at the top of a flight of huge stone steps. The
house roof had slipped over it like a hat on someone asleep. Under
the *bolet* was a low stone arch, the entrance to a vault.

I saw it little by little. It was not safe to go in then. Because his
mother had been born there, he said, he was reluctant to take the tiles
off the roof. But it was not of use to him. We talked about how it
might be fixed up; and later, as a mason from the valley, with trucks
and assistants, jacked up the roof, replaced rafters, wrapped the tower
in a harness of iron straps and bars and covered it with an ugly coat
of cement which was supposed to help hold it together, I watched the
work and came to know the house well, as it was then.

The courtyard, I learned, was paved with immense stones three or
four feet across. The house sat at one end of its enclosure which ran
the whole length of the green. In front of the house was the courtyard
and then the raised threshing floor which divided that end of the
enclosure from the grove of plums, lacquer trees, walnut trees, and
acacias beyond it. Running through the brambles in the middle of the
grove was the low wall that had once surrounded a garden. A hollow
deep in the shade, that was damp until midsummer, was all that
remained of what had once been a shallow spring. It might still be
there if one dug down. There were two entrances to the house: one,
double width, facing the courtyard at ground level, and the other at
the top of the flight of stone steps, where one door had opened onto
the stone porch and a second one had opened from the stone porch
into the house.

Around the south corner of the building, under a tangle of brambles,
was one more stone oven, built against the stone end of the house.
The oven itself filled the few feet between the house wall and the wall
that bounded the stony field to the south. The familiar shape: at waist
height, set on a pedestal of stone, a broad stone shelf. In the middle
of the ledge the dark half circle that was the oven opening. The twelve
feet or so in front of the oven was deep in rubble, and it turned out
that here too M. Vert had removed the tiles and rafters of a roof and
carted them off, years before, throwing the rest of the rubble into a
square stone duck pond that had been cut with great labor, at one
time, into the stone of the upland, outside the ground-floor entrance
to the house.

I was curious about the oven because it appeared to be a later addition, something that had been added long after the house itself had been built there, part of some rearrangement, whereas many of the ovens on the *causse* looked far older than the houses near them. Many of them stood alone like solitary cells, separate from other buildings—a precaution, no doubt, against fire, for the dry brambles that heated them burned with a wild riotous rush. The ovens enclosed under roofs had wide chimneys built above the openings, and the faces of the stones or bricks above the ledges were still black or burnt red from the fires.

There must have been many redistributions within that house's enclosure during the centuries that the building had stood there, and I wondered whether there might have been another oven there at one time, within the walls, but I never found any sign of one. Some ovens had been used communally, and the occupants of the house might have used the other ancient oven nearby, over on the green facing Michel's cellar. That one stood by itself, massive and dark, and apparently in perfect condition. A vine ran along the south side of it.

"It's solid," Michel said. "We take care of it. It still works, like thunder. We still use it."

"Do you?" I asked. I had seen the baker's small delivery van come picking its way over the rocks of the lane, setting the dogs barking, and had watched Michel or his mother carry into the house several heavy round *tourtes* of bread, to set in the rack hanging from the black beams.

"Not often, now. From time to time. If we want to."

M. Vert said that the oven on the back of the big house was the only one there had ever been inside the enclosure, as far as he knew.

A huge acacia, dying now, reached its gnarled limbs out over the ruins of the oven and the choked duck pond. A grove of plum trees ran from the duck pond to the south wall of the enclosure, and then along to the trees by the threshing floor. In the early spring when the whole region was white with clouds of plum blossom the courtyard of the house was filled with its own shining cloud, floating below the still bare limbs of the walnut trees. The nights were cold then, and even on sunny days the broad sky of the upland was hung with drifting veils. Both orioles and nightingales haunted the trees beyond the threshing floor, and in the half-ruined house chaffinches and redstarts had found corners in which they had nested. The mason changed his plans to avoid the nests until the young birds had flown.

It was a stone place. Built on stone, of stone. The air inside was the air of stones. The house had four stone arches. The first, outside under the stone porch, the flattened arch built of big stones, like the span of a bridge. The base of the tower held one end of it and the foundation of the stone staircase held the other end. Through the arch, in the house wall, was the stone lintel of the heavy, oak, iron-strapped double door to the cellar, studded with hand-forged dia-mond-headed nails an inch across.

The cellar, like the tower, indicated that the house had been a place of some importance. The room had been dug into the rocky *causse* almost to chest level, and the whole square, some eight or ten paces each way, was roofed with a stone vault—the second of the arches. Inside stairs led up to the next room, the one off the courtyard. And that room, like the courtyard outside, was paved with huge stones, each more than one step across. The kitchen, M. Vert called it—which was the name for a main room with a fireplace.

And on the south of the room, facing the door from the cellar, was the fireplace: immense, occupying most of that wall. The opening was some ten feet across, and I could step inside it, under the mantelpiece made of a single piece of stone, without having to bend my head more than a little. Two pieces of stone, kin to the mantelpiece, formed the ends. Inside, the stone shaft, draped with waving cobwebs, narrowed and filled with light. I was happy to discover that the dimensions of things in the house bore no consistent relation to the metric system.

In the embrasures on each side of the fireplace, high up on the wall, was a small window. Under the one on the left, at waist height, a deep stone ledge crossed the embrasure, and below it the face of the stone was pierced with a half-moon opening like a small oven door. That was the ash box, built into the fireplaces of the region so that someone, at bedtime, could shovel the last of the fire into it and cover the coals with ashes. In the morning they could be dug out, still glowing, and start the next day's fire. The other embrasure, like the one down at the ruin, had been for firewood.

To the west, facing the entrance door and the courtyard, was the third arch, a perfect vaulted recess with a minute window in the end of it, well below eye level, another stone ledge around the sides, and a shallow stone sink set in the floor. That was the *évier*—the whole arch was the *évier*—where the dishes were washed. In the right-hand wall of the arch a low doorway led into a low-vaulted room, the fourth arch. Another cellar, or a larder, a cave made for some use that was later forgotten. Carefully sealed and, as M. Vert said, "deaf."

Inside the entrance from the courtyard another flight of stairs led up through the wall to a door into the room off the stone porch. The stairs made clear one of the peculiarities of the house: the north rooms and the south rooms were not on the same level, so that one climbed through the house as one climbs a staircase with landings. Had the two ends of the house been built at different times? There was no way of telling. It had housed two families, that was certain. The room at the top of the stairs was, once again, as M. Vert said, a "kitchen." Facing us across the floor was another huge fireplace, the twin of the one on the floor below, with a stone ledge and ash box to the left. The chimney was the one that could be seen from the green.

Stone steps through an opening in the wall led up to a loft, on two levels; and above that, beside the tower, the bedroom with a low door leading into the pigeon loft.

When I lived there a big dormer window, like the upper door of a hay barn, looked out from the lower loft, across the pastures, toward the line of woods and the minor valleys leading down to the river. I spent part of most days up there, by that window. Directly below the dormer was one side of the rough domed roof of the abandoned oven. The wall that ran beside it continued to the west, leading out from under the window to divide fields, with walnut trees at intervals all the way along it as far as it could be seen. They were middle-sized walnut trees, not giants like the one on the other side of the house, over the courtyard, which must have stood there for at least two centuries. That was one of the old *corn* walnuts of the *causse*, a variety which was no longer considered economical, though the nuts had the sweetest taste of all. They were too small, and the shells were too hard, for the wholesale trade. They were for local consumption, for cracking on the corners of the long walnut kitchen tables in the autumn evenings. Some of the trees along the pasture wall were of more saleable varieties such as the *candelou*, more recent than the *corn*, planted probably in the latter part of the nineteenth century, perhaps during the flurry of change that accompanied the coming of the railroad and the leveling of the road across the *causse*. Walnuts had been planted along many of the roads at that time.

The dealers in walnut wood still knew the lineages of the trees and their value for purposes that the trees had never considered. They knew the individual walnut trees for miles around, and could point to majestic veterans standing alone in plowed fields and say that they were worthless. They had frozen. Water had found its way down through a fold and had frozen and cracked the trunk.

Then there was the color of the wood, and all the rings of ritual and dogma surrounding it. The wood of a green tree had no color, and you could not simply cut down a healthy tree in the field. To get the real color, the dealers agreed, you had to wait until the tree began to die. It would take three years doing it, and you could cut the tree at almost any time during that period, though there was an art to choosing the best possible moment. Once the tree had died it would begin to turn gray, and would lose its color completely.

The wood merchants carried long augers with which they could pierce the tree and see the colors of the wood in order. Core samples. You could get the law on them if you caught them drilling your tree without your permission. It was not good to have a tree pierced too often. Too many samplings could ruin the wood, or start the tree dying. And of course there were pirates who went around piercing trees without asking permission, and then came back with low bids for the wood. You had to watch out for them if you had trees above a certain size. Another thing that would kill a tree was *the ink*, a kind of disease that seemed to combine cancer and hemophilia; the whole family was prone to it. Its chief symptom was a black liquid that seeped out of the trunk near the ground, and out of roots near the trunk, darkening the surface of the soil with black bloodstains. The nuts went on forming in the great canopy overhead. A tree with *the ink* was dying, and it might have color or it might not, depending on when the disease had got its hold. The disease too could be diagnosed with an auger. And the tree pronounced valueless, while the owner stood by unable to argue.

Throughout the country the older inhabitants spoke of a general decline in the vigor, productivity, and health of the walnut trees, which were a kind of unofficial totem of the region. *The ink* was a symptom of the falling away. The ailment had not been common, the elders insisted, when they were children. In their grandparents' day it had been all but unknown. As they talked they would point to a dead tip of a branch high in a tree and say, "There." The first sign that another tree had been stricken and was doomed. There was a treatment for *the ink*, they said, but it was seldom worth the gamble. Digging the soil away from the roots out past the drip line of the tree, and then washing everything, roots and soil, repeatedly, with poisonous chemicals. They were suspicious of the process, found it alien and repellent, and took some satisfaction in telling of those they had heard of who had done the whole thing without success. It was certainly a long labor and expense, and it was agreed that often it did no good at all, or merely added a few years to the life of the tree, and the wood may have been rendered worthless in any case.

The malady, and the insidious decline of the walnut trees were ascribed to a variety of causes. Chemical fertilizers, poison sprays, the atomic bomb. But the suspect in the foreground was the tractor-drawn plow. Until the middle of the century, in most parts of the *causse*, plowing had been done with cows. Not oxen, usually, but the same red, long-horned, notoriously self-willed cows that supplied the rich milk on the farms, and the milk-fed veal, and the beef. Not cheese. The cheese was made of the goats' milk. The cows worked in pairs, with a wooden yoke lashed to their horns. Long nets, made by the inmates of the local prison, hung down over their faces to keep the flies off. The cows leaned toward each other when they were going uphill, or when the load was heavy.

Whoever was leading them carried a long slender rod about as tall as a man, often made of a hazel or willow shoot. The rod was not for striking the cows. If a blow was struck it was seldom heavy and was usually directed to land on the wooden yoke, clack, clack. The driver started the cows and urged them on with a deep belly syllable, some-thing between an "e-e-e-e" and a "u-u-u-u," a sound that echoed the cow's bellow. And shouted, *"Arrière!"* rolling the *r*'s hard, to stop them and back them.

And that was the point, they said, talking of the walnut trees. When the cows were plowing a field near a tree, and the plow hit a root, the cows stopped. One freed the plow and one went on. When a plow drawn by a tractor hit a root it kept going and cut the root. One could not cut walnut roots with impunity. There were only two periods in the year when you could cut the limbs aboveground—a few weeks in the spring, after the hard frosts but before the sap began its main rise, and in the fall, after the sap went down and the leaves fell but before the real freeze. Cut them at any other time and the tree might bleed to death or be so weakened that it would never recover, or would freeze and crack, and bleed away later. And the roots should not be cut at all. The tree might bleed into the field, unseen. The best roots were not far from the surface. When the cows drew the plow the share did not go very deep. Just below the surface. The old plowman would hold out his hand, pointing forward, palm vertical, to show the depth. But the tractor plow turned up the soil much more deeply. Too deeply.

And then there were the sheep. They used to spend much more time under the walnut trees. It stood to reason that the manure, and the urine, made a difference. Some places now the sheep never left the barns. The old *caussenard* sheep with the Roman noses, pop eyes, and long legs were being crossed with other breeds, such as the Bérichon, to provide thicker, shorter legs of lamb, or were being replaced altogether, in the brand-new sheep barns, by breeds imported from the Netherlands or from as far as New Zealand.

M. Vert shook his head as he spoke of them, but it was partly out of envy. He said he would not go as far as some of the farmers he knew, or knew of. Their farms shocked him. Like factories. It took capital to do that. The first way you could tell those barns was by the smell. They stank like rotting fish. In the summer, downwind, you could smell them a long way off, their stench wiping out the hot fragrance of the *causse*.

It was the middle of the sixties before that smell began to creep in—the smell of the world that claimed you the moment you bought your train ticket to somewhere else. M. Vert had a second cousin with a farm like that, and a brother-in-law who was talking of one—a small one. It took much less land to do it that way than to do it the old way, with pastures. You could build a barn. Buy the feed. Get used to the smell, which got into everything. On the open *causse* the droppings of the sheep smelled of sheep and of the stones and leaves. They were dropped in the pastures and in the lanes among the rubble of lime-stone, and they rolled into the grass at the feet of the blackberry canes, in a world of dogs and magpies and gates, and for the rest of the day they stayed black in the sunlight.

The new sheep barns, of course, were not built of stone with tile roofs, but of metal or prefabricated cement slabs. They might be several stories high, and there were wide-eyed conversations, indig-nant, revolted, among women at the fairs, talking of the delivery of lambs at Bordeaux, how they were flung out from the stinking hot hold of the ship in which they had traveled for weeks. Picked up by a leg or a handful of wool and thrown into the upper story of a truck, which drove them for hours and hours to the new barn, where they were unloaded the same way. And once they were inside they never saw the light of day again.

That was a minor part of the argument about the new "industrial" barns. The advocates dismissed it as sentimental. More serious was the fact that the operators needed water for their barns and for their slaughterhouses. The statistics differed depending on who supplied them, but they agreed that many thousands of sheep, over a period of months until they attained the desired weight, would eat, evacuate, and eventually bleed, and that the results would have to be removed continuously. And for this, the developers maintained, they must have water. It must come in clean, which was not difficult along the valley with its small clear crayfish streams winding through woods. On the downstream side of the new barns the current would emerge full of the warm contents of bowels, bladders, and veins of lambs and sheep fattened on chemically souped-up feed. The fishermen along the river were opposed. The neighbors everywhere were opposed—as much to the smell as to anything else. The suppliers of feed, huge national networks, made deals with local individuals who had political ambitions. Delegates to the National Assembly, officials at the prefecture, members of the local councils who raised sheep or simply sold them, and wanted to get ahead and needed a mortgage, whether or not they knew it yet. Representatives of feed companies initiated peasants in the modern hard sell, offering loans for building sheep barns, and for stocking and supplying them. The local *marchands de bestiaux* helped with propositions and threats. The main pressure was in the valleys, where big farms bordered streams near the river.

One rich peasant, M. Pouchou, whose farm was an entire hamlet with an ancient name, was among the first in the region to "convert" to the new factory production of sheep. He was already a local *conseiller municipal*. His one notable act in that office had been to slip through a permit for the demolition of a twelfth-century arch surmounted by a guardroom and tower. The building had been an outpost of the great castle on the hill which dominated the site of one of Charles Martel's crucial battles with the Saracens. It spanned the one lane of a hamlet along a clear trout stream. The arch was too low for the trucks of the big feed companies or of the *marchands de bestiaux*. Demolition crews were brought in and worked rapidly on a weekend. The other *conseillers municipaux* were not even aware that the permit existed, and the building was irreparably wrecked before they found that the document had been signed without proper authorization, and was invalid. At the next election M. Pouchou was elected mayor of the *commune*. He described his outlook and his political platform as "progressive."

Once in office M. Pouchou demonstrated openly some of the methods that had put him there. He had built a slaughterhouse inside his three-story sheep factory and had been slaughtering his own lambs and sheep there for several years and shipping the carcasses by the truckload to the north, to the cities, to the supermarket chains and to the army depots. Several steps in the process, including running his own slaughterhouse by the stream, were not legal, and accreditation for the slaughterhouse was not popular in the neighborhood, partly because of complaints from downstream.

But within a few years, by underselling to chain stores in the nearby market towns, and by making deals for butchering with the local *marchands de bestiaux*, the private slaughterhouse had managed to render the neighboring municipal slaughterhouse financially unsound. The new mayor pressed not only for complete "regularization" of his own slaughterhouse but for the closing for the municipal facility, which he claimed, with reason, was old-fashioned, inefficient, unsanitary, a structural hazard, and an economic drag upon the town that used it. He insisted that it would cost more to bring it up to legal standard than the dwindling use of it could justify. The municipal slaughterhouse was not, in fact, even in M. Pouchou's own commune, but in the one that adjoined it, to the north. But M. Pouchou's demands turned out to be part of a concerted campaign all through the region, which included among its backers not only "progressive" sheep enterprises, *marchands de bestiaux*, and the huge feed companies but figures in high positions in the national government. The sister of a cabinet minister, for instance, turned out to have a controlling interest in a supermarket chain that purveyed the "industrial" lamb, and to be the sole owner of an enterprise producing lamb's-wool vests, coats, and hats for chic stores. One object of the campaign was to close all the municipal slaughterhouses in the region, and to have public slaughtering become the monopoly of a cartel of "industrial" meat producers directed by the feed companies. It was an attempt to seize the whole market in one move.

Signs of hidden influence behind the campaign began to emerge. The mayor of the town nearest to M. Pouchou, in which the public slaughterhouse operated, was a young doctor who was originally a vigorous opponent of the new industrial sheep barns. He argued against them publicly and privately, on grounds of health, the pollution of the streams, the smell, the predictable impression on the summer vacationers. He deplored the long-range effects on the region if the industrial sheep barns were to become established there. He spoke of the self-sufficiency, independence, and self-respect of local communities and of the region as a whole. Then for a season the doctor was silent on the subject. After which, one day, he was quoted in a newspaper speaking at a Rotarian meeting in favor of the "progressive" methods of sheep production, describing them as a rational approach to agriculture, in the great tradition of the nation; as an essential response to a hungry world's need for meat; and as a hope for the economy of a backward area, if only one were open-minded and prepared to take the broad view.

M. Pouchou represented a more obvious operation of influence. The *mairie* to which he succeeded occupied a couple of rooms with bare board floors (it was not many years since they had been bedrooms) upstairs over a grocery store that had just been acquired by a national chain. The store, until a few years before he took office, had been a shadowy, piled, sagging, dusty general emporium on the ancient square of a village with a population of perhaps seventy. A backwater, at the confluence of two brooks, and the square had become a backwater even in the village: most of the sparse traffic was along a winding road that skirted the ancient settlement instead of passing through it. Everything on the square was small and venerable, built of limestone that had turned golden with age and the growth of lichens. One end of it was occupied by a Romanesque church, simple and unmarred, the fluted arch of its door resting on capitals whose intricate carvings had survived most of eight centuries. The façade at all hours and in all weathers seemed to be reflecting the sunset. A high wall next to it hid the cemetery. Another, along the far side of a lane that led into the square from the valley to the north, was the boundary of a plum orchard. The store faced the orchard, across the square.

And across the square from the church was the one remaining private house on the *place*, with a long stone porch looking out over dahlias, hollyhocks, roses, and an iron gate. There by the stone balustrade the present owners, a mason and his short round wife, who wore her brown cardigan winter and summer, would sit at the end of a day's work and sip a glass of their own ratafia, and wave to friends passing by. M. Toronne, the mason, came of a line of artisans that receded into the history of the old buildings of the region. His father had been a man who walked to work every morning, however far, in his wooden shoes, with no leather slippers but simply a handful of hay stuffed inside them. He had been famous as a builder and repairer of vaulted ceilings, and had been the best cutter of dressed stone for miles around. He had refused to learn to read, regarding it as a foolishness and a waste of time.

M. Toronne, son, had not followed him in that. He read two local and two national papers, the publication of a regional historical society, a magazine devoted to original views of health and diet, and a farmer's almanac. He kept his glasses in an old case inside the cookie tin. And he saw no reason to deny himself woolen socks inside his iron-shod *sabots*, or the occasional admission that the knee broken years before in a soccer game was giving him trouble because of the damp. But in other respects he had yielded little, and was proud of it. He was leaner than his father, not so massive but just as sinewy. He was proud to be the mason preferred by the Beaux Arts in that whole area for delicate restoration of ancient churches and medieval architecture. He said he knew every feudal structure in the region and had each one in his head. He saw no point in owning a cement mixer. His *commis* or his apprentice could mix the cement better by hand, get the mixture just right for a particular purpose, and learn something as they did it. In any case, *béton*, concrete, in his vocabulary, was regularly employed as a term of contempt, describing ugly, mass-produced contemporary work done by the square yard, and the mentality that preferred it. He reserved his respect for stone, and for oak and chestnut, which he referred to without hesitation as the noble materials. He worked on modern villas built of hollow bricks, on occasion, but shrugged and described them as imbecile, which was what he also called the woman antique dealer's small imitation château with its yellow glass mullioned windows, wrought-iron grilles, and round towers, which she had commissioned him to build along the road within earshot and smelling distance of the beleaguered municipal slaughterhouse. And now there was a firm of architects and contractors, not even from the region, from whom you could buy plans for an "antique" villa that looked like a château. You could choose among four different models.

The work crew for those was included in the contract, but prospective future château owners who had grown up in the region, or newcomers who had made careful inquiry, often came to enlist M. Toronne's service, if only as a consultant. "To be sure," M. Toronne said, without specifying what it was that they wanted to be sure of.

He was not above giving them civil advice, but the structures were false, everything was false, and he was disgusted and preferred to have nothing to do with such operations. He said he would rather take small jobs building grave vaults or repairing family tombs in cemeteries.

And he sat in his socks and sucked in his cheeks and railed, in his hoarse tenor, at the military jets that had been breaking the sound barrier, for several years, over that part of the country. They were cracking the old stone vaults everywhere, he said. They were destroying the churches. The cathedral of Stuttgart would never be the same. They were making the stones from the seven-hundred-year-old castle on the hill, within sight of his porch, roll down onto the roofs below. They were imbecile too. "No, no, and no!" he insisted, shaking his head furiously, as he did when an apprentice did something he disapproved of. "Striking force!" he said, with a snort, using the phrase with which the government described its new military buildup. He had nothing but contempt for the military. He was one of a number from the region, several of them artisans, who had been deported by the Germans in the Second World War, and had escaped and made their way home and obtained false papers and fictitious disabilities, and had served in the Resistance with signal effect until the Germans were gone. He had not mellowed toward the Germans and had no wish to see any of them return to the region as summer visitors "no matter how much money they spend." Yet he shunned war veterans' reunions, which he also described as imbecile. As for the army, he referred to it generically as imbecile. In the war, he said, the military had been pompous sellouts and cowards, and now all they could do was talk big, waste money, destroy ancient monuments, and frighten flocks of sheep. They had not changed a bit.

He railed when the shadowy 15-watt general store, his neighbor, had its wooden casements with their small panes torn out, and a single pane of glass put in instead, though at least the Beaux Arts had insisted that, since the church and everything in front of it was a national monument, the glass must be set not in cement but in stone. M. Toronne had been disgusted the day he came home and saw the new chain grocery further defaced with a huge red sign half the size of the building, and he had got the Beaux Arts to force the chain to replace it with a small discreet row of gold capital letters.

He spoke with the same forthrightness that he used for the army when the subject turned to M. Pouchou, the new mayor, and the move toward "progressive" sheep barns, which M. Toronne referred to as factories unless he called them Dachaus. He knew the pressures, the threats, the deals, that had won M. Pouchou the mayoral office, and he sat on his porch in the evening and snorted over his paper the day he came home from work and saw that they had begun to decorate the square for the ceremony at which the new mayor would be invested with his office. He glowered over his spectacles at the familiar strings hung with little red, white, and blue paper flags, that were dangling here and there, attached but not yet finally in place. They were draped from the brackets over the white enamel shades like tin plates, above the bulbs of the two light poles on the square. And from the limbs of a walnut tree that reached out over the orchard wall. And from the front of the church, and out of the windows of the *mairie* itself, which was bibbed with red, white, and blue bunting gathered at the sides to frame the plate-glass window of the grocery store as though it were a stage. He observed, above his newspaper, the platform set up in front of the *mairie*, and dropped his eyes in disgust.

On the day of the ceremony he took his wife calling on friends in the country, in the truck, driving out before any of the officiants had turned up, before the cars began to edge to a stop by the ditch at the bottom of the street, or the volunteer firemen's band had arrived, in uniform, for their *aubades* and procession.

And M. Toronne was tireless in spreading the news far and wide when the new mayor, almost immediately upon his investiture, set up a schedule of compulsory hearings, requiring every resident of the commune who raised sheep for meat, and every *exploitant* of agricultural acreage, to come in alphabetical order, at fixed times on fixed days, to appear, one by one, before M. Pouchou himself and three of his cohorts seated behind the desks of the *mairie* as at the bench of a tribunal. And there the *exploitants* were to declare themselves for or against the closing of the municipal slaughterhouse and the official sanction of a private slaughterhouse owned by M. Pouchou to fulfill its functions. And they were to affix their signatures accordingly, before these four witnesses, one of whom had been made a notary public for the occasion.

The schedule of hearings, with names and times filled in by hand, was posted weekly on the door of the *mairie*, upstairs, and the announcement suggested onerous and costly consequences for anyone who failed to cooperate.

There were two small cafés at the bottom of the one winding street, with a stream and the open fields across the road from them, and another small general store a few houses farther along. On the first morning of the hearings the cars began to arrive and pull off the road a little hesitantly, as for a funeral. And the *exploitants* and proprietors, men, women, and their seconds—sons, wives, brothers, sisters-in-law, grandsons—climbed out. Many of the cars were veterans: tall as cupboards, black, green, brown, rusted, a spare tire on one running board, a battery on the other, a crate lashed to the luggage rack behind. And more than half of the *exploitants* were of the generation that, as they themselves put it, had "made the '14 war." Gaulish mustaches, gray and stained orange; the wide, new-looking berets reserved for Sundays, fairs, weddings, and interments; corduroy jackets, black sateen jackets, striped black trousers. Women with round red faces, in straw hats. They all stood for a moment by the edge of the road, in groups, looking around as though they were strangers to the place, when in fact none of them had driven more than a couple of miles, and they were joined, as they stood there, by neighbors who had come on foot. They stood and consulted watches, and ventured opinions as to what it could all mean, and bits of news, and careful information about the times of their appointments, every word of it in the language of the region that was older than French. And then they drifted into the store or the cafés, from which they emerged in twos or threes or singly, at intervals, to shuffle up the narrow street with its overhanging upper stories to the *place* and the *mairie*, where a small crowd formed through the course of the morning, as the bell in the church struck the quarters, and struck the hours, each time twice.

M. Pouchou was a large, burly man with heavy hands and a habit of bringing them down on the table in front of him to emphasize his sentences. Two of his companions at the long table were beefy, stolid presences with closed, inimical expressions. They said nothing. They nodded if M. Pouchou addressed a question to them. It never required anything but assent. They, like M. Pouchou, kept their hats on. They were wearing berets, and he a gray porkpie. Outside, on the square, those who had been dismissed discussed the identities of the two heavy individuals. One had been employed by M. Pouchou for years and was currently the head butcher at M. Pouchou's sheep barn. The other, who looked like his twin, was a more recent employee. Neither of them had grown up in the region. The third assistant, the notary, wore a white shirt and a suit, and typed parts of each deposition, asking the deponents to repeat themselves more slowly.

M. Pouchou spoke in the regional tongue part of the time, but used French with chilling effect when he wished to sound particularly lofty and official. He was menacing in both languages, and the procedure he had set up, the questions he asked, were designed to make each proprietor in turn feel that the object of the interview was not to solicit an opinion but to exact a justification. Some of the *exploitants* began with obvious doubt as to whether or not to keep their hats on. They were asked to name themselves, last name first. M. Pouchou had known most of them all his life. Then name their properties—on many of which he had played as a child—and their acreage, and the numbers on the tax map, and to produce evidence that they had paid their property taxes. The first days many of them had not brought the relevant papers and information with them. This was treated as a delinquency, and in some cases they were asked to return at a later date. That depended, clearly, on how they spoke of the subject in question. If any of them expressed the slightest misgiving or hesitation, M. Pouchou began to turn the screws.

It was easy to begin with taxes, if there was any irregularity there. The notary at the end of the table riffled through his files and produced evidence, which M. Pouchou had gone to some trouble and expense to procure, concerning any other debts incumbent upon the property, upon the proprietor or other members of the family, and any loans outstanding to local banks, to neighbors, in some cases to M. Pouchou himself. Also indebtedness of other kinds, and any family disputes over title to all or to part of the property. Old ghosts that the *exploitants* had supposed to be long since at rest were hoisted up and paraded before them. And if M. Pouchou's researches had revealed nothing of the kind, threats of other sorts were invoked, including suggestions of violence to property or persons, the confiscation of land—whatever might be necessary.

It was a part of the world in which the German occupation during the Second World War had never really "taken," as they said. The local population, from the valley towns, the *causse*, the chestnut forests of the *ségala*, bourgeois and peasant alike, had simply closed ranks, with notable exceptions. They had spoken their own language, fed themselves and each other on their own exchanged produce, and supported an extremely effective Resistance movement on the *causse* and in the *ségala*—a guerrilla band that was powerful, mobile, and coherent enough to maintain its own field hospital, radio station, and underground publication. The Jews in the towns had been adopted into farm families for the duration—there had been only a few dozen of them. A single local Fascist collaborator had led the Germans to the ones he could learn about, and there were not many of those. Nobody on the *causse* knew anything. Nobody in the *ségala* knew anything. The Resistance managed to get gasoline. Its members ran cars, drove motorcycles, carried messages. They moved sheep, whole flocks of sheep, at night, when the Germans were due to show up to requisition meat in the morning. The owners had no idea what had become of the sheep.

"Don't you have sheep?"

"No."

"It says here you keep sheep. Don't you keep sheep?"

"Yes, when we have them."

"Where are they?"

"We used to keep them."

"What happened to them?"

"They were stolen. Every one."

"When?"

"It must have been in the night."

"How could they have been stolen?"

"We don't know."

"You have dogs. Don't they bark?"

"Oh yes."

Then the searches. In one town the Germans machine-gunned every garage door one day, but it made no difference. The members of the Resistance got everywhere, and kept the sheep out of reach of the Germans. When the Germans went to burn sheep barns, whole patrols disappeared on the *causse*. The remains were discovered at the bottoms of potholes after the war. For three years the Resistance had three foreigners, English and American, up on the *causse*. Liaison officers. A number of peasants knew who they were. No one said anything. The officers arranged a parachute drop of arms and medical equipment onto a designated spot on the *causse*. The Resistance had ambushes waiting beside all the roads.

It was a high, bare, open, stony place. The wild aurochs must have roamed there in the days when the caves were being painted. A slightly domed tableland, at a point where the valley could just be seen, over the edge of the *causse*. Stones all around it, walls and standing rocks. Lanes leading off under small trees, past ruined stone barns and houses, through woods. On the morning of the 14th of July after

D-day, the planes came over at the scheduled time and the parachutes opened above the country of the cave bears and bison and vineyards overgrown with brambles. When the planes had gone and the chutes had collapsed onto the stones, peasants leading pairs of cows and heavy wagons emerged from the woods, from all sides of the bare tableland, where they had been waiting since the middle of the night. They gathered up the crates and parachutes and headed home with them in the carts, at the pace of the cows. The Germans were less than fifteen miles away. The Resistance came by each farm and picked up what the carts had brought in.

Days later, at the request of one of the liaison officers, a contingent of the Resistance—boys, some of them, and old men—about forty of them all told—were asked to delay a particular German troop movement that was heading north, led by an elite regiment. If possible, the partisans were to delay that regiment for three-quarters of an hour. They agreed to try, set up an ambush at a narrow iron bridge at the outskirts of one of the towns, and held the bridge until the German tanks arrived—three-quarters of an hour later—losing a third of their number. Afterward they learned that the troop movement was part of the German mass rush of reinforcements to the north to stem the Allied advance in Normandy; that there had been a tight schedule of troop movements because so many bridges were down and the number of places where the army could cross the wide rivers was limited. As they crossed, they were particularly vulnerable to attack from the air. The RAF had acquired part of the schedule of troop movements and knew that the regiment in question was scheduled to cross the Loire in the last hour of darkness. The delay meant that they reached the river after daybreak, had to cross in daylight, and the RAF was expecting them. Few of them, it was said, ever reached Normandy.

Most of the people of the region had not considered their own behavior during the war at all remarkable, even when they knew how people had behaved in other parts of the country, in the north, in cities. They were proud of their distance from cities, and always had been. They did not expect much from there. They said that they had acted as they had because that was what one did.

But M. Pouchou was from the region, and he managed to perturb them. They had known that the Germans were transients—it was a question of waiting them out. With M. Pouchou it was a different matter. They knew him, and he knew them. They remembered him as a boy. What he was like then. Already not so good. They had seen how he got his money together. Sly and ruthless and shady. Yet in conversations about him and about the sheep factories, sooner or later some original thinker was likely to suck his teeth, sigh, and conclude that you can't stop progress.

Which might mean that the speaker had already decided to evolve, as the saying went, with the times. To be modern, after all. To advance. And to profit by it. If only for the sake of the children. For the children.

Or it might mean that the speaker saw no way out, and felt trapped by a process that was destroying everything that he knew and cared for and had believed in. Or that the speaker would not face the choice at all and used the words to shut it off, having picked up the phrase from earlier conversations. It was said with satisfaction, with disgust, with belligerence, with resignation, with hypocrisy, with grief, with raised shoulders. Nobody knew what progress was, but they all spoke as though they did.

And some said, "I'm glad my father never lived to see this day." Some who spoke against the sheep barns were wondering whether they could afford to install one. Some couldn't decide anything at all. If the barns made money for you, God knew you could use it. Some always wanted to try the newest thing. If there's money in it it's right. Some spoke deliberately about why they meant to do it. And some who railed against the whole thing voted for it when they were faced with the mayor and his assistants.

M. Pouchou's barn and his commune were in the valley, and the main resistance to his aspirations came from the *causse*, outside his jurisdiction, where each hamlet and each family had its traditions of sheep raising in the walled pastures, winter and summer, taking the sheep out to pasture, bringing them back, according to the season and the weather. The soil of the *causse* was far poorer than the valley soil. Sheep were more important to the inhabitants. But on the *causse* too opinion was divided. On the one hand those who resisted change or could not afford it, and on the other those who after all could not stop progress, and had no wish to if it meant money.

But the mayor of the commune on the *causse* nearest to M. Pouchou was actively opposed to his neighbor's ambitions and to his methods, both. He was among those who rallied political opposition to M. Pouchou's tactics in the prefectural offices and the national government, and the opposition succeeded, before the vote on the issue of the sheep barns was complete in M. Pouchou's commune, in bringing about a legal challenge to what M. Pouchou was doing. M. Pouchou

was enjoined from proceeding. He declared that he would continue
the legal battle, but he had been seriously delayed and his position
had been shaken. The municipal slaughterhouse near him continued
to operate, despite threats to those who ran it and to those who used
it. M. Pouchou's private slaughterhouse was not officially sanctioned.
Yet M. Pouchou went ahead with a new addition to his prefabricated
sheep barn, with revolving fans on each floor. He stocked it, increased
his feed orders, and schemed at the prefecture to acquire a permit to
widen the road that led from the nearest feed supplier and rail center
on the *causse*. The road was widened part of the way. Land was
requisitioned to make it possible—the edges of vineyards on the slope,
the lower fringes of plum orchards. Which did not endear him or his
plans to the owners.

Widened or not, to reach M. Pouchou's commune and his farm
the road had to cross a small stream, over a narrow stone bridge of
unknown age. The *marchands de bestiaux*'s trucks could just barely
squeeze through between the stone parapets. Some of the smaller
trucks of the feed companies, the proportions of medium-sized moving
vans, could not get through at all, and others left paint and loosened
stones at the corners. Both were above the permitted load limit. And
the big semis of the feed companies could not even make the turn to
get their cabs onto the bridge.

In the middle of the arch on one side was a recess, a walled bay
jutted out over the stream. Nobody knew just why it had been built
there—possibly to stand in if you happened to be walking across when
a cart came by with a load of hay, filling the whole bridge. Or possibly
for fishing. It was used regularly for both. And the boundary between
the two communes ran down the middle of the stream and divided
the bridge halfway across, so that you could stand fishing in the recess
with one foot in one commune and one in the other. M. Pouchou,
continuing in the same role that had rid his own commune of the
ancient fortified archway, applied for a permit to replace the bridge
with a broad modern structure of steel and concrete. His neighbor,
the mayor on the *causse*, not only managed to have the request denied;
he declared that even if his neighbor were to succeed in widening his
half of the bridge, he would keep his own half at its present width.

The feud was carried into a new phase the following winter when
the stream flooded and part of the bridge was mauled by flotsam. The
damage, in fact, seemed to be greater than the flood could account
for. It was, after all, a small stream, and had flooded many times before

in the life of the bridge. On the other hand it had been a fairly severe flood, the bridge was old and had cracks—particularly in the few years since the big trucks had been using it in defiance of the posted weight limits—and there was no clear evidence of the kind of deliberate human agency that was immediately suspected as soon as the damage was known. In fact, if M. Pouchou and his staff had contrived to lend the flood a hand at that spot, with a view to assuring the need for extensive renovation, their efforts backfired. The mayor on the *causse* had fostered some historic research into the history of the bridge which indeed proved to be older than anyone had supposed, though its exact date of origin was still unknown. And as soon as the bridge was closed because of flood damage it was fenced off and posted by a team of archaeologists from the capital with authority to keep it closed for as long as their purposes required. Their examinations went on for the rest of the winter and most of the spring, and the results pointed to greater antiquity than anyone had believed. The present bridge, they learned, had been built over a still earlier—and narrower—cobbled arch that may have been Roman. In any case there was no question of its being widened or remodeled in any way, nor of its being used for further heavy traffic of any kind. It entered a new category in the index of national monuments, and received the corresponding surveillance of the national government. The feed trucks coming from the main warehouse next to the railroad station on the *causse*, on their way to M. Pouchou's barn, and the *marchands de bestiaux*'s trucks coming to his slaughterhouse would have to go round some twenty miles farther, along winding roads that had not been widened to suit them, and crawl behind flocks of sheep, and cows, and loads of hay.

As the struggle wore on, the views of it on the *causse* grew more varied. The feed companies stepped up their campaign to encourage sheep raisers to develop intensive sheep barns. Representatives called at remote farms to suggest studies of the present methods of exploitation and point out how they could be improved. They worked in collaboration with banks and government advisory agencies. Loans could be offered for building modern steel barns of appropriate sizes, and for stocking them, and for feed. Of course, the old walls along the lanes would have to be cleared away to allow the trucks to come and go.

For the most part it was the larger and more prosperous farms that received the special attention of the companies and agreed to smash out the ends of existing stone barns to extrude steel additions and make whatever changes were necessary for "progressive" sheep production. The owners included some of the best and most careful farmers in the region, families proud of their care of their land, which had been in the same names since before there were records. They had neighbors and friends whose tenancy was as old and as honorable who were unalterably opposed to the new form of sheep raising, which came to be referred to simply as "chemistry"—a term extended from the new agricultural techniques based on bag fertilizers and synthetic toxins.

But the conservative peasants too were being dragged into the use of these things year by year with the advent of machinery, which meant that they no longer worked in each other's fields and ate together at each other's tables on several working days each week. Nitrate of ammonia in the fields, for wheat. Superphosphate in the pastures. Then the old copper knapsack sprayer that for decades had misted the vines with *bouillie bordelaise*—plain copper sulfate and lime, and "bad enough," as they said—against mildew, was filled with some new product that had leaked out onto the back of a man in a neighboring village and killed him. Cancer all down his back. They moved reluctantly, helplessly, resentfully into debt and the use of unknown forces that they had been told were bettering them and that they knew were taking them over and would obliterate them. They also were convinced that the new substances were insidiously threatening not only their physical health, their stamina and longevity, but their relation to the world, their lives. They scolded like crows about the spraying which they saw in the market gardens, even as they were herded into using chemicals themselves in the fields. They continued to grow their own vegetable gardens without the new products. The word "manure" took on the ring of the word "honor," and the notion that they would spray their own lettuces was rejected as though it implied incest.

And many of the more prosperous sheep raisers, those who had a hundred or more sheep all year round, took to dividing their sheep into two flocks. One, a commercial flock, raised intensively, or semi-intensively: largely or entirely indoors, on bought feed with additives, implants of hormones, and other novelties suggested annually by representatives of the feed companies or by the government advisers, both of whom came round visiting regularly, carrying samples, like salesmen from American drug companies. And the other flock, a smaller one, would be raised in the old way, out in the pastures for all or part of

the day, into the barns only for shelter, or to be fattened at the end
on wheat and fodder beets grown on the same farm, until the butcher
took them away for local consumption, or shipment to specified
butcher shops and restaurants in Paris. Occasionally one was illegally
butchered there on the farm and divided up among the neighbors.

And in the butcher shops and restaurants in the region mutton and
lamb raised in the traditional fashion were plainly labeled "*Brebis du
Causse*" in the window or on the menu, and the purveyors stood ready
to prove their claims, and name the farms. No one wanted to eat the
stuff from those barns that stank of rotting fish. "Have you read the
labels on the feed bags?" they asked each other, shaking their heads.

Many small farms on the *causse* continued to raise sheep only in
the traditional way. Some of them kept sheep only for part of the year,
buying five or six ewes with lambs, two each, at the autumn fairs,
fattening them on the autumn pastures, feeding them the summer's
root crop, and selling the lambs in the spring, and the ewes sometime
later. They spoke, as of a bedrock under all changes, of the eternal
days before the war, when each family, they said, had had its own
secret formula for feeding the lambs during the last weeks. Thyme
and marjoram and carrot tops, and other things about which they
remained mysterious. You could tell from the taste, then, which family
had raised the lamb. But then, of course, they had eaten their own
lamb, taking turns, one farm after another butchering and dividing it.
Now it was like the work in the fields: it was no longer something
that they all did together. Even the *brebis du causse* were all bought by
the butcher in his truck, and "they" could have the law on you if you
butchered your own sheep. Maybe the butcher promised to save you
some, and maybe what he said was yours really was, but you could
never be sure. Sometimes it had already been reserved for somewhere
in Paris before the butcher even came by to pick up the living animals.
In the sixties some of the larger farms, with two flocks, bought freezers,
which they paid for month by month, in which they could store their
own traditionally raised lamb, or their neighbors', after the butchers
had slaughtered it. Then the owners of freezers worried about the
cost of electricity, about thunderstorms cutting off the power, about
generators, and about rumors of new taxes on the freezers according
to their cubic capacity. And those who clung to the traditional system
railed against the Common Market, which allowed the mass impor-
tation of cheap factory-raised mutton from the Netherlands and elsewhere, just as the spring lambs from the *causse* pastures were ready

for sale, so that the price of local lamb dropped until the whole of the winter's herding, and all of the chopping of beets by hand, went for nothing. "A few years like that," they said, "and we're ruined." They could not keep the lambs, they said. Once they had started fattening them they had to be sold. They could not come back off the fattening diet, and if they continued on it for too long they would simply get sick and die. So by the time they reached a certain age they had to be sold at any price.

M. Vert and his methods carried on somewhere between the traditional and the "progressive" systems. He thought of himself as "evolved" and forward-looking. His house, on the road that crossed the *causse*, was not one of the ancient farmhouses, built on several levels, with towers and deep porches, that stood here and there, mostly in ruin, on the upland, and were clustered together like a sprawling château, in the village with a population of twenty-two, three miles away. A farmhouse must have stood on the same spot for some time, but its existence was attested not by the form of the present house but by the small ancient barn that M. Vert still used for hay, which sat back from the road some distance to the west, on a lane that diverged from the later road. It was not only the gray weathered stones of the barn that told of its age. It was their massive size, the great lintels and sills and corners, the amplitude of its proportions, the way it sat in the side of a hollow, with one of its doors facing an upper level and one opening into a lower enclosure of grass sunk in towering brambles—what must at one time have been a barnyard. Beyond that, to the east, was one of the old dew ponds that dotted the *causse*: hollows that had been scraped out of the bare sloping rock, and cobbled in the crevices and along one side, so that they would collect rain or dew. The road that ran past it had been paved for less than a decade, and Muscovy ducks still dabbled and paddled in the green muck, ignoring the occasional cars.

M. Vert was a hurried man, with an obsession for gainful employment. He did everything without a moment to lose, so that he could be doing the next thing. All of his motions were rapid and upward, sudden leaps against the law of gravity: the gestures of his hands, the way he flung up his chin, his cheeks, or one corner of his mouth. He walked as though he were jumping a series of puddles. And old stones left undisturbed made him feel that something in his own life was running to waste. He was impatient to find a way of turning them into some new profitable purpose of his own devising. He talked of removing the tiles from the roof of the old barn to use them on a new extension of his own traditional sheep barn. It was that or a metal roof, which might be best after all. If he took the tiles off, then he could use the stones for the wall of a new barn.

M. Vert's passion for moving stones led him to feel it as a personal triumph each year when the government sent machinery to "reclaim" a few more square miles of *causse*, bulldozing the rocks and outcrops as well as the thickets of sloe bushes, the tangles of brambles and eglantines, the may trees, the scrub oaks and bird cherries, marjoram, thyme, honeysuckle, box, bulbs of autumn crocuses and bee orchises, pushing them all into piles, rubbing out the long lines of walls around fields and pastures and along worn lanes, and scraping the lanes away. Once I came back from an absence through which I had remembered each wall and tree to find that M. Vert had got the reclamation crew to bulldoze and grade away the stones of one of the high walls along the narrow winding lane from the paved road near his house to the green. It had been replaced with posts and five strands of barbed wire.

He modernized, using the materials that he moved from other places. His own house had been built that way. The original structure must have been small—like the old barn along the road. One or two rooms at ground level. Perhaps only the room with the fireplace, on the wall nearest the road: the kitchen and entrance, the first room you came to now as you passed through the gate. It had all been rebuilt in M. Vert's time, by his own efforts, in the first years of his marriage. The wall along the road had been tumbled and remade using stones from nearby buildings, everything set with mortar this time, and the whole thing topped with a broad cap of cement in which a series of lengths of galvanized pipe held up a two-foot strip of chicken wire. The new wall ran some yards past the house, to the west, and a little way past the main barn to the east, and then reverted to the old dry stone boundary wall again. The iron gate was the same age as the renovations.

And the house had been expanded by simply adding rooms, one behind the other, on the side away from the road, and running a hall along the west side, each room with a door on the hall and a window on the barnyard. The stones came from other buildings which M. Vert owned or had acquired in land swaps—that was where the door and window stones from the ruin by my garden had gone. During those years he too had been a mayor for a while, of his own commune of Monteferre, and had made enemies for life by using the information and powers of his office to threaten land seizures for back taxes and debts, and effecting subsequent transfers of land in his own favor. He had land for miles around. Mme. Vert, a sunny, pretty, kind woman with a clear laugh that told of a strong, good, but reserved heart, had brought to the marriage land in the valley, and they worked, down there, a vineyard of several acres, a plum orchard, wheat fields. Their house, when the moved stones had been rearranged by the valley mason who usually built barns, was covered with the old tiles taken from roofs in the neighborhood—including the tiles from my ruin. And the whole building had been *crépi*, as a final touch, with two coats of mortar.

Over the years as the roof had been repaired the old dark tiles had been replaced along the eaves with new, bright *tuiles mécaniques*, which would take over more of the roof each time it was overhauled and the tiles cracked by the frost were pried out and thrown down. The mortar had shaded to a mottled gray, almost like the stones. The grapevine had grown up the wires along the southeast side near the front door, and the wall around it was airbrushed a pale green by the Bordeaux mixture that was sprayed on the leaves in the summer. In a few decades the house had an age of its own.

So that the fly curtain of yellow plastic streamers at the door, and the frosted-glass visor above it, looked new as party hats. And M. Vert's mother, in her eighties, wearing her perennial black dress with its print of a snowstorm of minute flowers, her gray apron and her wide straw hat, looked completely at home as she wandered back and forth along the earth-stained cement slab beside the house, carrying flowerpots or old cans full of geraniums, flowering cactus, dahlias, or in the autumn, chrysanthemums. She set them on top of the wall inside the chicken wire, or on the bench by the door to get some sun if she had brought them out of the house. The additional rooms had been built right over the ancient garden enclosure and she had never got used to that. To her it seemed as though the change had taken place a few months ago. M. Vert had run some sheep fence from the end of the house out to the wall by the road, closing off a triangle around the lid of the cesspool, and he had dumped loads of manure in there from time to time, and his daughter Jacinthe managed to grow a few hollyhocks in there, but not much else. The earth inside the triangle still harked back to the stony red subsoil dug out at the time of building, and that was why it was "ungrateful," M. Vert said. But his mother simply shrugged and smiled and said that nothing had

ever wanted to grow just there, and nothing ever would. There was
another old garden enclosure beside the open-fronted cart shed opposite the entrance door of the house. It was full of rich black soil
built up with manure out of the barn next to it, and in there M. Vert's
wife grew most of their vegetables: giant lettuces and cabbages, tomatoes, onions, carrots, leeks, and sorrel.

The long barn itself had been altered little by little. The façade
facing west, across the barnyard from the house, still showed some of
the original stonework. The cows filed to their stalls through the
massive stone doorway under oak beams whose girth approached their
own. M. Vert had pulled all the tiles off part of the barn and replaced
them with the gray hexagonal shingles of some patent composition
that had been pushed, for a few years, by the vendors of building
materials, and then had been all but abandoned in favor of corrugated
roofing, which covered the high lean-to that M. Vert had tacked onto
the end of the barn, and the industrial shed that he had built farther
back to house machinery: tractor, hay rake, manure spreader, old truck,
buzz saw. He had ripped out part of the back of the barn and built a
wing as large as the whole of the barn, for his sheep, and that too was
roofed with corrugated metal and never seemed finished, perhaps
because he himself dreamed constantly of adding to it, but still in
stone, using the stones from the ancient barn beyond the dew pond,
which was another of the structures that he described as "nothing but
stones."

The peasants who defended the traditional methods of sheep raising
shook their heads at the metal roofs. No insulation. Too hot in the
summer. And certainly the heat added to the smell, in the barns where
the sheep were fattened on the new bag feed with its list of polysyllabic
additives in fine print on the tag in the seam of the sack. The old
barns smelled of ammonia and straw as one came into the cool darkness. The new ones shimmered with an acrid stench of decomposition.
M. Vert did not plan to follow the full "progressive" practice and keep
his sheep in a closed barn all their lives. But he began to add sacks
of the modern feed to the mangers in his barn, and the odor began
to seep into the barnyard. "But not much," he said, jerking his head
toward the piles of sacks. "Only to finish them. For fattening." And
he kept a few sheep apart and fed them on nothing but what was
grown on the place. They were for the family freezer. In the daytime
they all went out to pasture together.

From the hayloft window at the back of the house in which M.

Vert's mother had grown up I watched them come in to the pasture below. In the first hours of the morning in the summer they scattered over the rocky acres, moving like clouds among the clumps of sloes, through the shadows of brambles, clattering on the loose stones, the lambs calling. The few bells clonking and tonkling. I could hear the small teeth snapping the coarse grass close to the ground, and grinding it. The voices of cuckoos echoed from the far trees, and by nine the shrilling of the cicadas was rising like a tide, and a faint smell of mice wafted under the house roof. As the sun climbed, the sheep moved closer together and gathered in the shade of the walnut trees: under a big one standing alone out in the pasture, and under the smaller ones along the wall just below me. In the late morning they pressed tightly against each other, their heads down, the ones by the wall butting the stones. The mass of gray backs washed slowly from side to side as in a tide pool, the sheep pushing to try to get deeper into the shade, and from time to time one of them who had been shoved out at the side until the whole woolly back was in the sun would pull out from the crowd and gallop around the rim of sheep butts to dive in somewhere else, tail twitching, sometimes repeating the process two or three times before finding a spot in which to burrow for a while. Some of the lambs managed to squeeze among the legs and find their mothers' teats. They disappeared as though they had drowned. By noon the swarmed sheep were almost still, and the whole *causse* grew hushed at midday except for the cicadas.

One morning just after the summer solstice the sheep appeared without their wool, looking pallid and famished. They were scored with the marks of the electric clippers, from behind their ears to halfway down their legs, as though they had been gnawed by rats. They clattered faster than usual on the bleached stones, constantly startled, and they huddled earlier in the shade, twitching their short tails incessantly against the flies.

Until only a few years before, the sheep had been shorn by hand. Those who had raised sheep all their lives, and the professional shearers who went from farm to farm in the season, appeared to move their shears over the recumbent sheep almost as fast as the clippers went, and the sheep, when they were finished, looked as though they had been made by a wood carver who had left them covered with the marks of the adze.

That was the way Michel and his brother the roofer sheared their flock, outside the barn behind their house, the next Sunday. One by one as the shorn bodies were released they were turned out onto the green. We stood by the oven, late in the afternoon, and they surveyed their work and told me how many bags of wool they had shorn, and rehearsed the virtues of wool.

"It's the only thing," Robert the roofer said. "*Causse* wool."

"Nothing like it," Michel said. "For the health. But it has to be raw wool."

"Winter," Robert said, "it's the only thing. It keeps the feet warm."

"Best thing to sleep on," Robert said. "Wool mattress."

"We don't sleep on anything else," Michel said.

"Sweaters," Robert said.

"You put it against your back," Michel said, pushing his hand up inside his red sleeveless jersey, "like that. Pure wool. For rheumatism. For the kidneys. It draws it out. My mother puts it there. My father put it there."

"It warms you," Robert said.

"It absorbs," Michel said.

"It absorbs everything," Robert confirmed, with a gesture of his hand like a magician's about to draw a handkerchief out of the air. "Primordial."

"Even wet," Michel said. "It's good in the rain. Impermeable. The old shepherds' cloaks."

They both nodded.

"To the ground," Michel said. "My grandfather wore one. That was all they needed. You could live in it."

"You wrapped it"—Robert showed me with a gesture—"like that, to carry a lamb."

"When it rained," Michel said, "you just pulled the cape over your head. And you stayed dry."

"But it just got heavier," Robert said. "Thousand gods, it got heavy. With the water soaking into it." He laughed. "How they ever walked home under it—" He shrugged.

"Me, I don't mind the rain," Michel said. "Only a little, in the winter. I use a sack, that's all, over my head. And my umbrella." His huge ripped umbrella.

And he was the last, no doubt, of the shepherds on that part of the *causse* who sat, in bad weather, in any of the remaining shelters built into the boundary walls of the pastures, echoes of the stone ovens and the beehive houses of the Gauls, so deftly fitted into the slopes of the ground and the meanders of the walls that some of them were all but invisible unless you stood directly in front of them. Some of them were cramped and narrow, but most of them were a pace or so across, wide enough for two shepherds to crawl into at once, if need be, and sit facing each other on the stone bench that was part of the wall, and they were high enough inside so that the shepherds could sit out of the wind under the flat stones of the ceiling and look over a broad landscape of *causse* with lines of woods, dips of valleys, clouds. One shelter not far from the green had been set on a steep slope that was part of a long valley. A standing cave. It was crouched between two huge rocks, in oak woods that ended just in front of it, so that the shelter was hidden from behind and above, and looked out on a broad hollow that wound away like a river.

Each of the shelters was sited to watch over a wide expanse of grazing land. Each of their arched doorways framed a place that was like nowhere else. Sockets. Michel would never have admitted to sitting in one. Never. Not as a child, when they were regarded with awe. Children did not play in them. The huts were the abodes of figures of the past, and were spoken of as though they were haunted, though it was never said, and there were no stories. In the present age there was a certain shame attached to the notion of actually entering one and sitting there, taking shelter in so rude and small a place, the kind of protection that humans had been making for themselves in that region, out of the stones lying there, for thousands of years. Nobody wanted to be thought of as backward. Almost no one in the region had sat in the huts for a long time. Roots came through the roofs. Trees grew up through them. Every year the reclamation project devoured a few more, along with the walls into which they had been built. But Michel sat in them, unseen, and looked out on pastures that were his own and on others that were not. He emerged from them cautiously, and looked up at the open air overhead, while his sheep flowed around him.

I waited for M. Vert to ask me whether the neighbor had shorn his sheep yet, and then to tell me that they had to do it by hand because they were too tightfisted or too poor to pay the shearers, and because they had no electricity.

"Imagine," he said. "They didn't *want* electricity when it came."

I said that I sympathized, but he never heard it.

"The line could have gone down to the green for nothing, when it came past here," he said. "But they wouldn't have it. The mayor tried to make them have it, but they wouldn't." He touched his forehead.

The top of his head was pressed into the flank of one of his cows, one of the red-brown Salers, and his hands went on milking into a pail between his legs. He still kept Salers for the milk for his family and for the calves, but he had introduced several of the black-and-white Friesians. Their milk was thinner and poorer but there was more of it. I came up the lane every evening with the scalded-out bottle, for milk, and was barked at, inside the gate, by Montagne, who then greeted me. I looked for the owl that came and went from the top of the barn, and listened for the sound of M. Vert talking to his cows, *"Là! Là! Meh! Eh ben!"* Mme. Vert would come out of the kitchen and say, "He's milking," and we would go together into the barn and begin the round of the day's gossip, while the cow swayed, stamped, swatted around her with her tail, and was told to stand still. M. Vert called her a slut, buried his head into her side, which had made the top of his beret shine like patent leather, and he screwed his face around to look up as he talked.

He straightened up and put the funnel on top of the bottle and the piece of screen in the funnel for the cow's hairs, and poured the bottle full. Suddenly it was warm in my hand. If he was finished milking we went into the kitchen, some evenings, and stood for a few minutes reviewing the local news, with M. Vert's mother working at the big range set in the embrasure where the fireplace had been. A band of red-and-white-checked material a few inches wide hung from under the brown painted board of the mantelpiece. Pieces of antique polished copper, brass candlesticks, a coffee mill, on the mantel itself. The walls had been painted yellow. The post office calendar with a picture of the yacht harbor in Saint-Tropez hung over the long Formica-covered table. The TV stood on top of the refrigerator, and it was on. M. and Mme. Vert's harelipped younger daughter was watching it from a chair at the table.

I paid for the milk once a month if they would allow me to. Usually they refused, saying that they used water from the big house for the watering trough in the pasture, or telling me that it didn't count because I had been away for a few nights. I helped with watering the fodder beets when the Verts transplanted them into the field, and with picking peas and beans when they came on too fast, and those were cited as payment for the milk and for the vegetables from their garden which Mme. Vert pressed on me most evenings, even when I had brought them vegetables from my own. A lettuce (when I had more than I could eat). New potatoes. "We'll only give them to the pigs," she said. Sometimes she said, "Wait," and disappeared for a moment and came back with a few eggs wrapped in newspaper. "We have too many," she explained.

If I helped with anything invested with ceremonial importance, such as haying—or even if I didn't, and they were engaged in it—I would be invited to the great banquet that always followed it, at tables of planks and trestles set up in the courtyard if the weather was fine, or in the cart shed across from the kitchen if it looked like rain. I entered a bubbling of humanity, startling after the wordless *causse*. They were sitting at the long benches, the men in their hats, laughing and interrupting. Workmen and neighbors and members of the family who had helped with the job or were owed some favor or were simply invited because they were always invited. Noodles in the soup, to begin with, instead of bread, as the sign of a special occasion. The soup plates, once the soup was emptied, rinsed out with half a glass of the thin dark wine from the vineyard in the valley, which was then drunk from the plates. Then the glasses filled, to accompany the omelette and the farm pâté. Rabbit and chicken and lamb. Potatoes and peas and salad. Goat cheese from the village. Fresh cow's-milk cheese— a rarity—from the farm. Camembert from the grocer's truck that stopped once a week at the gate. *Baba au rhum*, or *clafouti*, and coffee, and fruit if it was in season. Cherries and strawberries at haying time. And then the clear bottle of plum eau-de-vie, passed around the table with the coffee, to pour into it, or into the cup when it was empty.

"Not for me," M. Vert said. "It's bad in the sun."

A huge load of hay towered above the flat trailer hitched to the tractor at the end of the courtyard, and he planned to unload it into the barn that afternoon when the guests had all filed out, picking their teeth, to the cars parked by the gate.

Somebody was sure to tell me again that it used to be like this all the time when they worked together in the fields, and ate at the farm where they had been working.

"Now we don't see each other," they said. "There's never time."

And I was asked politely whether I still liked living down on the green in the big house, and whether it wasn't too quiet for me or too lonely, and how I was getting along with the neighbors.

Coming back in the afternoon, the green was still, surrounded by the glare and the unending high note of the cicadas. Michel's door was closed, with the plastic fly curtain pulled back. There was nobody home. The rotting five-bar chestnut gate at the entrance to the court-yard of the house with the tower had been propped in place with sticks. A narrow path led in through the tall cow parsley and vetch, but it was not possible to see from the gate whether or not the house was even inhabited. The walnut tree and the tower and heavy walls behind its shade were enfolded in silence. M. Vert said that the house had been there during the Wars of Religion. Some of the local in-habitants said so too, though they were perhaps as likely to exaggerate as he was. There was the usual legend which went with houses of comparable antiquity on the *causse*, of an underground passage that led out from the cellar, under the fields, and emerged in one of the steep ravines that ran down to the valley. M. Vert said he knew where it came out but that the place was hidden now. He could have been describing a root.

The walls of the house held the cold of night all though the day.

"It's cool there in the summer, isn't it?" M. Vert asked, with a certain proprietorial vanity. When the *causse* shimmered with heat and the sheep pressed hard into the shade, the house had a chill like deep water. A breeze from under the cellar door flowed up the stairs and out onto the stone porch, and on up and out of the upper windows. When the sheep began to move out again across the pasture I would slip out at the gate, carrying a can of water down the lane to the garden, or if it had rained I would go over the wall at the foot of the old acacia, and along the edge of the lower field, the long way around, to come to the garden from the other side of the Roman road.

The brambles retreated and the cultivated rows advanced across the walled triangle of the garden. The narrow *causse* hoe, the *bécou*, made for me by a blacksmith friend from an old carriage spring, sang in the stones. Before long, even that first season, I had more to take home in the evenings than I could eat. I invented new salads of what was available: young white squash, green walnuts, mushrooms. I tossed chopped young cabbage and garlic and tarragon together in grape-seed oil. Tomatoes ripened on the windowsills. When I went out to get them after dark they were warm.

Friends came to visit, but almost no strangers found their way to the green. I was amazed one morning by a knock at the door and the delivery of a telegram by a young woman who had parked on the green. From then on such messages reached me from time to time, or in bad weather were left for me at M. Vert's. The Jehovah's Witnesses from a town an hour's drive away showed up one morning to inquire about the state of my soul. They had asked, at Michel's house, whether the house with the tower was inhabited, and Michel's mother had confessed that it was. They questioned me about how long I had lived there, and for a moment I could not remember.

The other house across the green, due north, the one full of furniture, with the date 1819 carved over its door and the last trees dying around it, continued to shed its tiles suddenly in the still nights. Michel let his sheep in around the house and I saw him from time to time peer in through the loose shutter of the west window. I looked in myself every so often to see what I could of the bed with its crocheted spread, the table with its cloth, everything in there rotting as the rain got in. It seemed as unlikely as ever that the house would be repaired, but one day during a week of cold rain in the summer a thin young man and thin young woman turned up on the green in a rusted 2CV. They drove in at the empty gate, stopped by the front door, and got out in their raincoats, stepping on the cracking border of broken tiles, and the young man fished out a key as long as a table knife, struggled with the rusted lock while the rain poured down off the eave, and got the key to turn at last. Then he tried to push the door open. But it was stuck, and they both put their shoulders to it and heaved. It let go all at once, a foot or so, and a rotten board from above it, and a bushel of plaster and rubble cascaded onto the floor in front of them. Very carefully they slipped through the opening and into the house.

They emerged a few minutes later carrying half a dozen dinner plates, which they set out in the rain, and then in spite of the weather they started pitching their tent between the house and the wall along the green. The rain stopped when they had finished. The young man dragged pieces of dead trees up near the tent and they managed to start a fire. The next day I took some pieces of dry wood across to them and Michel turned up at the wall and joined us. The young couple were from a city on the Mediterranean. They were both students. They spoke very quietly—so quietly that they were barely audible. He would have liked to study history, he said, but was training in pharmacology "to make a living." She was studying to be a schoolteacher. He was a son of one of the owners of the house, and he was trying to persuade the rest of the family to let him have it so that he could fix it up. He had loved it all his life, he said, and had always dreamed of having it to come to, and living in it on the empty *causse*. I asked her how she liked it and she said she liked it very much. She thought it was beautiful. She loved the country and did not mind that it did not have all the comforts. She loved the silence, she said, and the rain.

For days they dragged things out onto the grass to dry in the sun, once the rain had really stopped. Half-decayed quilts, drunken chairs, a crooked spinning wheel. A cradle, miraculously undamaged. Kerosene lamps. Bowls, and iron cooking pots. In the evenings they made fires, using pieces of disintegrating floorboard, and we talked about what they hoped to do to the house—restore it as it had been—and where they hoped to have trees and a garden. Ten days later they put all the things back into the house in a pile, and brought a sheet of plastic and covered them, and hauled the door shut and locked it carefully and drove off up the lane to the north under the big lime trees.

A year later, in high summer, they were back, looking as much as ever like a pair of fledglings, and they were followed, a day later, by another 2CV *fourgonette* crammed with two more couples who turned out to be architecture students, disciples of a man of whom they spoke with awe, a professor of architecture and a historian of architecture whose passion was restoring ancient domestic and agricultural buildings. The four young architecture students and several of their friends had already restored two old farms farther south, and we all spent several evenings planning the restoration of the house full of furniture, and of the ruin beside my garden as well, which they agreed must have been built by the same mason at about the same time. They spoke of both houses as particularly pure, beautiful examples of the *causse* shepherds' houses of the period just after the Revolution. "They've got *dog*," one of the students kept saying. And the students talked enthusiastically of bringing their professor, and trying to get the whole of the green protected by the government.

They too drove off up the lane some days later, and the first young couple followed. And then nothing, until the word came back that the family was still a problem and that at least one of the heirs was refusing to cooperate, but that the young man was still trying to persuade them all. The next year the young couple did not come back at all.

The autumn comes late there. In September a haze veiled the sky above the *causse* and the evenings and mornings were edged with mist along the walls. The house grew cold, as it had been in the spring. The warmth of the day never entered, and I stayed closer to the fireplaces and to the wood stove up in the room with the hayloft window

over the pasture. In the afternoons, when Michel came past the garden
with his sheep and stopped to ask, each time, "Well, you still working?"
the sun would be filling the lane with long rays but the day would be
growing chill, and we would discuss the likelihood of frost that night.
Some of the firewood was already stacked for winter.

The corn grew well in that garden, despite the shallowness of the
soil, and when the first frost seemed to be almost upon us I had several
short rows with ears just forming, from the last planting. I picked
them all and took them home. Husked, they were the size of little
fingers, and I steamed them and had an autumn feast. I could not
have given them away, for none of my neighbors would have touched
them.

Dry windstorms at the end of summer. Then days at a time of cold
rain. The first yellowing leaves. Afterward the days seemed to return
to summer, but the green of the plums had begun to take on a blue
shadow. I sickled the grass under the trees, and took an old wine
barrel and rinsed it out and stood it under the big walnut tree with a
few inches of water in the bottom. Several times a day I rocked the
barrel, sloshing the water up the sides to swell the wood and close
the cracks.

The tomatoes had been harvested and still lined the south windowsills, on which the shutters were closed at night. The garden was
full of leeks and cabbages, brussels sprouts, broccoli, endives, sorrel,
a spreading bush of lovage in one corner. The last hollyhocks were
blooming on the tops of their dry stalks against the curved back of
the oven, and there was even an autumn damask rose blooming, grown
from a cutting taken from the garden of a ruin miles away on the
causse.

But as the autumn came in there was less to do in the garden and
I spent more of the afternoons wandering on the *causse*. If the day was
clear the air was warm by that time, and the sky was bright. There
was bronze in the earth and leaves and lichens on the stones, in the
rust of the eglantines' foliage around their clusters of scarlet hips, and
everything looked like its own reflection in clear water.

The lanes led out through the woods past ruined towers and farms
which I knew room by room, window by window. They disappeared
in thickets and reemerged winding along hillsides among the golds
and black of the oaks, down through overgrown farmyards into small
valleys that opened out like estuaries. They arrived in fields just
plowed, with solitary walnut trees standing in them, the leaves already

looking like leather. The *causse* smelled of the changed season, of black humus among the roots of moss. I found my way into caves in the woods that shelved down under the tableland into the dripping maze of galleries and streams and caverns with walls still showing the animals of the Great Hunt. Three steps into the earth and the silence seemed absolute.

Most days I went on foot, but I had also acquired a bicycle, just as Michel had. Only his was a stripped-down racing model on which he traveled occasionally to see his brother or to visit someone miles away. He bent over the handlebars, pumping with his massive legs, muttering to himself phrases with which the sports announcer, in the summer, had described the Tour de France. Mine was of a design called, frankly, a Wanderer. The short, muscular bicycle salesman who had sold it to me had clearly been disappointed that I had not chosen something more like Michel's. Something, he said, with which I could hope to enter the *rallyes*, the bicycle races that wound through the villages decorated with strings of flags, in the fetes at the end of summer.

Mine was, unfortunately, purple—there were no other Wanderers—but it was otherwise perfect, and I traveled on it farther and farther away. I came to know more of my neighbors as the summer receded.

Then one morning, after a night of rain, the blue plums had begun to fall. Every day after that, as long as they went on falling, they were picked up from the grass. It was a regular round, with a couple of buckets, that began with the trees just beyond the former duck pond outside the door, in the courtyard, and continued tree by tree around the walls and over them into the next field, to the old trees around its edges, between the trunks of the walnuts.

"Are you picking up the plums?" M. Vert asked.

I assured him that I was. We discussed once again the matter of barrels, the excellence of the vaulted cellar, and his offer to use his own *patent*, his own permit, to make eau-de-vie, later in the autumn, from the plums I gathered, as well as from his own. The *patent* was his by right as an agricultural *exploitant* who had been able to claim that said situation had existed unchanged since before a certain date, and that his or her parents, furthermore, had been on the land for a certain period before that. It was a serious offense to make eau-de-vie in any of the clandestine ways that might have suggested themselves to a people so independent and so fond of providing for themselves.

The government's zeal to control the manufacture and above all the sale of eau-de-vie had its roots in the excise laws and the revenue they produced. It is in the nature of government to need absolutely every bit of money it can raise. The government's traveling inspectors, the revenuers, were the *gabelous*. They were detested and feared, and were the heroes of jokes. There were peasants in the region who still boasted of a time, preserved in verbal as well as written history, when the King had utterly failed to collect taxes in those parts for decades on end, and the royal collector who came to try was thrown into the river. It was spoken of as a Golden Age.

The laws suppressing home manufacture of alcohol had been administered very strictly in latter times as a result of a government campaign against alcoholism. Every year the peasants who still made eau-de-vie lived in fear of new legislation that would prevent it entirely. Finally they seemed fairly secure, for the time being: those who already had a permit to make eau-de-vie from their own plums would continue to be able to make so many liters a year, for their own lifetimes. But there would be no successors, and no new permits would be granted.

It was a campaign, in the view of the peasants, fomented by the *licoristes*, the commercial manufacturers of alcoholic drinks, in order to prevent competition from the homemade eau-de-vie, which was pure fruit alcohol, and vastly superior to the doctored and colored syrupy stuff that they sold in the stores with phony antique labels and a lot of hoo-ha about their traditional vats and ageing, when everyone knew the guys who worked there and how much burned beet sugar they used. The *licoristes*, for their part, affected a disdain for the eau-de-vie from the villages, which "tastes of the burner," they said. But they evidently felt threatened by it. According to the peasants, the *licoristes* just wanted them to be unable to make eau-de-vie so that they would have to buy the stuff the *licoristes* sold in the stores.

"Never," Robert said.

"Never," M. Vert said.

They bought, each, one bottle of dark rum (Negrita) a year, for the coffee, on special occasions, because that was what you did.

"It's not that we drink the eau-de-vie ourselves," M. Vert said. "It's useful. One uses it. And one sells it."

The *patent* gave each qualified agricultural *exploitant* living on his or her own land the right to make 1,000 degrees of eau-de-vie a year, which, at the alcoholic strength that the distillers reached—about 108 proof—worked out to roughly nineteen liters each. Or that was the accepted mathematical explanation of the nineteen-liter limit that peasants and *gabelous* agreed on.

The windfall blue plums were the principal source—the plum was a kind of quetsch, called locally the St. Antoni, or pig plum (St. Anthony's animal is a pig), because they used the plums for fattening pigs. Windfall greengages were used, by anyone who had them. And more rarely, mirabelles: small, gold, transparent. But those were the only kinds of plums that were used for eau-de-vie. The big round black one that was sold half ripe, to be shipped to Belgium as a dessert plum, was no good for it, and the Agen, which was dried to make prunes, was tolerable but not valued for alcohol.

The plums had to be picked up from the ground. They had to be ripe enough to fall by themselves. The filled buckets were emptied into barrels and left to ferment. There was a time in the autumn when almost every inhabited house in the country whose owner had a few plum trees—and both the blues and the greengages grew wild throughout the region—had a barrel or two bubbling away in the cellar, plop-plopping like cooking cornmeal.

A full barrel of plums, depending on how good the summer had been, how much sugar the plums had made, and how much juice, would produce close to twenty liters of eau-de-vie. The plums poured from the buckets into the barrels, to begin with, making a soft thunder on the wet wood, and then an excited staccato splashing, too fast for the notes to be distinct, as the barrel filled. All the later buckets, day after day, were poured through a cloud of gnats that closed over the barrels as the plums came to rest.

But first they had to be gathered. Gathering is older than agriculture and the gatherer knows it. Gathering is on happier and calmer terms with the unforeseen than are the later efforts of our kind to control the living world so that there can be more of us in every measured part of it. Gathering fallen fruit is a stage beyond picking it from its branches. When you pick you choose the fruit. With fallen fruit the tree and the fruit have made the decision before you. You have to find where the fruit has gone on its own. In the autumn nights when there was no wind I could hear the plums falling in the dark.

I went out in the morning and they were lying in the wet grass among the stumps of sloes and brambles, and in the crevices between rocks. They were the color of the sky a long time before sunrise just after the stars go out. The cold night had covered them with clear dew. It is better to leave them until they are dry, to let the sun get to them after they have fallen. Water is a great enemy of your eau-de-vie. So some picked them up in the afternoons, some in the evenings. But there were those who didn't care, or had no other time, and picked them up in the mornings, still hard, with the chill dew on them. Some picked them up a bucket or two at a time. Some rushed to fill a couple of barrels all at once, and then collected more later on, as there were chances and barrels. Sometimes a whole family picked them up together, late in the afternoon, backs bent and turning in the mottled shade. It was not a furtive labor but it was private and followed a different pattern in each household, just as each family's fields and trees were laid out differently.

It is a ruminative hunt, likely to be silent even if several are engaged upon it. The mind of each gatherer turns separately, out of focus. More than one sense is called upon. Where a tree leans over a fallen wall the plums are piled among the stones like eggs. The top ones show, but usually there are others below that found their way there first, and you grope along the damp faces of the rock, feeling for them, and hook them out one by one with a finger. In the shade under the brambles the plums often cannot be seen at all, and you reach in slowly, so as not to stab a finger with a thorn or thrust your hand among unseen nettles, and you pat your way through the base of the grass until you touch the cool, smooth skin of a plum, and you roll it out if it can't be picked up. The vipers are still awake at that season, and you remember it, if the sun is hot, but they are rare, even among the stones. In the rain the plums feel like part of the rain come to rest. You stand up and the horizon is a surprise each time, and the size and color of the world come back from far away. The buckets are stained with the red of the plums that are already fermenting. You wipe your fingers on the grass that smells of moss. The sheep eat the plums you miss or the soft ones you leave. From the edges of the pastures you hear the small teeth cracking the seeds.

Before the month is out, after the moon has turned old, the mushrooms begin, and it is the same hunt, but in different shadows, under different trees, the mushrooms appearing like muted lights in the wet grass or the moss or among leaves, their skin powdery to the touch, softer than plums, making it seem as though the gathering of the windfall fruit had been the introduction to the true secret hunt, the search for mushrooms. The plums go on working in their barrels in the cellar, domestic and hidden.

After the mushrooms appear—psalliotis, marasmius, girolles and chanterelles, cèpes and morelles, bluets, oyster mushrooms, trumpets of death—the walnuts begin to fall, cracking on the walls in the wind. The gathering retraces the steps of the plum hunt, weeks earlier. A day might begin with gathering mushrooms and go on to picking up walnuts, which were dropped with a clatter into wooden baskets, and then poured, rattling lightly, into burlap sacks, to be spread out in lofts to dry. There was an annual war over them with the rats, who found their own, under the trees, and carried them off deep into the walls where they could be heard gnawing at all hours—a sound that was the successor to the cicadas, as the days grew short. Later in the autumn the dried walnuts were shoveled back into the sacks to be sold. Some farms first dipped them in *eau de javel* to remove the last of the husks and bleach the shell, but others frowned on the practice.

By then the weather was cold and rainy. The seething and bubbling of the plums had quieted in the barrels, and the rumor began to circulate that the *brûleur de cru*, the distiller, was about to arrive in the village to make everyone's eau-de-vie. Some of the old farms had their own stills: big copper vats with double bottoms and walls, copper swan's necks reaching out from their lids to enter the essential part, the piece that was registered with its own number in an official tome, the part mentioned with a certain awe, the holy of holies of the still, the *serpentin*—a coil of copper tubing suspended in a copper box. On each of the old stills hidden away in barns the *serpentin* had been locked shut and sealed with a wire and a lead wafer marked with a number, and the date when it was sealed.

"Oh, you don't dare touch that," the owner said. "If the *gabelous* find that broken, it's serious." Of course, if you had a still and a *patent* you could, theoretically, use the big engine once a year to make your own nineteen liters. But that would involve filling in forms in an office in town, an application in many phases, in order to have an official come and remove the seal on a certain day, and the official would almost certainly be one of the *gabelous* who would go sniffing around the place, poking into corners, checking on how many liters of plums you had gathered, asking how much you had made last year and whether any was left and where was it, and making sure you did not make more than your limit, from your own plums off your own trees. Whereas if you did it when the *brûleur* came to the village, owner after owner explained—and did not finish the sentence but simply dropped the corners of his mouth, nodded, and raised a finger. So the private stills were used less and less, and some were being sold off to antique dealers, piece by copper piece, usually without the *serpentin*. M. Vert himself did not have one, but the reason for that was never divulged in so many words. The lack of it appeared to be a part of the relative rawness of his farm, which had been subjected to so many changes in his own time. The subject of the still faded into the general impression which M. Vert gave, much of the time, of preferring to forget the past.

When the date of the *brûleur*'s arrival was definitely known it was relayed in a hushed voice, though his work was officially sanctioned and his itinerary registered. It was as though a spotlight came with him. No one could be sure whether or not the *gabelous* would be by in the course of the day or two when he would be distilling in the neighborhood, and everyone felt a flutter of anxiety at the moment of actually signing the application for distilling. The preparations for the deed were carried out as though they were part of a secret mission. The froth and the layer of skins and seeds floating on top of the liquid in the barrels was scooped off and tossed aside in some spot where the quantity would not be apparent. Then the fermented juice was dipped out with a bucket into *comportes* used a few months earlier for the grape harvest: heavy wooden casks, open at the top, which was wider than the base, and with wooden cleats like small stiff arms on the sides, under which poles could be slipped, for carrying them. They were transported in one vehicle or another to some spot near the village *place* where the *brûleur* was already at work.

It was usually raining at distilling time and he would have set up his great engine under a big lime or walnut tree and opened an enormous café umbrella over it, orange sections alternating with white advertisements for aperitifs, to protect the operation and the equipment and himself. The copper still on its chassis and wagon wheels resembled a small, burnished, antique locomotive or a particularly magnificent popcorn stand, and the *brûleur* himself looked as though he might be peddling things to eat at a fair: a short, pink-faced, sunny officiant, whom everyone knew, the rest of the year, as the owner of a small pig farm and village store specializing in homemade sausages, some miles away in the *ségala*.

Along with the juice, and the money to pay him for his work, each *patent* holder had brought some oak logs for firewood. Each in turn went through the paperwork, the signing under the umbrella, so much a liter for taxes and distilling, and brought out the first *comporte* from around the corner, and a round, wicker-covered glass jug, a *bonbonne*, with a capacity of twenty or thirty liters. Then the bearers stood by as casually as possible, in rubber boots, their black umbrellas swaying under the drip of the orange-and-white dome in the middle, while the distilling took its slow course. The smoke from the firebox under the vat rose around the umbrella, and floated out through the rain; and wisps of steam slithered upward from the alembic. The *place* shimmered with the smells of fermented plums, warm alcohol, wet clothes, rubber boots, the smoke of burning *causse* oak and of black tobacco, the rain and the rotting leaves. The vapor of the heated juice climbed into the swan's neck and then passed into the coil of tubing in the *serpentin*, which was kept cool by running water through the outer casing. The warmed water trickled away down the cobbled gutter at the edge of the *place*. The first condensed drops of clear alcohol began to drip from the bottom of the *serpentin*, and the *brûleur* filled a glass with the alcohol and dropped his floats into it to determine the proof, and made adjustments accordingly, rearranged the fire and poured water on the thick layer of wet straw between the casings at the bottom of the still that was there to keep the juice from overheating. The flow of alcohol continued and he tasted the result and passed the glass around to the owner and the bystanders, each of whom sipped and made a face as though the taste were an abomination to them, and then smiled and nodded. The rest of the glass was tossed onto the ground to show that nobody cared.

All around the *place*, on stone porches, in doorways, in windows, at the ends of lanes, neighbors stood and watched for a while, then disappeared, returned to watch some more, came over to gossip. The oldest man in the village, gaunt and white, sat on a stone bench at a corner of a porch and told everyone within earshot all the stories about eau-de-vie that he could remember.

"Once when we were young," he said, "we bet a young apprentice that he couldn't drink a whole liter. He was a young fellow, not from around here. From somewhere else. So he took the bet. He took it. And he drank it. The whole bottle. And he died."

There was an appropriate silence. "We thought he was just sleeping it off, there in the barn in the hay. But when we tried to wake him— not possible."

Another silence.

"Ah yes," said one of the neighbors.

"Ah yes," said another.

"He was just going to be married," the old man went on. "We had had a little of it too, you know, but we slept it off. It's too strong," he said, smacking his lips. "We didn't tell anybody. That was one time."

The *brûleur* put nineteen liters into the first *bonbonne*, which was then set beside a wall in full view. Then if there was no sign or word of the *gabelous* another *bonbonne* was brought out, and another *comporte*, and so, with luck, it went, until all the *comportes* were emptied and it was the turn of the next name on the list. The *brûleur* was paid for the extra amount, and the *bonbonnes* and empty *comportes* were loaded up. The permits covered not only the manufacture but the transportation on the roads of the legal amount of alcohol, between x hour and x hour of x day, and the first *bonbonne* was loaded last and placed more conspicuously than anything else in the vehicle, which made its way home with as little waste of time as possible.

Even then the suspense was by no means over. Every villager could tell of one big farm that made a thousand liters a year—either with the *brûleur*'s permit or its own—and sold it in the valley, through the liquor dealers, wine dealers, restaurant owners, or ordinary word of mouth. The *licoristes* bought it to mix in their vats with whatever else they had there, and colored it and resold it under quaint names, in sanded "antique" bottles. The big farms never had their barns searched, for reasons one could only guess at, but as for everyone else, the *gabelous* were capable of turning up at any time—it was said that they preferred the week or two before Christmas.

One village across the valley buzzed all winter about a visit from the *gabelous*, with orders to search, two nights before the end of the year. In that village they made what, for the region, was a great deal of wine, and rather than waste the mash they made *marc* out of that, as well as the eau-de-vie they made from their plums. But their permits were the same as everyone else's, and it stood to reason that they all had much more than the legal amount of alcohol tucked away in their farm buildings, for sale as the market smiled on them. They had begun to think that the *gabelous* were a thing of the past when suddenly the official van turned up at a farm at the bottom of the village that foggy evening when everyone was still recovering from Christmas. And it was remarkable, the neighbors said, how many farms in the village immediately felt the urgent need to move loads of manure up the mountain in the middle of the night.

In the winter the *causse* became at once more secret and more open. You could see farther than you had come to think was possible, through the leafless trees, across the snowy slopes full of the gray outcroppings of stones and the drawn shadows. It was bitter cold in the big house then. The heart of the tower was icy, and the air in the rooms was colder than the day outside.

There was food all winter in the garden. Leeks, cabbages, brussels sprouts, endives, turnips. It thawed to mud in January, but there was hard white ice in all the hollows again in February, the coldest month. The sheep moved over the pasture, darker than the snow, gray like the stones. They found stubble to eat. Their breath was whiter than they were. In the evenings they were brought in early and the barns were warmed by their droppings trampled into the straw.

In March the snow of the plum blossoms, the sky rising like a curtain above them. Clouds appearing everywhere, even in places where one had forgotten that there were plum trees. The plum grows wild there and for a moment it fills the world with its own whiteness, after the snow.

By the second year the brambles were gone from the garden. They had been piled in the gaps in the walls and filled them, to the delight of the mice. Down the middle of the garden, only an inch or so below the surface, I had found a limestone ridge, part of a fault, a spine of the *causse*. It was shattered like a fallen column, and there was good soil in the crevices. I filled them with thymes and herbs, more savory, rosemary, oregano, tarragon. The garden changed and filled but was the same place. Month after month that corner of *causse* fed me. I worked there hearing the upland talking to itself, feeling the air pass over it. In the spring and early summer the birds were present all day and the nightingales sang until noon. The cuckoo changed its song twice in that season. The strawberries ripened in the shade of the north and east walls. In early summer I could stand at the end of the day and look over the wall of the garden, up the lane which the sun, setting in the oak woods beyond the house and the long pasture, was flooding with dazzling yellow light, and could turn and look the other way, under the walnut tree, and see the sky already the color of a plum, and across the cut, by the ruined house on the far ridge of oak trees, the full moon rising.

As I stood watching it one evening M. Vert came down the lane and we talked of the things of summer. The long twilight stayed around us after the sun had gone down and the gold had gone out of the lane. By the twilight and moonlight we discussed the hay and the garden. The main haying was just over. The *causse* smelled of hay and honeysuckle. M. Vert pointed into the garden. He asked what was growing here and there, and I showed him, and told him, and he nodded. He stood with his chin on the wall, nodding and smiling, twisting his small pointed face, but would not come in. He told me what the garden had been like when the old woman had lived there and grown her potatoes. He forgot whether she had grown flowers too. Then he remembered that she had. In the white moonlight I put the tools away in the oven and walked with him the long way around, east along the Roman road to the paved one, and then west with the full silver-white moon behind us, floating above the railroad bridge.

He told me of sinister events in the region. Sheep rustling at night. For several years it had been going on, as everyone knew, but recently it had been getting worse. Up on the high tableland near the Black Stone, the big meteorite the color of dried blood that lay out in the open all day by itself under the sky it had fallen from, sheep had vanished from pastures. Two at a time, four at a time, six at a time. The tire tracks had been found. There were signs that the sheep had been hidden for a time in half-ruined barns out on the *causse*. A few sheep had been butchered right there. The dogs had found the remains. It had been happening all over the *causse*. The worst had been on the night of the policemen's ball in the shopping town. During the dancing. The rustlers had been busy that night. Four or five places on the upland.

"Keep an eye on the pasture," he said. "But they won't come there. All the way down the lane. They know somebody would see them. The dogs would bark."

The moonlight made him think of a trick he had pulled as a young man. He told me of a sickness of cows called the White. A fatal chill, he said, in which they are covered with a white frothy sweat. We were walking up the road that was silvered with moonlight, our shadows stretching out ahead of us growing darker as we walked, though the sky was still light in the west.

"I brought a cow home from the fair," he said "and two nights later I heard her breathing hard, gasping for breath." He gasped and gagged to show me how it sounded. "I opened the barn door and there she was, as white as that. At first I thought maybe it was the moonlight, eh?" He stopped, facing me, to make his point. Then we walked on up the hill. "Like snow," he said. And then he told me what he had done after that, how he had got her warmed and given her hot medicine so that she seemed to recover, for a few days.

"But they never recover from that," he said darkly.

"I got her to the next fair, along with some others," he told me, "and she looked all right, if you didn't know. And I sold her well."

And again he said it had looked just like moonlight. He was glad to have the hay in. Elated. Last week the hay from the valley. This week the hay from the upland fields and from the shallow valley up behind us. We returned to the subject of the old woman who had lived in the ruin, and he told me that his mother knew more about her than he did, and we would ask her when we got to the house and while he was milking she could tell me what she remembered—he was late tonight. But when we got there his mother had already gone to bed.

When I went by the next afternoon and saw her out in the courtyard arranging flowers, long-petaled dahlias, in a jar, it was not a good time to talk. The doctor was expected any moment. He was coming to see her. Her heart, she said. And she was arranging the flowers for the doctor's visit. "I love flowers," she said. "And I don't like to have anything the matter with me. I'm not used to it, you know." She laughed. "But I'm old. Just the same, one doesn't want to go. The day is never long enough." She was eighty-seven. The doctor never turned up that day.

That spring, while I had been away, M. Vert had cut down many of the oak trees at the far end of the pasture, to make more room for grazing. He put the cows in there more often than before, and they spent most of the day almost out of sight, in the shade of the farthest trees. From the house I could not see the rawness of the stumps, the tangles of cut brush, the stacks of logs sawn for firewood. The grass still appeared to run all the way to the woods, which seemed to be a little farther away. Serins were nesting in the rafters of the stone porch. The sheep were turned into the pasture at night, and spent the first hours, usually, up close to the house, near the water trough. I could hear their hooves on the stones, the teeth tearing the grass off short, the jaws grinding.

At the hayloft window I read of Vietnam, of Watergate, suffering and shame. Piled by a deck chair, the books I was reading, written in other years about other places. I put out the light. From the open window I watched the gray shadows of the sheep moving below me. From the other window, facing south, I saw a row of square lights suddenly emerge, as from the wing of a stage, at the edge of the field where it dipped toward the small valley beyond. The late train. Shadows at the windows. Lives. The rank of yellow rays moved over the field like fingers crossing a table, showing the lower ground in an alien glow, vanes of light turning. Then they were swallowed up. I had scarcely heard the train. The silence came back brushed by the sounds that slipped through it. I went down the dark stairs and out into the courtyard. In the night sky the long wands of the aurora borealis swayed, sank, vanished, returned. Some nights I slept out on the threshing floor and watched the moon pass through the branches of the old acacia, turning pink before it set. A woodpecker worked on the acacia trunk in the moonlight. A barn owl came to the top of the tower and shrieked to the mice in the pasture.

Some mornings the summer sun rose bright red, in mist. Stonechats sounded like clapped pebbles outside the kitchen. Magpies echoed them over and over from the edge of the woods. A large falcon slipped among the walnut boughs. Black kites, up from the valley, sailed over, adjusting their tails to the wind as though they were surfaces of water. Goldfinches clicked in the thistles. Wood larks disappeared along the foot of the wall, where their nests were. One morning, heavy wind and black sky, and that evening a bat flew up and down the stairs of the house, and then out a window, and back, and out, and then the night was still. In the morning the summer had entered its next age, and butterflies, hundreds of them, clung to the south wall above the demolished oven. They were there all day. I went around to look, in the afternoon, on my way down to the garden. Powder-blue ones, yellow ones, fluttering on the warm stones in their one summer.

As the afternoon sun was filling the lane again with long rays before it went down, I straightened from hoeing and weeding in the garden and saw, on the other side of the wall, M. Vert's mother walking slowly toward me. She was moving slowly, with small steps, as though she were balancing as she came. From where I was standing I could not see her shadow moving ahead of her down the lane, and I was startled to see her advancing in that buoyant light. She was just across the wall and I had not heard her.

I greeted her with surprise. It had been weeks since I had seen her at all.

"I just wanted to go for a little turn," she said. "I felt that I wanted to. It's such a beautiful evening. It was such a beautiful day."

"Besides," she said, "I wanted to see for myself. I wanted to see the house. My son told me about it, the way it is now. I wanted to see your garden. It's good to see it as a garden again. I was thinking about that, and I wanted to see it. It's lovely what you have done."

I asked her whether it looked at all as it had when the old woman had lived there.

"Oh, it's different. But she liked to grow things there too, and she had flowers, I remember, she had them there, and there. Not so many, maybe, but she had to keep the goats out, you know." She laughed. "And she was old. She kept the goats there." She pointed to the eastern end of the ruin, the wall that had held up the lean-to roof against the house. Brambles filled the old goat shed.

"She liked it, living there," she said. "She was alone."

"Was it her family's?"

"Oh yes. They were all shepherds. She was the last. She had a few sheep. And the goats. I saw her come and go here. Almost every day we talked. She was older than I was. Like my mother, maybe, or older. She washed her dishes there at the window. She used to sing. Like the shepherds, you know. People sang then. That was how it was. When they worked in the fields together they sang. We all used to sing." She laughed.

"When did it stop?"

"Oh, I don't know. Not so long ago. We sang until the war."

I asked her to come in and sit down, but she said no, she was fine where she was. She liked to see for herself.

"I remember when she died," she said. "That was years ago. The roof was there then, the door was there. I brought the sheep back up along the lane here in the evening like this and she was not here. She was not at home. I could see. The key was in the lock and the door was closed. There was a gate along here with a wooden latch. I took the sheep up to the barn on the green. It is not there any more. Only some of the stones. I came up to the barn and her dog came up to me. My dog knew him and let him alone. I put the sheep in the barn and left my dog in there with them. I came out and her dog was waiting and wanted me to go with him. He took me along to a pasture she had there, a little way down the lane on the other side of the green, going toward the village—it went all the way then. The sun was down and he led me there, and she was sitting up, in the pasture, on the grass, with her back to the wall and her head tipped forward as though she had fallen asleep sitting up, you know, watching the sheep. She had some knitting in her lap. She was good at that. She made things, all the time. And that's how it was."

"I couldn't believe she was gone, even after the funeral. I came back, in the evening, past the empty house. It went to a nephew, he was, in the village, and he didn't care. I was sorry when the roof was taken off. And when the door was taken away. What a beautiful evening."

Again I asked her in, to sit down.

"No," she said. "I'm going. I came to visit and I've done it."

"I'll walk along with you."

"No. Thank you. I'm fine. I'm fine. I came all this way by myself. I'll be all right."

"But it's all rocky along there."

"I know. I'll be all right."

"I'm very glad you came."

"So am I."

And we said good evening and I watched her teeter down the lane and over the rocks, slowly, and I walked under the truffle oaks and through the marjoram to the wall in the farthest corner from the garden to watch her slip out of sight climbing down the rough end of the land, and then turned to look at the evening through the ruined house across the cut, by the lime tree, and went back up to put the tools away, and then along the lane to the house, and to M. Vert's farm for the milk. She was already home, and in bed.

"She went for a walk," M. Vert said as he milked.

"She came to visit me."

"She took it into her head. She said she wanted to go for a walk. By herself. She wanted to see the green and the house and your garden. So she went, like that."

"I was anxious about her coming back, on the path."

"She didn't want anybody with her, she said. She was tired when she came in, she said. That's all."

"She told me about finding the old woman who lived in the house by the garden, the night she died."

"She wanted to tell you that, she said."

We went on explaining it all to each other without understanding anything. A few nights later she had pains in her chest and they sent for the doctor but by the time he got there she was unconscious and by the morning she was dead. The cemetery of the commune was on a steep slope facing southwest. It was a small group at the churchyard. Cars always had a hard time parking outside it, along the road, on the hill. At one moment during the ceremony I turned and looked up the slope behind me and saw Michel's mother in her everyday faded dress, with no hat, standing at a distance, watching.

Late in the summer there was an exhibit, "Shepherds and Sheep," in the market town, in the medieval municipal building, from which most of the offices had been removed. Some of the panes in the old casement windows were broken. The rooms had been painted the pale butterscotch color called *crème* early in the century. There were posters: "The Shepherd. An Exhibition," with the head of a sheep. "A Thousand Years of Shepherds," with a sepia photograph of a man in a cloak, and a dog. There were shepherds' crooks and cloaks on the walls, carding combs, spinning wheels, sheep bells of all sizes. Paintings, photographs. Not much. The exhibit had been announced on the bulletin boards of the Syndicat d'Initiative and a few tourists wandered in, going somewhere else. On the wall there was a large, long photograph of the country just outside the town, and a record of local dances was playing over a p.a. system—a remote, marginal continuo. It was not at once clear whether it was part of the exhibit or the record player of some neighbor across the narrow street.

I went from there, one afternoon, to an ancient mill farm where the owners, who had become friends of mine by then, had taken to raising trout in the millrace. The matriarch at the farm, and a contemporary of hers who lived up on the hill near them, both made willow baskets, and she kept a pile to sell. I brought home some trout in a basket. On my way across the valley I saw the big falcon again, as I waited at a railroad crossing while the train came through very slowly, the driver high in the air at his wheel. The train, for some reason, was scarcely moving. The whole world stopped while it glided through the crossing and along the line. Then the gates went up like an intake of breath. Just before those of us who were waiting resumed our ways I saw the country for an instant, the broad bending valley, the limestone cliffs where the Gauls had held out, the edges of the uplands, green and amber and white in the light of the late afternoon, late summer. Stone façades on the slopes, towers above the trees.

I crossed the river and went under the railroad bridge and on up the empty valley: plowed fields and walnut trees along the bottom, woods around the side. And emerged at the top at a stone well with an iron arch above it, no longer used: the site where several lanes came together, the palm of an open hand. A stone cross at the corner of a wall. Beyond it the broad *causse* with its huge sky. It had rained in the morning after a long drought, and there were still dark clouds rushing over the upland. The gray stones, the plowed fields, the dark of the woods looked washed, the colors clear. The last miles over the *causse* were easy and I always went slowly to make them last, looking at it all again.

I went out through the kitchen into the pasture and brought in some brush for the fire. The sloe bushes were loaded with night-colored fruit, washed by the rain. I stopped to watch the sunset. The sky more vast than ever, after the rain. One enormous sweep of the west an intense luminous orange through which two jet trails hung glowing scars. Farther to the north the whole sky was a green turquoise, the color an old man once told me meant that there was an earthquake coming somewhere, and balconies were about to fall. As I stood there watching, the sheep were turned into the pasture. I could not see the gate or who had brought them. They flowed out into the open, a gray river, with their bells and their baaing. The wool had grown back and all but hid the purple numbers with which they had been stamped a month or so earlier. The numbers went up to more than 140—both flocks together, the one for local consumption and the others. They spread across the pasture in the long sunset light, and drifted to the far end, and out of sight. A few of them paused at the water trough and at the salt licks in yellow plastic basins. I looked at the lambs saved from the spring, part of the home flock, big as the others by now, but the faces still short, the eyes less prominent, looking out to the west, across the pasture, to the lower pasture, where they all seemed to be going, to spend the night. I imagined looking at the pasture as a place where I would spend the night, and how I would see it. I wondered at their going straight to the lower pasture that way, before dark. It must have something to do, I decided, with the rain on the grass, after the drought.

I went down to the garden to pick corn and beans to have with the trout that evening. The train went through the cut as I picked, going south. I scarcely noticed it anymore. It was twilight still when I came up the lane, but when the lights went on indoors it turned dark outside.

As I was cooking in the vaulted kitchen I heard the train whistle in the dip beyond the pasture, before the tunnel. The northbound train. The sounds were clear like the colors after the rain. The night was cool, the breeze from the pasture coming through the kitchen door.

The main summer all at once was over. Long, distant note of the whistle. A young driver, I thought. I stepped out of the door into the pasture. The turquoise sky had turned yellow. When I came back in, the big room looked enormous, with its wide fireplace and high ceiling full of shadows, its long table, the old lamp hanging over it, the stone floor that was cold in all seasons. As I set the table I thought I heard a motorcycle, a strange sound, in the lane. Going and then passing again, and I looked out but saw nothing. Then the evening was quiet.

Under the hayloft window the *causse* was silent, the sheep nowhere near the house. I sat in the dark looking out at the deep night above the walnut trees and the pasture. From that window with its wide view across the woods and ridges there was not a light to be seen. Only the stars, with the clouds moving across them.

Then the sound of motors. Headlights turning, coming from the green, the beams sweeping the walls. Michel's dogs quiet. I saw two 2CVs ease out into the pasture, one behind the other, and watched the red taillights bob like the quarters of running sheep until they disappeared in the first dip, retracing the route that I had taken a few hours earlier to fetch brush for the fire. The lights reappeared, searching part of the pasture, picking up some of the sheep, which stood, and then ran back into the dark. The cars disappeared again. I sat thinking of the stories about sheep rustling, but could not believe that the cars were up to anything of the kind, coming with their lights on, no attempt at secrecy. And Michel's dogs had not barked once. Suddenly I was seized with a feeling that something terrible was happening, and that it was already under way, and I was just sitting there. I went down the stairs with no light, and crossed the big room and let myself out the back, through the kitchen. Not knowing who was there, I took a flashlight but did not turn it on. I climbed the fence into the pasture.

Walking fast, in the dark, I felt as though I had been picked up and was being carried along through the night air. A few brambles and eglantines brushed my face but none of them hurt me. I could not have run there so surely in the daytime. I heard sheep near me, heard them run, pause, then rush away. Their bells made little sound. I remembered how loud they had sounded a few nights earlier.

I came in sight of the cars again, turning, catching more sheep in their headlights. Then turning to drive along the line of cut brush full of birds, at the end of the pasture, and out of sight again at the lower end. I followed, across the dip, the groove of valley that appears to be nothing but broken stones, where a vineyard was growing. I missed

the stakes and vines and followed to the break in the sloe hedge, and
the lower pasture. There was no way out of there for a car, except
the way it came in. An imprudent spot to have picked if they were
rustlers. The possibility seemed more and more unlikely but the feeling
of dread remained.

The gate of the lower pasture was open. The cars were far ahead
of me in the woods on the other side. I could not see the headlights,
but I could hear voices, local voices, speaking in patois, and the beams
of flashlights fluttered through the trees. M. Vert's voice, here and
there, a choked tenor, the words wrapped in distance. Sheep ran past
me like ghosts in the dark. Bells came closer, tonkled frantically,
receded. Some sheep managed to run with their bells scarcely making
a sound.

The moon came out, the last quarter, bitten, and I could see the
sheep clearly, running, pausing, circling in small groups. Disappearing
when they huddled against a wall. Some of them began to follow me.
It started to rain again, with the moon shining, and the night seemed
very warm. I touched sloes in the darkness, like wet fingertips.

The car lights reappeared, turned, and came toward me. I stood
still at the open gate of the lower pasture. The first car came up to
me and M. Vert got out and I stepped toward him.

"The sheep," he said, in a kind of rushing daze. "They got out at
the bottom of the pasture. We found the place. A hole. The wall down,
just a few stones. A gap in the bushes. We found it. We found where
they got out. They got out. The got onto the tracks."

He stood looking up at me.

"Did you hear the train whistle?" he asked.

I said I had, a couple of hours before, while it was still light.

"Yes," he said, "still light. But the driver couldn't see them in time.
He came around the bend. They were all there at the end of the cut.
He blew the whistle. He put on the brake all the way. He couldn't
stop in time. Right into the middle of the flock."

"What can I do to help?"

"Nothing. Nothing. We've got the living ones out."

I looked into the car. There was a man I did not recognize. Jacinthe
was driving the car behind.

"Were many killed?"

"Thirty-two. They stopped the train. It stopped. They sent somebody out right away from the station to clear the track. They called
up the *poste publique* in the village to find out whose sheep they were

and somebody in the village who had a pasture by the track, Ricadou, you know, he came out to see. You know, who raises the pheasants in cages. Who uses all the modern sheep feed. He was afraid they were his, got out. He went along with them, and found them. You could still see, even then. He found them there on the tracks, lying there. A few standing there by the tracks. They could read the numbers and that way they could see whose they were."

"We've got the living ones out," he said again, and I imagined he meant that they were in the back of the *fourgonette*, and peered in again, but saw none. "The ones that were hurt only," he said.

"Were there many?"

"I don't know," he shouted, jumping back into the car, wringing my hand through the open window, with his stumps of fingers, and driving off calling, "Thank you."

The passenger in the second car, Ricadou himself, with a bandage over his eye where a branch had caught him earlier, reached out and seized my hand and asked me if I would shut the gate behind them. I walked back across the pasture, hearing the voices of sheep behind me even after they were far out of earshot, and checked the gate on the green, and then walked back to the house through the dark. The rain had stopped. The moon came out again and its misted light came and went in the pasture. Smells of wet oaks, lichen, mushrooms. Of autumn. Smells of box and of sheep, the one turning into the other, sides of a door.

I returned to the lower pasture. I went along the wall with a light. An old wall, but sound, with a high thicket of sloes above it, black as cypresses. At the foot of the wall the sheep tracks appeared to be evenly stamped in the mud. The track of a sheep's hoof is a pair of drops. Two strands of barbed wire above the wall. The sheep were silent, wherever they were, shut in the upper pasture, or dead by the tracks, or helpless in the woods. I looked for the gap where they had got through. The light on the stones kept shining on the faces of lichens, with their rings, their shapes of ripples on pools, of amoebas, ears, clouds, galaxies. A little owl called, close beside me. The warning note of a wakened redstart.

The gap was almost nothing. A few stones had rolled down. A sheep could squeeze under the wire, snatching at the shoots under the sloes, and then going on. One had started it, the rest had followed. The pattern of tracks swerved there. They had all gone through an opening too small to have driven one of them into. A bird shifted on a branch

and a few drops fell on me from the wet tree. I could not help the
sheep and I turned back. In the upper pasture the lights reappeared,
coming toward me.

It was M. Vert again. When I got up to him he told me that he had
come to take the rest of the flock home, herding them up the lane
with the car. He asked me, suddenly diffident, whether I would help
him round them up, and again I was walking across the dark pasture,
sending the sheep toward the gate. The stragglers became a flock.
Still frightened. It yawed and smoked back and forth. I wondered why
he had not brought the dog. Did he not trust him, with the bleeding
sheep?

At the gate he stopped and I went over. He told me again that he
was taking them home to the barn, since he hadn't been able to fix
the gap in the fence, in the dark. I asked whether this was all of them.

"All except the ones that can't walk," he said. "They're still back
there."

"What about them?"

"We can't do anything until tomorrow."

"They have to stay there all night?"

"The vet won't come in the dark. Saturday night."

"And the slaughterhouse?"

"It's closed. They're all closed. Closed all day. It's already Sunday."

"What will you do? Will you shoot them?"

"No. I don't want to shoot them. The insurance inspector has to
come and see them first. He won't get here before morning. Nothing
can be done until the vet gets here at least. As it is, we have *un million*
of loss, pure loss. The most they're likely to give me is five hundred.
And I might lose the insurance, any of it. They'll say it was my fault."

I had been telling myself that it had been no worse for the sheep
than the end prepared for them anyway. That perhaps they had, in
fact, come out of it better, escaping the frightening loading onto the
trucks, the long crammed, jolting ride to the slaughterhouse, and the
arrival and the reek of blood and guts. Instead, the train taking them
by surprise, the headlight rushing toward them like the sun, over-
whelming them. But now M. Vert told me of the ones down in the
woods by the track, and in the pasture, lying with their bones crushed.

"They're all right," he said. "They're not thrashing around. They
have their kidneys broken." He meant, more or less literally, that their
backs were broken and they could not move.

"We got them off the track," he said. "They're propped so they can't roll. They'll stay where they are until daylight. There are a few with broken legs still out in the woods but we can't do anything about that tonight. They just try to run, and get hurt worse. I'll fix them in the morning if I can, when the vet comes. I'll be able to use help then."

He told me that they had figured out how it had happened.

"The sheep were nibbling the tips of the brush that we piled along the fence. We just built it up again last week. They pulled some down and made the hole, and then they just went on through."

The flock had passed through the gate and the cars followed. I saw the taillights of one car stop at the other side of the green, and Michel in a nightshirt talking to them through the car window. I shut the gate. It was raining again.

It was still raining and not yet daylight when I heard the cars coming back down the lane. Jacinthe opened the pasture gate. I saw Michel run across the green in his shorts and boots and get into the back of one car, and they rocked on across the muddy pasture. I went out through the kitchen door and followed their lights. By the time I got to the gap in the wall of the lower pasture I could see my way without a light. They had cut a path through the brush farther along, at a place where the wall had collapsed, and had trundled an old wheel-barrow through it, out to the tracks. The railroad cut and the woods were full of mist. They seemed to be working in a white cloud. The tracks, for a hundred feet, looked like the floor of a slaughterhouse, dark red. Blood, pieces of bodies, bits of heads, wool, intestines. M. Vert, his wife and daughter and Michel, had begun dragging everything off the crushed rock of the embankment to a pile at the edge of the woods by the gap. All the wool had turned darker in the night.

M. Vert was piling the larger pieces of bodies into the wheelbarrow. Where he dragged them the blood still looked fresh. The pieces sank into the wheelbarrow as he let them go. Bellies swelling. An udder. Milk on a teat. He dumped them out near a spot where he could bring the tractor. His wife and daughter, Michel and I, loaded smaller pieces into feed and fertilizer sacks and dragged the sacks to the pile.

The hurt sheep lay in the woods facing the tracks. From time to time one of them would shift a leg or try to stand, even flounder a step or two, and then fall again.

Another car eased into the lower pasture. New. Pale green. The vet. A man older than M. Vert by a decade, and over a foot taller, helped himself out of the car and looked around like a general arriving on the scene of the battle. He was the shape of the udders and bellies in the wheelbarrow, and his face was much the same color. The bulges of his body rolled under his lavender nylon shirt that fluttered in the dawn wind. He was wearing a dark pin-striped suit with a gold watch chain crossing the vest, and over the suit a long black *marchand de bestiaux*'s smock, flowing open. Thin, short hair, the scalp showing. He reached into the car for his black felt hat. Rubber boots. The rain stopped for his arrival. In his eye a peasant was a peasant and an animal, an animal.

M. Vert deferred to him. The vet's report would make all the difference in the insurance claim. With the maimed and mutilated sheep lying under the trees, the vet launched into a speech about how the insurance applied to railroad rights-of-way. The insurance premiums were supposed to go up in each area as the railroad changed over from hand-operated crossing gates to automatic crossing gates. He and M. Vert agreed that prices of everything were going up.

"Faster than the price of meat," M. Vert said, and the vet agreed.

Then they talked about hunters. There were more of them every year. The local people were all right. They did no harm, the vet said. M. Vert was not so sure.

"They damage the fences," he said, "and never fix them."

He and the vet agreed that the real culprits were the strangers to the region, mere acquaintances of the local residents who had the right to hunt, or the sort of people who bought a little piece of abandoned land solely in order to be able to claim hunting rights. It was people like that, they both said, who left the gates open. And they returned to a subject familiar to both of them: the night a few years before when hunters had left a gate of another of M. Vert's pastures open, and several of his sheep had got out onto the tracks and had been killed.

"And the insurance paid, that time," the vet reminded M. Vert.

"Yes."

"That will make it harder this time," the vet said. "You can be fined, remember. If the railroad wants to treat it that way. It's your responsibility, remember. If they get on the tracks you're responsible."

"I know, I know."

"How many dead?"

"Thirty-two. More. Three more died in the night."

They talked about which of the sheep that had been hurt could still be taken to the slaughterhouse.

"You should have got some of them there last night," the vet said.

"I had to wait, for the insurance," M. Vert said. "I had to wait for you to see them. And the slaughterhouses were closed."

"There's always one open for emergencies. You know that."

"I didn't think there was anymore, now that they've closed the one at Eylac, which is where we always used to take them."

Eylac was where the vet lived, in a large cranberry-pink villa surrounded by a high chain-link fence. The small slaughterhouse there had been closed the year before as a result of the same campaign that M. Pouchou was waging in his commune farther up the valley, but the industrial sheep barn that was to have been built at the edge of the town to replace the closed slaughterhouse had never been started. The permit had been blocked at the prefecture. The vet had invested in the enterprise, and chose to blame the whole course of events, including the closing of the municipal slaughterhouse, on the opponents of the new industrial sheep barn. When M. Vert mentioned the slaughterhouse, he exploded.

"And what are they going to do with it now?" he asked. "Their great corpse of a building. Turn it into an asylum for all the people in the town who were afraid of the industry coming, afraid of progress? You can't stop progress."

"Ah yes," M. Vert sighed.

"They wanted to keep it residential. All residential." Eylac had a population of 317.

"So what do they have in Eylac now? The cemetery." The vet looked at me with hatred, and then turned in disgust and glanced at the injured sheep lying under the trees. He walked a few steps toward one that was having trouble breathing. M. Vert told him its back was broken. He took another few steps toward the gap in the hedge. M. Vert pointed to the place where the sheep had got through, and told him about the two with broken legs still out in the woods.

"You'd better burn them," the vet said, pointing to the dead bodies.

"I'm going to, of course," M. Vert said.

"Or the Health will fine you."

"I know."

"The wool," the vet said. "That burns too."

M. Vert nodded and said, "I burned them the last time." They walked away from the ones that were propped here and there, and over to the green car, and stood talking for a while. Then the vet got in and drove carefully out of the pasture.

M. Vert came back and asked me whether I would mind making a pile of brush in the near end of the upper pasture, to burn the bodies. There where I'd come to get the firewood the night before. He told me of a big cow of his that had been killed in the woods a few years back, and how he'd burned that with diesel oil and it had worked very well. But this time we had all that brush right there.

I went up and started, carefully laying the brush of the oaks that I had watched in their lifetime from the window at the other end of the pasture, building a pyre some fifteen feet across, as the sun rose. M. Vert came alongside in the car.

"I'm going up for the straw," he said. He meant the load of straw on a trailer at the end of his barnyard, where he had brought it with the tractor four days before, and no one had found time to unload it, so it had stood outdoors in the rain. He drove off and I built the pile and he came back in a while with the tractor, and the high load on the trailer. The sun was well up. The air was wet. The mist was burning off, and the ground was steaming here and there. The straw was bright yellow against the dead brush that was all shadows, brown, rust, and gray. We pitchforked it into the openings in the pyre.

M. Vert took the tractor down into the bottom of the lower pasture and turned it so that its back was to the wide gap in the fence. Out in the woods he tied the legs of dead sheep, that were still attached to bodies, together with twine from the bales of straw, and then hauled them to the end of a wire towing cable hooked to the tractor.

Mme. Vert, with her hands and arms stained with mud and blood, stood watching and shaking her head and saying that it wouldn't work. The bodies would fall apart, she said. But he said no, she shouldn't worry. They were fresh.

He made a pile of ten of them at the end of the cable, and tied them with wire and started up the tractor. The wire tightened and rose in the air and the pile of bodies began to move. It slid over the wet ground leaving a track in the mud and across stones, bits of wool, blood, the heads catching as they went on brambles and stumps. He got them up to where we had built the pyre and I stayed and piled on brush while he untied the bodies and went back for another load.

Michel came with a load of full sacks in a wheelbarrow, and dumped it out onto the pile of bodies. M. Vert came back with his second load and Michel came and went with the wheelbarrow, and I went on building the pyre higher and thicker. With the last wheelbarrow load Michel brought the heavy *serpette* that they had used to cut the hedge, and a sheep's head. The lips were black. He threw it up onto the pyre. The first thing there, by itself, like the head on the posters at the exhibit, but the one on the poster was green. This one's teeth were bared. Small teeth, like children's teeth. M. Vert left with the tractor to fetch the forklift. I went on building the pyre, over the head. By the time he got back the pile was as tall as I was.

He came back driving too fast, with the forklift raised at a rakish angle, and pulled up beside the mound of bodies, slid the forklift under the edge of it and the fork rose slowly into the air with limbs and guts cascading from it, swinging, and he turned the tractor, with the load still rising, and rolled the few feet to the pyre and stopped abruptly, lowered them, withdrew the fork carefully. It had worked. He went back for load after load. The second time he kept dropping them, but he went on scooping them up until everything was on the pyre except the patch of blood and wool and mud where the pile had been, and the trail where they had been dragged there, and the bloody paths leading to that spot. It began to rain again. But the wind was turning around to the north. It was going to be clear, now that the moon was past the quarter.

Mme. Vert and Jacinthe went home in the car. Michel bade M. Vert a grave, ceremonious farewell in a low voice, with a small bow, which was returned. They shook hands, and Michel walked away across the pasture. M. Vert and I stayed to pile more brush over the bodies, and some big logs on top of the brush. M. Vert said that would be like a hearth, whatever he meant by that. And it would burn them well. And their own grease would burn them, he said, half talking to himself, his crumpled face sweating, flinging on more wood.

"The ones out there," he said to me, talking to himself about the sheep with broken legs, in the woods, two in one place, standing, and four in another, lying down. He was saying something he had already said to himself many times, trying to find a way around it. "The ones out there. Better not go near them yet. It makes them run."

"We have to make the pile big enough," he said. "Because of the smell. So the smoke is more wood than sheep."

But the pile was already as high as we could throw the brush. A hill, the shape of the hives and the ovens and the shelters in the walls.

"Will you light it?" he said. And I lit the straw. Oak. Three-lobed maple. Juniper. Bird cherry. Sloe. Wild plum. The lichens on the oaks and plums caught fire first and were gone in an instant as though they had practiced. The oldest creatures there. The pyre caught and we stood back from it, in the morning sun.

"I'm going to the house," M. Vert said. "I'm going to wash." I realized that we both smelled.

"I have company today," he said. "It's Sunday."

"I'll stay," I said. "But what about the ones by the tracks, there in the woods?"

"They won't move."

"What can you do for them?"

"Later," he said. "Nothing to do. Nothing to do." He lurched away, on the tractor, driving too fast, and I watched the pyre. It looked enormous, roaring in the daylight, bright as a furnace door, the bodies of sheep appearing in long landscapes of fire. I circled the fire, but there was really nothing for me to do there. The morning pushed past me into the fire.

As the brush sank, the bodies appeared through it, moving, the fat burning, the bones pulling apart in the orange caverns. The ash sifted through them and around them; the fire sank from its first mountain. The breeze was from the northwest, blowing the smoke, with its stench of burning fat and wool and its scent of oak and smell of lamb chops, down toward the railroad tracks. The heat shimmered in a high column around and above the pile. A ring of ash grew around the fire. The smoke turned blue, transparent.

I went down to look at the wounded sheep in the woods. There were dogs nosing along the embankment, where the blood was turning black. They had found scraps. And they were eyeing the four sheep in the underbrush. The sheep were frightened, watching them, rolling their eyes.

The fire was burning steadily. The breeze had dropped, around noon, and the damp air was hot. I went up to the farm to tell M. Vert about the dogs. The harelipped daughter was in the kitchen with the serving dish. She motioned me toward the hall and the next room, which had become the dining room after the death of M. Vert's mother. M. Vert was all washed and shiny, his sparse wet hair plastered down, no hat on, his upper forehead white, his shirt white. Striped suspenders. The guests were a large silent woman with gypsy features and a loose lock of gray hair over her forehead, and two large men with round red cheeks, white foreheads, broad smiles over their soup plates when M. Vert introduced us and we all remembered that we had met before, out in the farmyard, one day when sheep were being delivered. We remembered that we had mutual friends on the *causse*. The meal paused while we rehearsed the details. Then I told M. Vert about the dogs. Mme. Vert was worried at the news, and the men said they would be down soon, to do something.

They came down to the fire with the tractor and began tossing more brush onto the charred bones and flesh, and unloaded more straw from the trailer and packed it around the edges, and we went down to the animals in the woods. By then only two of them seemed to be conscious, trying to snake their heads up sideways from the ground, pawing the air feebly with a foreleg. The other two scarcely moved. M. Vert and the younger of the men heaved them into the wheelbarrow and trundled them to the trailer that had brought the straw and laid them on it, the same two still trying to get up, heaving their heads a few inches into the air. The younger man climbed onto the trailer beside them and sat down. As the tractor started across the pasture he stroked the neck of the sheep that kept trying to stand.

The two with broken legs, in the woods, were exhausted, and M. Vert and the older guest went back and carried them into the guest's 2CV *fourgonette* and drove them up to the farmyard to wait, between the trailer and the entrance to the sheep barn. The man from the slaughterhouse was said to be on his way.

Everyone stood in the farmyard waiting, talking of insurance and of sheep fairs and cows. The guest's wife and Mme. Vert, Jacinthe, and the harelipped daughter sat on the bench outside the kitchen door turning the pages of a book of wallpaper patterns, discussing which would be best for the dining room. After M. Vert's mother had died, all the rooms along the hall had been shuffled around. The present dining room had been the girls' bedroom for years, with no wallpaper at all. But now M. and Mme. Vert had moved into the room that had been M. Vert's mother's, and the girls had moved into the room that their parents had used. M. and Mme. Vert had considered giving the girls separate rooms, but had decided it wasn't necessary, Mme. Vert said, giving her guest's wife a knowing look. Jacinthe and the young man, the son, Mme. Vert told me in an aside, were engaged to be married but it had not yet been announced. Jacinthe might not want me to know. Jacinthe pretended not to have heard, but she turned red and bent over the book of patterns, and her sister giggled and covered her mouth. I congratulated Jacinthe. She smiled and I kissed her on the cheek. Her sister got up with evident impatience and stamped into the kitchen.

I congratulated the young man, and his father and M. Vert, and Mme. Vert, and the men beamed, and Mme. Vert smiled and looked at the ground.

"Your fire is a success," M. Vert said to me. "They were fat," he said, turning to his guest. "That burns well. You'll see. There won't be anything left. It may burn all night, until tomorrow, but there won't be anything."

The sun had moved around onto the four sheep lying on the trailer. I pointed it out to M. Vert.

"They don't mind," he said.

A high red truck drove up and stopped by the gate. The butcher from a town on the *causse* where there was no question of closing the slaughterhouse. M. Vert explained to me and to his guest that this was the butcher on call over there. They always had somebody, day or night.

"Oh yes," his guest said. "Of course. Have to. Emergencies." He beamed at me.

The butcher was in his shirt sleeves. A pleasant, open face. He got out of the truck and put on a black *marchand de bestiaux* smock and walked in. Stained pants, boots. Smiling. Round, red. M. Vert went to meet him and they walked toward the sheep.

"I wasn't sure about bringing the truck in until I'd seen them," he said.

"The vet has seen them already," M. Vert said. "I told you." They were speaking in patois.

"And until we had agreed on the price," the butcher said.

"Oh, we'll agree, surely," M. Vert said—the ancient formula in the region at the beginning of negotiations, and a plain fact this time, when M. Vert was in no position to bargain. They walked over to the *fourgonette* and peered in. The butcher opened the back and reached in and felt the backs, through the wool. Then they turned to the trailer and he examined the four lying there, touching backs and legs, making sure the quiet ones were alive. M. Vert told him they were fat. They talked for a while out of earshot, and shook hands, and the butcher went back to the truck and drove on down the road and in from the lane through the place where the wall had been bulldozed to allow machinery to come into the farmyard.

He drove in, and another man, young, silent, broad, a face like a post, got out of the other side, and they opened the back of the truck, and then the back of the *fourgonette* and began to move the two with broken legs. The younger man grabbed and hauled them by anything he could catch—legs, tail, wool—and they heaved the two sheep into the back of the truck, and the butcher climbed in and put a rope around them to hold them still. The younger man was already dragging at the ones on the trailer.

"Don't pull them by the ear too much," the butcher said. "Don't pull all the weight by that. That's not wool. You could hurt them." They carried the sheep, together, from the trailer, and let them down like hammocks in the truck, and slammed the back shut and put the chain up. The young man got back into the truck and sat there without having exchanged a word with anybody.

"You'll have a little something," M. Vert said to the butcher.

"There's no need," the butcher said.

"Yes, yes. Have to," M. Vert said. Jacinthe appeared with glasses on a tray, and her mother handed them around. The younger man got back out of the truck to take a glass, and Jacinthe went round with the bottle from the dining-room table, turning red again as she filled the glass of the young man she was engaged to. The butcher's assistant drank his glass at a gulp and then breathed out hard, ha, and flung the last drops onto the ground, put the glass back on the tray that had been set down on the trailer, and climbed into the truck again.

M. Vert and the butcher and everyone else raised glasses to each other and drank. M. Vert and the butcher brought up the subject of fencing, speaking a little formally, in French, then slipping back into patois as they warmed to the subject. More fence was needed, they agreed. And it was expensive, and hard work. But no way around it. M. Vert showed the butcher the new wing of his sheep barn, the stone wall of the old building broken through to make way for the cement-block extension from the side of the old barn, toward the road. And the bright tin roof.

"It gets hot in there," he said, and they agreed about that. The butcher said the new wing was fine.

"It's the only way," M. Vert said. "My brother-in-law," he said, with long-standing rancor in his voice, "kept telling me that I should go to cows, give up sheep, the way he did."

The butcher shook his head. M. Vert's guest shook his head. He told the butcher that he had a herd of young steers, and they were beautiful. He went on shaking his head.

"Oh, as for being beautiful, they're beautiful," M. Vert said.

"But they don't make money, the way things are," the guest said.

"You can't sell a cow," M. Vert said. "I tell my brother-in-law. These last two years you can't sell a cow for anything. He can't either."

"The market's ruined," the butcher said.

"That's what I tell him," M. Vert said. "Sheep are still what brings it in. Now he talks of building a modern barn himself."

"You'll have some more," Jacinthe said, returning with the bottle.

"No, no. That's not politeness. Honestly. I have to be going."

And they said goodbye and everyone shook hands all around, and the red truck trundled off and turned the corner and drove past the gate.

"About half price," M. Vert said to me, answering the question I had not asked. "What can you do? It's bound to be *un million* pure loss," he repeated. "Forty of them gone. I'll see the insurance man tomorrow."

I declined another glass and turned to go. "Will you be up for the milk?" he asked.

"Will that be all right?"

"Of course. Has to be. Like every night. Only it may be a little later tonight. With the guests. Come when you like. You don't mind keeping an eye on the fire?"

I told him that I did not mind.

"Keep it burning," he said. "I'll go down when I have a minute. Or my wife. Or Jacinthe. There's no danger. The woods are wet. There's no wind."

The fire had burned down and some of the black bones were protruding again. The smell of meat and grease was still in the smoke. I piled more brush onto the remains and went down the lane to the garden.

I spread sheep manure on the damp earth around the base of the one rosebush, and picked tomatoes and lettuce and corn for supper. I heard Michel scolding and cajoling his sheep, bringing them along from the woods. As he came up the lane I was standing in the corn with the basket and he stopped, and his eyes widened.

"What a catastrophe," he said.

"Terrible," I agreed.

"How many, in the end?"

I told him.

"Did he sell the hurt ones all right?"

"Not so well. What can you expect?"

"Ah yes. It happened before. Up the tracks that way. Six years ago. But there weren't so many that time. Four or five."

"Bad enough."

"Ah yes. That's how it is. My faith. You made a good fire."

"The brush was there."

"We must help our neighbors. We're neighbors."

"You're right."

"Eh, the beasts!" he exclaimed. The sheep had gone straggling up the lane, doing no particular damage, but he waved goodbye and ran after them. The clouds were low and there was no sunset as I walked back, put the vegetables in the kitchen, and went out to the fire to pile it up again. I turned to see that Michel had come to join me, and we worked together, dragging and tossing the branches, and stood watching them burn for a while. We could hear crows down along the tracks. Titmice in the wall. A hen clucking. The pasture gate was standing open and the hens were wandering in the empty expanse.

"Forty," Michel said. "My faith." It was about the size of his whole flock. We walked back across the pasture.

"Wait a minute," he said, and motioned me to the gate of his house. He went into the kitchen and came out in a minute cradling a small bundle held together with newspaper as though in a handkerchief.

"You eat eggs, surely, don't you?"

"Yes, of course, but there's no need—"

"You'll make an omelette, certainly."

I protested.

"We only have too many," he said. "With the hens. And we're neighbors. Take them. They're fresh, I can tell you. We give them nothing but the wheat. You can go with that. And the rest they find for themselves. You will tell me if they're good."

At the farm M. Vert was milking, his hat against the cows. He talked of the sheep that had been killed and the ones he had sold.

"They were beautiful," he said. "They were well chosen. They were fat. I never had better. They were like flowers."

All night the fire fluttered against the black band of trees at the western end of the pasture, and all the next day, burning out at last toward evening, leaving a few smoking embers in a wide disc of ash. A few bits of bone, pieces of skull, teeth, nothing adhering to them.

The weather cleared and the hot days came back, but the pasture stayed empty. One day the two yellow plastic basins for the salt licks were gone. The water trough was emptied. M. Vert's harelipped daughter, with nothing to do until school reopened, brought a puppy on a string and put it in the trough to tease it, and ran past Michel's house with it to set the dogs barking. The hens took over the pasture.

The year seemed to hang suspended, with the days turning under it. Michel's mother was sick. She had seemed to be only a little sick for a few days but now she was in bed all day, Michel told me, leaning on the gate. Robert came that Sunday and we all talked, on the green, in low voices.

"I don't know what's the matter," Robert said. "It's age."

They went over the symptoms, sparing no detail. From the description it could have been anything.

"It's worrying," Michel said.

"We'll have to get the doctor," Robert said.

The doctor came the next day, and parked on the green. Michel's sheep were folded in the farmyard just down the lane from their back garden, one of the properties they used that did not belong to them.

"The old woman is sick," M. Vert said as he milked. "They never want the doctor. But they need her pension. What are they going to do?"

"I don't know," I said.

Michel stayed home most of the time, the next days. The sheep were folded in small fields near the green, none of which were his. He kept running out to make sure they had not got out through the rickety fence. He took them along the lane for an hour or so at a time. The doctor came again, and that evening Michel was very subdued.

"He says she will have to go to the home," he said. "They will have to look after her better there than I can do."

"What will you do?" I asked.

"I can look after myself," he said, "as for that. It's just that one doesn't know. What we will do."

The ambulance came a few days later and she was led out, and then she was gone. Michel followed on his bicycle. I saw him on the green the next day.

"She's well," he said. "She's even very comfortable. It's nice for her there. The national medical insurance pays for it all. It's good."

He went to see her on his bicycle, penning the sheep in the barn when he went, and taking them out at night.

"She wants to come home," he said, when we talked on the green. "But they won't let her. They say I could not look after her. The medicines. Needles. It's true. It's worrying. One doesn't know."

He confided to me a week later that she might not come back. He would have to face that. And what was he going to do?

"As for living alone, I like to live alone," Michel said. "I don't need anybody, if it comes to that."

"He'll sell his sheep," M. Vert said. "He'll have to. He can't keep them like that."

"I have the sheep," Michel said. "I have to take care of them. I like that. That's what I like to do. That's what I do. It's that it's a long way to the home. All afternoon, over there and back. In the winter I don't know."

The pasture seemed silent in the mornings of early autumn, although the cicadas were still clinging to the summer and the titmice were gathering in flocks. I had been planning a trip in September and I began to pack. I told M. Vert that I would be gone, and made arrangements with him for my absence. I told Michel, one evening when he came up the lane in the old way, with his flock. There seemed to be fewer than I was used to seeing.

"I sold a few," he said. "They were fat, but they were getting older anyway. I would not have bred them for lambs again. It's easier like this. I only had too many."

I told him that I was going on a trip, and his eyes widened.

"You'll be back, won't you?"

"Of course," I said. "I have to take care of the garden."

"Oh, if it's only that," he said, shrugging. But then he said, "It's beautiful, your garden. I love coming past and seeing it like that."

He asked me where I was going on my travels and I told him. He looked at me, not taking in a word.

"It's far," he said, "isn't it?"

"Yes," I said.

"Is it better there?"

"No."

"It's good here, isn't it? It's good for us."

"Yes, it is."

"Do you like it when you go away?" he asked.

"No. I don't like leaving."

"Why do you go?"

"There are other places I think I want to see, things I imagine I have to do there. And friends. After all, I wasn't born here."

"That's true. You weren't born here. But you're from here." He pointed to the lane.

"Thank you."

He went up the lane without saying anything more. On my way back with the milk, later that evening, he came out of his door and waved me over to his gate.

"Wait," he said. "I have something for you."

He went back in and came out with whatever it was in both hands and held it out to me.

"You'll take that," he said. "I give it to you."

It was a heavy brass cow bell, a steep, flattened cone.

"You said to me a long time ago that you were looking for one," he said. "You said you like the sound. Of the cow bells here. It's old, this one. From when we had cows. We don't have cows any more. We haven't had them for a long time. I still have other bells. You take this one."

His door was closed when I left the green in the afternoon a few days later, but I had already said goodbye. I took the train that came through early in the evening, going north. I climbed on and watched the patches of oak woods slip past, the cliffs turning away, and the gardens, the villages, the light in the pastures, the animals standing on their long shadows.

Blackbird's Summer

"IT IS BECAUSE the moon is old," Blackbird whispered hoarsely, and the sentence came from under his breath, from nowhere in the darkness.

Each of them could hear both of them breathing, and it sounded much louder and more isolated than usual. They could hear the brushing of their sleeves as they walked. The velvet-smooth fabric of Blackbird's worn cotton moleskin jacket and the flapping folds of the priest's threadbare cassock. The sound of their feet echoed in their ears. Blackbird was in the habit of walking quickly with his legs apart, swinging his arms and shuffling a little with each step. It was an ungainly affectation that he had evolved early, like a deliberate lisp, something to do with being knowledgeable and in a position of responsibility, and now that those things scarcely mattered any longer he was too old to change it, and that was the way he would walk day or night as long as he could walk. But he was having to swing himself along more slowly than came naturally to him so that the priest could keep up with him. The priest took short steps in his heavy laced ankle boots, as though his feet were hobbled to each other with a piece of rope. Or as though his pants had fallen down, Blackbird thought, and shrugged. They realized that back between the walls of the village they had been setting their feet down like wool.

They were already past the oval of beveled stones around the pool by the stream, the mirror under the trees where by day some of the women still washed clothes, slapping them in the smooth flat limestone.

The soap-whitened ring gleamed faintly in the darkness but Blackbird and the priest never glanced at the eye of water as they passed. The last light of the village no longer reached them from its pole against the garden wall of the mayor's house, beside the road. They had crossed the first of the walled stone bridges over the series of small streams that wandered through the wooded length of the broad upland valley. Along the ridge, far to their left, several springs, each with a legend about its origin, each with a name and a character ascribed to it, welled up among trees, and some of the streams disappeared again among stones, miles beyond the village and long before reaching the cliffs above the river. Dogs were barking in the village, but dogs were always barking, and the dogs were not paying attention to Blackbird and the priest but to their own conversation. You could tell the hour of the day or night by listening to the barking of the dogs, and the echoes.

The priest was behind Blackbird, trying to stay in his footsteps as if he were Blackbird's shadow. Though it had been Blackbird who had been in the priest's shadow as they had left the village with the light behind them, and now it was too dark for any shadows at all. Blackbird was no longer anything more than a rocking darkness just ahead of him, a little blacker than the night on either side, and it was becoming harder and harder to be sure he was seeing that shape at all and not imagining it. But the priest was afraid to look away for fear of becoming completely lost. He was a head taller than Blackbird, and was concerned about tripping over something, but he would not have dared to take Blackbird by the arm or put a hand on Blackbird's shoulder. The sound of their feet came to him, he thought, from very far below him. When he walked in the village in the daytime he always felt that he could be seen over the tops of the walls, and it added to his feeling of being a stranger there, of not having been born there, not having been a child among those houses and the sounds of those gates.

"It's better like that," Blackbird whispered, chiefly to say something. It sounded at once vague and determined. He was referring again to the darkness. He had chosen that night because he had known there would be less chance of their being seen, and they had agreed about it without further discussion.

"You can see?" Blackbird croaked.

"Oh—" the priest answered. A hundred years before, children from Blackbird's family who would become his ancestors had watched some of the long stones being set point first in the loose dirt of the road, pounded in with mallets, and then the gravel swept over them, and Blackbird had known the knuckled surface as soon as he was able to walk.

"I just follow you," the priest said, listening for the sound of Blackbird's breath.

"Do the glasses help at night?"

"I need them," the priest murmured. "Without them I couldn't see at all."

Then nothing but shuffling and listening. That day someone had cut the first hay of the year, and they could smell it in the night.

"After all," Blackbird whispered, with a trace of self-righteous irritation, "it does no harm to go there. It's done. That's what it's there for. It's well known."

The priest said nothing, but followed.

"It's true, not many people go. It's been some time. That's how it is."

A long pause, with only the sound of their feet.

"It's not far," Blackbird said, after what seemed to the priest like at least half an hour.

"Wait," Blackbird whispered, and the priest heard the shuffling stop, and imagined that he saw Blackbird raising an invisible hand in the night. They both listened. The priest heard the barely audible rustling of the trees, and besides that the trickling of water.

"You see?" Blackbird asked, and the priest was not sure what he meant.

"Here's the gate," Blackbird said. "You've seen it. You've been past here."

It was true, the priest thought. He had probably walked past here in the daylight, quite a few times in fact, especially during his first summer in the village, when he had allowed himself an occasional meditative stroll along the road before the evening office, something which he soon gave up and came to blame himself for as a thing inexcusably affected and idle. And of course he had been driven past here on his way to administer last rites, and on the way to the "nightingales"—the convent school for retarded girls in the larger village down in the valley where he was invited from time to time to officiate in some ceremony, and where the local curates convened once a year in the refectory. No doubt he and Blackbird had not walked as far from the village as it had seemed in the dark, and here they were at a gate he had seen but never noticed, since he had known nothing about it.

"Put your hand out," Blackbird whispered.

The priest groped ahead in the darkness and the sleeve of his cassock caught in a tangle of brambles. For a moment he felt nothing else, and then his bony fingers bumped against a cold rough rod, an upright bar of a tall gate.

"You have it?" Blackbird asked. "It's iron."

"Yes," the priest said.

"It's locked," Blackbird said. "It's always locked. That's how it is. One could have brought the key. There's a key, of course. I know where it is. But it's not worth the trouble. Nobody does that. You go in this way."

The priest heard bushes thrashing and snapping, and then a pause.

"You see?" Blackbird asked. And indeed, now that they had left the road altogether it seemed to the priest that his eyes had adjusted better to the night, so that some shapes seemed darker and others less so. Just in front of him there was a deep darkness but to the side there seemed to be something paler.

"The wall has— This is the wall," Blackbird said. "You go in here." And the priest felt Blackbird's hand under his right elbow, guiding him forward over a jumble of fallen stones. He put out his left hand and felt a piece of rock and an edge of mortar that crumbled and fell into the leaves. A section of broken masonry. He supported himself against the jagged surface cautiously as he inched his feet forward.

"You step over it here," Blackbird whispered. "Here's where you step down." Rocks turned as the priest set his foot on them and Blackbird's hand was no longer under his elbow. He reached out and caught his hand in brambles. In front of his foot he felt nothing. He let himself down onto his left knee and let his right foot slide forward and then down, down. Suddenly he was overwhelmed by an immense sweetness in the still air. The scent of lime flowers with the sound of water trickling through it. For an instant, one knee on a rock, one foot in midair in the night, he forgot where he was. His foot touched something solid, on a lower plane.

"You're down," Blackbird said. "It's not hard from here. It's level. Like a road. You can walk along. You could drive a carriage. In the old days they drove carriages here. I saw them."

The bushes and weeds caught at the priest's legs as he tried to follow Blackbird.

"It's hard to see, under the trees," Blackbird admitted from farther ahead. The priest heard Blackbird pushing through long grass and branches, heard sticks snapping, tripped over something and almost fell. He thought he heard the cuckoo that still had not changed to its summer tune, and then he heard Blackbird's feet, and his own. And then one nightingale. Then another.

"It's this way," Blackbird said, and the priest felt himself pulled forward by his sleeve, faster than he wanted to go.

"This is the way," Blackbird repeated with new assurance. "I know it well. One's always known it." And the priest felt bare ground under his feet, a path, perhaps a drive. He followed through the deep smell of lime flowers.

"One always came," Blackbird said, something happy in his voice.

"Over there one played," he said, but the priest could not tell what direction Blackbird must be indicating. "That's where they had their—buildings, at one time. There are walls. That was long ago. Olden times. It's nothing but stones. We go this way." And the priest followed obediently along what seemed like a gravel walk netted over every few feet with vines and weeds, while the cuckoo was echoed by another and the nightingales sang one behind another and the sound of water grew nearer, louder.

"One might come for nothing but the lime flowers," Blackbird said, "for tea. But there are so many at home. These trees are old. So many of them. There are plums over there. Quinces. You should see in the daytime. It's along here." The priest felt himself drawn forward and to one side by his sleeve, and all at once the sound of water came from directly in front of him, almost at his feet.

"Here we are," Blackbird said, and the priest realized that he had stopped.

"It's just stones here," Blackbird said. "You can sit down. We're here."

"This is the water?" the priest asked. "The—pool?"

"Well—pool. It's more, you might say, like a basin. A little deeper here. There is watercress up there in the stream. That tickles. There is less now because of the shade. There is water mint over on that side but it's muddy there. There has to be some mud, after all, in a stream. It's natural. The spring flows into the stream. It's sandy right here, by the spring. When you walk out farther you have to let the mud settle."

"You know of cases," the priest began, hesitating. "Cases—where it has effected a cure?"

"Indeed," Blackbird said. "No end of them. It's celebrated. It's sovereign. At one time this spot was—I might say frequented. You've heard of the waters of Liru. They were in vogue a few years ago. There were postcards. You've seen them. There's no comparison. But these waters were never public. What is called a private source. A knowledge that the neighborhood preferred to keep to itself."

"And what kinds of sickness?"

"Many kinds. With some troubles it has been more effective than with others, as you would expect. The digestion, for instance. It establishes a regularity. That is beyond dispute, even in the most obstinate cases. It was legendary."

"That is not my problem, I should tell you," the priest said.

"Possibly," Blackbird agreed.

"I eat very plainly."

"I suppose. It's the mama who makes your soup?"

"Sometimes I make it myself. She's not very lively, you know."

"Is that so? I scarcely ever see her."

"She comes to mass," the priest said, "sometimes," and Blackbird smiled in the dark to hear the light reproach, the suggestion that he, Blackbird, was seldom to be seen in the church.

"I hear her call the hens," Blackbird said.

"She still does that. She feeds them. I can't call them," the priest said, and it occurred to Blackbird that he would feel awkward about addressing the priest directly. He knew that his voice would inevitably convey a trace of something that would sound like unfriendly irony if he called him "my father," as many in the village did. He might try, but it would not seem right. And yet addressing the man by his title as the curate would seem oddly formal in these circumstances. Perhaps, Blackbird thought, he would not have to resolve the matter, at least for the time being.

"The hens would rather come to women," Blackbird said, though he knew it made no difference and that the hens came just as well to old Foin, who lived alone now in the one-room stone house out on the upland with only his donkey and his dog and cat and hens for company. He said it as a jab at his son-in-law from town, who embarrassed Blackbird by doing all sorts of woman's work around the

hotel—including calling the hens—and who was in almost every way
a disappointment to Blackbird.

"She can kill them too, I suppose," Blackbird said.

"We don't eat chicken very much," the priest said.

"And you don't have a pig?"

"You know, some of the people of the parish are very good to us,
and when they kill a pig we always have quite enough."

"It's true," Blackbird said. "There are some who make sausage
here in the vicinity—you won't find any better. Very talented. They
always were."

"One has to drink the water, then?" the priest asked.

"Of course. A fair amount. One must get a taste of it, as they say."

"What does it taste like?"

"As for the taste, that's not what you'd drink it for. In any case I'm
not a great appreciator of water, you know. In my calling. The kidneys.
That's another thing. It's known to be a veritable rebirth for the
kidneys."

"My kidneys are very well."

"So much the better."

"Your complaint—was it anything like mine?"

"No, no. But the source is recommended for so many things. My
great-uncle had a brain inflammation. A torture. The family talked
for years of how the waters relieved him. He didn't die of the brain
inflammation, you may be sure."

"You have tried it yourself?" the priest asked.

"In the distant past."

"What did you take it for?"

"Something of little importance. I have to admit that for our family
ailment the water has proven salubrious but not altogether curative.
With us it's a professional affliction. It's the liver that's our fate. My
great-grandfather was a wine merchant. He died of the liver. My
grandfather the same. The liver. My father the same. The liver. What
can you do about destiny? I'll die of it too, if not of the heart. With
me it's the heart as well, they say. If it weren't for this water in my
youth I imagine I would have been gone long before this."

Blackbird smiled to himself, remembering some of the nightly visits
to the spring in his youth, and pleasures that were with him even now.

"But you see how I am," he said. "In the strength of age. A little
—you know—perhaps, around the eyes, but how old would you say
I was?"

"I wouldn't dare guess."

"Sixty-eight."

"I would never have thought it. I wouldn't have said fifty."

"I roll every keg myself, at least up to the size of the *demis*. It's I who roll them. It costs me nothing. I'm happy to do it. It keeps me young."

"But it did cure—what you came here for."

"No question," Blackbird said.

"And cases like mine—"

"Above all. It's famous for its benefits to the skin. Why else do you suppose"—he dropped his voice to a whisper again—"why do you imagine the ladies used to make their way here? And they would go to some lengths, I can assure you. They came from all points, from distances—you'd be surprised. Women of all ages. Sometimes they came together. Even mothers and daughters. So I hear. Sometimes they came alone, to bathe at this very spot. There were those who came in the daytime, and there were those who came secretly, at night. For their complexions."

"And they bathed here?"

"They took the complete cure."

"One must get into the water altogether?"

"That's essential. Especially for the skin."

"Mine, you know—I've suffered from it for a long time."

"That's a shame."

"Since I was a child. This eczema on the arms and legs, sometimes on the torso. That's quite bad enough."

"Aggravating."

"One longs to be scratching. One lies awake longing to scratch. It spreads. Sometimes on the face, as you know. You've certainly noticed the scars on my face. That's embarrassing, but I thought of it as my cross, something sent to humble my vanity."

"Who knows?" Blackbird said.

"A penance, I told myself. I tell myself that all the time when it attacks me in the parts that one does not reveal. The armpits. And of course—"

"That would certainly be unpleasant," Blackbird said. "And one cannot scratch very well in public. In the middle of mass, for instance, or at a wedding or funeral."

"You understand," the priest said. "And I wonder whether this would help with something so established."

"It's up to you," Blackbird said. "I don't see what you have to lose. I've known the water to heal skin conditions that were due to imprudences of several kinds. Some of which I would have thought more difficult than your—penance, after all. But it's not my affair."

"So," the priest said, and took a deep breath. "One begins by drinking the water?"

"That way it's clean."

"I should have brought a cup."

"There used to be one here. Wait. Behind this stone." Blackbird rustled in the bushes.

"For the pilgrims," Blackbird continued, rolling the phrase as he rolled most of his phrases, as though they were sips of wine on the tongue, which gave the syllables a roundness, richness, depth, and a touch of conscious irony. "It goes back into history," he said, "if it's still here. But who would have taken it away except the water itself? Sometimes it overflows in the winter. Ah, here, where it's supposed to be. One has only to rinse it out a little."

The priest heard the sound of splashing, and then Blackbird pressed something against his chest and said, "Don't set it down when you've finished. We could misplace it in the dark. Give it back to me to put it where it belongs. Sometimes one needs a cup—"

The priest took the cup and knelt on the stone. He groped forward and felt the water, cold in the night, and he filled the cup and sat up and sipped from the rough rusty edge of metal, and the water ran down his chin and cassock. The water had a rank, eggy iron taste.

"Sulfur," he said.

"I should think so," Blackbird said. "It's good for the mildew, if you have mildew." The priest took another gulp. It was not easy to get it down. But the next swallow was not so hard.

"The whole cup?" he asked.

"Oh yes," Blackbird said. "Even two, the first time." As the priest drank he closed his eyes, and the stream and the nightingales and the cuckoos beyond them rang in his ears and he swallowed them and came back from a long way to catch his breath.

"That's the way," Blackbird said.

"It's even refreshing."

"Possibly."

"You won't have any?"

"Not this time. Have another."

The priest leaned forward and filled the cup again and drank, this time with his eyes open, looking up into the black night, and the sounds of the water and of the birds and of his swallowing were even louder than before. He stopped and took a deep breath. It was not a pleasant taste at all, but the smell was not so bad as he had thought at first.

"There," he said, holding out the cup to Blackbird, who took it.

"Make yourself at home," Blackbird said. "There's nothing to worry about."

"Is it deep?"

"Up to—the thighs, if you'll permit me to say so. You won't drown. You can think of it as a kind of baptism."

"Perhaps," the priest said.

"You can give me your clothes so that you know where they are, to put back on. I have known cases where garments were left at the scene of the crime."

"One removes everything, I suppose."

"It's more efficacious, no question about that."

The priest sighed and began to unlace his boots. He felt confused, not knowing in what order to take his clothes off, as though he did not take them off every night to go to bed, and take them off to bathe, standing in the washtub by the potato bin. It seemed to him that he was many miles away from anything he knew or had ever known, and as he unlaced his boots he found that his eyes were tight shut and he was looking at a blue-gray wall of chipped damp plaster, scratched, stained, shadowed, under a washstand in the bedroom he had shared with his parents when he was a child, and he stared at the base of the wall and could not remember whether his father was alive or dead, and then he remembered that his father had been dead for forty years and he opened his eyes and took off his glasses.

"Here," he said, and handed them to Blackbird. He stood up and pulled his cassock up over his head and folded it in the darkness in front of him without being able to see it. He seemed to be folding the darkness, and he shivered.

It was encouraging to find the stone still warm when he sat on it again, and he finished unlacing his boots, took them off, peeled off his socks and stuffed them inside. "Here," he said, and gave those to Blackbird and stood up. He was still wearing his long-sleeved undershirt with its medals pinned over the left breast, and his long underwear, which he himself had washed on Monday evening. It was too much for his mother, now, to do their laundry, and Mme. Espeyrie,

the widow who lived two doors down the street, did most of it for
them, coming by with her basket and her small bad-tempered dog on
Sunday afternoons, to pick up the modest pile. She said she had
nothing else to do and that it was her offering to the church—along
with the plucked chickens and the eggs she brought in the basket,
and the dandelions, corn salad, lettuces, carrots, and peas, now that
it was spring. Mme. Espeyrie's attentions to them, he reflected, standing there in the night, were inexhaustible. A manifestation of the
Divine Providence. Every few days there was something else, "since
my poor husband died," as she kept saying. But the priest could not
bring himself to give her his underwear to wash. He did that himself
on Monday nights if it was not raining, and the socks afterward, and
hung them outside when he went to the outhouse at the end of the
garden, before he went to bed. He hoisted the undershirt into the
dark above him and then folded the sleeves carefully over the holy
medals so that they would not fall off. "The saints are inside there,"
he said as he handed the undershirt to Blackbird.

"So much the better," Blackbird said. The priest felt how cold
his own narrow chest was. He was stoop-shouldered, and he straightened up.

"The river Jordan," he announced to the night in front of him, and
undid the drawstring of his underpants and let them down around his
ankles. Bent over in the darkness he was unsure of his balance and
did not dare raise a foot for fear of falling over. He groped around
for something to lean on, found a rock, and lifted his feet free of the
last of his clothes.

"Here," he said, handing the folded underpants to Blackbird and
standing naked. "Since it must be."

"It's a fine evening," Blackbird said. "For that. Safe."

But the priest shivered and crossed himself and began praying under
his breath in Latin. Blackbird sighed. A Paternoster. Then Hail Marys
and a prayer to St. Christopher. Blackbird cleared his throat.

The priest crossed himself again, reached down to the water and
took some in his hand to sprinkle on top of his head and then on his
chest. It felt very cold.

"It's cool," he said.

"It has to be," Blackbird said. "It's fresh."

The priest took a step into the water and gasped, but said nothing.

"All right?" Blackbird asked. It was too soon for an answer. The
priest took another step. The sandy streambed shelved away steeply

and he sank up to his knees and gasped again. His other leg came splashing to meet him to keep him from falling over.

"It's better to get in right away, squarely, all at once," Blackbird said.

"Maybe," the priest said, feeling a fluttering in his abdomen.

"You could kneel," Blackbird said. The priest found the suggestion annoying, especially as he had been considering doing just that.

"I should have brought a towel," he said. And then he sank to his knees and pitched forward, and his hands and arms plunged and splashed ahead of him. He slipped sideways and capsized into the black water so that he was lying with the stream up to his neck. His feet began to drift off the bottom and he was short of breath.

"Good," Blackbird said. "Congratulations."

"Thank you," the priest said. His teeth were chattering.

"You have to submerge the head, at least once."

"It's cold."

"That doesn't last. You'll see."

"I'm going to submerge the head," the priest announced, shivering, as though he were about to dive into oblivion.

"Hold your nose," Blackbird said, as he would have spoken to a child.

The priest obediently seized his nose, then let go of it to cross himself again, resumed his grasp, squeezed his eyes shut, and drew his head down under with the rest of him. He felt that he had entered a wholly unexpected world, full of sunbeams and archways and a ringing sound like the afternote of a bell, and then he raised his head above the surface, released his nose and opened his eyes to the darkness.

"You did it?" Blackbird asked.

"Of course," the priest said. He had rolled back onto his knees. An ache began to unfold somewhere in his legs and yet a new vigor ran through him, chill and fever at once.

"It's not so cold," Blackbird said, "is it?"

The priest was surprised to find that, in fact, the water no longer seemed cold, but the night air chilled his head.

"It's more effective if you stay there for a while," Blackbird said. "I'm not in a hurry." For a moment they said nothing. The water rippled on the stones and around the priest's shoulders. He heard the nightingales like reverberations of the stream.

"It's the apple, mainly, and the pear, where you come from, isn't it? Rather than wine, I mean," Blackbird said, expressing polite interest.

"They make some wine too."

"Is that so. But exclusively for their own use, I suppose."

"That's true."

"Rather than for general distribution as one might say. I've scarcely heard of the wine of that region."

"They also make a fortified wine."

"Ah, that's another matter."

"It's virtually a quinquina. There is a special grape—"

"Yes, I remember."

"Color of a ripe greengage."

"Yes, yes. It's a little like what we call the Ermemon. It has a flavor—" Blackbird smacked his tongue gently against his palate, searching for a word for the taste.

"Orange," the priest said.

"Perhaps," Blackbird agreed. "A little. We have one of those varieties here, something like that. Now they are trying to stamp it out. The government."

"So it goes," the priest said. "I remember hearing of such a move there too."

"They say it has ether in it," Blackbird said, and made a popping sound in disgust. "It's forbidden. No longer planted. They fine you if you have it. They give money to dig it out. Think of that."

"One never knows," the priest said.

"How is it now?" Blackbird asked.

"Not bad," the priest said. "I'm used to it."

"The—affected areas?"

"I can't tell. I can't feel them at all."

"And before you got in?"

"I was trying to ignore them. It's true, they were itching as usual, and for the moment they're silent."

"You see."

"But I can't stay here," the priest said, with a small laugh.

"It indicates something. Or at least it may. It's not for me to make claims," Blackbird said.

"Suppose I were to get out now?"

"It's reasonable." The priest rose as though he were climbing up himself, and stood dripping. Then he stepped cautiously up onto the stones of the bank. Now it was the air that felt cold, and he shivered again.

"I'll wait to dry off a little before I get dressed," he said.

"Rub yourself," Blackbird said. "Friction. Activity. That does it."

The priest began to rub his limbs and his torso briskly and as he was doing it he heard a sound like a cork popping.

"Passable," Blackbird said, evidently talking to himself. "Here," he said. "This counts for something too. Reach out your hand."

The priest reached and felt the cup again and took a sip.

"Good," he said. "Thank you."

"Nothing special," Blackbird said. "But an honest Auxerrois. One of the noble vintages of the region. It may go back as far as the time of Henri IV, how would I know. It doesn't keep reliably. This is three years old. A small property. They always produce something I think well of. Though this was merely their serviceable ordinary. It does not seem to have been too troubled by our little promenade."

The priest felt the warmth of the wine as Blackbird spoke of it. He handed back the cup and heard Blackbird pouring from the bottle.

"It was kind of you to think of it," the priest said.

"A kind of necessity, more or less," Blackbird said, handing him the cup again. The priest drank slowly while drops of water continued to run down his back.

"Thank you," he said, handing back the cup.

"Is one ready to dress?" Blackbird asked.

"I think it's time."

"The linen," Blackbird said, handing the priest the folded underpants, and the priest took them, balanced precariously in the dark, stepped into them, tightened the drawstring, and took a deep breath. The long underpants stuck to his wet legs.

"The upper garment," Blackbird said, handing him the undershirt, and the priest unfolded it carefully, checked the medals, and slipped it on, smoothing them into place afterward. It stuck to him, front and back.

"Here," Blackbird said, and swung the boots to him with their laces dangling. The priest's feet were wet but he sat down and pulled his socks on, and then the boots, and laced them up.

"Next," Blackbird said, giving him the cassock to put on over the wet underclothes. The priest was surprised at the way his hair went

on dripping when he had so little of it. Drops were running down
inside his clothes everywhere.

"And there," Blackbird said, passing him his glasses. The priest
put them on, straightened his shoulders, and saw nothing, just as
before.

"You need this to keep from sneezing," Blackbird said, and the
priest felt the cup in his hand once more, and he drank.

"Excellent," he said, and waited for Blackbird to drink.

"The darkness has an effect, I've noticed," Blackbird said. "On
the taste, I mean."

"Very possible," the priest agreed. It seemed to him also that the
wine and the tingling of his skin from the cold water were lifting him
from the ground. The cup was in his hand again.

"No, no," he said. "That's quite enough."

"You must avoid a chill," Blackbird said. "You are susceptible."
The priest drank obediently and handed back the cup.

"We are in the habit of consuming very sparingly in our house,"
he said. "Wine, that is. We water it, when we have it."

"Perhaps," Blackbird said. He did not ask where the priest and his
mother got such wine as they drank. It would not have been correct
for him, as a wine merchant descended from wine merchants, to
inquire. And besides, he knew. "Parishioners' wine, wine of the
parish"—the phrases said everything one would care to know on the
subject. Black, sour, and thin.

"What did you think of the bottles from the Sylvinette's baptism?"
Blackbird asked.

"Ah," the priest said, "that was generous of you." Sylvie was Blackbird's granddaughter, and his voice softened when he spoke of her.
At her baptism during the winter he had made the priest a present of
half a dozen bottles of a fine Cahors that he had bottled several years
earlier. He had inscribed the labels in elaborate copperplate script,
signing them and stamping them with the family seal of a blackbird
holding a piece of grapevine.

"To tell you the truth," the priest said, "we have not yet found the
occasion that merited opening one of those. They have been put aside
for a celebration."

"Oh, there's always some occasion to contribute to," Blackbird said.
"One mustn't wait for the angels. As it were." The priest heard him
rustling in the bushes.

"Putting the cup away. For another time," Blackbird said.

"How your granddaughter is growing," the priest said.

"She talks to me like a bird. She has a grip of iron," Blackbird said.

"I owe it to her, after all," the priest said, wanting to put it tactfully, "that we have become acquainted. That adds to the importance of your gift."

"Nothing to speak of," Blackbird said.

It was at the dinner after the baptism, at the Hotel Blackbird, that he and the priest had found themselves trying to make conversation and in some desperation had clutched the subject of the priest's health and the eczema to which he was a martyr. Under ordinary circumstances, as Blackbird said to himself later, he would never have mentioned the spring by the stream. "I talk too much," he said to himself. But after all the man knew nothing of the region, he was a stranger, practically a foreigner, he was in need, he listened to Blackbird with evident intelligence and appreciation, it was the Sylvinette's baptism, there was no harm in informing the man about a matter of local interest, and it gave them something to talk about, as Blackbird's daughter, Françoise, had said when she came upon them with their heads together and their voices lowered, at the end of the table.

"Ah, you have found things to discuss, I see," she had said in her rasping way, bearing down on them with a smile that raised a question. The priest complimented her on the dinner and said that he must be going.

"Another piece of cake," she had said, but he had declined that, and more coffee, and had risen to leave, thanking her. She had slipped into the kitchen and returned with a basket containing Blackbird's six bottles, and a baptismal dinner packed up for the priest's mother, and then she had said, "I must go and see to my daughter," and had shaken the priest's hand as he repeated his thanks, and had vanished into the kitchen. Blackbird had seen the priest to the front door. It had been the priest who had raised the subject of the spring again, as they stood there, asking whether Blackbird thought it was true, what they said about its curative properties and so on, and whether it would be possible to go there sometime for a visit. Blackbird had named an evening and a time, weather permitting. He thought afterward that the priest would forget, but again it was the priest who had emerged from the lane across from the hotel, a few days after Easter, and had asked Blackbird whether he was still willing to show him the spring of which he had spoken.

"I think it's late," the priest said.

"It's not midnight," Blackbird answered, and as he said it they heard the clock in the church tower strike, sounding far away. They listened, counting. Eleven.

"Eleven," they both said, and it struck eleven again.

"I didn't hear it strike ten," the priest said. But Blackbird had already started along the path.

"You can see?" he asked as before, from several steps ahead. And the priest followed, the wet clothes cold when he moved. He was afraid of sneezing. He kept close to the sound of Blackbird's shuffling, the thrashing of leaves, and it seemed a long time before they came to the wall by the gate, and the gentle slope along the road, which looked pale after the darkness under the trees.

"The next time you'll know the way," Blackbird said, and laughed.

"How many times must one come?"

"It depends on the state of your health."

"I could never find the place by myself," the priest said as they walked along the road. "And I would not dare to come alone." Blackbird said nothing.

"If I have begun a cure," the priest said, "it would hardly be worth the trouble you have been so kind as to take if I did not continue it, I suppose. Though that is asking a great deal of you, to come out at night, to take the time."

"Don't mention it," Blackbird said, and they agreed on a night in the future when the moon would be dark again. They had reached the laundry pool at the edge of the village and were talking in whispers again, and then they walked on into the village saying nothing more, and came to the lane off the main street, which was the back way to the vegetable garden behind the presbytery. There was a streetlight at the corner and they waved good night to each other and parted without a word.

Blackbird's wine business was not too big for him to handle by himself, including what delivery needed to be done. "It makes me circulate," he said. For a few days in the spring, a spell of settled weather that came every year near the equinox, he bottled some of the wines he wanted to keep, but most of his trade was in unbottled wine in quantities ranging from kegs or *fûts* of forty to fifty liters to *demis* of a hundred-odd and *pièces* of over two hundred. Some of his clients had kegs and barrels of their own which they left with him to be filled. Often they dropped them off in the course of the winter, and the orders that were attached to the drumheads were commonly the result of ritual deliberations on cold afternoons brushed by gray shreds of smoke—smoke of the short lichened oaks of the upland and even, these days, of coal and oil.

Blackbird's depot, as he called it, was scattered through an assortment of buildings on both sides of the road that led past the hotel to the main square of the village of Aylac. From the stone gateway of the hotel courtyard you could look along the road—somewhere along in there it had become a street—to the square, and across the square to the church, which was obviously much too big for the village as it was now. It looked, in fact, too big for itself: a bit of undistinguished ungainly late Gothic, put up sometime after the sixteenth century and the Wars of Religion, when Aylac had recovered from the devastations of that age and was aspiring to a certain importance based on politics far away in the north. The shape of the square revealed something of its history. It was widest at the top, in front of the church, which was the part that had been constructed with calculations, plans, ambitions. The masonry of the two or three buildings that faced the church across the square was smooth, blank, with neoclassical doors and windows, and fluted columns in bas-relief. One of the buildings now housed a bakery and one a grocer's.

The church itself had been rebuilt on the site, incorporating the stones of a smaller one that had stood there before, a Romanesque nave whose crypt was still there under the chancel of the later structure. The squat stone pillars of the crypt supported a low vaulted ceiling, and behind the rough altar a carved slab was said to seal the tomb of a saint from the age of Charlemagne, a knight who had been to the Crusades and returned to live as a hermit on the windswept barrens where, as the phrase still went, "there is nothing but stones." Most of the inhabitants of Aylac would not have been able to recall the name of the saint, and the tomb was left to itself except when the priest needed something to show a visitor.

Houses, shops, part of the market roof, had been built up against the lower wall of the old church. Some of them had survived the rebuilding or returned soon afterward, and they straggled down the paved slope. The lane from behind the church meandered behind them too and finally turned, making of them a tapering island in the square. And the square itself, as it descended, narrowed to a street that led past a few shapeless edifices with their backs to the village: the slaughterhouse, a tanner's barn, a bottle warehouse, the old train station on the line between Mujeac and Renat, where passenger trains stopped a couple of times a day during the week. After that the street was a road again, crossing the tracks and an arched stone bridge and leading away into the pastures and woods.

Along to the south, overlooking the small valley, was Aylac's principal claim to fame, the château—a Renaissance pile erected by a local Count who had acquired fame and a considerable increase in fortune as a military adviser to Henri IV. His particular service to the Crown had been the modernizing and improving of French artillery, an arm which—some of the ancient families of the region never failed to point out—was never the oldest or the noblest, and they would go on to suggest that the Count, indeed, had been something of a clever arriviste and that the château confirmed it: huge, cold, pretentious, distinguished chiefly by the quantity of its Italianate decorative bas-reliefs around doors, windows, the stone ribs of the ceilings, the stone stairs, the walls, and particularly by the friezes repeating everywhere the family device—a flaming grenade and the crossed cannons of the artillery. The Count's heirs had even adorned the church with a band of stone carved with the same device, which ran all the way around it like a broad ribbon as though the church were part of their estate. Among the memories of Blackbird's youth was the image of that frieze on the apse of the church by moonlight in summer when the high box hedge there had been a favored nightly rendezvous.

The Hotel Blackbird, behind its courtyard shaded by old lime trees, was of unknown age and of a style, at least, that was older than the château. A great barnlike building with black creosoted oak timbers set in white plaster walls, and across the whole length of the building a painted frieze, scarcely visible in the summer through the dense green of the leaves. The hotel frieze must have been a rustic reflection of the Italian reliefs in the château. It portrayed, on a yellow ground, a running pattern of grapevines and leaves, and at either end of the ornate letters forming the name "Hotel Blackbird" a blackbird holding a vine.

Behind the hotel was the long vegetable garden which Blackbird's wife had tended while she was able to, and with which his son-in-law, as Blackbird admitted, had done wonders—but he admitted it in a way that made it sound like a waste of time. Along one side of the garden a row of aging barns faced outward onto a lane flanking the hotel. The one farthest from the hotel still housed an old carriage. Blackbird's truck occupied part of the next: a gray diesel Peugeot with iron hoops and a canvas top over the bed.

But Blackbird's own headquarters was down across the road from the hotel. The barn doors of what must have been a farm, a century or two earlier, gave straight onto the road, and above them was a shallow balcony with a wrought-iron railing and faded green shutters in the stone window frame. What would have been the barnyard had been roofed over at some time in the last century, and Blackbird had inherited it already full of old winepresses, stacked barrels, pieces of wagons and harness, bottling machines functional and retired, loops of hose, barrel hoops, funnels of different sizes, deep vistas of dusty cobwebs. His current ledgers often spent the night on top of the barrel he used for a desk in the place, which he sometimes referred to as his atelier. Another door led into the cellar of the stone house and there the wine *tonnes* lined the wall from one end to the other. By the door to the cellar a flight of stone steps with an old bent iron railing led up the side of the house to a stone terrace and the door of the kitchen.

He called the rooms of the old house his bachelor quarters, and the front room, next to the kitchen, his salon. After his wife had died of cancer, more than ten years before, he had taken to spending more and more time at his atelier, and he had amused himself, as he put it, setting the old place to rights, more or less. It was none too soon. He began by having the roof repaired and he went through the attic. Worm-eaten cradles, chairs, beds, four-armed spinning wheels, kneading troughs, all piled together. Trunks full of crocheted bedspreads, linen nightshirts such as he remembered his father and his grandfather wearing, pieces of uniforms, account books in writing that he could barely read, the ink faded to the color of wine stains.

Everything in the attic had to be moved first to one side and then to the other as the tiles were lifted from the roof and the laths renewed. The roofer lived over behind the church and had been repairing the Blackbird family's roofs since he had been an apprentice. He and Blackbird had grown up together. When Blackbird was working in and out of his cellar with its wet floors and its hoses for washing out barrels—practicing his calling, as he put it—he wore battered wooden shoes, as the roofer did when he was off the roof. They stood together in the attic talking in patois about the condition of the crooked beams, which were still sound, and the old chestnut laths which had been split with the grain and must have lasted for a hundred years or more. The new ones would be mere poplar, sawn in a mill, and twenty years would be the longest one could hope for from them. Blackbird and the roofer sucked their teeth and agreed that that was the way things were.

Some of the relics from the attic found their way down the stairs into the front room, which was already filled with a continuation of the assortment overhead, though most of the assortment downstairs was a bit younger, and in both places Blackbird kept finding things he remembered from his youth. A baby carriage. An old bicycle. A bayonet. More ledgers. The front room had been a bedroom, and huge plain armoires stood against two of the walls. Blackbird had been burrowing through the attic and the rooms for several years in an unsystematic fashion—picking up things, examining them in the half light, carrying them to the door, or to the fireplace in the kitchen, finding somewhere else to put them—before he had laid bare one of the armoire doors and opened it. It was full of linens: bed linens, shirts, nightshirts, tablecloths, undergarments, wedding dresses, hand-kerchiefs. Some he took across the road to his daughter, Françoise, who was running the hotel, and she received them without interest, lifted the corners of the sheets looking for mildew or worse, shrugged, and said they would have to be washed. That was the sheets. The other things she drew back from when she saw them, laughed, and asked what they were.

"They're old," she said, drawing the word out so that it meant everything she did not want, and later Blackbird took them all back to the armoire, on which the lock still worked, and he put the key on a hook in the cupboard in the kitchen.

The room on the other side of the kitchen must have been a bed-room too at one time, but since then it had been used as a hen house, and there were old rabbit hutches against one wall and ancient wooden chests that had held grain and potatoes, and more recently generations of rats. By the time Blackbird had got back there carrying objects that he had not yet decided about he had learned which of the warped floorboards had succumbed to age or damp and threatened to give way just when one had one's hands full. There were boards like that in the attic too, of course, and at last his neighbor the carpenter had to be brought in to replace some of them. In the course of that work more relics came to light. "But no money yet," Blackbird took to saying, as he described to friends the course of his gradual repossession of the house.

In one of the armoires in the front room he found a pile of old books—an apothecary's manual, sermons, a volume by Labastide on pruning fruit trees, a few on wine—and he set them up on a shelf with several of his own ledgers beside them. When he got to the window over the road, rags of lace still haunted the inside of it, tangled in cobwebs. The windows ground open, and the shutters on their heavy hinges, and when the afternoon light burst into the room for the first time in over half a century it caught the armoires and the shelf of books as though it had done so every day. "My office," Blackbird murmured sententiously to no one, and he hauled out a table from under one precarious pile, and a skeleton of a chair from a corner and stood considering them. Yet when he had occasion to consult one of his ledgers in the house he did so in the kitchen. He had had electricity for years down in the cellar by the wine *tonnes*, and a light outside the cellar door above the drain, and two in the roofed yard over the barrels and presses and bottling machines. Eventually he had the wires extended into the upper rooms and provided one dangling socket for the middle of each ceiling, but for some time there was only a single bulb among them, like the eye of the Fates, and that was in the kitchen.

He did most of his rummaging in the old house on rainy afternoons, an hour or so at a time, stumping and scuffling back and forth. He had a habit of keeping a piece of round loaf and a goat cheese or two in a tin box in the cellar, for *goûters* when he was working there in the afternoons, and he ate standing up, washing down the bread and cheese with wine drawn directly from one of the *tonnes* into the wine-glass that stood there on the one nearest to the door, upside down, having long since lost its base. After the house roof had been repaired he got into the habit of taking the bread and cheese and a small pitcher of wine up into the kitchen and putting the bread and cheese on a plate, on the table, but there too he usually ate standing up, looking out through the open door onto the stone terrace, the iron railing, the traceries and translucent pale leaves of the Chasselas vine climbing a trellis of chicken wire attached to the eaves, and the road and roofs beyond. It occurred to him one day that he had spent years reclaiming the house and had almost never sat down in it.

He slept over at the hotel in a corner room above the kitchen, to which he had gone to lie down during the months when his wife was dying. After she did he had tried the main family bedroom again but had said it echoed, and had moved back into the corner room looking down through the lime trees into the front courtyard on one side and the lane that led to his barrel yard on the other. There were four staircases in the big old building, and one of them led past the corner room and down around the back of the kitchen fireplace and out into the lane, so he could wander in and out as he pleased without having to go through the hotel. Françoise, and her husband, Gérard, and Sylvie, took over the family bedroom.

After the war Françoise, who was Blackbird and his wife's only child, had moved into Mujeac, twenty-five kilometers away, and had taken a job in the automobile parts factory. During the occupation the Germans had converted the factory to produce Messerschmitt parts, and one night two men from the Resistance had driven in dressed as mechanics and had blown the place up. In the postwar reconstruction the plant had been greatly expanded and modernized, and for young people who went into Mujeac looking for work it was the world of the future. Françoise was some years older than most of the workers who were just beginning there, and she had had two long arrangements that had appeared to be *fiançailles*, and had been referred to as such by everyone in Aylac, though more often by others than by Françoise and the young men. But in the end both of the friendships or whatever they were had flickered out even though Françoise was one of the most substantial prospective heiresses in the village. She had insisted that she would not have wanted either of the men as husbands, and it may have been true but it did not keep neighbors from speculating about her marriage prospects and why she was still single. It was noticed that both of the men were a few years younger than she was, but that did not seem to explain much. And that with her voice like coarse sandpaper she was notoriously outspoken, but there were women in the village and the country around it who were certainly no different in that respect and who had produced large families. It was true that she treated the local young people of her own age as though, someone said, they were working for her and she did not think much of the way they were doing it—but it was possible to point to several marriages in the neighborhood in which the women were clearly unimpressed by anything their husbands did or said.

"What can you expect?" Blackbird's wife said to him once quite late in her life. "She's your son."

Which troubled Blackbird without making sense to him. But in the end no one was surprised that Françoise did not marry in the village, nor that she went off to Mujeac, nor even that when she came home at Christmas she had had a permanent and her hair was a reddish blond, which made her heavy eyebrows and the shadow of hairs on her upper lip look darker than ever. "I like that," several of the women said of the transformation, as they stood outside the church after mass. "I think she looks nice like that." Something they might not have said if Françoise had been more attractive.

When her mother had become sick Françoise had given up her job and moved back from Mujeac to her childhood room at the hotel, to take care of her. By then she had a beau, as she referred to him. Gérard, whose father was the freight agent at the Mujeac railroad station, and who worked himself as a waiter in the station restaurant, as Françoise said with a lift of her chin, and who read books. She brought Gérard home to meet her mother. He was younger than Françoise, with thin, light-brown hair and small features.

"He looks nice," one of the older women who happened to be passing slowly, just as they arrived, said to her companion.

"He's a child," the other said as they nodded and walked on.

He looked smaller than Françoise, though in fact he was a hand's breadth taller, with a light, deferential voice, and he carried himself bent slightly forward, his face and eyebrows raised as though he were waiting for an answer. Françoise spoke to him with a tone and manner she had for no one else, barely audible, and she smiled when she looked at him. Her mother said that she too approved of the young man. "He will be very nice," she said. In the latter days of her mother's illness Gérard came regularly from Mujeac to see Françoise and to help out, but by then her mother was too sick to know he was there, and after she died it was over a year, of course, before there was any question of marriage, and most of another year before it took place, in the early summer, naturally, when the cherries were ripe. The conflict of feelings with which Blackbird gave his daughter away at the altar was aggravated by his knowledge that Gérard had never liked the taste of wine, and never drank it. Even at his wedding banquet what did he drink? A thimbleful of champagne—and what champagne!—and when he did it he looked as though he had sat on something. With Françoise it was one thing: she had never appreciated wine but she could swallow something when it was the moment to do it—with two fingers toward heaven, and the rolled eyes of the saints.

But if they were both going to be that way, Blackbird said to himself,
sometimes it seemed like a merciful stroke of fortune that there was
a different flight of stairs from the corner room down to the kitchen,
so that he did not have to pass them too often.

And then it had been years before there was any sign of children.
There was talk about that in the village, needless to say. Mme. Farlat,
the baker's wife, wondered to her customers whether it was true, as
she had heard, that dyeing the hair could have a harmful effect on
things of that kind.

"Well, she doesn't have forever," Mme. Boumie, next in the line
of customers, answered as she fished for change. "She's losing her
first teeth."

"It could be the husband," the widow Gaire, standing behind her,
answered from under her black straw cloche hat.

"I wouldn't know about that," Mme. Boumie said, drawing herself
up and sniffing, as the baker came in dusting his hands.

By the time Françoise became pregnant the neighbors were ready
to discuss their surprise, and when she miscarried they considered
the possible causes for that. And Blackbird, as they knew, had been
hoping for an heir.

In the summer after the wedding, in the hot weather when thunderstorms threatened the vineyards with hail, he had dragged an old
sleigh bed out of the pile under the stairs in the house across the
road, and had set it up in the front room. He had wiped off the
casement windows inside the shutters, and then washed them carefully,
which he said to himself made it more cheerful in there. He had made
up the bed with linens and old bedclothes from the armoire, and when
he felt like it, on days when there were no deliveries, he would cross
the road after the midday meal and a glass with friends under the
lime trees, and clomp up the broken stone stairs in his *sabots* or his
heavy shoes, shut the door behind him with a glance at the condition
of the Chasselas as he did so, and take a little nap. Then it happened
once when he came home from a day of deliveries and a dinner with
clients that he took the truck up to the barn behind the hotel, but
then, instead of going in through the back door, he wandered on down
across the road and gazed up into the moths on the white enameled
reflector of the streetlight, and shuffled down into the roofed yard to
look at the empty barrels sleeping on their feet. The rounded iron
railing on the stone stairs sent a chill up his arm, and he felt the first
touch of autumn and went up to bed in the bachelor house. In the

morning he made up the bed carefully and returned to his corner room at the hotel, feeling that he could have a night out if the urge took him.

When Françoise became pregnant the second time the neighbors were surprised all over again. And Françoise was not well. The nature of her problem was not divulged but the doctor had her taken to the hospital in Mujeac for her confinement, and there after a terrible delivery Sylvie was born. But it was no secret, for long, that Françoise would not have another child. Sylvie was the hope of them all, Françoise and Gérard and Blackbird, though their hopes for her were not altogether alike.

She certainly had no lack of love and attention. As soon as she could be carried it seemed that one of them always had her on a lap, on an arm, her head on a shoulder. Françoise had the crib in the kitchen, but she had only to turn her back, she said to Blackbird, to find it empty, and have to run out looking for Blackbird, who might be anywhere—out with his drinking companions at a table in the courtyard, or up the lane where the truck was kept, or on the way to the roofed barrel yard, jogging la Sylvinette on his arm and mumbling nonsense in her ear. Françoise realized that she could not remember when she herself had crossed the road and set foot in the shed where the barrels were stacked and the bottling was done, and that the smell of the wine cellar, which she found acutely distasteful, must be something she remembered from her own early childhood, for she could not recall standing in that cellar since she had been old enough to decide where she would or would not go. It occurred to her that she had never once climbed the stone steps on the side of the house and looked in at the door, and she knew that she would not do so. She did not so much as consider whether Blackbird would have welcomed her at that doorway—she could not imagine herself there. She knew that she did not want him to take Sylvie over there but she knew also that to forbid it would be to create an unhealing dissension with her father. Neither of them spoke of it. She found Blackbird once, with Sylvie on his arm, standing on the road at the entrance to the barrel shed. She could not hear what he was mumbling to the child. He had not taken a step down the slope into the shed, and when he heard Françoise behind him he had turned and walked back toward the hotel.

"I never know where you are going to be with her," Françoise had scolded, but she had said no more, simply taking Sylvie from him as she usually did, and carrying her back toward the kitchen, saying that it was time to feed her.

"She wasn't crying," Blackbird had said, watching Sylvie's sleeping head on his daughter's shoulder.

In the spring after Sylvie's christening they had agreed that the Hotel Blackbird should be rejuvenated.

"It certainly needs it," Françoise said.

"It's more or less time." Blackbird nodded. "A little attention."

All the time that they had been getting ready for the christening banquet she had clucked and growled and sighed about how shabby and old the hotel looked. The paint on the wooden panels along the lower parts of the walls was chipped, and the walls looked smoked and dingy, as she kept pointing out. Blackbird admitted that a coat of paint would do no harm, and that early spring, before what he spoke of as the inundation of summer guests, was the time to do the work, if his painter-decorator friend from Brimon, M. Milibou, was free to do it.

"Yes," she said, with evident scorn. "No doubt it will have to be that one."

"Of course," Blackbird said. Milibou had always done whatever painting and plastering was needed at the hotel, and it was no secret that Françoise had despised him for years.

"He'll be free," Françoise said. Milibou, who had a face like a huge cherry and a belly like a demijohn, always managed to fit any work for Blackbird into his overbooked schedule, and one reason for that was clear enough to Françoise, who had noticed that the man was never more than a few steps away from a wine bottle standing among the tools, and that when the bottle was empty Milibou wandered off with it toward Blackbird's barrel shed. Blackbird carried the key to his cellar on a string around his neck, but when Milibou was working for him he would pick up the row of empties from the foot of the stone stairs, on his way into the cellar, refill the bottles, and leave them waiting in the same place for Milibou and his assistants, who generally shared his interests.

"He's a liar," Françoise said.

Blackbird blew out through his pursed lips. "It's a big word," he said, though he knew what she meant. Milibou, he conceded, was not altogether reliable. One had to allow for that.

"He gives me a headache, the way he talks," she said. "Why does he have to gabble-gabble that way?"

Milibou talked like a deck of cards being shuffled by a sharper, and not everyone, even among those who wanted to, could understand him. Children tried to imitate him and gave up in fits of giggles. And in a region that took material honesty with the utmost seriousness it had been noticed that objects had disappeared from houses while he and his assistants were working there.

Blackbird shrugged his shoulders. "His wife is sick," he said, as though that had anything to do with it.

"I would be too," Françoise said. And added, "She's fatter than he is."

"You want the work done," Blackbird reminded her in a most reasonable tone. And it did seem to him quite natural that Françoise should speak her mind about Milibou all over again, just to get everything in place before the estimates were made, the colors chosen, and the work scheduled. Blackbird noticed that Françoise did her grumbling about the dinginess of the hotel only when no one else was present, which he thought tactful of her. But this time the topic had followed them out of the kitchen into the main dining room and back, and in the kitchen when they returned Gérard had come in from the garden with a basket full of peas and was standing in the corner looking down at Sylvie, who was asleep in the crib.

"If you don't like that painter—" he began.

"Oh well," Françoise said, dismissing the whole thing.

"Isn't there somebody else?" Gérard asked.

"It's the country," Blackbird said. "That's who there is."

"You don't even inquire," Françoise said.

"I travel. I go everywhere," Blackbird said. "I have an idea of who there is. Of course, if you wanted to bring someone in from Mujeac or Renat, and house them and pay them three times as much, plus the insurance you have to pay them these days. Milibou, you should remember, has worked here for a long time and he charges accordingly. And he gets the work done."

"Better in the morning," Françoise said.

"I could do some of it myself," Gérard said. "I've done that kind of work."

"You?" Françoise said, shocked at the suggestion.

"It's no good being proud," Gérard said. "It would save money. But I would not be as fast as they would."

"No, no," Françoise said.

"It's a big undertaking," Blackbird explained to Gérard with more

deference than he usually showed to his son-in-law. "Large surfaces.
They need their ladders and boards and drop cloths and all kinds of
things."

And Gérard began to ask what they were thinking of painting and
redecorating. Blackbird realized that Françoise had not discussed the
matter with him except in the most general way, and that Gérard
assumed that she and Blackbird had it already planned.

"We have not quite decided on the color for the dining room," he
said.

"The chimney smokes," Françoise said, "Whatever color you put."

"When the wind is in the west, or the southwest," Blackbird admitted. "It stands to reason."

"Look," Françoise said, walking in and pointing. "And when you
paint it still comes through." Blackbird did not look at Gérard.

"One could paper it," he said. And in the end they agreed to see
what wallpapers M. Milibou had in his books of samples, though
Françoise said she knew everything in those books and that they had
not changed since she was a child and were all drab and lugubrious.

So Blackbird planned one of his early-spring rounds of deliveries
to include M. Milibou's establishment above the river at the place
called Brimon. It must have been a village at one time, with several
houses and a lane wandering among them—"twenty chimneys," a
neighbor boasted. It was set on a windy promontory with rolling country behind it, the limestone buttresses dropping away to the valley in
front of it, and the road winding up to it along a narrow side valley
under curving lines of tall poplars by a stream. They made a loop
around a massive apron of walls, the remains of a small *château fort*,
before emerging onto the upland where pieces of ancient masonry still
showed among the brambles. Fragments of stone window frames and
carved fluting. Broken lintels under sloe bushes. The sheep and goats
and cows kept them visible.

The grass shone with the translucent green of early spring. Two
goats were tethered under a plum tree by the tumbled remains of a
wall, near the mossy wreck of a small truck and the rusted chassis of
another under a cherry tree, with an arrangement of defunct tires and
rusted gasoline cans from the Second World War leaning around them.

M. Milibou's house, where the road came out onto level ground
after the climb from the valley, was a narrow stone building that
appeared to be all that had survived from larger structures all around

it. Perhaps at one time they had all been parts of the château built into the face of the cliff. To show what he was capable of, M. Milibou had stuccoed the stone façade of his house from top to bottom, giving the stucco a surface like wet fur and painting it a color of his own invention, something neither pink nor purple but reminiscent of both, and he had troweled the stucco smooth around doors and windows, for trim, and painted those borders canary yellow.

"It makes it brighter brighter brighter," he said, repeating himself like a stammerer and beaming at it when visitors remarked on the change in the appearance of the simple old house. And that remained true, of course, even though the colors edged a shade or two closer toward common brown with each passing season. M. Milibou did not repaint the whole thing but he tried out new colors on the door. It was a shade of viridian on the morning that Blackbird drove up in his gray diesel. Formations of clouds were racing over the wide sky of the uplands, and the complicated web of clotheslines stretching the full length of the straggling orchard of plum trees beside the house was under full sail with enormous laundry. Everything looked much too big for the house. Blackbird maneuvered the truck carefully off the road, parked under a walnut tree opposite the front door, and got out to see who was home. He saw a pair of huge hands rise like pink moons over a distant clothesline. That would be Mme. Milibou, no doubt, and he set off in that direction through the flapping maze.

Mme. Milibou was, as Françoise had said, a person of remarkable size but that did not seem to impede her movements. When she bent down to drag the next bit of washing from the basket she looked like another mountain of laundry, but when she straightened up she was more than a head taller than Blackbird and perhaps four times as thick. And whereas M. Milibou's face was round, hers was long as a sack of onions, and solid, with nothing small about it but the eyes. Fortunately she was a woman of apparently tireless cheer, which shone forth at the sight of Blackbird.

"*Te*," she said, "we have been talking about you."

"That's nice of you," Blackbird said.

"Yes," she said, "because of Lisette." Blackbird raised his eyebrows. Lisette was their only child, a young woman who was larger than either of her parents and had a walleye besides.

"She is very good-hearted," the women of the neighborhood said instantly whenever Lisette was mentioned. And it was true. She seemed to have inherited her mother's even and amiable disposition, and added a certain delicacy entirely her own. Her father's talk was a full kitchen cupboard rolling downhill and her mother had a voice like a frog in a cistern, but Lisette's way of speaking was downy and thoughtful. She always smiled when she spoke and she seemed thoroughly kind but she looked at the person she was speaking to from a greater distance than her parents did, a slight remoteness that was not merely the effect of the thick glasses she had worn ever since childhood. It was into her broad lap that one cat or another climbed as soon as she sat down. She had a way of looking over her shoulder, whatever she was doing or whomever she was talking to, as though she were expecting someone. "She's no fool," was another of the things that were said about her. It was also regularly asserted that she was a very fine cook. "She'll make someone a good wife," the women would say somewhat defiantly, and at that the young people, and the young men in particular, would look away trying not to smile.

"She's getting married," Mme. Milibou bellowed over the flying laundry.

"That's serious," Blackbird said. "Congratulations. Has it been announced?" He knew it had not because he would have heard about it from someone.

"We're getting ready to announce it," Mme. Milibou laughed. "Yes. Yes."

"Who is marrying her?"

"You know—Rillac."

"I'm acquainted with the family. They are even slightly—among my clients." Indeed he knew them. They had the kind of reputation that the neighborhood bestowed without hesitation on gypsies and the laborers and performers who traveled with fairs. But the Rillacs had been in the region longer than anyone could say. Down beside the river where the poplars ended in a grove of much older trees they lived in a slate-roofed house sticking up like a two-story railroad station, which it may have been originally, for the tracks ran along there between the road and the river, and to get to the house a car had to drive up the embankment and down the other side and along it for several hundred yards, "so they could see you coming," as people said. But life in their house was turned toward the river. The Rillacs were, among other things, fishermen both legally and illegally, and spoke of the river as though it were part of their property. There was an island across from them, to which they stretched their nets at night, walking in the shallows. The place was no longer inhabited but it was said that at one time the family had lived over there. It was called Thieves' Island.

"Which Rillac?" Blackbird asked.

"The little one," Mme. Milibou told him, fluttering her large hand out in front of her like a cat shaking off drops of water. "You know. Robert. He came and apprenticed himself to my husband."

"The one who was in the—"

"That's right."

"The Legion?"

"Yes. What they call the paras. Paratroops."

Blackbird nodded. "I've seen the beret," he said, "that he wears." He remembered the young man confiding to him, a few years back, that whenever he went tickling trout or setting nets of forbidden gauges he wore his para uniform. He was an agreeable young man just the same, Blackbird thought, and he would come up more or less to Lisette's breastbone when they stood up together, he imagined, but he did not pursue the image.

"He works very well," Mme. Milibou said. "The other three as- sistants that we have," she went on, "are fine too, and they have been with my husband for years, as you know, but none of them really likes responsibility."

"I see," Blackbird said.

"They're good, they're good," Mme. Milibou said, "and if you tell them 'do this,' they will do it all day, and they do their work with great care—I'm only telling you what my husband says—but— And one of them is only part-time, and we needed more help. There's always more work than we can manage."

"So much the better, I suppose."

"And this one came along."

"The answer to a prayer," Blackbird said.

"We knew him years ago. He used to come up to the stream here for crayfish when he was supposed to be in school."

"I can imagine. So he knew the ropes, in a way."

"We need someone to carry on the business one of these days."

"I understand. I think of that myself."

"So we have put together an order for the wedding. The champagne, the wine, all that. My husband has to be here so we can talk about it together."

"With pleasure," Blackbird said. "Where is he working at the mo- ment?"

"He's just over at Aubillac, at the château. They are redoing the paper in some of the bedrooms, exactly the way it was. They have to by law. It was old. It's beautiful. It had to be sent from Paris. He's getting them started today. He'll be back for his soup, because he had another job to see about this afternoon. I thought he'd be back by now."

She had picked up the empty basket while she talked and had led Blackbird behind the lanes of wet sheets and around to the front of the house. The door was ajar, hens and cats coming and going.

"Come in," she said. "You'll take something. Stay and have the soup."

She buttoned herself through the doorway without waiting for an answer, and Blackbird followed into the smell of soup and laundry in the narrow room with its smoked yellow walls and low black-beamed ceiling. She picked up the lid of the soup pot on the stove and set it back with a crash.

"How is your health?" Blackbird asked. "I heard that you were sick."

"Oh, it was nothing," she said. "Angina, they said, but I think it was just the liver, like everybody." She turned toward the door. "Here he comes!" she shouted, "as I said," and stood for a moment listening, until Blackbird too heard the sound of a small truck with a hacking cough struggling up the valley below them.

"What can I give you?" she asked. "Ratafia? Our own."

"No, thank you," Blackbird said.

"A Pernod."

"Not that either, honestly."

"A drop?"

"Dear me, no," Blackbird said, for a "drop" meant straight eau-de-vie. "I must take care of myself."

"Then—a touch of your own Minervois."

"That's just possible," Blackbird said. He purveyed several grades of wine from unnamed small vineyards in the Hérault for his simplest *ordinaires*.

"A little left from the autumn," she said. "We put some in bottles."

"Well," Blackbird said with a deprecatory nod. That vintage, in his estimation, was scarcely worth bottling, but it was not the time or the place to say so. She brought a bottle from under the sink.

"Or something in the food," she said, returning to the subject of her ailment. "I see how they spray the fields and the truck gardens.

See," she said, showing him the bottle, "it's already open." To make him feel at home. Blackbird heard the asthmatic truck make it to the top of the hill, pant to a stop, and the door slam.

"*Te*," M. Milibou puffed before he appeared, "we were talking about you." He pushed his way through the doorway, one hand held out to take Blackbird's.

"So I hear," Blackbird said. Mme. Milibou had poured a glass, which she handed to him. She went on to pour one for M. Milibou.

"Well," she said, "it's an occasion," and she shook out a glass on the drainboard and poured a few inches for herself.

"Health," said M. Milibou, and they all solemnly touched glasses and drank. M. and Mme. Milibou emptied their glasses in one breath.

"I've brought you the spring reinforcements," Blackbird said. "And now you have things to celebrate."

"She told you," M. Milibou said. "It's good it's good. We have the future future to think of."

Mme. Milibou had filled their glasses without a word, and they raised them again.

"It was good, that," M. Milibou said to Blackbird.

"Let's get the new one," Blackbird said, "while we have it in mind."

They went out to his truck and he dropped the tailgate and slipped into the back like a badger into a burrow, pushed out a length of ramp, one end of which M. Milibou settled on the ground, and together they rolled the *demi* down the slope, then around the side of the house and down to the small dark cellar set into the cliff. Then they bent over the barrel with their berets butting together between the tops of their heads, counted to three, and rocked the barrel one more step onto a cradle of beams. Its empty predecessor was already waiting beside the door.

"Is it clean?" Blackbird asked.

"Clean clean," M. Milibou said.

Blackbird pulled out the bung and put his nose to the hole. "Seems healthy," he said, and they rolled the empty to the truck, closed it all up, and went back to the kitchen to settle the account. Mme. Milibou had put three plates of soup on the table, half a loaf like half of a tan moon, and three clean glasses. They crossed themselves, passed the loaf and carved slices off it to put into the soup, and then they bent low to the bowls until their noses were almost to the rims, and for a moment the only sounds were those of the spoons and the slurping of soup and the unrequited flapping of laundry. Mme. Milibou passed the bottle and each of them sloshed a little into the bowl, swirled it around, and drank it.

"Thank you," Blackbird said.

"You'll stay and eat something," Mme. Milibou said, filling the glasses.

"No, no, I can't. I have my clients. An itinerary," Blackbird said, pushing the invoice across the table to M. Milibou and handing him a pen. M. Milibou fished out a battered spectacle case and put on his brass-rimmed glasses.

"Delivered," Blackbird said, pointing to a line on the form. "That's the place." M. Milibou signed, and Mme. Milibou handed him a roll of money, from which he counted off a number of large notes and handed them over with the slip. Blackbird tucked them together into a billfold, and they drank.

"Well, this wedding," M. Milibou said, and Blackbird pulled out another notebook, wet a finger on his tongue, opened it, and found the right page, and they fell to placing the order. Besides the provisions for the wedding party it included two dozen bottles of a particular vintage as a wedding present for the young couple, "for occasions."

"And I have some work to discuss with you besides," Blackbird said, and told M. Milibou about the redecorating plans for the hotel. "Could you manage something of that kind?"

"We're always in demand," M. Milibou said. "You know that. No end no end. But I'll find a moment a moment. You can count on it."

"When can we expect that?"

"I'd better fit it in before the next large project," M. Milibou said. "In a few weeks, maybe. After the château there is Dr. Garrigues. After that—"

They arranged for M. Milibou to come over to Aylac during the following week to see what would be needed, and Blackbird drove down the winding road with the books of wallpaper samples lying under his account books on the truck seat beside him.

He turned left on the lower road and along the river to the small town of Florème, where the priory next to the church, inside the château walls, had been converted first to a doctor's residence and then to a hotel. The floors and ceilings of the bedrooms remained more or less as they had been for four hundred years, with nothing added but a few coats of walnut-husk stain and furniture wax. The Hotel Blackbird, come to that, was old, and had changed little for generations, but its antiquity had never been evoked as an attraction. The hotel at Florème was a different kind of establishment. It was advertised in publications in England and the Netherlands, and most of the guests there at any time were foreigners, though the dining room attracted a certain number of local residents, especially on Sundays—depending on who was known to be doing the cooking.

The main entrance was just inside the château gate tower, a step from the columned portal of the church. Blackbird did not go in that way, but drove up the lane beside the walls and opened the door that led across a back courtyard to the kitchen.

Everyone there knew him. The first person he saw was the smiling, massive, ruddy adolescent in a white apron who divided his time between his work there and helping his father raise pigs across the river. At that moment the young man was walking a garbage barrel toward the door, destined for his father's pigs. He let go of it to kiss Blackbird on both cheeks.

"I have a *pièce* in the truck," Blackbird said to him. "We have to put it to bed. Eh, little one," he said to the small, dark, sharp-featured young woman who turned to him from the huge stove. "How is your grandmother?"

"Not too well. It's the arthritis."

"She can get around?"

"There are days—"

"And her customers?"

"Oh, she cooks well enough on Sundays if she knows who is coming. But it's hard for her now."

"It's Blackbird!" Mme. Grunie, the plump woman in white at the stove, exclaimed, rushing over to him. "How deaf I'm getting." She flung her arms around him and they kissed each other's cheeks and asked about each other's health. "But it's the *patron*," she said then, dropping her voice, "who's not doing well. Not at all." She raised both hands and sighed.

"Bad as that?" Blackbird asked.

"I think so. He doesn't eat anymore. Nothing but medicines. A little chicken broth. How can you live on that?"

"What does he have?"

"It's complicated. He had it before. They say he got it in the colonies."

"That's bad," Blackbird said.

"How is Josette?" the dark girl who appeared to be scarcely more

than a child—her name was Hélène—asked. Josette was a woman
somewhat older than Hélène who had worked at the hotel a few years
earlier and now was the housekeeper at a château not far from Aylac.
She had been pregnant when she left the hotel, and her departure
was a subject that still prompted the young man working within earshot
of them to raise his hand at the mention of Josette and roll his eyes
toward the other end of the room, where the door had opened and
Mme. Becquer, the owner of the château, had come in.

An elegant woman, indeed a beautiful woman, who looked much
too young to have had an entire life in the colonies with her husband
before his retirement and the return to metropolitan France and a
second career running a hotel. Everything about her was long and
fine. Her dark hair was drawn back in a glossy chignon and she carried
her head with her chin slightly raised. Pearl earrings, a dark skirt
almost to her feet, a close-fitting jacket with long sleeves that alluded
to the tropics. As she stepped into the kitchen it was clear that she
was in charge, and Mme. Grunie and Hélène both turned to the stove.

"M. Blackbird," Mme. Becquer said from the far end of the room,
scarcely raising her voice. She moved forward smiling, and Blackbird
shuffled toward her.

"Mme. Becquer."

She offered her hand and he took it and inquired about her health
and her husband's.

"He is courageous," she said, "but it is difficult. He has always
been so vigorous."

"It must give you a great deal to take care of."

"I'm used to that. It's just that one feels that there is so little one
can do."

"But you have help with him."

"There is a nurse with him all the time. Dr. Mirot recommended
her highly, and she seems capable. How can I tell?"

"And are you ready for the season?"

"Let me show you." She started to lead him out the way she had
come in.

"I've brought you your *pièce*," Blackbird said. "It's out in the truck."

"Albert," she said, addressing the young man who was muscling
the garbage out the door, "will you put M. Blackbird's *pièce* in the
cellar?"

"I'll have to help him," Blackbird said.

"He'll be all right."

"I'll go and get Michel," Albert said over his shoulder.

"It's clearly marked. You'll see 'Florème' on the paper." Blackbird growled the name for emphasis.

"It will be fine," Albert said.

"You know how to move it?"

"Like a baby."

"Four more just arrived," Mme. Becquer was saying to Mme. Grunie, at the stove.

"Four?" Mme. Grunie asked.

"English. Two couples."

Mme. Grunie nodded to Hélène. "The hors d'oeuvres," she said.

"In two cars," Mme. Becquer said, at the window, looking down from the château and across the road. "You'll stay to lunch," she told Blackbird, and led him to the door into the dining room.

"We made good use of the winter, you see," she said, "even though we had a charming couple from Scotland here for over two months, and you remember how cold it was in January. That made some company for me. And the renovations were kept out of their way as far as possible. But as you see—"

The walls of the long dining room, once the main hall of the priory, had been plastered and painted with a scene framed by the columns of a painted pergola with grapevines rioting over them. On the wall facing the windows a rose garden was portrayed, with paths narrowing toward a distant line of poplars.

"It's impressive," Blackbird said. "Who executed it for you?"

"A firm from Meysse, whom we heard about. They sent a team. They were very meticulous."

"They were artists, one might say," Blackbird said, sucking his teeth.

"I'm still getting used to it. It's a little strong. But it gives the room more light. It was so cold and somber."

"Perhaps. And the rest of the hotel?"

"Here and there, a few things. But with my husband's illness— And my son was here too, briefly. He's an officer in the navy, as I believe you know. I did not want the place too torn up. It's never easy to schedule these things."

They had made a circuit of the room and were back at a table near the kitchen door. A screen across half of the end of the room separated the dining room itself from a large counter and set of cupboards outside the kitchen. Mme. Becquer paused at the table by the inner wall

near the screen, and it was clear that she meant for Blackbird to sit
there.

"You'll take something with me before lunch," she said.

"Mme. Becquer," he protested, "I did not dress for the occasion."

"You're perfect as you are," she said. "If you please." Her hand
seemed to indicate a place at the table facing out into the room, and
he pulled out the chair. "Sit down. What can I bring you?"

"I think, perhaps, a Salers."

She disappeared into the kitchen. It occurred to him for a moment
that he should take off his old beret, but he knew how strange he
looked without it by now, how much older, how much it had become
a part of his face, the person he was in the world, Blackbird. He could
not decide what to do, and in the end he left it on.

Mme. Becquer was back soon, followed by Hélène with a tray and
two glasses. Hélène set Blackbird's Salers in front of him, and the
other glass, filled with something pale like lemonade, across from him,
and was gone.

"I will be with you," Mme. Becquer said, and vanished into the
kitchen.

Blackbird was aware also that he was in his old working blues, the
bib of his overalls showing under the faded jacket. He had noticed
with an appreciation that had become habitual that no color faded so
variously as blue. The bright blue of his shirt, whose cuffs, he saw,
had suddenly become frayed and not clean, was subsiding into a
metallic gray. Then his working blues themselves: the trousers had
worn to shades of cloudy mauve on the upper parts, and the jacket
echoed them. Where wine had spilled on them it had contributed
purple shadows that were also fading. He had noticed shadows with
those same colors in his face and had wondered how long they had
been there. Dimmings and blotchings that came and went but mostly
stayed now. He knew that when he pushed his beret up in front his
forehead underneath was a polished azure, that there were traces of
indigo under his eyes, of violet creeping over his cheekbones and nose,
laced with a very few fine red lines. Remarkably few, and barely
noticeable, he told himself. His eyebrows were still dark, after all, and
his eyes gathered up all the blue of the rest of him. They were strange
eyes, it seemed to him sometimes when he caught a glimpse of himself,
shaving. The whites looked like penumbras of the irises, a last stage
of blue, and they occupied a wide space below the irises themselves,
which were a little flattened, like saucers. When he stood still he leaned

slightly forward, and that, and the way his eyes looked up, made him appear to be expecting something. It was a trait he shared with his son-in-law so strikingly that it made them look like father and son. It grew more obvious the longer Gérard was with the family, and yet none of them seemed to have noticed it. Blackbird reached for the glass and saw that there was a purple wine stain on the back of his right hand, which he put in his lap and picked up the glass with the other.

"You don't look it, Blackbird," he growled to himself, remembering what the priest had told him about how old he looked, and he paused and rolled the unspoken sound of his name with a slow curiosity, savoring it and the endless visions of himself that it suggested, humming and rumbling far down in his throat until the resonance had acquired vowels and echoes and an audience of its own, and was cast unmistakably in the accent that Blackbird had evolved out of his decades of listening and his admirations. An articulation that was wholly his own, though it evoked reverberations of stone cellars, and the quacking vernacular of Paris picked up in the First World War, and even remnants of half-swallowed barks from the imbecile marking of time in uniform all those years ago.

"It's all right," he said to himself about nothing in particular, and he felt it. He looked up to see, on the wall above his head, a framed photograph of M. Becquer standing in bright sunlight, wearing shorts and high socks, his hair cut flat on top like a brush, one hand on the barrel of a gun and the other resting in an attitude of casual possession on the wrist of a dead gorilla that had been hauled up by ropes into an upright, dangling position beside him.

"The devil!" Blackbird exclaimed, and looked away. And then looked back, trying to decide how old Becquer must have been when it was taken. It was the same blunt face he knew, a cluster of small bulbs and a tuft of mustache, the hair receding, a smile, but the eyes somewhere else. Blackbird had half risen from his chair to look more closely.

"That's him all right," he said. "He didn't change." Except, of course, to get older, gray and white, chapfallen, avuncular. Blackbird decided that Becquer must have been about forty-five at the time of the picture, and he was about to try to remember life at forty-five when he heard the kitchen door behind him and sat down quickly.

"Ah yes," Mme. Becquer said, and he half rose again as she positioned herself in her chair.

"From the colonies. I put away all the pictures that were here, before the work began. And then—pictures don't really belong in this decor, as you can see. But my husband was disappointed to think that none of them would be seen at all, particularly the ones from the colonies—this one. I put it up to please him."

"It's hard to see you having had a whole life there."

"Why?"

"You don't seem old enough. You look many years younger than your husband."

"Very kind."

"Not that he looked older either, of course, the last time I saw him."

"His illness is aging him."

"Your health, Mme. Becquer." He looked at her directly and with undisguised admiration, over the rim of his glass. It was her green eyes, he thought, as much as anything, that made her still so attractive, but she had the skin and the features and the slender fingers of a woman who might be barely out of her thirties.

"I'm enchanted to see you, M. Blackbird," she said, laying a hand lightly on his wrist, and for a moment he thought of M. Becquer's hand claiming the wrist of the dead gorilla in the picture hanging just above him.

"Will you excuse me?" she said. He saw that the two English couples had entered the far end of the dining room. She went to greet them and to seat them by a window overlooking the island below, and the river beyond it, and the broad valley. Other guests arrived, and she seated them, walked back to the kitchen, smiling to him on the way, and Hélène came in to take his order. Mme. Becquer reappeared, went to chat with guests at one table and another, vanished into the kitchen again. Blackbird listened to the foreign voices, ducked his beret over his food when it came, and ate with a running commentary of low growls as though he were agreeing with himself all the way through. The food, he thought—well, Mme. Grunie was a capable woman and it was more hotel-like and done-up than the fare at the Hotel Blackbird, but to tell the truth it was no better. In fact it was not as good, he had to say it—to himself.

The meal was almost over and some of the guests were leaving and he was waiting for a coffee, before Mme. Becquer returned.

"A coffee?" she asked.

"Thank you. I spoke with the little one about it," Blackbird said.

"Something with it?"

"No, no. You treat me too well."

She sat down again facing him.

"I thought of you," she said. "I have a neighbor. She has renovated the old artist's tower and now she is about to open an art gallery upstairs inside the old wall. I am sure she would appreciate what you carry. The authentic. She said as much when she tasted our wine—your wine—here. I can introduce you, if you like, after lunch."

Blackbird mumbled assent.

"It would add to your reasons for coming over this far."

"It's profitable, an art gallery?"

"We shall see. It's only for the summer. She's from Paris. The antique shop next to the church is doing well after two years."

"They can thank you for bringing the foreigners."

"As for foreigners—do you still see your neighbors the Canadian with the Italian wife, M. and Mme. Bright?"

"I deliver wine there."

"They still have—that same young woman?"

"Oh yes."

"And the child?"

"She's growing up. At a convent."

"Good."

She's still thinking about that, he thought. "That same young woman" was Josette, about whom Hélène had inquired. According to Josette, Mme. Becquer had been no pleasure to work for, had paid miserable wages, grudgingly, irregularly, and had treated Josette harshly. She had taken advantage of Josette's tireless industry to get her to scrape and wax floors and stairs on hands and knees, besides the regular work as maid, waitress, and kitchen help. And when she discovered that Josette had a lover whom she met late at night after the hotel was supposed to be locked, she berated and threatened Josette, who was already pregnant. It had happened during the winter that the Canadian historian Gavin Bright and his Italian wife were staying at the hotel at Florème while the château that they had just bought over near Aylac was being renovated. They had seen Josette's distress one morning in February when they had all been shut up for days by heavy rain. Josette had come to clean their room when they were still in it, and the whole story had come tumbling out: the child-hood in a prefecture in the north, parents dead, an older lover who drank and beat her and whom she left, a subsequent lover by whom she was pregnant but who was married. And Mme. Becquer, who would undoubtedly get rid of her soon. In the course of the winter at the hotel M. Bright and his wife had come to feel they knew Josette, and when their own house was ready for them to move into, in April, Josette went with them. Mme. Becquer had pretended to be delighted with the arrangement. Josette had had her baby at the employers' château, the following summer, and thereafter had been fiercely devoted to the Brights, their household, and their well-being.

"It's simply that I have not seen M. and Mme. Bright for a year or two," Mme. Becquer said, and Blackbird explained that M. Bright went off to some university somewhere for a season or so at a time, and was away at that moment. And Mme. Becquer turned to business matters: the accounts, orders for wine, and then led Blackbird through the far end of the dining room, down the stone stairs, out through the main doorway of the hotel in its round tower, and across the medieval street to another stone doorway with a new sign announcing in carved Gothic letters an art gallery. Up one flight of stairs, a smell of fresh paint, and there a woman standing at the foot of a ladder in a large empty room gave a shriek of welcome and rushed toward them. Mme. Becquer introduced Blackbird to Mme. Jorne. The walls were white, the windows were full of glare, and she was almost upon them with open arms before Blackbird could see that she was a slender middle-aged woman in very tight white trousers and a very tight white blouse unbuttoned most of the way down, several necklaces, short-cropped dark hair around the sharply pronounced features of her face. She greeted Mme. Becquer as though she had been searching for her for some time, and she professed a deep-seated interest in Blackbird when she learned who he was. Mme. Becquer left them together, laying her hand once more on Blackbird's arm as she said goodbye to him, and smiling at him, as he thanked her, in a way that left him musing.

Mme. Jorne was telling him something about her plans, and before he left she ordered wine for her own house and for the opening of the gallery, plied him with brochures to pass out at his hotel, and promised to visit him, to sample the cooking at the Hotel Blackbird. Perhaps, she said, she would drop by on one of her trips to the prefecture at Mujeac. The prefect, she confided to Blackbird, would certainly be at the opening.

. . .

Blackbird was surprised to find that it was no later than it was as he drove out of Florème toward the river, past the old stone sheep barn built into the hill, which was always plastered with posters for some circus, usually one that had taken place months earlier, one that it seemed he had never heard about. Each time that he passed, the dates on the flapping bright tatters of paper evoked in him a sudden floating absence of reference, and on the curve as he drove he could not remember what year it was, where he was going. It was not unpleasant, that recurring moment, though it had something of the feeling of having a kite string slip out of one's grasp. He knew perfectly well where he was, and everything else was always back in place the moment he got to where he had to decide whether to turn left and cross the water meadows and the iron bridge, or to go straight along the road under the old trees, beside the river.

This time, before he got to that point thoughts of Mme. Becquer had reclaimed him. He could feel her hand on his arm as she left him. The scent of her perfume was still there.

"Why was she so particularly agreeable today?" he asked himself, raising his eyebrows. "It can't be my blue eyes," he said, though he lingered on that possibility. "I suppose she's lonely," he said. "Becquer so much older." It occurred to him that Becquer must be more or less his own age, and he turned from the thought at once. "But no," he said, "let's be reasonable." And for the next few minutes he continued to be reasonable. "She needs friends, there with a hotel to run all by herself and a husband who's not up to much. She finds my company, who knows, interesting. After all, I know the region. I know a thing or two. I am, in a sense, a colleague you might say, with a hotel of my own. It's better to help each other, it's only reasonable."

He remained reasonable all the way to the outskirts of the small market town of Saint-Ricque, and the delivery of another barrel of excellent Cahors to M. Moulade, a tall swollen dealer in building materials who owned two sand and gravel dredges on the river, and was known to have advanced his fortunes through large-scale corruption dating from the days of the Vichy government during the German occupation. He had bought up a number of the most venerable buildings in the town, to tear them down and rebuild on the site with government funding, as part of a program that he had helped to steer into place, and he was currently running for mayor. Blackbird

noticed the new red iron cranes in his warehouse, the calendars on
his office wall—poplars by a stream, an old stone bridge—the kind
of thing M. Moulade would have got rid of. M. Moulade was always
smiling, Blackbird thought, at some tall person above Blackbird's
shoulder. M. Moulade's house was next to his office, and he had two
of his employees remove the full barrel from Blackbird's truck and
put an empty one in its place. Once they had agreed on the next order
and a secretary had taken care of the paperwork, Blackbird nosed his
truck across the *place* and around the corner to park just beyond the
open gateway of a large edifice, an anomaly in the town, an apartment
building that apparently had been converted from something else in
the age of de Lesseps, in unpracticed imitation, no doubt, of urban
architecture in large cities of the north and on the Mediterranean.
Around the small, rectangular cemented courtyard that sloped into a
drain in the center, a series of gray, painted wooden balconies rose
on three sides, four stories of them, which made the building very
high for Saint-Ricque, but it was set back among other structures so
that it was scarcely noticeable until one was inside the gate and looked
up. At each level lines of laundry hung above the courtyard looking,
Blackbird thought, as though they had been there for months without
moving. The wooden balconies were not bounded by railings but by
solid enclosures of boards, like low walls. Even so, it was possible to
catch sight of piles of crates, boxes, interesting accumulations that
appeared to be upward continuations of the stratified storage and
jetsam below the balconies, at ground level.

A choir of large dogs roared and echoed overhead as Blackbird
picked his way over an arrangement of collapsing crates, past a rusted
kitchen stove, toward a broad open doorway at the end of the courtyard.
Nothing but darkness inside that doorway, which seemed to lead into
a cellar. From the opening a deep, rank, powerful smell was filling
the courtyard. Blackbird felt along the wooden doorframe in the
shadow, found a series of buttons, and pushed one. Nothing. The
dogs went on barking, a little absentmindedly. He rang again. Nothing.
He bent and peered closely at the buttons and the smell rushed up
at his face. Something seemed to have been written beside the button
he had been pushing. He took out the small flashlight that he carried
to find his way around wine cellars, and read, "Shit. Three times."
And below that, "I am dead." And below that, "Moved," with an
arrow pointing downward. "Wit," Blackbird said to himself, and
stepped back into the courtyard and called, "Labadie."

The dogs responded with a happy frenzy of barking, and a round, sour woman's face appeared over the second-floor balcony railing and stared down at him. He touched his beret and made a slight bow to her but her face did not change.

"Labadie," he called again. Her stare had settled onto his beret like a foot. The smell was composed, he decided, of the back premises of the shoemaker's shop facing the next street, an outhouse somewhere in the cellar, vegetable garbage consisting chiefly of cabbages and potato peelings, wine from the next-door cellar of M. Ruscayre, whose spectacles seemed to have been made from the bottoms of bottles. Blackbird was refining his analysis when another head appeared above the third-floor balcony on the side facing the gateway. A man no longer young, dark hair cropped short to his skull, a swarthy cast to his complexion with shades of verdigris, hollow cheeks, large, dark, piercing eyes, a look of intelligence and cultivation. Even peering down from three stories overhead he looked subterranean. Blackbird thought he was wearing a velvet jacket. "Be quiet," the man said to the dogs, and they stopped barking.

"Ah, Labadie," Blackbird repeated, dropping his voice. "I've brought you—" He waved his hand to indicate the truck beyond the gate. It was not up to him to inform the woman of the details of his business in that place.

"I'll join you," Labadie said, in sonorous, deliberate syllables that for an instant transformed the courtyard and its balconies into a theater. Labadie disappeared and then Blackbird heard feet descending the reverberating wooden stairs, and he saw Labadie on the second floor framed in stacks of boxes, on the side across from the woman, who went on exercising her right to stare.

"Mme. Brojolle," Labadie greeted her in a low voice, inclining his head. She tipped her head forward just perceptibly in acknowledgment and stood still to supervise. Labadie went on down the stairs to emerge from behind a pile of mixed storage, near Blackbird.

"M. Blackbird," he said, in the same grave tone, and extended his hand. Blackbird saw that what he had on was an old brown corduroy jacket faded to gold here and there, so that it seemed to be catching the afternoon sunlight.

"And the papa?" he asked, when they had inquired about each other's health.

"The same. Which is to say, worse," Labadie said with modulated gloom.

"He recognizes people?"

"Oh yes. Remembers more than is good for him, I'm sure. He will be delighted to see you."

"If there's time," Blackbird said. "I don't like leaving the truck there at the gate."

"Because of the neighbor," Labadie said with immediate sympathy. The neighbor, M. Ruscayre, he of the glasses, was also a wine merchant, a retailer dealing principally in ordinary *vins du pays*. Outside his shop a blackboard, chalked with an elaborate script, announced the day's bargains, a 9 degree at such and such a price, a 10 degree at another, the writing so small that no one driving past could read it without stopping. Inside on the wall another blackboard, larger, repeated the same information and told more of what M. Ruscayre had to offer, including several grades of Corbières, a local white, a house blend like those for sale in the grocery stores, but cheaper. M. Ruscayre was one of the old school who encouraged his customers to bring back their empty bottles. If those were clean he would fill them from the barrel, and cork them with a plastic stopper that neither he nor his older customers thought much of. If the bottles were not clean enough to suit him he gave an allowance on them and put them in the back room to be washed. In there it was full of pyramidal metal "hedgehog" racks studded with washed bottles drying upside down in the gray light from a single high window far away among cobwebs. From the black coils of a hose on the floor water dribbled without end, and the cement floor was constantly awash. M. Ruscayre accepted even mineral water bottles, aperitif bottles, and champagne bottles, and had some destiny in mind for them. His customers tried not to stare at his glasses, but children on the way home from school sometimes stopped in a band and stood silently watching him move his face with its heavy spectacles to within a few inches of what he wanted to see, and by common agreement it was a wonder that he did not make mistakes with everything from the wine to the change.

His glasses themselves were something the children wanted to return to. They were not only so thick that they looked like fishbowls, they were hollowed out in front, and in each of the hollows M. Ruscayre, the whole of him, appeared again at a distance like someone at the wrong end of a telescope, only since there were two lenses there were two of him. You had to keep looking to figure it out, and he would turn away and it never seemed quite possible.

"He doesn't see you," one of the children would say.

"Yes, he does," another would answer, and they would go on watching him.

The miracle, to everyone, was that he too drove a truck to fetch barrels and deliver crates of bottles. He did it rarely, it was true, and preferred to have his son—a huge, even-tempered young man, round as a cheese in his stained white apron, who seldom heard what was said to him—do the driving. Unfortunately, as M. Ruscayre had come to realize, the young man was not particularly bright, and his father did not like to entrust him with anything except the most routine errands. The ideal, of course, was for both of them to take the truck, but that meant leaving Mme. Ruscayre in charge of the shop, and it was hard, heavy work for her. She had rheumatism, and there were things that she simply could not manage. But when M. Ruscayre was at the wheel, the word spread quickly. He never drove very far, and of course he knew the town inch by inch. The truck crept along at walking speed, the bottles in the back jingling without hope. The inhabitants of Saint-Ricque had come to recognize that sound and moved cautiously out of the way.

There was no reason why Blackbird should not deliver wine to the building next door to M. Ruscayre's. He knew for a fact that Labadie was a regular customer of M. Ruscayre, for everyday wine, which was quite as it should be. Yet it always made him feel uneasy to park his own truck practically in front of M. Ruscayre's door in order to deliver wine of a quality which was not M. Ruscayre's specialty. Blackbird and Labadie walked to the gate and Blackbird found himself dropping his voice as they unloaded the small *fût* and rolled it into the courtyard. They were headed toward the dark, open doorway at the end.

"Still the same place?" Blackbird asked, in case there was a chance that it might have changed. Labadie nodded. Blackbird tried to avoid rolling the barrel through unidentified puddles and piles in the courtyard, and he could not approve of leaving the wine among such odors. As they passed into the darkness at the doorway he went so far as to say, "The air is not healthy. It's not good for the wine."

"The temperature remains very steady," Labadie said. "Never hot. Never freezes. Never."

"It's the air," Blackbird insisted. "It would encourage"—he waited for the word to fall to him—"mold." Mold could mean everything.

"It's a little damp sometimes," Labadie admitted. "That's due in part to the canals, as I imagine you know."

Blackbird grunted. He was used to cellars, after all, but there was not much light at all, and this place was full of oddities. They rolled the keg around several vast bales that were contributing an acid, sweaty note to the general emanation—the cellar was used for storage by M. Leyme, the antique dealer, who had begun and who continued as a ragpicker, something which he had done so profitably that now, besides his antique shop, he had a hardware store and was opening an outlet for children's clothing, on a back street.

"The canals," Blackbird repeated to the fetid shadows.

"Indeed," Labadie said, pulling an empty keg out of a corner. "The Avenue Masséna, where your truck is parked, was a canal less than a century ago. And Pouillet Passage, just behind here, was also a canal."

"This is your empty?" Blackbird asked, rolling it out of the way.

"It is yours," Labadie said.

"Indeed," Blackbird said. "And this one belongs to you." They heaved the full one into place and Blackbird began rolling the empty keg toward the doorway.

"The three small rivers flowing into it," Labadie continued as they reached the light of the courtyard, "and the network of canals through the main thoroughfares, led to Saint-Ricque being referred to at one time as the Venice of the southwest."

They rolled out into the daylight and Blackbird did not look up.

"Is it sound?" he asked, rapping on the empty barrel with his knuckles.

"Oh yes."

Out of habit he began to open the keg to sniff the inside, but he decided to wait until there was less olfactory interference, and they rolled it on across the courtyard.

"It must have been beautiful," Labadie said as they got to the gate. "The Guizat Palace there"—he nodded his head up the street behind him toward the venerable complex of turrets and balconies visible above high garden walls—"had canals in front and in back."

At the truck Blackbird opened the keg and sniffed, raised his eyebrows, nodded his head from side to side.

"It will survive," he said. "Just."

"And then they were all covered over. In the interests, as they pretended, of public health."

"Public health."

"But you've seen prints of the town as it was," Labadie said.

"Perhaps," Blackbird said. "I'll move over there."

Labadie watched from the gate as Blackbird swung the truck across the broadening end of the Avenue Masséna, to park it with its nose against a low stone wall surmounted by a tall iron fence that was draped with climbing rosebushes, the garden of what had once been a private house and was now a girls' boarding school. Blackbird returned to finish his business with Labadie.

"I have some things I wanted to show you, if you can come up for a moment," Labadie said.

Blackbird followed him up the thunderous stairs, telling himself that Labadie was a good fellow with no luck. On the way up he noticed that the old woman had disappeared, and that the balcony overhead was sagging, and he wondered whether the whole structure might be about to collapse. He imagined that the old woman was probably watching from somewhere inside, and he decided that if she had nothing better to do she might as well do that. At the top of the stairs a wooden garden gate kept three large dogs in: a red setter, some kind of dark pointer, a soiled Dalmatian, all of them lined up to greet Labadie and his companion. The smell of the third-floor landing was simpler and more definite than the odors below. The source of it was visible in piles here and there on the cupped floorboards.

"You remember them," Labadie said solemnly. "They're too friendly. Don't let them jump up on you. They don't get enough exercise. I don't hunt, you know." The dogs raced around the balcony stepping in everything.

Labadie led the way to the back, where a main double door was standing open.

"Denise," he called. "She gets harder of hearing, my cousin," he explained to Blackbird. "I don't know what we would do without her."

A heavy woman with a face as pale as a plate appeared in the room inside the doorway, smiled, and was gone.

"M. Blackbird is here," Labadie said to her retreating back. "What would you like?" he asked Blackbird. They walked into what seemed to have been a dining room but was so crowded with furniture that it was hard to say what its present function might be.

"Nothing, thank you," Blackbird said.

Inside, the smell was a compound of old clothes, damp wood, the kitchen, with reminders from the balcony.

"A *vin paillé*," Labadie suggested.

"If you like."

Labadie took two fine crystal liqueur glasses and an etched decanter in the shape of an hourglass from an Empire cabinet.

"Well, and this violin?" Blackbird asked, as Labadie poured.

"I play, as always. After all, it's my profession. I teach it, as I must, for a livelihood." He pointed to the music rack and the shelves of music, and to the violin on a piano in one corner.

"Come and see Papa."

He led the way into a shadowy bedroom that smelled unopened. The walls were paneled with painted wood that was barely visible behind the pieces of furniture shouldering each other on all sides, and on a large four-poster bed with burgundy curtains gathered at the corners an old man lay talking to himself.

"Papa, it's M. Blackbird."

The talking stopped and the figure on the bed waved to Blackbird as to a friend in a crowd.

"I'm delighted," he announced. "Do you play cards?"

"Rarely," Blackbird said. "And only *manille*."

"And there are only three of us," the old man said. "Maybe someone will turn up later."

"I want to show M. Blackbird a few things," Labadie said to his father, "in the library."

He drew Blackbird into the next room, which was lined with cupboards.

"We may have to move," Labadie confided darkly to Blackbird, "and I may have to sell some of the books. I'm not happy to part with them but perhaps the hour has come."

"Why are you going to move?"

"The building has been sold."

"To whom?"

"The cartel. The building materials combine. You know M. Moulade."

"I do."

"It fell into his hands."

"He'll raise the rent, I suppose."

"He'll tear it down."

"Are you sure?"

"It's going to be a bank."

"A bank." Blackbird blew out through his lips and looked around the room, gazing at the ends of things.

"Where will you go?"

"It's not certain. We may not need quite so much room. But I have to stay in town for my students. We don't like the new buildings at all, of course, and besides, the rent there—"

"So I hear." They spoke as though the new buildings, along a street on the far side of the old school, were a foreign country.

"They will earn you a bit," Blackbird said, vaguely surveying the furniture. Labadie shrugged.

"If we come to sell any of the family pieces," he said. "The antique dealers, as you know, are robbers, without shame and without exception. They have made a profession of that. They have been stealing from the country people for years, and they take it for granted by now that it's the way to behave. They carry something around the corner to their shop, dust it off, and add two or three or four zeros to the price."

"And your family?"

"As you know, I have not married. There was a young woman, but—there are my parents to look after. I have cousins, but they're in Lyon and we don't see each other."

He had opened a cupboard, which turned out to be full of books in leather bindings.

"Some of these are beyond price," he said. "I prefer to let them go, myself, to friends who will appreciate them, rather than let the dealers get hold of them." He ran his finger over a set bound in black and gold. "Fénelon," he said. "Complete. Fénelon may not be someone you are interested in yourself, but it's a fine set. Here"—he took out two volumes—"are some of the old engravings of Saint-Ricque."

In the dim light he opened one of the books and showed Blackbird an engraving of a canal curving between high garden walls under trees, a church tower, cobbled lanes on the other side of the canal, arched bridges, horse carts, men with broad hats, women with voluminous skirts. "You recognize the Guizat Palace," he said, and Blackbird said he did.

"This is not for sale, of course."

"I am not a regular consumer of literature," Blackbird said.

"That may be. I thought you might find something of interest even so. Not for money, you know."

"You're not giving them away?"

"I thought that a few of them might"—Labadie dropped his voice and his enunciation grew more than ever like a recitation from the classics—"somewhat reduce the bill for the current delivery. Only if you would like to make such an arrangement, of course."

"That depends," Blackbird said.

"This one," Labadie said, "is a present. I put it aside for you."

He held up a volume on winemaking, bound in green: "Eighteen seventy-four," he said, and handed it to Blackbird.

"That's nice of you," Blackbird said, clearly interested in the book. He turned the pages. "Oh, the cow," he said, looking closely at an engraving of a large winepress, "where is this supposed to be?"

"The book is yours," Labadie said. "Sermons, now, would not be for you so much."

"I'm not a connoisseur."

"Though there is an edition of Bossuet that is rather fine. *Funeral Orations.*" Blackbird was continuing to turn the pages of the volume on winemaking.

"More sermons. A cousin of my father's was a priest in Tonkin. Voltaire. Balzac. Do you fish?"

"Not since I was a child."

"A lovely book on fishing, translated from the English."

Blackbird took it from him. "How much would that be?" he asked. "I have a friend with a weakness for fishing."

"Put it with your book and we'll decide later. *The Healing Fountains*—"

"What's that?"

"A little book on the subject of springs that are said to effect cures."

"Vichy. Evian."

"No. More spiritual. Lourdes. Puy-de-Dôme. Miracles."

Blackbird put his hand out for it.

"You're interested in—?"

"The waters," Blackbird said. "In my profession one takes an interest in the waters."

"Perhaps so."

"Health," Blackbird said. "It's precious. If we lose our health—"

"True."

"And my daughter is fervent about that sort of thing." Blackbird put the book with the other two.

"Liquids," he said, raising a finger.

"There are some odd works here," Labadie said, "that I'm not sure what to do with." He opened one of the casement windows and pushed a shutter ajar to let in more light. Then he drew from behind a stack of books a folio-sized volume bound in red vellum, much worn, and opened it carefully to an exhaustively detailed scene in full color showing two men and two women engaged in complicated sexual activity. He held it open for some time, then turned the page to another scene of the same kind, with a new set of characters differently positioned.

"The whole book is of this nature," Labadie said. "And there are others. Quite a number of them, and of the same quality. A remarkable collection, it seems to me. I suspect they may be valuable."

"It's possible," Blackbird said.

"What to do with them—" Labadie said.

"There must be—amateurs."

"I'm sure there are. If one knew how to find them. And the value of the books."

"These were in your family?"

"An uncle of my father's, I believe, assembled them."

"And your father appreciated them?"

"Oh, you know Papa." Blackbird knew that Labadie's father, after a career as a notary and member of the town council, had been seen, so it was said, sitting out on the balcony with a pair of binoculars fixed on the windows of the girls' school across the street, which had led to his being referred to in the café around the corner as Old Spyglass, an allusion sometimes accompanied by an obscene gesture.

"I have no competence in these materials," Blackbird said.

"It seems there is a new interest in things of this kind," Labadie said. "There was an international exhibition of erotic art in Denmark last summer. I saw it mentioned in a number of places."

"You should have sent them these," Blackbird said. The thought of the new art gallery in Florème crossed his mind, and he smiled to himself but said nothing. He started for the door, mumbling about time and accounts. Labadie closed the cupboard carefully and locked it. His father seemed to be asleep as they filed through the bedroom with Labadie carrying the books, but the old man sat up, seized one of the columns of the four-poster, and seemed to be on the point of getting out of bed. This time Blackbird noticed the ancient wheelchair by the night table.

"Very good of you to come, M. Blackbird," the elder Labadie said, holding out his hand. "You'll excuse me, I trust. I seem to have caught some kind of bug."

"Yes," Blackbird said, "it's going around."

"The doctors are no help."

"It may be nothing but fatigue," Blackbird said. "Liquids, I'm told, are always beneficent. I'm on my way. Goodbye, M. Labadie." The younger Labadie had slipped out into the dining room, where they did their accounts and Blackbird lowered the price of the wine in consideration of the two books, allowing about half of what Labadie suggested they were worth.

"This keg is yours," he reminded Labadie. "The one I'm taking home is mine. It's just as well it worked out like that if you're moving."

"It won't be for a while," Labadie said. "Not for a year or so. We like to think it won't happen at all. We should be planning the next delivery."

"Maybe you should wait until you are sure of the address," Blackbird said, and shuffled out the door, carrying the books. "Thank you for the present," he said, as the dogs nosed his hands, leaping around him.

"You like dogs, don't you?" Labadie asked.

"As a rule," Blackbird said, treading carefully along the balcony. At the gate he turned and said goodbye, shook hands, and then went briskly down the steps without looking back. As he crossed the street he shook his head and he did it again as he started up the truck.

He drove across the main *place* of Saint-Ricque, turned right into a tiny medieval street that led to a small marketplace, where he parked under a sycamore tree, and ducked past rows of cans overflowing with vegetable garbage, into a narrow defile between scarred stone buildings. He emerged on the Rue de Paris, the main street of the town, turned right past a men's haberdashery with old rolled-glass windows set in varnished wood, and a grocer's, to a café whose red-and-white awning bore the enigmatic message FOOT BILL SIX SHOTTER.

No one in Blackbird's acquaintance had ever managed to learn what the words meant or were supposed to mean. The present owner of the café did not admit to being their author, and inquiries about the intention and etymology of the phrase—it was unclear whether it was supposed to be a name or a description—led only to conversations as inconclusive as the phrase itself. In the past they had led to several fights, to unseemly rowdiness, and to offending customers being pushed out into the street. Such conversations had usually followed lines such as this:

"What do you mean, what does it mean?"

"What does it mean?"

"You know English?"

"Yes, I know English. Enough."

"Well."

"Well what?"

"It's obvious. *If* you know English."

"It's not obvious to me. What is obvious?"

"You know what is 'foot.' "

"I know 'foot.' "

"Well."

"Well what?"

"Foot is foot."

"The foot or the game?"

"So you don't know."

"The game is actually foot *bol.*"

"Who said it's the game?"

"What is it then?"

"Pay for your drink."

The regulars would not have dreamed of raising the subject, and questions about it came only from transients and summer people.

The café, like the one off the green behind the church at Aylac, had indeed long been the habitual meeting place of soccer fans, among whom Blackbird was well known in the region as the author of a column about the game in a local newspaper: "Talking Foot." For a decade and more he had published the column twice a month, but in those days he had managed to attend most of the principal matches in the region. In recent years he did not get to the events nearly so often. The column appeared irregularly and much less frequently than before, and it focused increasingly on the careers, lives, opinions, expectations of those caught up in the sport either as participants or as spectators. He continued to visit the places where the players and devotees of *futbol* met to talk about it, and his own pronouncements, now that he published them only occasionally, were accorded even more importance than in the years when he had attempted a fuller coverage. He was free to speculate, digress, cite partisan views from corners of the region not often represented. When his column appeared it was eagerly studied in the cafés where soccer fans gathered, partly in the hope of finding a quote that someone present might claim as his own or could at least ascribe authoritatively to someone he knew or knew of. When Blackbird arrived at one of those haunts they gathered around and fed him hearsay, prediction, anecdotes already rehearsed at those same tables for just such an opportunity, and their fervor increased when Blackbird drew his notebook out of the bib of his overalls, licked his thumb, and made a few notes on a blank page. It was odd, because Blackbird did not have the soul of a gossip. The game fascinated him and his attention lit up in following the actions of those who were drawn to it.

The doors from the street were standing open and the proprietor hailed him from behind the bar as he came in.

"Eh, my poor friend, no luck. There's nobody here," he said.

Blackbird looked around and it was true, none of his soccer friends was there. It was a quiet afternoon in the small café and most of the tables had been piled against one wall. Someone had started to sweep the floor and given up halfway. The broom was stuck in a pile of chairs.

"Thursday was the fair," the proprietor said. "Saturday there was an anniversary party. Everybody's tired. There are days like that. What will you have?" he set a glass before Blackbird.

"*Te*, Blackbird," a short figure called from the glare of the doorway, waving and coming on in.

"Oh, thousand gods," the proprietor said under his breath.

"Good day," the man said, with a touch of ceremony.

"It's Pierrot," the proprietor said.

"That's right," Pierrot said. "M. Blackbird knows me." Pierrot was wearing a felt hat of no preponderant color between gray and brown, with a brim turned down all around, and a wool jacket a few sizes too large for him, a shade or two darker than the hat. He appeared to have had a drink or two on the way.

"I saw your truck," he said to Blackbird. " '*Te*,' I said, 'that's Blackbird's.' " He laid one finger alongside his nose and winked the eye above it.

"I guessed where you would be. How are you?" He held out a rather unsteady, not very clean hand, which Blackbird shook. From behind his back Pierrot produced, in his other hand, a bunch of salmon-pink carnations.

"I brought you a present," he said.

"Thank you," Blackbird said, taking it.

"For Madame," Pierrot said.

"Mme. Blackbird," the proprietor said with contained exasperation, "is no more."

"My regrets," Pierrot said.

"I will give them to my daughter," Blackbird said, turning away.

"I was on my way back from the garden," Pierrot said, "with the flowers for tomorrow. Work, work, work."

"How is Lulu?" Blackbird asked, with the toneless inflection of someone who does not want to contribute unnecessary momentum to the conversation. Pierrot's wife—or his partner, no one was sure—Lulu ran a flower shop in an ancient building on another small square. The pair had come from Paris some years before, with the savings from years of working in a restaurant, and a dream of living in a country town. Pierrot grew some of the flowers and bought some at reduced prices from the market gardeners. Lulu arranged and sold them. They both drank relentlessly, often to the point of paralysis, and the inhabitants of the town could tell at a glance how drunk either of them was, could do it at some distance and prepare whatever evasive action was possible. Beyond that their general feeling about the two from the capital was divided as categorically as the sheep are to be divided from the goats. The locals were used to seeing Lulu staggering along the street in her man's felt hat, her dyed blond hair cut in a bowl around her head, her doggie face blotched purple, the big bow tie dribbling down her blouse, the checked tweed sport jacket, which looked like an allusion to a racecourse, flapping around her. "Poor Lulu," they would say, even as they turned a corner to avoid her. That was more or less normal. When it got worse she might be glimpsed sitting on the curbstone in front of the flower shop, vases of carnations, roses, mignonettes, gladioli massed on tables behind her, the pebbled sidewalk awash from a recent hosing, the water running to the puddle at her feet, her tartan slacks splashed and muddy, occasionally leaning back to raise the bottle to her mouth, mumbling in her deep, hoarse voice to the cats watching her in a ring.

"Poor Lulu," the passersby would say. "She's at it again." And when she keeled over someone would be there almost at once to pick her up gently, carry her into the shop crowded with potted plants and cut flowers, through the damp twilight heavy with final fragrance, everything tended, fed, arranged, waiting, and on into the back room that was chaos itself with sinks on one side, a dish rack, a stove, another smell altogether, and unmade beds against two walls, each piled with clothes, boxes, newspapers, cats. They would make a space for her on one of them and there they would lay her and leave, saying, "Poor Lulu. It's Pierrot. He beats her."

He did, and sometimes she appeared with a black eye and said that she had had a fall, or—confidentially—that Pierrot had been drinking. Sometimes after one of Pierrot's most uncouth orgies Lulu would undergo a reformation. She would appear with everything washed, cleaned, pressed, everything neat and orderly from the minute feather in her hatband to the wide braided laces in her polished brogues. Her face would look as pale as though it had been hibernating under a stone, and her breath would be almost bearable. A ripple of relief would pass through the town, and one by one, as they heard, inhabitants would come to greet her as though she had returned from a long journey and they would exchange pleasantries and buy quantities of flowers from her, to encourage her. And she would always make them a present of more flowers than they paid for, and often give them back too much change, and leave the money they gave her tucked between vases on a table in front of the shop, and someone would find it and tell her to put it away. If only, they said to each other, she could keep Pierrot from getting his hands on it. If they saw him lurking somewhere around the corner or in the shop they glowered at him.

No one carried him home if they happened to find him collapsed against the back of a building. They simply told the next person where they had seen him, and both shook their heads over it. If they came to buy flowers from Lulu and she was nowhere in sight but he was there instead they were not quick to mask their disappointment. If they bought anything from him he too was likely to make them a present of flowers with it, but they would receive it as a miserable attempt at bribery, and would thank him loudly to make it clear that everything was open and aboveboard. They said he stole.

"She's not well," Pierrot said. "It's the liver," he confided to Blackbird, who nodded.

"Medicine's expensive," Pierrot continued. "Ampoules. Extract. Beef-liver extract. Artichoke extract. Who knows what's in them? Injections. Suppositories. Everything is money, money. I work. I was happy to see your truck. '*Te*,' I said, 'Blackbird.' "

He raised his hand as though he were lifting a glass. "I'll let you buy me one."

"That's enough, Pierrot," the proprietor said. "Let my customers alone."

"I know M. Blackbird, don't I, M. Blackbird? I'm almost a customer of his."

"How's that?" Blackbird asked out of pure curiosity.

"I would prefer not to be limited to retail consumption. To whatever they happen to have at the Economat." His tone became increasingly confidential and the street Parisian accent heavier. "If I had the space for it I'd have my own barrel there, to draw upon when I saw fit. One of your faithful. I'll drink to that if you'll treat me."

"Enough," the proprietor said, raising his voice and pointing to the door. "Out."

"I can pay myself," Pierrot protested. "You can't refuse me. I'm a paying customer."

"Yes, yes, Pierrot. Fine. Have a good trip." He bundled Pierrot out the door. The half dozen customers sitting at the few tables that were in use had turned to watch.

"It's ignoble," Pierrot said, stepping into the street. "Ignoble!" he shouted, and walked on.

"He'll be back," the proprietor said. "A red? It's still the good Fronton."

"That will be fine," Blackbird said.

"Deliveries?" the proprietor asked politely, with his little finger crooked, after they had touched glasses. Blackbird nodded.

"Necessary," the proprietor said.

"I took some to Moulade," Blackbird said. "Getting big, his establishment."

"That's how it goes," the proprietor said, with a hint of bitterness.

"Still the cartel?" Blackbird asked.

"Cartel, cartel. It has a long reach. It goes all the way. Now he's all friends with the old families. Giddy Guizat pushing him now for mayor. If you can get those two together, what will be left?"

"Will he win?"

"The way things are going. And another dredge on the river will be next."

"And his daughter?" Blackbird asked.

"She runs the business better than he does, that one. Solid. Well, it's nothing to me, after all."

"And I took some over to Florème, the hotel."

"Oh?" The proprietor raised his eyebrows. "And how is M. Becquer?" he asked.

"I didn't see him. Doesn't sound good."

"So I hear. But Madame is very well, I hear."

"Certainly appeared to be."

The proprietor gave Blackbird a suggestive leer.

"No sign of the subprefect?" he asked. Blackbird shook his head.

"I understand that he has been very concerned about the state of M. Becquer's health this past winter. He was buying flowers from Lulu every few days. For the sickroom, he said. But that was not where they went. They were for Madame."

"Is that so?" Blackbird said, without interest.

"Everybody knows it. I know where the flowers went. You know her neighbor, who fixed up the artist's tower and is opening an art gallery, I hear? Well, who has the key to the tower when the neighbor is not there? They say it's very nice the way it's fixed up now. The young subprefect spent many afternoons over the records in the mayor's office at Florème this past winter. After all the years when the office was open only one afternoon a month, or by appointment only. He's a public servant. He gets the medal."

"Thank you," Blackbird said, setting down his glass. "Blackbird had better get on the road."

"Your friends will be disappointed," the proprietor said, "when they find out that they missed you."

"There'll be other times," Blackbird said, and they shook hands.

The leaves of the poplars along the stream beyond the slaughter-house shone translucent in the afternoon light of early summer as Blackbird drove west out of town, then took the south fork up along the cliffs to the open upland, the rolling wooded sheep pastures, hills covered with scrub oaks. The shadows stretched longer as he followed the empty winding road on which he found himself sometimes in his sleep. When he got home he rolled the barrels down into the cellar, rinsed them, stood them to drain, took the books upstairs into his bachelor quarters, and put the truck away. Then he went into the hotel to tell Françoise about Milibou, and have dinner.

He found Gérard alone in the kitchen, and he sensed at once that the day had not been without event. Gérard was busy at the stove, and carrying dishes into the larger summer dining room. Blackbird went to the doorway and looked in, watching Gérard, in his white apron, moving among the tables. There was the schoolteacher in her brown woolen suit, who came two evenings a week. The retired pharmacist who lived alone near the château and never looked up from his folded newspaper. A Belgian family who were friends of one of Blackbird's regular annual customers. Several others about whom Blackbird knew nothing. He felt weary, and he shuffled to a counter in the kitchen, poured himself a glass of wine, paused at the stove to gaze vaguely over its familiar landscape, and sat down at the cleared end of the main kitchen table.

"Where is Françoise?" he asked Gérard when the young man re-appeared.

"In the bedroom, with Sylvie."

"All right?"

"Not too."

He was off again into the dining room with a tray.

"Get you something to eat?" he asked when he came back in.

"Lamb tonight," Blackbird said. "A little salad."

"Peas and potatoes from the garden."

Blackbird nodded. He finished his glass, hesitating to ask an ordinary question in his own kitchen. But if Françoise and Gérard were at odds, did he want to find out about it from his son-in-law? He watched the young man, who set down a bottle of wine in front of Blackbird without looking at him, on his way into the dining room with another tray.

"Speak," Blackbird said to him when he came back.

"Françoise did not feel well."

Blackbird seized, for a moment, at a sense of relief that it was something so simple. But even as he did so it seemed to him that there must be more to it.

"How was she sick?"

Gérard touched his fingertips to his lower abdomen, then spread them in front of him with a gesture indicating his own lack of knowledge. He turned to the stove.

"The normal?" Blackbird asked. It was no secret in the family that Françoise suffered from menstrual cramps, sometimes severe, that seemed to follow various patterns, about which she had theories that they had all discussed at that same table.

Gérard shrugged and shook his head. "I don't know," he said.

"When did it catch her?"

"We were making dinner. She stood over the table, holding on." He showed Blackbird how she had stood there.

"I've seen her do that."

"She said she'd take Sylvie upstairs, and then she said she'd stay up there for a while. She looked white."

Gérard set Blackbird's dinner in front of him, then picked up the tray and started for the dining room. "Then she tells me she's been feeling that for a while," he said as he left.

Blackbird pushed his beret up on his forehead, stared out into the middle of the room seeing nothing, feeling a sudden flush like a fever, and the loss of his wife. Gérard brought in some dirty dishes.

"More Belgians, those," he said, nodding toward the dining room. "He makes in the apples, he says." Gérard and Blackbird both laughed.

"They had the *soubise.* They say they'll be back."

"That will do no harm."

"We had another visit. The housekeeper from down at the Canadian's château. The one with the daughter. You know her."

"Yes. The Josette. Someone was just asking about her. How did she get here?"

"Oh, that!" Gérard said.

"She came to make an order?"

Gérard nodded.

"Usually makes them by telephone," Blackbird said. "In fact it's usually Monsieur himself, the scholar, who makes them, and unless it's something out of the ordinary he generally comes in person."

"It was a little out of the ordinary," Gérard said. "She said that Monsieur and Madame are away."

"Strange that she came, then. Who brought her?"

"That's it. It was Popeye."

"Who's that? I've never had the honor."

Gérard was off to the dining room again, leaving Blackbird eating absentmindedly.

"He's not someone—I would have brought home," Gérard said, returning with another pile of dishes. "I knew him a while back in Mujeac. He's not stupid. But you can tell what he's like with one look. He's been hanging around the château when Monsieur and Madame are away, getting his hooks into the housekeeper."

"I wouldn't have thought he was the type," Françoise said, suddenly appearing in the doorway. She gave an imitation of a mincing walk, a pursed mouth, a languid approach, and a limp "Enchanted, madame."

"She's a fool," she said.

"He impresses her," Gérard said. "She thinks he's sophisticated. He pretends to have an education. Maybe she thinks he's like Monsieur, her *patron* at the château."

"I told you she's a fool," Françoise said. "Nice that he has a car." She turned to Blackbird. "He's this high," she said, putting her hand out at breast level, "and somebody has wrung him out like a rag."

"Oh, he can work," Gérard said. "When he gets to it. You'd be surprised."

"Work? Setting himself up with Josette, that's his kind of work. He needs somebody to keep him. Better if they have a château. That way he doesn't have to send them out on the street."

"It seems he did not impress you." Blackbird smiled.

"He disgusted me."

"What work did he do?" Blackbird asked Gérard.

"He calls himself a decorator," Françoise said. "It's just painting."

"He does plaster too," Gérard said. "He did a café in Mujeac. He had three working for him then. A team. They did a good job. But—" He made a gesture of drinking. "So he got other jobs in Mujeac. People heard about him, you know. And then he got around Josette, and then Madame at the château gave him some decorating to do when they were away. Once he got his foot in the door— Why do you think they came up here?"

"What did they order?" Blackbird asked.

"Nothing," Françoise said. " 'Oh, if M. Blackbird is not here—' I can't stand that woman. She looks out like a Duchess from her carriage, and who is she, come to that? It was all because he wanted to see things up here, what might be here for him. Too bad. It's not a château."

"Who told him we are considering repainting?"

"Anybody could have told him," Gérard said. "People talk."

"You should have seen them," Françoise said to Blackbird, "standing out in front looking at the hotel sign. 'It's charming,' he said. 'It's in the old style. You don't find them like that anymore.' He said to me, 'Bravo.' I felt sick."

"How are you feeling now?" Blackbird asked.

"Better. It passes." She looked in at the dining-room door and went on in with a tray.

"She sounds better," Blackbird said, and stood up.

" 'Do you have someone in mind for your decorating?' he asked me," Françoise said, her voice back to its full searing blast as she returned to the kitchen. " 'M. Milibou,' I told him. 'Oh, M. Milibou,' he said, like that. 'I know him,' he said. 'Is that so?' I said. 'Yes,' he said, 'he's been at it a while. Isn't it too far for him to come?' 'He's a family friend,' I told him. 'Oh,' he had the nerve to say, 'that explains

it then.' And all the time she's there with that little smile on her face.
'And what color are you going to have here?' he asked me. 'And what
are you going to do here? Something amusing? There's a great deal
of style here in this building. One would have to do it with taste. Is
there someone who does the plastering for him?' 'I know he has
whatever he will need,' I told him."

"I hope you didn't hurt his feelings," Blackbird said, laughing.

"You know, he's nothing. I wouldn't trust him out of my sight, but
she's the one who annoys me. She comes up with him driving her in
that little blue car of his. You'd think the car was hers. A 5CV. For
her royal visits."

"When are Monsieur and Madame coming back?"

"Soon," Gérard said. "Two or three weeks, she wasn't sure.
They're in Paris. So he won't be able to spend so much time at the
château."

"And they need some wine?"

"Who knows?" Françoise said, and she gave her imitation of Josette.
" 'Oh, if M. Blackbird is not here—' It was all a farce."

"Curtain," Blackbird said. "Good night." And he turned and
thumped up the stairs to his corner bedroom looking out over the
unimproved courtyard.

M. Milibou went over to the Hotel Blackbird within a week and
his prospective son-in-law came with him. Their arrival looked as
deliberate as a ceremony. M. Milibou was driving. He approached
the front of the hotel slowly, drove past as though he were looking
for some place he remembered from his youth, reached the square
in front of the church, made a slow circuit, came back to the hotel,
and stopped outside the front gate, blocking the entrance. Then nothing. He sat there for a moment without moving. Suddenly both car
doors popped open and M. Milibou began to hatch his bulk from the
cab. It took him a moment to do it, and in the meantime Robert had
emerged from the other side and stood looking around, not officially
there yet, delaying his own arrival so as not to draw attention to how
long it was taking M. Milibou to get, at last, to his feet. It was a
sequence so often rehearsed that they performed it without a trace of
self-consciousness, and then walked through the gate and across the
courtyard together. An incongruous pair: M. Milibou rolling on his
rubbery legs, Robert small, dark, neat, light on his feet.

Blackbird had thought it best not to tell Françoise too much about

Robert, whom she had never met. Even so, it was clear that she was halfway to assigning him, on sight, a place in the crowded gallery of her disapprovals. He was obviously too good-looking, too feline, watchful, quick, for her to advance him any trust or liking on the basis of first impressions. Besides, Robert arrived in the shadow of M. Milibou, whose place in her esteem was not high. But he had brought her a present of half a dozen trout lifted from the river that same morning. And he addressed her from the beginning with a particular conspiratorial deference which eroded her defenses. M. Milibou conferred with Blackbird but Robert spoke to Françoise, inferring an understanding between them whose details could be worked out as they went along.

That much had been established by the time M. Milibou and Blackbird had had their first round of drinks at the kitchen table and she and Gérard stood looking over their shoulders as the books of samples were opened. Robert too was standing, and could meet Françoise's and Gérard's eyes, so that the three of them could form a kind of league of relative youth when it came to choices.

If they were going to go to wallpaper in the dining room, Blackbird said, he favored something with leaves—he turned through the books to a pattern of green stripes on a white ground, with vines climbing up the stripes. The eyes above the table let it pass. For the smaller dining room facing the garden in back Françoise had decided she wanted a scene that showed, in red, teams of horses arriving at an inn, sometime in the long ago. She and M. Milibou were in immediate agreement about that, and suggested covering the lampshades in the same paper. They had no serious disagreements at all, and decided to paint the kitchen a conservative shade of what was known as *crème*.

The façade, everyone said, could be done at any time, depending on the weather, and no decision was made about whether anything would be done with any of the upstairs rooms.

"Who does the plastering now?" Françoise asked.

"I do," Robert said, and Françoise nodded her approval. "Sometimes Matthew works with us."

He brought Matthew with him a day or so later in another old truck loaded with ladders, planks, drop cloths, tools, and materials. Matthew was a few years older than Robert, and beginning to go bald. He was Polish, he explained to Françoise, and Robert told her that Matthew was capable of fixing just about anything from plumbing to eyeglass frames. At the end of the war, when Matthew had arrived as a refugee, he had put together a bicycle repair business on a back street in Florème, and had gone on from that to repairs of whatever needed repairing—hot-water boilers, gas stoves, electrical appliances. He became everyone's elf, and he seemed to manage it without difficulty. He married, had two children, took a plastering job and then steady work with M. Milibou, and still did repairs when he had time. He poached in the river with Robert (who did not see why the fish should be left in the river for the summer people) and got along with everybody. He and Robert invaded the winter dining room first, where they could stay out of the way of the rest of the hotel, and the whole building soon smelled of wet paper, paste, damp cigarettes, paint. Robert brought trout every few days, and he and Matthew ate in the kitchen with Françoise, Gérard, and Blackbird while the work moved ahead.

But the visit of Josette and Popeye had set a weed growing in Françoise. She kept hearing Josette's patronizing murmurs, her air of someone on an afternoon's outing from the château, and Popeye's soft, knowing comments. Before they had come she had thought she knew what she wanted, more or less. She had wanted to have the hotel looking nice, fresh, looked after, brighter, maybe a bit more color. When they had gone she kept sweeping them out of her head and there they were again, and it seemed that what was being done at the hotel day by day, the painting and papering, was not having the effect she had hoped for. Some of the time it merely looked raw to her without looking new. Sometimes she thought the old walls had looked better. Something was missing and she could not decide what it was, something that would change the tone of those two in her head, startle them, undo them.

Her lack of enthusiasm for the work as it proceeded did not go unnoticed, and yet everyone including Françoise could see that Robert and Matthew—despite the amount of Blackbird's Cahors that they consumed every day—were working well and steadily, doing a good job, and she told them so.

"You can't tell anything now," Matthew said to her. "It never looks good halfway through. You have to wait until the ladders have gone and the furniture is back."

But she knew it was not the whole truth, and she kept wanting something that would not have come out of M. Milibou's sample books, something superior. Her broodings settled on the hotel façade, and she concluded that it would be a good time to change the sign painted across the whole front of the building, the name "Hotel Blackbird" on the frieze of vines and blackbirds. Maybe no sign on the building at all, but just the one out at the gate.

She raised the matter one day when they were all at the kitchen table, and nobody said anything.

"We could have a look at the sign," Blackbird said, "before we put it out for the season." Clearly he thought she was talking about the painted placard that stood by the entrance during the summer, an addition that Françoise had wanted a few summers earlier.

"It probably could use touching up," Blackbird said.

When Françoise made it plain that she was talking about the sign on the plastered and timbered façade of the hotel there was silence.

"What did you have in mind?" Blackbird asked at last. And when she told him there was another silence.

"What kind of modern letters?"

"You know what they are. Like—" She thrashed around vainly for an example.

"I know what you mean," Robert said.

"Yes." Matthew said, trying to be helpful. "Modern. You see it everywhere. Filling stations. TOTAL. Like that."

"Even neon, maybe," she said.

"Neon," Blackbird said.

"You could do that, couldn't you?" Françoise asked Matthew.

"No doubt," Matthew said. "But that would be a whole different undertaking. Probably expensive. There are companies for that."

"I don't think I would like that," Blackbird said.

"And the vines, and the birds," Matthew said. "That would be complicated."

"We don't have to have them," Françoise said.

"Oh, they are the sign of the place," Robert said. "Vines. Blackbirds."

"For the time being," Blackbird said.

"I know, I know, they've always been there," Françoise said. "Things change. We're in the twentieth century. The vines, after all—"

"They don't run on forever," Blackbird said.

"I would not want to lose them," Gérard said.

"The vines?" Françoise said to him in surprise. "What do you care about the vines?"

"And the blackbirds," Gérard said. "They are what is here. I don't want them not to be there."

"So we'll paint it all over again exactly the way it is," Françoise said with suppressed exasperation. "Vines. Blackbirds." She imitated Popeye. "It's charming. The old style. You don't find them like that any more."

"That's true," Robert said. "But we can do it."

"People like it," Matthew said to her. "It will look good when we've finished."

Françoise left the table and she and Gérard rattled around the kitchen without saying anything.

"Well," Blackbird said, and they all stood up slowly. No one was happy about the argument, and it followed them as they left the table.

That afternoon Blackbird drove down to the château and called on Josette to ask what she had wanted to order the other day. He went up the hill and in through the long carriageway lined with huge ancient plane trees that almost hid the round towers of the small château, which was a remnant of a much larger building virtually demolished during the Revolution. The enormous trees probably dated from the time of the first bourgeois owners in the Napoleonic era, who had built a wing on one end of the château to house servants and impoverished relatives. M. and Mme. Bright, the present owners, had bought the château and its farm from a retired customs inspector, narrowly outbidding a furniture manufacturer who later revealed that he had been interested only in the trees. He had planned to cut them down for furniture and then resell the property, and he regretted having bid too low and missed the chance.

White fantail pigeons were circling on the freshly cut grass in front of the château as Blackbird drove up, and a blast of rock music was pouring through the climbing white rosebushes around the kitchen windows. He imagined that Josette's daughter, perhaps, was home from school, but it was not a holiday as far as he could remember, and the girl, he thought, must still be a little young for music like that. Then he smelled paint and walked in at the open door. A small, thin-faced, youngish man with receding fair hair, dressed in spattered painter's overalls, was sitting in an armchair covered with newspaper, smoking and reading a magazine, with a glass of wine in his hand and a half-full bottle on the floor at his feet. The music was coming from a radio on the floor beside him. He did not look up until Blackbird's shadow had almost reached the bottle, and then he nodded and gave him a quizzical look. Blackbird walked past him into the kitchen. Only then did the painter get to his feet and take a few steps to see what Blackbird was up to.

Blackbird stood looking around the large familiar kitchen. Vegetables piled on the big table. Everything spotless, orderly, the mid-afternoon breeze blowing in from the grass, the din of the radio holding the room in a suspended deafness.

"Who are you, monsieur?" he heard, in a hoarse voice behind him, over the sound, but he acted as though he had heard nothing and at that moment the door at the far end of the kitchen opened and Josette came in, carrying in her apron a plucked chicken.

Her face brightened. "M. Blackbird," she called, over the voice of the announcer, and rushed to lay the bird on the table and shake his hand. Her own was very cold. She waved past Blackbird to the painter, patting the air in a gesture to him to turn down the noise, and then waited until suddenly it collapsed like a curtain, and through the echoing in their ears they heard, in the huge cave of light, the sounds of the afternoon that had been there the whole time, the leaves rustling, the pigeons on the grass, a tractor on the road. Josette greeted Blackbird over again. The painter slipped back in, walking carefully and looking around him to make sure he was leaving no footprints.

"This is M. Popelin, who is doing some decorating before Monsieur and Madame return," Josette said. "M. Blackbird."

"Enchanted," Popeye said, and Blackbird tried not to see the imitation of him that Françoise had given. She had been fiercely accurate, as he could see. "I have heard a great deal about you," Popeye said, and to Blackbird the words were like the touch of cold water. He thought nobody ever said such things except old women in hats with veils on Sundays. Popeye's voice sounded like Françoise's imitation softened and muted. It was rough, constantly hoarse, but whereas Françoise forced her voice like a jet on an acetylene torch Popeye dropped his to hollow tones and a series of confidences.

"I allow myself a break about now, most afternoons," he said to Blackbird. "Your Cahors from three years ago is doing very nicely." He smiled.

He seemed to slide as he talked, Blackbird noticed, and nodded. He thanked Josette for her visit and said, "I thought you might want something to be here when the *patrons* come home."

Josette was setting fresh homemade cheese, bread, and wine on the table, and she invited him to sit down.

"I wanted to let you know when they were coming," she said. "It is not my place to make an order, of course, and I believe we are provided for the moment. But I wanted to make sure you had some of that Cahors that Monsieur mentioned last autumn."

"Oh, I remember," Blackbird said. "We ran a little short of that a year ago. It's the foreigners."

"I know," Josette said.

"There's enough for the time being," Blackbird said. "I bought the whole production from those two vineyards last fall. Monsieur tasted the *vin nouveau* in November."

"He mentioned that. That's the one."

"I was very pleased to see your domain," Popeye said. "Your hotel has cachet." Blackbird glimpsed what annoyed Françoise. "I have even thought I might order something on my own account," Popeye said.

"I'm in the trade," Blackbird said. "Where is your cellar?"

"I could pick it up myself, one of these days," Popeye said.

"I'm delivering," Blackbird said. "I'm often away." He thought it would be as well to avoid another encounter between Popeye and Françoise.

"Well, if I miss you it will still be an occasion to have something at the end of the day's work, at one of the tables under your lime trees."

"As you please."

"I hear you are doing some decorating yourselves. If ever you need a little help, I can show you what I've been doing."

"I noticed. I saw it. Very fine."

"You can't tell anything from that room. Let me show you."

"Perhaps later," Josette said.

"The light is perfect at the moment," Popeye said. "If you are free."

Blackbird pushed back his chair.

"Now is the time," he said. "I see that you want to get back to work." He followed Popeye out and across the drop cloths in the adjoining room.

"Be careful where you walk," Popeye said, "so that we do not track paint into the other rooms."

He opened a plain, elegantly proportioned door that had been stripped back to the bare wood. "We worked together stripping these," Popeye said. "The former owners had everything a finger deep in junk." Inside was a simple, pleasant, immaculate room looking out into trees on the slope behind the château. Two of the walls were lined with bookshelves. The other two had been recently papered with a design of small flowers in quiet colors on a grayish-green background. To Blackbird it looked calm, subtle, delicate, with a suggestion of lightness and depth.

"Monsieur's downstairs studio," Popeye said. "But there are so many books. They had to build new bookcases upstairs." He shut the door and led Blackbird across the round entrance hall with its broad wooden staircase spiraling against the wall, and opened a room at the far side.

"You know the dining room," he said. Blackbird was surprised to see it transformed with a new paper, pale blue with vertical bands of small white flowers. It looked airy, high-spirited, inexplicably appetizing.

"Where do they find their patterns?" he asked.

"They have the papers sent from Paris and London," Popeye said.

"Very fine." He thought that it was something that had happened in his own lifetime, even in the latter part of his life, this introduction of light and lightness, this opening in places that had been kept dark. He thought over the work that was being done at the hotel—but then the hotel, he said to himself, was different. A different *époque*. People expected something different of it.

"I've heard that when Monsieur and Madame bought the château," Popeye said, "this room and the one next to it and the entrance were all paneled in brown-painted wood, brown over brown over brown, so that you couldn't see anything else."

"That's the way I remember it," Blackbird said. "When I was young."

He stepped back and shuffled away across the dark red tiles of the entrance hall.

"I have subjects to discuss with Mademoiselle," he said as they reached the drop cloths again, "so I will say goodbye here." He shook Popeye firmly by the hand and thanked him.

"I look forward to continuing our conversation soon," Popeye said.

Blackbird smiled, bowed slightly, and was off to the kitchen.

"Monsieur and Madame will be pleased," Josette said to him. "He works so well."

"So I see," Blackbird said.

"How your Sylvie has grown. She's so pretty."

Blackbird inquired politely about Josette's daughter, and then returned to the subject of the wine order.

"You will tell Monsieur, then, if you please, that some of that Cahors he is interested in will be expecting him. He can come by and see what he thinks of it now, or I will deliver it, as he pleases." He was starting to leave.

"He showed you the dining room?" Josette asked.

"Yes."

"He's clean, you know," Josette said. "He doesn't get paint all over the house. He appreciates things. That's what it is. Yes." She agreed with herself, saying "yes" with an intake of breath. "He has his refinements."

"How did he find you?"

"He worked for some friends of Monsieur and Madame on the other side of Mujeac. People from the theater. English. They talked about his work. They were very content with what he did for them. But some people have taken advantage of his good nature."

"Indeed."

Again Josette's "yes" like a small gasp. "People have been very unkind to him. They have misunderstood him. Even as a child he was mistreated because he was small. He had a very unhappy childhood. His mother was abandoned. A sad story."

"I'm not surprised."

"And he is so good with my little Laura. He has manners. It makes company having him work here."

"Well, that's important," Blackbird said, and made his way out of the kitchen by the end door, and around the woodpile, with Josette following to see him off.

"And how are your decorations going?" she asked as he got into the truck.

"According to schedule," Blackbird said.

"I'm sure you are doing interesting things," she said.

"Ordinary renovations."

She waved to Blackbird as he drove off through the shadows of the plane trees.

The weather continued fair as they approached midsummer. Blackbird went on his deliveries in the region. It was too early to tell much about the grape harvest but so far it looked promising. Better than usual. The painting and papering progressed steadily at the hotel but the bloom of the first days was gone and something sullen had taken its place even though Robert turned up regularly with trout for the midday meals and he and Matthew addressed everyone at the hotel, and Françoise in particular, with a deliberate good cheer polished on all sides like an apple. Françoise had one recurrence of her abdominal pain—or one that Blackbird knew about. He suspected, from the way she spoke of it, that there may have been at least one other, about which she had said nothing. He told her that they should have the doctor look at her. The subject came up in the evening, after dinner, when she and Gérard and Blackbird were alone in the kitchen with ladders and scaffolding along two of its walls, and half the furniture piled up around one end of the table like the nest of a monstrous bird.

"Pah!" Françoise said. "The doctor. We know how much good that does."

Blackbird realized that he was sitting in the same chair, at the same place, where he had felt the ice slide over him again and again as his wife's sickness grew worse. It seemed as though he had never moved.

"I've always had it," she said.

"It's the wrong time," Gérard said.

"How do I know?" she said. "I've never been regular."

"I don't like it," Blackbird said quietly.

"You think I ordered it?" she snapped, banging a lid onto a soup pot.

"What harm would it do to have a little examination?" Blackbird asked.

"I know these doctors," she said, "and so do you."

They knew them indeed, Blackbird thought, and in their different ways they had no faith in them. He had done what he could, all his life, to avoid them, and his experience had done nothing but confirm and deepen his well-founded suspicion of them. Françoise had inherited his distrust, her own temperament had intensified it, and her anger as she watched her mother die had included the doctors at each step. She and Gérard, as Blackbird knew, spoke of their resolve not to fall into the hands of the doctors. It was part of the rationale for Gérard's hours of work every day in the big vegetable garden, the pride that they took in the fact that everything was grown "in the old way" without chemical fertilizers, with nothing but manure.

"That's the way that garden was always grown," Blackbird had said, yet it had seemed important to both of them to feel that "the old way" was something new and different. And it was true that Gérard had the farmer who supplied them with cow manure bring three or four times as much as before, and bring it more than once during the year. And he and Françoise had ordered sheep manure besides, from a farmer on the other side of Aylac who raised his sheep in the old way without bag feed and additives. They were scornful of the way the vegetables in the stores were grown.

"I've seen the way the truck gardeners spray them," Françoise said. "And then we eat that. And give it to the children."

Gérard had watched sadly when Blackbird sprayed the Chasselas vine over the door of his house across the road, and Françoise had fussed about poisons.

"You have to," Blackbird said. "It's Bordeaux mixture. For the mildew. That's how it's always been."

"No, it isn't," Françoise said. "What did they do when they didn't have Bordeaux mixture?"

"How do I know?" Blackbird said. "They had mildew, I suppose."

"They survived. They were healthy. The grapes survived."

"It doesn't do any harm," Blackbird answered.

"Copper. Sulfur," Gérard said.

"It's normal. That's how it is. You put it on the tomatoes."

"No, I don't," Gérard said.

"Then they'll die. The first day the weather turns damp you'll wake up and the leaves will be black."

"We'll see," Gérard said. He had sprayed the tomatoes with some kind of powdered seaweed from up north, and when it rained for a few days in early summer Blackbird had been surprised to see that the tomato vines continued to look green and flourishing, and the young tomatoes went on growing.

"And the potato beetles, what are you going to do about them?" Blackbird asked. Gérard was less successful with that pest, but Blackbird had refrained from mocking his son-in-law and had felt a certain admiration for him when he realized that Gérard was walking along the potato rows early every morning picking the fat pink larvae off the undersides of the leaves and dropping them into a bucket of lye water. The potato leaves were chewed but they lived, and Gérard and Françoise ate the new potatoes as though they had never tasted anything like them, and they talked about the sprays that were being used in the potato fields.

"It's not that I love the doctors," Blackbird said to Françoise. "But they're what we've got. If you go on that way—"

"That's enough!" she said. "It's my own business."

Blackbird saw that Gérard was watching him from across the table.

Aylac was not a large place, but in the normal round of his days Blackbird seldom set eyes on the priest. As the end of the next lunar cycle approached, and the night on which they had agreed to meet, he wondered whether the priest would remember the appointment or would still want to keep it. He realized that he himself was rather looking forward to it. "As though one were young," he said to himself, and he was relieved, early one evening as he crossed from the hotel to his cellar and bottling shed, to see the priest standing a little way along the road talking to an old woman who tended a garden inside the wall there. Above them the cherries were ripening on a big tree that hung over the road. The priest was facing toward the village, toward Blackbird, and Blackbird could see at once that the priest was waiting there in order to see him, and to nod to him, as he did, in confirmation of their arrangement. The lane that came from the back of the presbytery joined the road at the stone cross on the corner of the garden wall.

That was where they met, a few nights later, as they had agreed to do, and slipped away in the young darkness toward the iron gate and the stream flowing through the old park.

"And the ailment?" Blackbird whispered, once they were past the laundry stones.

"Maybe a little better," the priest whispered. There was a light breeze that brushed out the sounds they made.

"And the mama?" Blackbird asked, after a while.

"I can't tell," the priest answered. "It's always bad. At her age I suppose that's not surprising. She complains, of course."

"What does she have?"

"It's complicated."

"Oh. That."

"She has arthritis. That's plain and simple."

They climbed over the wall in the dark. The priest had been enjoying a small wave of confidence, a pleasure in knowing where he was, in the dark. As he let himself down on the far side of the wall he lost his footing and fell into the bushes, giving his ankle a twist and scratching his right hand and arm.

His ankle hurt and his hand was bleeding. As he put it to his mouth he found that he was laughing and that he felt unaccountably pleased with himself. He limped after the sound of Blackbird on the path, tripping over the runners of brambles, almost falling again several times, his arms flailing in the night around him, and the ridiculous pleasure continuing to well up inside him so that he went on laughing quietly to himself. He bumped into Blackbird.

"You all right?" Blackbird asked.

"Completely."

"I thought you were crying."

"No. Excuse me." That too seemed amusing to the priest. He did not laugh very often, and it came to him as something new and pink and reckless.

"Have you been drinking?" Blackbird asked.

"No. I was just laughing. Because we are here."

"Oh yes. Of course. We're funny."

Blackbird shuffled on.

"We would be even funnier," he said, "if we could be seen. Think of that."

It was a sobering thought: the park suddenly full of daylight just at the moment when he dropped his old underwear and stepped into the water. Then it too seemed funny.

"I brought a towel," the priest said.

"Comfort," Blackbird answered. "One must look to the future. Plan."

They reached the edge of the stream, the spot where they had been four weeks earlier.

"This time you know the ritual," Blackbird said. "I hold on to the clothes to keep them from wandering away."

"It's just as cold as before," the priest said, trailing his fingers in the spring.

"Always the same," Blackbird said. "In my experience."

He heard the priest's clothes rustling.

"Have you had to do with other waters—of repute, let us say?" Blackbird asked.

"Not personally," the priest answered. "Stories." He gave Blackbird his towel.

"What is the place where you lived before Aylac?" Blackbird asked, as though he had just forgotten the name, but it occurred to him, like a glimpse of a doorless corridor opening in front of him, that he knew really nothing about this large, ungainly, ungraceful, hollow-cheeked, ill-shaven, gray-faced, asymmetrical man with the voice of an old sheep, his neighbor more or less for several years of both of their lives, a time that had vanished unclaimed and without a trace between them. He saw one by one the walls that stood between the room where he, Blackbird, shut the door and went to sleep, and the room where he assumed that the priest lay down at night. They could not have been as far apart as one side of the village square from the other side, or the back of the hotel garden from the road in front of the hotel, and if there had been no buildings there, between the places where they were alone, they could have waved and hailed each other and had conversations all that time. But there was first the wall of Black-bird's corner bedroom in the hotel. And then the back wall of the old carriage house, and then—Blackbird counted on his fingers the walls between the room in which he slept with the whole village in his head, and the room in which he imagined the priest went to sleep at night, though he was not sure which room that was. Counting kitchen walls and the walls of the lane and the goat shed he concluded that there were sixteen or maybe seventeen stone walls between the two rooms, in that little distance, and they had been there all his life. He could not be certain about the inside of the presbtery. He did not recall having been in there since he had gone with his mother, as a child. He tried to remember why they had gone there then, or indeed whether he had ever known. It seemed to him that the buildings and a great deal besides in Aylac had been more spacious then, and easier to see and know, and that it echoed as he remembered it, and now it was growing deaf and foreign.

"Roche-Quentin," the priest said, and the name passed Blackbird like a single leaf falling, nothing to do with anything he knew, and then he remembered what he had asked the priest, who handed him the pair of boots swinging by their laces.

"It's in the north, isn't it?"

"The north," the priest said, his voice muffled by the cassock that he was pulling over his head.

"A city."

"No. Not much bigger than Aylac."

"The country, then."

"No. It used to be the country. Now it's not country, it's not city, it's between everything. Between the Route Nationale and the old road, between the railroad and the Louze. Between the embankment and the flats. Between the new asphalt they put down after the war when they took all the rubble away, and all the wires you see when you look up. Like fences over you." The priest said it as though he were giving directions to someone who did not know the way, and he handed Blackbird the cassock.

"You have family there?"

"None at all. It's true they used to call me 'father,' " the priest said, and laughed as though he were grunting.

"You have friends there just the same," Blackbird insisted.

"Yes?" the priest asked. "Friends. I don't see anyone from there. Sometimes I get a card saying that somebody has died. Most of the people I knew there were older than I was." He gave the folded shirt to Blackbird.

"The young, you know," he went on, "I christened, I saw them at catechism and first communion. Then they were gone. Maybe I saw them to marry them, and then maybe I never saw them again. That's the way it is. I was in between, you see."

"I see a little," Blackbird said, rummaging in the bushes. "But you grew up there, just the same."

"Not at all. I was not even young any more when I went there."

"But where you came from—it was the north too."

"Yes. It was the north too."

"The cup," Blackbird said, handing it to the priest.

"The—things," the priest said, handing Blackbird his long muslin underpants and standing naked on the damp ground.

"I saw the north," Blackbird said, "in the war."

"Which war?" the priest asked, "if you'll excuse me for asking." He crossed himself and drank. The water ran down his chest, down the bulge of his stomach, on down.

"The '14 war."

"There's almost nothing left from then," the priest said. "You would not know the place."

"Even if it hadn't changed," Blackbird said, "I probably wouldn't know it. Where did you come from?"

"You wouldn't have heard of it."

"That's possible."

"Moudan," the priest said with the cup at his mouth, and choked.

"All right?" Blackbird asked.

"All right," the priest answered a moment later. "It was the water. Sulfur." He drank again.

"That happens," Blackbird said. "It's a good sign. So they say."

"Moudan," the priest repeated with determination. "That was still country. Almost." He drank more water. "The cup," he said finally, and gave it to Blackbird.

It occurred to Blackbird that he was not in the habit of asking so many questions unless it was about football. It seemed strange to him. And it was true, it was something he was unlikely to do except with a stranger, someone who was not from the region. But having got so far he thought it would be too bad not to try to find out things that he was curious about, or at least a few of them. He heard the priest mumbling under his breath, and then heard him step into the water.

"How did you become a priest?" Blackbird asked. He heard the priest gasp.

"It's complicated," the priest said.

"No doubt," Blackbird said. The priest took a step deeper into the water.

"I tell myself it's the family," the priest said. "It was because of the family. It's true. It was because of the family."

"I understand," Blackbird said. "The mama."

"Yes. The mama. And her mama. My father—" The priest took another step. The water was almost to his knees. "Worked in the village when I was a child. He did this and that. He was the *cantonnier*. He cut the grass along the road. Poor man." The priest took another step and lowered himself to his knees in the water, gasping again.

"He's dead?"

The priest picked up water in his hands and clapped it to his face.

"Years ago," he said. "I scarcely knew him. I was very small. He went away."

"You have brothers and sisters?"

"My elder brother," the priest said, "went to Lille. Then there were some problems. We don't know where he is. My grandmother said that what was needed for me was education. Latin, she said. Latin was the secret of success." The priest flopped full length into the running stream, bruising a knee, swallowing more water, and rolled over, coughing, propping himself on an elbow.

"It's a good sign," he said, as he coughed.

"I can see how it was," Blackbird said.

"My mother worked," the priest said. "Like everybody. Laundry and sewing and housework. The priest there helped me. He got me into the seminary. Latin." The priest laughed. "Success. It's cold." He could see blurs of light that were stars through the black of the trees. "It's good," he said.

"It's not a calling," Blackbird said, "that one inherits."

"I don't know what I inherited," the priest said, splashing himself. "Maybe my complaint. They say such things are hereditary."

"Who are your friends, principally, in Aylac?" Blackbird asked with some hesitation. "We don't frequent the same circles."

"My friends," the priest repeated, as though it were a strange idea. "Mme. Gaire, the widow. She brings flowers. She comes to see my mother. Several of the old people. Women, you know. Older than I am. The children. Of course, I teach them their catechism—" For a moment there was no sound from the water. "I hear that you play football," the priest said.

"I don't play any more," Blackbird said. "I could, but I'm out of practice."

"Last year when I was at the gathering of the clergy at the nuns' school I met a young priest who has the presbytery at Montcaille. He plays football. He is there the way I am here: he has his mother with him. It's true, he has an old car. His mother bought him that, he told me, with her savings. But he has four parishes to minister to. And he plays football. I thought that if I had learned to play football when I was younger—" Blackbird heard the priest get to his feet in the water and flounder out onto the stones beside the spring.

"The towel," Blackbird said. "I know the man."

"How busy he is," the priest said, "with four parishes."

Blackbird handed him the underwear, then the shirt.

"And you," the priest said, "with your business. You must have a great many demands on your time. You are very kind to come out with me for the sake of my health. At night. Do you do everything yourself, in your business?"

"In effect," Blackbird said, giving him the cassock and taking out a bottle almost in the same movement.

"The barrels must be heavy to move."

"They've never bothered me. I like rolling them around. We have an understanding. In the war the sergeant asked who could be relied on to take care of the wine supply for the outfit. I told him that I had some essential experience of that. I said it did me no harm at all. And that was how I got to spend the war rolling barrels, putting them to

bed, opening them up, inspecting the contents. I didn't suffer from
it, that I know of. That was what I was brought up to. Taking care
of things that were maturing. But I need a successor in the line."

"I see. Your granddaughter cannot be expected—"

"Eh, no. The son-in-law drinks milk. The nephew—what does he
know about wine? Once I took him to taste the wine at a vineyard, in
the autumn. He couldn't tell the wine from the soup. No. I will be
the last," Blackbird said. "Ter-min-us." The priest heard the bottle
open, and the sound of wine pouring. "It ends well," Blackbird said,
and handed the cup to the priest.

"Your health," the priest said, and drank. "It's not the same as last
month," he said.

"What do you think of it?" Blackbird asked.

"It's finer. It has more light in it." The priest drank again. "I can
taste that when I breathe out."

"Maybe you should be my successor," Blackbird said, and laughed.
"You seem to have the spirit." The priest gave him the cup and he
filled it again and drank.

"The taste of that piece of ground," he said, "and that year. They
have pigeons, the family who grow this. Cauchois. Wings like pheasants, you know the kind. They win prizes for them, for the wine and
the pigeons both. Three sons, two daughters." Blackbird drank. "It's
on the slope, the way it always was, the way it has to be for this. Now
with the new hybrids they plant everything down on the flat so they
can run the tractors between the rows. It's all right. But it's not the
same thing." He drank and filled the cup and passed it to the priest.

Blackbird fished the book on miraculous springs out of his bag. "I
found something you might be interested in," he said, and gave it to
the priest. "Do you like to read?"

"When I have a chance."

"The paper?"

"Sometimes."

"Do you take the *Southwest* or the *Dispatch*?"

"Neither the one nor the other."

"I see," Blackbird said. "We get them both, if you wanted to drop
by the hotel."

"That's very kind," the priest said.

But Blackbird knew that the priest would never do that.

"Thank you for the book," the priest said. "I will return it next
time."

"It's a present."

"Thank you again. We are coming back, aren't we?"

"If you like."

"I would prefer to give the waters a chance," the priest said. "They certainly have done me no harm. The purgative effects, of course, on the following day or so. That was to be expected, I believe."

"It's indispensable," Blackbird said. "Primordial." And this time they emptied the bottle before they made their way back to the gate and the road to the village.

Robert and Matthew had finished the papering and painting indoors and they had set up scaffolding along the façade of the hotel and started repainting the frieze when M. Bright, the Canadian historian, and his Italian wife arrived one afternoon. Blackbird was just waking from a siesta in his bachelor house. The weather was hot and dry, and the shutters on the window facing the road were hooked slightly ajar and the top half of the door propped open to let a breeze through. Blackbird had taken down the tatters at the window and put up ancient lace curtains out of one of the armoires. They were swaying slowly as he opened his eyes and heard the car stop and knew at once who it was.

He hitched up the shoulder straps of his overalls, put on his shoes, rubbed his eyes, splashed his face in the kitchen, and lurched out onto the stone terrace, where the grapes on the Chasselas vine were the size and color of early peas. The afternoon light was so bright that everything appeared to be blurred in a luminous haze, and for a moment Blackbird stood on the top step, a little dizzy, and nothing moved in the world except the echo of waves in his ear. It became the sound of a breeze in the lime trees and then he heard the voice of M. Bright greeting Robert and Matthew. The foreigner's voice, raised and tight, holding up a smile. Blackbird clumped down the wide stone steps, one hand on the iron railing, a young man and an old man at once, and shuffled into the dazzling road.

M. Bright's red car was parked just beyond the outer doors of the cellar. As Blackbird walked past he saw books, maps, an umbrella, a felt hat inside the back window, as in a tourist's car. But on the back seat there was a coil of hose and a tangle of irrigation tubing and connections, and on the floor there was a jumble of buckets and tool handles. Blackbird crossed the road and walked through the arch of rusted trellis that was the entrance to the hotel courtyard, passed under the wisteria vine into the shade of the limes. All he could see of Robert and Matthew was their legs in the splashed trousers above the scaffolding, one pair faded blue, one pair dirty white. The rest of them was hidden by the branches, as though they were ascending into a dark green heaven.

M. and Mme. Bright were standing looking up at them, talking with them. M. Bright was laughing. Blackbird felt that he had surprised them in a secret. M. and Mme. Bright looked perfectly accustomed to bending back that way, talking up into the air. And so that was where Josette had learned to hold her head the way she did now. M. Bright's laugh, with his head back, was regular and deliberate, and several times deeper and older than the light voice that conveyed his neatly rolled syllables when he talked. Mme. Bright's voice flew higher and with more abandon, and her voice dipped, skated, rushed, and made Blackbird smile. M. Bright's thinning curls had turned a shade or two grayer than Blackbird remembered them, but there was still enough of their fair color to see why one local wag referred to him as "the Archangel." Blackbird told himself that M. and Mme. Bright were friends of his, after all. In a sense, at least. They were standing there rejoicing in the repainting of the "Hotel Blackbird" frieze across the façade, most of which Blackbird could see from the entrance to the courtyard. The pattern was the same as before, but the dimness had been eclipsed, the colors were new: a canary-yellow background, green vine leaves, black blackbirds, their white eyes with jet pupils clearly seeing something. "A work of art," Mme. Bright was saying. Blackbird realized that he had not seen M. and Mme. Bright for months, not since the early autumn. People always looked different after a winter, as though they had been covered with dust and then wiped off. But how strange they looked to him, standing there like a picture of people singing. How far away it all looked. The next moment he swung forward to greet them, just as Françoise appeared at the open French door of the kitchen and shrieked to welcome them.

"M. Blackbird," M. Bright said, smiling with open mouth and clamping Blackbird's hand in a tight grip. He said it as though they were survivors of the same recent disaster. Mme. Bright kissed him on both cheeks and he remembered that she was a *Contessa* by birth, and shrugged off the thought because he liked her. Gérard came to the doorway with Sylvie in one arm rubbing her eyes after her nap, and the Brights turned to exclaim over the child, who buried her head in Gérard's neck. They complimented Françoise and Gérard on the repainting of the façade and the smile on Françoise's face shrank and she looked at them with a trace of suspicion as they said they were eager to see all the work they had been hearing about which had been done while they were away.

"Oh yes," M. Bright said to Blackbird, "we've heard about the visit that Josette paid you." He laughed, and Blackbird was not sure what he was laughing about. He looked at Mme. Bright and saw that she was watching him. Everybody was watching everybody else, and he saw that nothing, probably, was going to be revealed.

"Yes," he said, "Mademoiselle came to call. We've just done a slight rejuvenation of the dining rooms." He shuffled ahead of them, waved a hand toward the wallpaper and paint, and let their exclamations of approval float past him, watching Françoise out of the corner of his eye. Her face looked as though it had been set in plaster, and her dark eyes were caves. Blackbird wondered why he had not noticed before the way M. Bright talked with his head tipped back, and the reassuring way that Mme. Bright spoke. He saw how unlikely it was that her compliments sounded convincing to Françoise.

"We will have to come up here for dinner very soon, in the new dining room," Mme. Bright said. She stayed in the kitchen with Françoise and Gérard and Sylvie as Blackbird and M. Bright walked out into the courtyard.

"Josette tells me you have saved me some of that excellent Cahors we tasted in the autumn," M. Bright said. "I hope that's right, and that it hasn't all been bought by your Belgian tycoon."

"Oh, that one. He came when the black plums were ripening and bought the whole crop around here. They were on the dining-room tables in Belgium within a week, he told us. He bought a good deal of that Cahors again this year, but I would not sell it all. I have several other friends who appreciate it, and I want some for myself. There is still quite enough."

They paused at the entrance to Blackbird's bottling shed, and M. Bright stood looking up at the barn roof, the tiles, the swallows' nests, the mountain ranges of old winemaking equipment and stacked barrels, pieces of wagons and harness lining the walls. They ducked under the low lintel into the cellar. Blackbird pulled the string to turn on the light and they walked between the stone wall and the row of *tonnes*, engaged in the serious business of tasting. Besides his broken-stemmed wineglass upended on a barrel, which Blackbird always used for himself, rinsing it out at the tap by the door each time, he found a kitchen glass for M. Bright, washed out the cobwebs with expert speed, flinging the water on the cement floor and drying out the glass with a towel that had taken up residence on a nail in the mortar. They began their comparisons, the rehearsals of the histories of vintages Blackbird thought well of. It was a ritual they had conducted many times in the past, and apart from what Blackbird had to recount about each wine it was carried out without much talk. M. Bright would take the half-filled glass from Blackbird's hand, swirl the wine in the glass to watch its meniscus move on the sides of the glass, sniff it, sip it, stand with his head back for a moment like a drinking bird, smile, say "yes" and then something complimentary but noncommittal, perhaps sip again, hand the glass to Blackbird, who would empty out the rest, rinse it, and turn to the next. Within a half hour the decisions had been made, the order placed, the arrangements for delivery agreed upon, and Blackbird closed his order book. M. Bright turned for a last look around the cellar and they ducked out into the summer daylight, where their voices changed, and the way they talked, the expressions on their faces.

As Blackbird closed the cellar door, M. Bright said, "It's good to see that it's just as it was."

"It's old," Blackbird said.

"That's it."

"It was like that when we hid in the barrels," Blackbird said, and laughed.

"I never saw that door open before," M. Bright said, looking up to the stone terrace at the top of the steps.

"I have my own quarters up there, you might say," Blackbird said. "The place keeps me amused."

"Was it the family house?"

"There was always someone in the family living there. My mother-in-law at one time, of course. One of my uncles. One of my aunts. There seem to be layers."

They were standing at the foot of the stone stairs.

"I love to look into old houses," M. Bright said.

"There's nothing to see," Blackbird said. "But if you like, you are welcome."

He clomped up the stairs with his rocking walk, pushed open the door, and went in.

"Ah yes," M. Bright said, coming in behind him, squinting his eyes, trying to see everything at once. "It's wonderful."

"Wonderful," Blackbird said, with a laugh.

"It hasn't been touched," M. Bright said.

"You could say that. The housekeeper is me," Blackbird said.

"May I?" M. Bright asked, picking up a corner of the crocheted bedspread on the unmade bed.

"As you please," Blackbird said. "I take my afternoon nap here, when it's hot."

"How long has the house been in the family?" M. Bright asked, deciding on the basis of what he had seen that it dated from the early years of the past century, somewhere between 1810 and 1820, the end of the Napoleonic era and at least a generation before the phylloxera ravaged the vines and ruined the inhabitants of the region. He thought of it as the Hesperidean age of the uplands, a time of agrarian serenity filled with the light of ripening harvests and the fattening of fruit. The architecture of those decades seemed an expression of that, and many of the trees seemed to date from then. The local limestone from which all the buildings were made gathered a rusty lichen on south and west walls and even in gray weather they gave off a glow of the late afternoons of summer when the square stones, the fast-shuttered windows, the bronzed roofs floated into the end of the long days' radiance. They revealed an age like the hour and season it resembled, which the light was about to leave. It seemed to have remained suspended wherever the stones had not been disturbed. M. Bright remembered, especially when he was away from the region, the worn gleam around doorways and windows, the faint gold stain like a cloud, just below the shadows of overhanging eaves.

"It was always ours," Blackbird said.

"But it appears to have been a farmhouse, at the beginning at least. Is that possible?"

"I suppose," Blackbird said. "The village, the country, there wasn't so much difference between them."

Even now, after all, M. Bright thought, the distinction was scarcely more than provisional, with the pigs and chickens folded in sheds beside the vegetable gardens, and the lines of red cows swaying along the road through the village every evening, the flocks of sheep seething in the lanes, the hay wagons jamming the street below the church at haying time, pigs butchered under lime trees, out in the lane, surrounded by rings of neighbors.

"My uncle who lived here," Blackbird said, "had a raven for a companion. The raven was the concierge here. A big bird. He would stand out there on the top step and decide whether he liked whoever it was who might have come to see my uncle, and whether he would let them come up to the door. My uncle had to shut him in the back room in order to be able to entertain anybody, unless M. Raven liked them, which was rare. My uncle called him Gabriel. That bothered my mother. Gabriel. The angel. How black he was. He was the black-bird of his day. After that, we came down in the world. Things got smaller. My uncle would put a little wine in Gabriel's dish when Monsieur had stopped eating, and sometimes Gabriel would refuse it but sometimes he would sip a little, put his head back, close his eyes, walk away—more or less the way I walk myself, turn around in the doorway to look us over. That's how it was."

"Was your uncle in the wine business?"

"He was a partner. My great-grandfather and my grandfather, back in their day, transported the wine from Mujeac by railroad to the warehouse down by the station. There was my old cellar over at the hotel, and this one. Good cellars. My nephew has the warehouse nowadays. He sells beer. He doesn't have the—name. I'm the last of the Blackbirds."

"I would hate to think so."

"It's progress," Blackbird said. "What can you expect? Who un-derstands the wines of the region now? I deal more and more in bulk, from the Hérault, because that's all that many of the customers want. It's not bad, the Minervois. It's not the noble stock. But it's agreeable. It goes down. After all, the Cahors is changing too, with the new hybrids and the new methods. The vintages are small and not famous. They don't fetch great prices. The young growers as often as not would rather grow more and sell at the cooperative."

"The choice vineyards too?"

"Not all of them, oh no. Not the ones I frequent for preference. The Blackbird tour."

"They'll go on, surely."

"They'll last my time, I imagine."

"Let us hope that will be a long time."

"Oh, I continue. I plan to have the back wall of the cellar rebuilt. It needs repair. The cellar is worth it. But when I'm gone—I am going to have the masons seal up a dozen bottles of the best, labeled by hand with the date, and each bottle inscribed with a dedication: 'To the Demolishers of This Building.' It will slow them down."

M. Bright winced and shook his head. His eye wandered to the

shelf of books behind Blackbird, to the titles. A much-worn copy of
Dr. J. Guyot's *Etude des vignobles de France* looked as though it might
be the first edition. He pointed to it.

"That's been used," he said.

"My grandfather's," Blackbird said. "He corresponded with vint-
ners. Médoc. Pomerol. Even Burgundy."

M. Bright touched the volume and looked inquiringly at Blackbird.

"Of course," Blackbird said.

"Eighteen sixty-eight," M. Bright said. "I believe it's the original
edition."

"Very possible," Blackbird said. M. Bright turned the pages. Blackbird watched him.

"Take it," he said. M. Bright looked up. "Take it with you. I know
how it interests you."

"I couldn't do that."

"Yes, indeed. Take it. I know the story."

"You are too generous. But it was your grandfather's. It should stay
in the family."

"In the succession. I've decided that you should be my successor."

M. Bright laughed his careful laugh.

"Indeed," Blackbird said, "it makes sense. You know more about
the wines of the region than anyone in my family now, or than most
of the people hereabouts. You care about these vintages."

"I'm an outsider."

"That's not a real obstacle. There are precedents."

"I have my own work. It takes all my time."

"It would permit you to stay here instead of having to go off here
and there to earn your living. It's the solution. It could be 'Blackbird
and Successor' or whatever you fancied. 'Blackbird and Bright'—that
goes well."

"I am very flattered. I am honored. But I could not possibly. I am
not a man of affairs."

"You run your farm."

"At a loss." M. Bright laughed. "And M. Dulsat does most of the
running. I could not take on something so—demanding. I would want
to do it well, and it would be more than I could manage."

"It's too bad," Blackbird said. "Perhaps you will change your mind
in a while."

"Surely there is—" M. Bright began, but recognized Blackbird's
situation and decided not to pursue the subject. "I think we should

be going. They will imagine that we have been carried away by our sampling. Thank you for showing me the house. I know my wife would love to see it."

As his guest walked to the doorway Blackbird restored the first edition of Guyot to its place on the shelf, and then followed, turning the big iron key in the lock behind him.

The hot, dry weather held steady and people began to repeat, "Bad year for the hay, good year for the wine." The summer had drifted into a sere trance in which the days turned through the amber light as though they were not moving at all and each one were in fact yesterday again.

The main decorating at the hotel had been finished for some time and the walls had retreated into the background with the arrival of the summer guests, but of course the work had taken rather longer than anyone had expected, and had not been quite finished when it was said to be finished, and Robert and Matthew had left some of their tools behind and Françoise kept thinking of other sections of wall—the upstairs behind the kitchen, part of the upstairs hall—that looked dingy now that the paint downstairs was fresh. She had come to like having Robert and Matthew around. She seemed to derive a certain reassurance from their capable, confident presence. She had faith in the authority and relish of their judgments. She had ceased to pay attention to their wine consumption. After the first few days she had laughed about it. Then she ignored it. And then, on occasion, she was heard to say something by way of justifying it. "They work hard and the weather is hot and the materials leave a disagreeable taste in your mouth, and if that's what they need—" And to Gérard she pointed out how much less they drank, after all, than M. Milibou himself. "They don't bother me," Gérard said, and they kept coming back for a day or two at a time, painting, fixing up one spot after another at the hotel, like family. They conferred with Françoise and Gérard about colors and trim and all the details, and when they told her that a color, or a finish, or the piece of work they had just completed had class, she believed them, for the time being at least.

Robert's wedding, early in the summer, did not seem to change anything very much. He and his new wife, Lisette, had moved into a small house that had been in Mme. Milibou's family and needed repairs, and Robert had spent a certain amount of time working there on his own, and he continued to do so. The result, oddly enough, was that, since he was not committed to all the main jobs that his father-in-law contracted for, he seemed to have more time for small jobs here and there. He was able to order his days more or less as he pleased, and he and Matthew liked working together. Matthew spoke well of Lisette's cooking. It sounded as though Robert had settled down.

Blackbird's nephew Pierre, who had the beer concession, got them to do some work over at his house below the church, and it meant that he was up at the hotel more than usual, conferring with them. Sometimes he would drop by toward the end of the working day and the three of them would sit at a table outside the kitchen, if there were not many guests, or would wander along to the café facing the pasture behind the church, or to a table outside the store which occupied the ground floor of Pierre's house. Pierre supplied the beer at both places, so a number of the drinks there were free. Sometimes Blackbird himself would turn up at the café, which was run by a widow with four small children whose toys always littered the cobbled terrace outside the front door and the yellow marbled tiles of the front room. It too was a football café and Blackbird had a circle of cronies who met there to discuss the sport and to play *manille* on Sundays. The meetings with Robert and Matthew and Pierre became more frequent as the summer wore on, an uncalculated pleasure bringing them all together for a while like a cloud.

Pierre was an amiable, broad-faced, swarthy man, a few years older than Robert and Matthew, losing his hair in front, not yet noticeably overweight though the conformation for it was in place: everything about him was rounded from his face to his feet. He spoke quietly, slowly, gently, but precisely, with a slight smile whatever he said. He got along with everybody and there were those who were saying that he should be on the municipal council, as Blackbird was though he seldom went to meetings.

Pierre suggested to Robert and Matthew, while they were repainting the inside of his house and the shutters on the square, that they might be willing to set up a brick-and-stucco wall at one end of the bottle warehouse down by the old railroad station, although neither Robert nor Matthew, as they said repeatedly, were masons. Blackbird was there as they discussed the work.

"Rustafic won't mind, I suppose," he said. M. Rustafic was the mason who did all the work in the village, as a general rule. "He always has more than he can do," Blackbird said, "and he's old. It wears you out, that work."

"Arthritis," Robert said.

"It's not much of a job," Pierre said. "A couple of days."

In the end they did the work, a plain, functional partition of hollow tiles and cement, and the evening they finished it Blackbird said, "If you're throwing in masonry with the other improvements I have a little corner, of importance only to me, that I'd like you to consider."

They could scarcely get out of that, and Robert and Matthew walked back with him that evening to the old house and ducked into the cellar after him, where they stood gazing in silent admiration at the row of *tonnes*.

"It's not there," Blackbird said, and led them along the wet floor. He pulled a string turning on a second dim bulb at the back of the cellar, and lit a stub of candle that he picked up from the top of a barrel. He slipped around the last of the *tonnes* and said, "Back here."

The illumination was poor, and their shadows washed back and forth on the massive stones. The architecture of the uplands had been lavish with stone since the days of the Gauls. There was limestone lying ready for use everywhere, and the builders had long performed prodigies of stone moving, using chains and rollers and the strength of the yoked red cows—not oxen but shod cows, the same that gave the rich milk of the uplands. The size of the stones in the base of the house told little about the date when they were set there, and there was no way of being sure whether they had been brought for the house or had been part of an earlier building on the site. Blackbird held up his candle.

"Here," he said, and ran his finger along a crack that zigzagged downward at the joints between stones. It began up at the corner of the vaulted stone roof and ran down almost to the floor. Most of it was as thin as a knife blade but there was one section where it was almost possible for Blackbird to get his fingers into it. The stones there were smaller than the ones below, and a piece of one was missing.

"What do you think of that?" Blackbird asked.

Robert and Matthew both looked carefully, with the candle.

"But it's not recent," Robert said.

"No," Blackbird admitted.

"It's been there a long time," Matthew agreed. "Maybe from the beginning."

"I have the impression that it's been getting worse," Blackbird said.

"I doubt it," Robert said. "I don't think it's moved for years."

"And with the vault sitting on it—" Blackbird went on.

"That's not where the weight is," Robert said. "Even if the weight was there it probably wouldn't matter, the way the stones are laid, and the size of those stones. But the weight comes down here—"

"I know," Blackbird said, impatiently.

"And here it's solid, thousand gods," Robert said, "that's not going to move. They knew what they were doing."

"And with these airplanes breaking the sound barrier," Blackbird continued. "I read last week of a mason who was building a cistern and they made their boom up there and the whole thing fell in on him. He's dead."

"I read it too," Matthew said.

"I thought I would rather not leave it that way."

"I wouldn't know where to begin there," Robert said. "What could you do? Bolts through here and there. Iron straps, maybe, and cement over that, but it's not worth it. That wall isn't going anywhere. Look at the vault. There's no crack up there. The wall settled a little, once, a long time ago and that's where it wants to be now."

"Yes, yes," Blackbird said. "I had considered, actually, making a small recess in the wall along there. A place to deposit a few things for the future. Seal them in, you know."

"I understand," Matthew said.

"I wouldn't touch those stones," Robert said. "Maybe you'll find a mason who would do it, I don't know about that. You don't want to have us playing around there. We could fill up the crack if you like, one of these days when we have a bucket of cement."

"Good," Blackbird said. "You'll know where to find me." And he filled what glasses they could find in the cellar and they stood and drank from his preferred *tonne* until Robert said, "On now. We have to be going."

It was a mistake to ask them, Blackbird thought as he locked the cellar before going across the road to dinner. Of course, the wall could not be rebuilt and that might not be the best place for the recess to hold the bottles he imagined walling up for someone to find. He had simply set it there in his mind without thinking about it practically. And he had felt reluctant to approach old M. Rustafic about the job. Rustafic was a gruff, impatient man a few years older than Blackbird, who had known him all his life. And Blackbird had liked Robert and

Matthew, the way they worked, their company. Now it occured to him that that was the wrong wall anyway, and he remembered, in the wall beyond the stairs, a niche already made, of the sort that one found in many of the house walls: one long flat stone above, and another one below. A place for keeping things. It was about the right size for a dozen bottles lying on their sides, and it seemed made for the purpose. He was smiling as he walked into the kitchen at the hotel.

Gérard was rushing around the kitchen, sweat on his face, looking pale and tired.

"Quite a few people tonight," Blackbird said, looking around for Françoise. He walked to the dining-room door and was surprised not to see her waiting on the tables.

"Where is she?"

"She went upstairs. An attack."

"How long ago?"

"Few minutes."

"Bad?"

"They all look bad."

"She's been having more of them?"

"She didn't want me to tell you. I think she's been having them and didn't tell me either."

"Which table?" Blackbird asked, as Gérard finished setting food on a tray.

"The four by the door. Woman with the pink dress."

Blackbird took off his dusty jacket, washed his hands, and took the tray into the dining room in his overalls. He went on serving the meal to the diners, working with Gérard, until everyone in the dining room had left and the tables were cleared. He came out finally and found the kitchen empty, and he served himself dinner, fetched the newspaper from on top of the old radio, and sat down at one end of the table to eat. He had almost finished when Gérard came back down the stairs.

"Well?" he asked.

"Not good," Gérard said.

"Same thing?"

Gérard nodded.

"Much pain?"

Gérard nodded.

Blackbird got up from the table and went to the telephone on the wall by the outside door and called the doctor, late though it was.

Gérard heard him say that, no, it was not an emergency but that it
was very serious and urgent and that he would appeciate a call as soon
as possible. He heard him arrange for the doctor to come the next
day, in the afternoon.

"There," Blackbird said as he hung up. "It's better to get him to
come here than to try to get her to go to him."

"She talks about her mother," Gérard said.

"I believe you," Blackbird said.

He looked up and Françoise was in the doorway, her face drawn
and greenish.

"I heard you on the telephone," she said. "I can always hear you
when you're on the telephone."

"You shouldn't be up," Blackbird said.

"Go back to bed," Gérard said, walking over to her and putting a
hand on her arm.

"The two of you," she said, laughing.

"It's not funny," Blackbird said. "The doctor's coming tomorrow."

"I heard."

"You should have seen him before this."

"There's too much to do."

"Too much to do, too much to do," Blackbird said, walking around
the kitchen, putting things away on shelves. She stood watching him.
Her hand rose to cover her mouth.

"Things can be arranged," Blackbird said. "You've got no sense.
You don't see."

"I could have gone to Mujeac to see him," she said.

"You say that," Blackbird said. "You didn't go. You should go to
bed." He went over to her in the doorway and gave her a kiss on the
cheek. "Good night," he said. She let her hand slide down his arm
and turned and went up the stairs. "You go too," Blackbird said to
Gérard. "I can close things up."

There was no preventing Françoise from helping with breakfast the
next morning, and with the big midday meal, and clearly she was
feeling better again. Sylvie, fortunately, was sound asleep when Dr.
Antaloube arrived in his large yellow convertible, a long-faced somber
man in his forties, dressed like someone in a men's clothing adver-
tisement, with a deep, smooth voice and an assumption of authority
that seemed one with the scent of his cologne. He and his elegant
wife were said to be prominent in Mujeac society. They lived in a

house that had once been a bishop's palace, and were reputed to have some of the finest antique furniture of any house in the region. Mme. Antaloube, so the rumor went, had helped to refinish the walnut floors with her own hands.

Dr. Antaloube knew the hotel both as a doctor and as a diner. He and his wife ate there occasionally, usually in the autumn. He ordered wine from Blackbird. He had been one of the doctors who had attended Blackbird's wife in her long last illness.

He spent three-quarters of an hour examining Françoise and would say nothing conclusive when he came downstairs except "There was definitely something there," whatever that meant. He spoke to Blackbird, all but ignoring Gérard, and wrote out a prescription for Françoise, for hypertension. He handed that to Gérard, addressing him as "young man." And he asked to have Françoise brought to the hospital at Mujeac on the following Thursday for a series of tests. As he left he inquired of Blackbird how a certain Cahors of the past year was turning out—the same one that M. Bright was partial to. Blackbird said it was fulfilling his expectations, and Dr. Antaloube said that he would find an opportunity to taste it soon. Some Sunday. They shook hands and each noticed that the other's hand was cold. The doctor turned, remembering at the last minute to say goodbye to Gérard, standing waiting in his apron.

"Don't worry," Dr. Antaloube said, "we're doing the right thing."

As Blackbird had expected, the tests indicated that an operation was imperative, and Dr. Antaloube managed to schedule one with unusual promptness.

Françoise insisted that she felt perfectly fine when she was not having one of her "crises," but Blackbird hung around the kitchen and he and Gérard did more and more of the work at the hotel. Adrienne, the young woman who worked during the summer as a chambermaid, was the younger sister of Pierre's wife, Martine, and she suggested that Martine might be able to come and help Gérard and Blackbird until Françoise was feeling better. Françoise had never paid much attention to Martine, who was just a few years younger than she was. She had got into the habit of ignoring Martine when they were both children, and she had taken no interest as Martine grew pretty, and married. Martine had always been quiet and exemplary and she seemed to have remained so through adolescence and marriage. Everyone spoke well of her; no one seemed to know her very well; she and Pierre seemed happy. They too had one child, a boy of six named Jean-Paul, who gave every indication of being as steady and capable as his parents. As Adrienne had predicted, Martine was perfect (and as Adrienne recommended her it was plain to Blackbird that she had other plans for herself). Once Martine was in the kitchen, Françoise liked her. It would have been hard not to. She did everything without apparent effort and with time to spare. She knew where everything was the moment she put on her apron. Blackbird had expected resentment and jealousy from Françoise and instead he saw a wave of relief and realized how tired his daughter was.

The operation was scheduled for the day before Blackbird had agreed to go again with the priest to the spring in the woods, and he realized that he would have to postpone the appointment. It made him more aware than ever of the oddity of the situation. Here they were, two grown men living in a village you could walk through from one end to the other in ten minutes, their roofs close enough together so that they could have sat on the tops of their chimneys and compared opinions of the weather, walking in the same streets and seeing the same people day after day, and yet not only did they go from moon to moon without catching sight of each other, but if by chance they had something particular to say to each other and wanted to do it without attracting attention it turned out to be like arranging an adulterous rendezvous. But to begin with, the priest, in everybody's mind, was simply the priest. That was what he was, and an end to it. A priest had the life of a priest, and this one was as poor as they came and it was known that he drank almost nothing but water, so conversations with Blackbird would not be related to the wine business. And everyone knew that Blackbird was Blackbird, who had never been one for church, and went to mass—funerals apart—not more than three times a year, at Christmas (sometimes), at Easter (sometimes), and on the Sunday nearest to his wife's saint's day (without fail). If he were seen talking to the priest it would mean that one or the other had made an exception to his regular habits, and all Aylac would soon have theories as to why they had done that. But what did they have to conceal, after all? Blackbird let it go at that. Neither of them wanted the nocturnal visits to the legendary spring to be a subject for village discussion.

Blackbird was not used to concerning himself with the neighbors' opinions of his activities. Even—as he remembered with a lingering pleasure—during the nights and days of clandestine meetings in the bushes behind the church, or beside that very spring in the old park. And so he felt altogether unsure of himself trying to devise ways of getting a message, undetected, to a priest who lived in a lane just around the corner. He considered leaving a note in the poor box. Unsigned. Cryptic. What would it say? What if it were opened by someone else? Even if that helpful person then delivered the message the priest might not understand it, and in any case would have to give some explanation, which would probably be inadequate and un-convincing and would provoke the very attention it was designed to prevent. Or the priest might not get it in time. No other form of communication occurred to Blackbird and he concluded that he would simply have to go over to the presbytery himself. The decision made him realize a number of things about his own customs and those of the village that he had not noticed before.

How seldom, for instance, he ever walked past the front of the presbytery. When he walked down the sloping square from the church it was always on the other side, the side where the grocery store with its outdoor tables, and the cobbler's shop, stood open. From there he could look across to the high wall of the presbytery, with its roofed gate, the plum trees spilling over the stones, the roof showing through them, the dark hollow of the stone porch—the *bolet*—and the lane running along the side. It had been a long time, Blackbird thought, since he had seen anyone go through that front doorway, up to that *bolet* and the front door. It was an indication of how different his hours were from the priest's. He wondered whether the priest used the front door at all. Come to that, Blackbird thought, it would be an uncommon sight in Aylac to see someone from the village knocking on someone else's door. It happened, but so rarely that the sound would bring heads to windows and to corners and to the grocer's doorway. If there was nobody home in a house in Aylac the fact was announced by a big front door key left in the lock on the outside. If there was no key and a neighbor came calling it was customary to walk into the front garden and stand there for a while. If there was a dog in the house, the dog would bark. If there was none the visitor might call at last, quietly, as though to the next room.

Of course, it was out of the question for Blackbird to go to the front door of the presbytery. Over half a century, he said to himself, threescore years since he had done that, as a child. Even then, when he had gone with his mother, had they used the front door or the back door? He might never have been up the stone front steps of the presbytery in his whole life, and the thought was like a surprising dream in which everything familiar was seen from an unknown side. Blackbird would have to go to the back door, along the lane, and he would have to do it during the hours of daylight. He tried to muster up what he knew of the priest's daily schedule. It was imprecise, but he knew the hours of the evening offices, and he decided that mid-afternoon, or late afternoon, would be the best time, and he made up his mind to drop around there on the following day.

He went over to his bachelor quarters for a nap, and lay in the bed thinking of walling up the bottles in the niche below the stairs. He considered carefully exactly what wine he would put in there, how he would use extra-long corks, double-sealed with red wax and his signet. Then he began to calculate how long it might be before his own death, and what would happen after that. He shied away from thinking of what might become of the old house and so it was not easy to have any clear idea of how long it might be before a crew came to tear it down. He saw it there just as it was, with him lying in the bed with the crocheted spread, the shutters slightly open onto the silent, sun-filled road. The men with their sledgehammers went straight to the cellar. The door was unlocked and they left it standing wide open. The light did not work. The *tonnes* were dry, cracked, with openings between the staves as wide as spaces in a pigpen. The floor was deep in dust. The men went to the niche and began to break open the cement with their hammers, very gently and carefully. It came away almost in one piece and they took out the bottles slowly, one by one, and laid them on the floor in the dust. They found Blackbird's old wineglass with the base broken off, and one of them, who looked like Robert, produced a corkscrew, neatly removed the wax from the first bottle, and began to open it. The cork was soft and came out in crumbs, and when he tipped the bottle above the glass what came out had no color. The man raised it to his lips and shook his head. Blackbird thought that he had not fallen asleep, but he woke shaking his head, and sat up, and then he shuffled, in his socks, into the kitchen and poured himself half a glass of good Cahors from four years earlier, from a summer that he stood there trying to remember. He washed his face at the kitchen sink, put on his shoes and beret, and went out.

He walked along the road on the way out of the village, making no more noise than he could help while trying to look as though he were simply going about his daily affairs. He turned at the corner where the lane branched off at a steep angle, the end of a triangular garden. The house behind his old bachelor quarters was empty. Almost no houses overlooked any part of that lane or the back of the presbytery. Next to the presbytery garden was an overgrown orchard full of tangled plum and walnut trees with a few old roses along the walls. The village was as still as though it were empty.

The gate to the presbytery garden was falling apart. The planks had been painted and painted, but in the far-distant past, and the paint had long since gone, allowing the worm-riddled boards to rot away until one could have slipped the fingers of a hand between them. To Blackbird they looked uncomfortably like the dried staves of the *tonnes* in his dream. He drew himself into the doorway in the thick wall, under the wide stone slab that roofed it, and pulled back the bolt without a sound. He decided that this must be the way the priest came and went every day, and not by the front door. The dust on the stone sill was scuffed and full of fresh footmarks, and the bolt had the shine of daily use. The gate opened easily, the hinges barely squeaking. As he stepped inside, Blackbird turned to look toward his old house, where he had just been sleeping. He could see part of the sagging roof of his bottling shed but the house itself was hidden by the empty one behind it and the big walnut tree that grew there. He closed the gate after him and looked around at the garden where he had not stood since he was a child.

He recognized it and yet it was more like a dream than the one he had just wakened from. He thought he remembered the way the old beds ran, the peach trees, the roses on the wall, the hen house, the rabbit hutches in sunlight. All overgrown now, their places filled with a dusty cloud. A patch of vegetables over near the foot of the steps looked utterly new, though probably it had been used for years. He looked up at the peaks of the roofs he could see from the garden, the few windows, all of which were shuttered. There were no birds at that hour. He went up the broken stone steps. The back door was ajar. He put his head into the darkness. "Is someone here?" he asked. Not a sound. He looked back to the garden. The elderberry bushes, the berries green, the tall dead stalks of grasses and brambles, teazels, the rusty stems of docks, all of it translucent in the sunlight despite the dust and the drying.

The door was pulled open. "Come in," the priest said.

"The arrangement," Blackbird said, stepping into the house, where, for a moment, he could see nothing. "I'm glad to have found you in."

His manner was suddenly hurried, that of a man caught up in urgent affairs.

"It's a pleasure," the priest said.

Blackbird, as his eyes grew accustomed to the shadow, was startled by the bareness of the place. He remembered a kitchen filled with all the things that kitchens normally overflowed with. Here was the cupped board floor, the long table of the same color, two old straight-backed chairs, a few plates in a rack by the sink, a loaf of bread hanging from the ceiling. A fire no bigger than a teacup was flickering silently in the big fireplace, and beside it on a bench against the wall he saw the figure of someone in black.

"How is your mother?" Blackbird asked.

"The same. She's asleep. She doesn't hear us."

Blackbird explained the alteration in his plans, and the priest said he was glad that Blackbird had not changed his mind about going to the spring at all.

"Blackbird would not do that," Blackbird said. "How is your health?"

"I'm improving," the priest said, a touch of excitement in his voice. "And I've been reading the book."

"Good. Does it talk about our spring?"

"No. But I've been wondering whether there are not any legends about it."

"There may be."

"None that you know of?"

Blackbird made a noncommittal gesture with his head.

"Maybe they've been forgotten," the priest said.

"A lot has been forgotten. Some of it I've forgotten myself."

Blackbird suggested a date in the following month, and the priest agreed. "If the weather is right," Blackbird said. "There will be a moon that night but we should be home before it rises."

The surgeon was a thin, tense young man known for his professional brilliance and his autocratic manner. He was said to be at the start of a great career, and most of his nurses, the younger ones in particular, were afraid of him.

Françoise was taken to the hospital two days before the operation, for more tests. The operation was pronounced successful and the surgeon said that the root of the trouble was not a malignancy but that it would bear watching and regular examinations. And he said that while he was about it he had performed a complete hysterectomy, since part of the reproductive organs had been removed already and the remainder served no purpose. It was probably safer without them, he said. He kept Françoise at the hospital for a week after the operation, and Gérard and Blackbird took turns going in to see her, Gérard taking Sylvie when he went. Blackbird and Gérard both went to bring her home, in the old square car with window curtains and flower vases that was kept in one of the barns behind the hotel, next to Blackbird's truck, and was seldom taken out any more except on state occasions. It pulled up before the hotel like a darkened parlor and Blackbird and Gérard both got out to help Françoise, who waved them aside.

"I'm all right," she said. "I don't need help." She walked out onto the stones of the courtyard as though they were ice. Sylvie was asleep in a basket, on a bench by the kitchen door, under the shade of a lime tree, with Jean-Paul sitting beside her. She woke up when she heard her mother's voice, and began to cry. Françoise bent to pick her up but Gérard put his arm between them and took the child from the basket.

"I'll carry her upstairs," he said. "You mustn't lift her."

"I have to," Françoise said. "It can't go on like this."

But she was obviously weak, and she let Gérard carry Sylvie, who was screaming fiercely, ahead of her. Blackbird stayed behind her and helped her to the top of the stairs, and then he went to put the old car away.

Françoise remained frail and she cried a great deal. After a few days she tried to resume some of the work in the kitchen. It was plain even to her how little strength and stamina she had. She kept having to sit down, and then tears would melt down her face. Nothing was said about Martine's going home, and Jean-Paul seemed utterly captivated by Sylvie. Martine actually seemed to be a comfort to Françoise, and Pierre too had taken to coming and having dinner at the kitchen table with Martine and Jean-Paul and Gérard and Blackbird. It went on just the same after Françoise came home, and soon was taken more or less for granted. They had a calming effect on the kitchen, Blackbird noticed, and he thought the peace was pleasant. But some kind of electricity was missing, and he would get up unpredictably, in the middle of meals, and shuffle into the dining room to see whether any of the guests were still lingering over their *digestifs*.

. . .

For several days in a row heavy clouds built up in the afternoons, and people talked of rain, how they needed it, but how they feared thunderstorms and dreaded hail, which could ruin all the harvests in a few minutes. They heard thunder in the distance but the clouds passed and no rain fell.

On the evening they had agreed upon the priest was waiting at the corner of the lane, and he and Blackbird walked out of the village without speaking. As they reached the gate to the old park Blackbird said, "How are you?"

"Converted," the priest said, and fell over the wall into the brambles. "Ow," he yelped, and he and Blackbird shook with laughter as he turned and tried to get up, only to roll and trip in the brambles. He went on trying not to say "Ow" too loudly, and they went on laughing. "I must look like one of the blessed martyrs by now," the priest said, and clapped his hand over his mouth. "Lord forgive me." He crossed himself and stood up, the laughter still welling up in him, and stumbled on into the darkness, following the sound of Blackbird snorting on the path.

"Bad boys," Blackbird said.

"I thought it was going to rain," he said a moment later, and as he said it the far-off thunder rumbled again. "The furniture," he said. "It could still rain."

They reached the edge of the stream, where the spring ran into it.

"Thousand gods, how it's gone down," Blackbird exclaimed.

"Can one still bathe?" the priest asked.

"Always," Blackbird said. "It never goes dry."

"Not dry, perhaps. But is there enough—"

"It'll be like a bathtub. At least."

"It says that's true of most of the sacred springs," the priest said. "They never run dry."

"Sacred? Is it sacred?" Blackbird asked.

"What do I know?" the priest answered. "I've read the book."

"Is it illuminating?"

"It leaves me wondering." The priest began to take off his clothes and hand them one by one to Blackbird.

"Have you noticed any effects?"

"Remarkable. I did not say miraculous. What do I know?"

"Indeed."

"But a very marked improvement. The condition I described to you—I might go so far as to say that I do not remember its having been so relieved. There have been times, these last few weeks, when it has almost gone entirely. All but a little healing up. One is tempted to hope, you know."

Blackbird groped under the bush and found the cup to give to the priest, who once again stood naked in the dark, on the pebbles. He stepped forward but felt no water. He could hear it running over the rocks and he took another step, then reached down and touched the surface. It was no more than a few inches deep there.

"I won't drown tonight," he said, and stepped farther into the stream.

"It's deeper up this way, near the spring," Blackbird said, and the priest followed the current until he came to a pool where the water was well above his knee. He reached down and filled the cup, drank, then drank another cup.

"Here is the cup," he said, handing it back to Blackbird, and sitting down. He gasped, for even after the months of summer the spring was cold. He said so.

"It's the limestone," Blackbird said. "There are rivers under us everywhere. They never freeze and they never get warm. They come up here and there to perform miracles."

"Whether one believes it or not," the priest said, lying full length in the water, his head on a stone, looking up into the black trees. "How is your daughter?"

Blackbird told him one thing, and then another, about the operation. Françoise, after all, was one of the priest's flock. She went to mass far more often than Blackbird ever did. Early mass at that, when she went. The priest lay in the water, occasionally asking a question that showed he was listening, and Blackbird found that he was telling more than he had meant to about Françoise, Dr. Antaloube, the surgeon, the hospital, how she had been before and after. He withheld the medical details. He thought it was for Françoise to decide whether or not she wanted people to know about those. It occurred to him that he must have been talking for some time.

"Aren't you cold?" he asked.

"It does me good," the priest said. "It's getting to me."

He asked about how Sylvie had been affected by the operation and Blackbird began to talk about Sylvie, about his hopes for a grandchild, and Sylvie's temperament, how she behaved, the things she seemed to know. Again he thought that he had said more than was perhaps appropriate. The priest sneezed.

"They'll catch us," the priest said, laughing.

"It's medicinal," Blackbird said, and he heard the priest stand up in the water, and reached out and gave him the towel. The priest sneezed again.

"Get dry quickly and put your clothes on," Blackbird said, and he handed the priest his clothes one by one. The priest sat down on the ground with his back to a tree. Blackbird got out his bottle and poured, and held out the cup.

"Try this," he said.

"Your health," the priest said, and drank.

"This is the finest—I can remember," he said.

"It was a good season," Blackbird said. "And it has improved."

The priest drank again. "There's sun in it," he said.

"I must verify that," Blackbird said as the priest handed him the cup, and he drank. "One can bear that," he said, "without difficulty." He filled the cup again.

"You can taste the place it came from," he said. "That particular slope."

They passed the cup back and forth.

"How many years?" the priest asked.

"It has another taste in the dark," Blackbird said. "A taste of what?" They sat tasting the wine in the dark.

"I thought, after you left, the other day," the priest said, "that you have known the presbytery much longer than I have, and that was strange."

Blackbird told him of going there as a child, with his mother, and the priest asked about Blackbird's mother, where she came from, whom she was related to, whether Sylvie looked like her, and Blackbird talked about his mother, what she had said to him when he was a child, what she remembered from before he was born, how she had been hard on his wife at first and then they had grown to like each other.

The priest asked then about Blackbird's wife, and Blackbird began to talk about her. He remembered and talked, and then stopped. Then he remembered some more and talked more about her. "I never talk about her," he said. But in a moment he was talking about her again, things she had said, her sickness, how he had known her before he went away to the war. Then the bottle was empty. Abruptly he felt that he was sitting in the dark with the women who surrounded his life—his mother, his granddaughter, his daughter, his wife. While the priest was there with only his mother, about whom he said nothing.

"You don't have a sister, do you?" he asked the priest.

"No," the priest said. Blackbird washed out the cup and put it under the bush.

"The bottle's finished," he said.

"I've been reflecting," the priest said. "My ailment has got so much better. I've been reading the book. I have something to ask you. I would like to bring my mother here. What do you think?"

"My faith," Blackbird said. But he said nothing else for a while. Then he took a deep breath.

"Does she suffer?" he asked.

"I don't know," the priest said. "All I know is that every time I ask her how she is feeling she says, 'You can't imagine how I suffer.' "

"What does she suffer from?"

"The rheumatism, of course. And the arthritis."

"I don't know that the water is recommended for those."

"She complains about her back. The doctor says she has kidney troubles."

"For that," Blackbird began, "possibly," he said, but without commitment.

"Who knows what else?" the priest said. "She doesn't tell me. There are things that I don't ask about."

"I understand," Blackbird said. "Does she go to the little—"

"Yes," the priest said, "but she has difficulties. I think that is an aggravation."

"No doubt."

"The waters, as you told me, are sovereign for that."

"Sovereign," Blackbird agreed. "*Te*," he said suddenly, and leaned forward with the bottle, holding it down in the small stream flowing from the spring until it was full of water. He put the cork back in. "Take her this," he said. "Get her to drink it. Maybe not all at once. At her age."

"Thank you," the priest said. "But I have a feeling that if we could bring her here, immerse her completely in the water, the result might be—"

"Miracles have always seemed to avoid me," Blackbird said, and at that moment they noticed that a faint silver light was entering the tops of the trees.

"Thousand gods!" Blackbird said. "It's the moon. It must be late."

"We'll be seen," the priest said.

"They'll all be asleep," Blackbird said. "Or we'll say they've been seeing visions." He laughed.

"Will you consider bringing her?" the priest asked.

"Bringing her?"

"Would it not be possible?"

"There is the danger of pneumonia."

"I doubt it."

"Have you talked to her about it?"

"I wanted to ask you first."

"She wouldn't want to come. Modesty, after all. It's very important."

"I'll ask her."

"Try her with the bottle first."

"Yes."

"The whole bottle. Over a few days."

"Yes."

"There's more where that came from."

They sat silently, with the moonlight imperceptibly sinking into the trees. Blackbird began to laugh.

"The two of us trying to get her here," he said, and the priest laughed.

"I don't know," Blackbird said. "After the bottle—" He stood up. "Well," he said. "The moon." He turned, looking at the beams of moonlight in the black lace around them. "We can go home another way," he said.

"Like the Wise Men," the priest said.

"Maybe," Blackbird said, "but I doubt it. Do you have the bottle?"

He stumbled on along the path by the stream. There was light enough for them to see where they were walking. They came to the larger lane, and a small stone bridge over the stream, which they crossed. The lane wound on through the woods.

"It's all the *domaine*," Blackbird said, "where they don't come any more." The lane curved to the left, and ahead of them beyond a tangle of moonlit bushes loomed a large building. "The house," Blackbird said, "where they used to live. There's nobody there."

"It's abandoned?"

"It's still theirs. Perlet over at Bastit is the caretaker. He comes every so often, I don't know how often. The house is respected. Up until now, at least."

"It's big."

"It's a palace," Blackbird said. "We go this way," and he turned left on a smaller lane that led past the house, around to the other side. "The carriage house is there," he said, "and the stables, and a court-yard that is full of brush now."

They went on until the house was out of sight again. Then out of the trees ahead of them a tall massive tower emerged.

"I thought I would show you this," Blackbird said. "Now be quiet."

They walked forward in silence along the path leading to the tower. The priest saw, as they approached it, that it was not round, as he had first thought, but apparently octagonal. The moonlight struck the beveled sides at different angles. The tower, as they approached it, seemed even taller than at first. They came to an arched doorway, with a single stone above it carved into shapes that the priest could not make out in the moonlight. There was a step in front of the door, a single huge slab of stone that echoed as they set foot on it. Blackbird got down on his knees and fished under the edge of the stone for something.

"Devil," he whispered, straightening, and then he felt along the door. "*Te.* Someone left the key in the lock. And never locked the door." He pressed the latch and pushed the door open with scarcely a sound, and stepped over the high threshold. Looking over Black-bird's shoulder, the priest was surprised to see that the interior was not utter darkness but that there was moonlight in there also. He followed Blackbird inside onto the floor, which glowed strangely white.

The tower looked even larger from inside. It was empty except for a single column that rose in the center like the mast of a ship, all the way, as he could see, to the black ceiling far above him, through which a few small patches of night sky appeared. The light came from several windows set in a spiral in the walls, which also were white except for rings of small black squares arranged one above the other all the way to the top. He saw that they were holes, recesses in the stone walls.

"The pigeon tower," Blackbird whispered. "They were always proud of it." They stood looking up. Blackbird pointed to the central post. "It still turns," he said. The priest saw that a spiral of spokes radiated from the post to a spiral ladder against the wall. "The ladder," Blackbird said, "is for getting the young pigeons, at night."

"Are they still taken?"

"Some of them. There are always too many. There are one or two in the vicinity who know where the key is kept." Blackbird turned and went back out and locked the door and tucked the key under the stone. "Only the seigneurs could have towers that stood by themselves," he said. "The pigeons went everywhere, into everybody's crops." He shuffled off past the tower, the priest just behind him, and they came to a high wall.

"The roses were always here," Blackbird said, and in the moonlight the priest could see the tangle of vines running along the wall, and here and there the gleam of a white rose. He heard Blackbird slide a bolt, and a gate opened in the wall. Blackbird went through and when the priest followed he saw that they were in another lane with walls on both sides, but the wall on the opposite side was only waist high, and inside it was a row of huge moonlit trees, walnuts, as he could tell even in that light, and beyond them a field of grain, white and shimmering. Blackbird turned left.

The lane followed the high wall of the old park for some distance, and then a jumble of collapsed roofs overgrown with brambles, more woods, fields, a farm, silent and dark. The priest saw then that they were on a rise, with the village below them, and as they went on he saw that the large building below a series of barns, on the right, the roofs white with moonlight, must be the hotel.

"Will we go again?" the priest asked.

"It's not long now until the grape harvest," Blackbird said. "I suppose we could go again, if you like. Wait." He stopped in the road to calculate the phases of the moon, then he told the priest a date and walked on.

"Will you think of my mother?"

"I will reflect about that," Blackbird said.

The main part of Blackbird's deliveries had been taken care of by the latter part of the summer but there were of course customers who placed or renewed orders throughout the year. Françoise grew stronger after ten days or so, and he began to plan another delivery trip to the far side of the upland. There was an Irish painter with a Dutch wife over there who had been customers of his for years. They lived in an old farmhouse with what Blackbird referred to as an estimable cellar. The building had been set into an immense ledge of the solid bedrock limestone of the upland, and the stone walls of the house seemed to be rooted in the underground cliffs and caverns of the plateau. Each time Blackbird went there with a delivery of wine he stood in the cellar with the painter, M. Riordan, and admired it:

the whole of the back wall, and part of another, was bare cliff, and the cellar kept a remarkably even temperature day and night, summer and winter. M. and Mme. Riordan had never put by the quantities or the variety that M. and Mme. Bright did, but still they had kept their house supplied with Blackbird's best wines. M. Riordan had even gone with Blackbird for several years in succession to taste the new wines at some of the growers' farms, driving over to Aylac the night before and staying at the Hotel Blackbird, getting up long before daylight the next morning and setting off, without breakfast, in the careening truck—Blackbird's driving was original by day, and in the dark it seemed to rely principally on Providence. It was important for Blackbird to have eaten nothing before the wine tasting, and all morning they went from farm cellar to farm kitchen to farm cellar to farm kitchen, tasting, before they reached the farm that Blackbird had chosen to be the last one for the day, and sat down to a table loaded with goose preserves and pork with prunes and an omelette of boletus mushrooms and *coq au vin* and goat cheese. It was called Blackbird's breakfast, and it was accompanied from the start with the wines that were the pride of the family. M. Riordan and Blackbird had not taken such a trip for some years now but each time they saw each other they agreed that they should do it again. And each time Blackbird admired the Riordan cellar he noticed that the wine rack against the rock face was not large enough for all the bottles, and that some were stacked in wooden cases piled on both sides of it. And he said to M. Riordan that he had another iron rack over at Aylac that M. Riordan should have, and M. Riordan agreed, but neither of them had done anything about it.

The day Blackbird loaded the truck for his next trip he got Pierre to help him and they hauled the wine rack out of the end of the hotel cellar, where it was leaning against the wall, and lashed it inside the truck, which it filled from top to bottom. It was a beautiful old bit of wrought iron with gates in front and a hasp and eye for a padlock, and iron vines and grape leaves twined along the top, joining in an iron heart.

"Sold?" Pierre asked.

"Not that," Blackbird said, but said nothing more.

"They don't make them like that now," Pierre said with admiration.

Blackbird usually slept well, but that night he kept waking up and thinking of the Riordans' cellar and the trip the next day. He felt as he did when he was playing cards, sometimes, and everything depended on something out of sight, though he seemed to hold it in his hand.

Françoise was there at breakfast the next morning. He decided she must be feeling better from the way she said, "I hear you're planning to do some masonry."

"Who told you that?" he said.

She turned to the stove. "Is it true?"

"I contemplated it. It's nothing of importance."

"It sounded important to me."

"I'm not sure what you're talking about."

"Rebuilding the cellar over there, that sounds important."

"Whoever you've been talking to has been exaggerating considerably." He noticed that Martine was keeping busy in the corner, with her head turned away. Robert and Matthew must have talked to Pierre, who had talked to Martine, who had talked to Françoise.

"I was considering a simple repair of no consequence, and in fact I've decided that it would serve little purpose and would not be practical or worth the trouble. Robert and Matthew would not be able to do it and I do not want to call upon the services of the good Rustafic for something so insignificant. Why do you ask?"

"No reason." Pause. "Only because I was thinking that if you were going to have some masonry done, there's some I would like to have done too."

"I've abandoned the idea."

"You don't want to hear what I was thinking."

"You'll tell me."

"The entrance out there, along the road. That old arch, and the high wall. That's the Middle Ages. The arch, we paint it every two years, it goes on rusting, the vine on it looks like a funeral. There are stones missing from the top of the wall like bad teeth."

"It's a point of view," Blackbird said.

"It's old," Françoise said with exasperation, slapping her apron with both hands. "It's mournful. People look in and what do they see? A wall. And it's dark under the trees. They can hardly see the name on the front of the hotel."

"We put out the menu in the summer. They can see that. In color. The smiling graduate from the *rossignols*, in the white chef's hat, holding a tray. Most of the people who come here know all about it without benefit of signs, and they come because they like it. You have to do with that," Blackbird said. "The food. And the service."

"What's the point of fixing up the dining room if the entrance looks like a cemetery?" Françoise persisted. "Now that you asked me."

"It has never reminded me of a cemetery," Blackbird said.

"Someday," Françoise said, "you are going to have to replace the stones along the top of the wall."

"That's nothing," Blackbird said. "I could do that myself in an afternoon with a few stones and a barrow of cement."

"Well, you haven't."

"That's certainly true."

"Why not take down that old arch, to begin with. And take off the top of the wall, down to the height of a table, say, and put some cement along the top of the wall once and for all, to keep it neat. You could put those posts in the cement, the way they do, and the wire fence attached to them, that people could see through. And just have square pillars at the entrance. With dice on top of them. You know the kind."

"Like the ones on the way in to the slaughterhouse," Blackbird said.

The kitchen was silent. Gérard was filling trays for Martine, who took them into the dining room. He was not looking at his wife or at Blackbird.

"You never want what I want," Françoise said. "You just want things the way they are."

"Well," Blackbird said, "for the moment—let's say no more about it."

He got up from the table. Sylvie began to cry, in her cot in the corner, and Françoise started over to her, passing Blackbird.

"I won't be early," Blackbird said. He kissed Françoise on both cheeks and went out the door. As he got to the truck he found that he had forgotten the old game bag with the few tools, the silver tasting cup, and the odds and ends that he usually carried with him. Gérard was alone in the kitchen and their eyes met.

"Until later," Blackbird said.

"You know—" Gérard said.

"Yes," Blackbird said. "Nobody's to blame."

"I wouldn't want that, out there," Gérard said. "But—"

"It's all right," Blackbird said. In the door he turned. "If you don't say anything about it," he said, "maybe she'll forget it. She has other things on her mind."

"Do you need any help loading the truck?"

"It's done. Thank you." Blackbird shuffled up the back lane to the barn, mumbling, "Repairs, repairs," as though he were humming a tune. He felt as though the day were ending rather than beginning. A fog drifted down the lane, an early herald of autumn, though the summer was far from over. By the time he got into the main road to Renat the mist had burned off. It was the beginning of another blazing day that would waken anxiety about thunderstorms and hail. He caught up with the tail of an army convoy on maneuvers and crawled along almost falling asleep at the wheel until they turned off just before Renat. In the main square a series of huge trucks blocked most of the thoroughfare. Sides of booths, decorated awnings, signs, Ferris wheel sections and seats, poles and machinery, were being unloaded for the fête. It's early for the fête, Blackbird thought. He thought of the traveling fêtes as events of autumn, but every year they seemed to begin sooner, gnawing at the end of summer. The music of the fête was already blaring from loudspeakers lashed up in the trees around the square, and the town was vibrating with it, deafened by it.

On the upland beyond Renat there was a place that he had always come to with pleasure, from either direction. A sharp curve where the road, following some ancient path, ran between a big old farm among veteran trees, on the east, and a duck pond in the bare stone, on the west. Coming from Renat, as you reached that corner, all of the upland to the north, and the wide valley beyond it, and the blue hills beyond the valley with their chestnut forests opened out in front of you. This morning as he came up the hill to that corner a flock of ducks was crossing the road, and a car full of strangers—you never failed to notice the Paris license plate—coming the other way. It was always a dangerous corner, but this time Blackbird saw the Paris car speed up, heading for the ducks, and run over one of them, and race on. Blackbird saw the men in the car laughing. He pulled over and stopped. There was no duck on the road. No feathers, no blood. He walked back along the road to see. The one that had been run over must have passed between the wheels unhurt. The flock had reached the pond. There was one of them at the end that looked untidy and kept walking back and forth faster than the others as though looking for something. Blackbird watched them drop one by one into the pond. The cicadas were already making the stones echo like a heat shimmer in the light. In all the years that he had passed there, Blackbird thought, he could not remember stopping. Never stood still there, hearing through the cicadas and the wind and the ducks the silence of the upland. He got back into the truck and drove on toward Aubillac with its château on the edge of the cliff over the valley.

The road dropped from the tableland, with its scrub growth of sloes and brambles, into a patch of oak woods, winding downhill. He was remembering the ducks, how often he had seen them at that corner and had thought they might get run over now that the road was paved and people drove so fast. As the road straightened out again between old walls with huge ancient walnut trees set at intervals along them, lining small fields, pastures, outcroppings of bare limestone, he began to laugh. In his mind the image of the ducks crossing the road had turned into an image of a trio composed of the priest and himself holding up the priest's ancient mother between them and staggering down the road to the iron gate of the overgrown park. The spectacle of their progress continued to entertain him as he drove along in the shade of the walnuts, and then it struck him that there they were, the three of them, stumbling down the road in broad daylight. That startled him for a moment and then he said to himself, "Why not?" and he laughed again. For he saw at once that of course there was no reason at all why they should not take the priest's old mother for a curative bath at the spring if that was her wish, and so there would be no reason at all not to go down to the spring in daylight, for what remained of the summer. It seemed like a remarkable solution, and he felt a current of exhilaration lifting him as he reached the crossroads and turned off on a smaller road to Aubillac.

As he came into the village where the road ended in a T he saw a man of fifty or so sitting astride a white motorized bicycle, a Mobylette. A man in a black new beret, a shiny black new jacket, shiny black new trousers, heavy black shoes, a large black mustache and matching eyebrows in a face that managed to be pallid with red cheeks from which black hairs waved. He was smiling at Blackbird, and Blackbird knew who he was. It was M. Gouli, who lived in the white-stuccoed two-story house behind him, with his old mother. He had a pension from his years on the railroad, and he farmed the field opposite the the store, in the corner of the T, and grew impressive leeks and artichokes. Blackbird even knew that M. Gouli had a reputation that made all the little girls who went to the school up on the hill keep a safe distance from him, and he knew that M. Gouli was referred to behind his back as "Don't move," because whatever you said to him, he would begin his answer with "Don't move," sometimes enforcing the command by seizing the other person's lapel if he could reach it. But Blackbird had no idea what M. Gouli was doing astride his white vehicle, in the middle of the road, smiling at passersby, and he nodded to him and drove on into the square to park under one of the big plane trees in front of the single café on his left. It was a building with a lane curving down the hill beside it to the cellars and an apartment looking out over the hillside, and a flight of stairs leading up in front to a stone terrace and the doorway under a red metal tube announcing that it was a tobacconist's.

On the bare level ground under the plane trees two men were playing an extremely aimless game of *boules*. Blackbird knew them too, and was rather surprised to see them there. They came from the hamlet of Nard, along the ridge, where Blackbird planned to deliver the wine rack later in the day. One of them was Micq, a widowed mason who lived by himself next to the roofer and his wife, and who worked alone and had bad lungs. A man with a long face white as a baker's, cavernous cheeks, and a deep, rasping, gentle voice. Micq was usually at work in the middle of the day, unless he was sick, or sitting outside his house in the sun recuperating from a bout of lung trouble. Silicosis. The other was Albert, his neighbor, who lived across the road from Micq with his brother Nestor and their bedridden mother. They lived, everyone agreed, on her pension, and they took care of her. "They'd better," the neighbors said. "When she goes, no more golden egg, and then what will they do for the red?" Both brothers were legendary inebriates, but Nestor, the good-looking one, was known also as a relentless hunter, stalking off into the upland with a smile and his gun, for rabbits, hares, partridges, thrushes, without regard to whether or not they were legally in season. And so he was referred to rather sardonically in the village as "the terrible Nestor" or simply "the hunter." He had held a job for a while in a slaughterhouse down across the valley, until the day when he was drunk and flew over the handlebars of his motorbike and broke his arm. But it was Albert who made everyone shake their heads. He was never sober, "the poor fellow," the neighbors said. And he was nice, they always added. And how long could he go on like that? But it was he who stayed home and washed out his mother's sheets every day of the week, sometimes twice a day, as somebody had to. The clotheslines behind their old house were always hung with sheets drying and there was usually a big cauldron out there, which had once been used for mixing food for the pigs, full of sheets soaking or boiling over a small fire.

They abandoned their game to hail Blackbird like a ship passing their island, and as he got out of the truck they stumbled over to him, Albert continuing to wave faintly until he was close enough to shake hands. Blackbird decided not to ask them what they were doing there, but after the greetings and the inquiries about health Micq said, "What a period of deaths since you were here the last time."

"It happens," Blackbird said.

"You heard about Delayre," Micq said—a declaration, not a question, as though everyone surely knew.

"The mason?"

"Delayre," Micq said. Delayre had built in dry stone without mortar, one of the last on the upland who really had the art. Delayre too had been inseparable from the bottle. He and Micq had sometimes worked together. Blackbird realized that it would be an offense not to have heard of Delayre, so he said, "How did it happen?"

"They thought it was the liver," Micq said in his voice like an echo from a vault.

"The liver," Albert repeated, raising a finger.

"The ambulance came to where you're parked. He was in bad shape. A crisis. He had not been feeling well. You remember."

"Certainly," Blackbird said. He did remember. Everyone had liked Delayre, who was slow and shy and said startling, comical things.

"But it wasn't the liver. Not just the liver," Micq said angrily, and spat.

Albert shook his head. "It was sad," he said.

"They kept making tests. They didn't know anything. He was getting worse. So they sent him by ambulance all the way to Mujeac. We had to go all that way to see him. To Mujeac."

"What did he have?"

"The pancreas."

Blackbird shook his head.

"So they operated." Micq spat again. "And I hear you can't operate that. We were there. Who else did he have? Pujol told me they should never operate when it's pancreas, but they went ahead. Once they get the knife in their hands— So he got better, they said. He said he felt better, only not very much. He said they were going to let him come home. Then he got worse and went into a coma, and that's how he died. In the coma."

"It was sad," Albert said. "It was unforgettable."

"It's already been a month," Micq said.

"I liked him," Blackbird said.

"I should think you did," Micq said. "Who didn't like him? And the month before that there was Foin, out on the upland. You liked Foin too."

"I met him right here," Blackbird said. "Years ago. At a fête."

"I should think you did," Micq said again. "Sometimes at the fêtes he used to drink, even too much."

Foin had been a legend in the neighborhood. His wife had died when they were both relatively young, and after that he had lived alone out on the bare upland above an underground spring, and had carried soil up from the cavern below and made a garden and vineyard and an orchard of pigeon-heart cherry trees, with walls around built of the superabundance of stones. There were so many stones that after he had built walls around everything he constructed a mound with a spiral track leading to the top, and he would ride his donkey up and gaze out over the upland. He had chickens, of course, and pigeons and rabbits. He would come into the village occasionally with his donkey, for some small thing he needed, and friends from the village would walk out to visit him every so often on Sundays in the spring and autumn.

"Mathilde was out that way with her goats and there was his donkey broken loose, so they led his donkey back home and that's how they found him. Sitting against the wall."

"He didn't suffer," Blackbird said.

"Just the same," Micq said.

"Yes," Blackbird said.

"Then before that, in the spring, you remember all that rain, that Mossac boy from down below there was out in those woods on the hill coming up to the château and his tractor rolled over on him just like that."

"He's dead," Albert said. "Like that."

"That's too bad," Blackbird said, turning toward the steps that led up to the café.

"That was just below the very spot where Bertrand's wife, the schoolteacher, that beautiful woman, was killed two winters ago when her car skidded on the ice and turned over."

"Dangerous place," Blackbird said. They followed him to the steps.

"We'll join you," Micq said.

Albert agreed.

"We must do that another time," Blackbird said, very seriously and confidentially. "I have some business to transact."

"I understand," Albert said. "Later."

"You have heard about Madame's mother," Micq said, but it was a question this time.

"She is—?" Blackbird asked.

"She died," Micq said, "at the beginning of the summer."

"Thank you for telling me," Blackbird said, and went on up and into the café. It was in fact Mme. Roche whom he saw first. She was watering the pots of geraniums and petunias on the terrace at the far side of the café, overlooking the valley: a handsome, dignified woman in her sixties, with large eyes set in a somber face, framed in a mass of gray curls. It seemed to Blackbird that she was always wearing a checked gingham dress and a checked gingham apron of a different pattern and color, both of which had just come from the ironing board, and he thought that it was she who was like a schoolteacher. She withheld her approval until she had heard what you had to say. But she greeted him like a friend.

"My sympathies, Mme. Roche," he said, "for the loss of your mother."

Mme. Roche thanked him. "It's good of you to come and see us," she said. "I will call my husband." She went out and leaned over the balcony and called. "Raymond. Come."

And they exchanged politenesses until a tall, heavily built handsome man with a round face, gray hair, and a gray Gaulish mustache appeared in the door.

"*Te*," he said, and stepped forward to take Blackbird's hand. "A pleasure." He too was a figure of considerable presence and authority. He was the most respected carpenter in those parts, but was more or less retired, leaving the business to his son, who kept expanding it on the far side of the village, mechanizing it, breaking down the walls of the original carpentry shop in its old house on a back lane. M. Roche had inherited land all along the ridge, in several hamlets, and his wife had brought more in her dowry. There were savings that both families had earned over several generations from the sale of wool and walnuts and walnut wood. M. Roche was still planting and grafting walnut trees and he had taken Blackbird once to see some young ones that he had planted in the old manner, with a pit full of wool dust from the carding gin under the roots.

"The *place* is busy today," Blackbird said, and M. Roche laughed.
"It's too bad," Mme. Roche said, shaking her head. "Those boys."
"Did they tell you what they're doing?" M. Roche asked.
"I didn't inquire."
"Waiting for a woman." M. Roche laughed. Mme. Roche turned away.

"They are making no secret about it," M. Roche said. "They gave us the details this morning. Gouli is in on it too. Their intentions— I suppose you might say they are honorable. At least they are not frivolous. As they tell it."

"That's something," Blackbird said. "And they have sent for her —out of a catalogue?"

"Albert and Nestor sold a field over in Nard. Lovely field. It was a pity. Going to brambles. They sold it to Pujol and they were drinking up the price of it at a terrible rate. Nestor fell off his motorbike coming over to Aubillac to buy red, and he has no license to drive, besides. He got all scraped up but he didn't break anything this time, fortunately. Albert doesn't have a license either, but he rode over on the same errand one day and rode into the ditch on the way home—over there past the crossroads where the ditch is six feet deep. Everybody was warning them about what they were doing. Albert was tired of boiling sheets and cooking. They decided they would use some of the money to get a woman. Micq was lonely and hates his own cooking and doesn't like looking after himself, and he said he would contribute some of his savings. He has been getting bigger pension payments lately, since his health has got worse, so he gave them some money. He seems to have some idea that having a woman established over there would make them all more respectable. They were talking to Gouli about it, and Gouli, you know—well."

"Raymond," Mme. Roche said, her tone indicating that he was saying considerably more than was decorous.

"Blackbird is a friend," M. Roche said. "You know, Gouli has never married."

Blackbird nodded judiciously.

"For a long time no one knew what his ideas on the subject were. Then for several years he lost his heart to Céleste—you remember Céleste, who lost her husband and serves meals in the little house up there around the corner, the alley."

"I remember her cassoulet."

"He bowed low when he saw her. He went early to her bistro and sat alone watching her, smiling at her. Apparently he never spoke to her of his ambitions but he began to tell people hereabouts that they were going to be married."

"Raymond," Mme. Roche said.

"It's not a secret," M. Roche said. And he went on: "Céleste said nothing for a while, and then when people began to ask her about it she laughed at the idea. She laughed at it, and everybody else began to laugh at it. Gouli was not pleased. That was last winter. One day a piece of wood exploded in her stove while people were eating there. Pieces of the stove were broken. Things flew around the room. Somebody could have been killed. While they were clearing up afterward and trying to find out how it had happened Céleste started looking through the firewood and she found about twenty pieces that had holes bored in them and shotgun shells hidden inside."

Blackbird laughed. "That's serious," he said. Raymond smiled.

"There was no proof who did it, you understand. It's true that Gouli had been seen haunting the alley outside Céleste's. Everybody had assumed he was trying to catch a glimpse of his true love. Nobody wanted to have the police mixed up in it, in the village. Céleste took matters into her own hands, as they say. She said it had gone too far and that this could ruin her business. Who would come to eat there if they thought the stove might blow up when they were in the middle of their cassoulet?"

"People like entertainment," Blackbird said. "Risk. So I hear."

"But not so close," Raymond said. "She'd had enough, she said, and she walked across the square with a piece of the plugged firewood in her hand, this big, and she banged on Gouli's door with it so the whole village could hear it. Nobody answered, so she stood there with the whole world listening by then, and she told him he was several kinds of disagreeable things, and that she had thought so since he had been a schoolboy without the sense to wipe his nose, and that if she ever caught him within sight of her front door again she'd take the firewood to him until he wished he had never thought of it, and then she said a few more things about his general character and behavior and walked home."

Blackbird saw that Mme. Roche was smiling in spite of herself.

"For the rest of the winter," Raymond said, "Céleste went over with her wheelbarrow and helped herself to his woodpile, and he never showed his face, poor fellow. And there they were, both of them, at the funerals, never looking at each other."

"One can think about other things," Mme. Roche said, from the far side of the room, where she was piling folded linen on a table.

"So when the weather warmed up Gouli got his white Mobylette and new beret and jacket and pants and started wandering all over the countryside looking for women. That's what he said. And he said he had some money, and so he was not a bad catch. Who knows where he went? They saw him here, they saw him there. By the fence at the new swimming pool in Saint-Ricque, at the bathing beach on the river, at all the fairs. He went down to the valleys at night, to the movies. And then when Albert and Nestor told him about their plan he said he would put his bit into the hat, since he was looking for a woman too. He was buying a share."

"What do you think of that?" Mme. Roche asked Blackbird.

"It's not my plan," Blackbird said. "What will *she* think of it?"

"Nestor came over yesterday and called up Frizat, in Saint-Ricque, you know. The garage where they have the taxi. They agreed on a price to take Nestor to Mujeac for the day. The price sounded very high to me, but Nestor said it was important. It was worth it. An investment, he told me. Something that would change the rest of their lives. If they divided it four ways, he said, it was reasonable. He had to agree to pay for Frizat's noon meal at Babette's in Mujeac, but he kept saying that it was important. So this morning Nestor and Albert and Micq and Gouli, all the shareholders, were here when it was hardly daylight. Nestor looked very fine. As though he were going to a funeral or a wedding. Best beret. His good corduroy. Everything. And he had a bow tie on like a Christmas present. Red. He's a fine-looking man, Nestor."

"It's very sad what that family has come to," Mme. Roche said. "Catherine over there alone in bed while the boys get up to things like this."

"It's the fair in Mujeac today," Blackbird said.

"Nestor decided that the fair day was the best day to go. He has a list of addresses that he's copied out of the personal advertisements in the newspapers and heaven knows what magazines. He seems to have been doing his homework for some time."

"The radio this morning said that there might be storms and rain over on that side of the upland," Blackbird said.

"I heard that," Raymond said.

"They're going to wait here all day?"

"So it seems," Mme. Roche said.

"Oh no," Raymond said. "Frizat said he had to be back by the end of the afternoon. Before dark. I imagine he'll have a good meal at Babette's, perhaps a little nap somewhere, and then be ready to start home so that he won't be too late."

"And what will Nestor do?"

"He had his addresses in some kind of order," Raymond said. "Beyond that, it's hard to guess."

The heavy click of *boules* reached them from the *place*.

"It's a casino over here today," Blackbird said. "I want to hear what happens, when somebody comes over near us. I brought you your *pièce* of the Minervois and the little *fût* of Cahors."

"It's the day for wine," Mme. Roche said. "Look." A new tan Peugeot station wagon was drawing slowly through the middle of the game of *boules*. It came to a stop facing Blackbird's truck.

"Mme. Lesage," Raymond said. Mme. Lesage was a wine merchant from Bordeaux, an attractive, expensively dressed widow in early middle age whose pretty daughter had married into one of the old monied families of Saint-Ricque. She traveled, as the phrase went, in Saint-Emilion, and the wines with which she regaled the guests at the wedding banquet had become legendary. She did the same for social functions at her son-in-law's large ancient house in town, and before long she had added a considerable local clientele to her list, and it continued to grow, like a rumor. She was at once condescending and amiable, extremely efficient, reliable and reasonable, and within a few years many of the older restaurants and cafés of the region had become regular customers of hers. And since she was willing to take orders as small as a dozen bottles or so, a surprising number of rural households had also begun to deal with her for the bottles they needed to bring out on special occasions. Her prices were far better than those in the store, and her wines were exceptional. The trade had been in her husband's family for generations, and her relations with her sources had been part of it. And she was evidently tireless. Every year she sent her customers a card at least once, announcing a visit, within certain dates, and came by with her current list of wines and prices, which she discussed in detail with her customers, and they placed their orders for that season.

"She said she'd be in the region," Mme. Roche said. "She sent the card." Mme. Roche lifted it out of the rack among the bottles on the bar. The car door opened and Mme. Lesage emerged as though she were stepping onto a stage. A beige suit, her fair hair piled elegantly on top of her head, a gold chain around her neck, medium high heels. She had brought the city with her. She cast an eye over Blackbird's truck as she walked past it, while Albert and Micq stared. As her gaze swept the *place* and rested on them for a moment Albert took off his beret and mumbled. Micq nodded. She nodded, from as far away as the winter, dropped her eyelids, and walked to the foot of the stone steps and up to the café entrance and the terrace with its trellis of vines, the leaves fading yellow with the end of summer.

"*Bonjour,*" she sang to no one in particular from the doorsill. Her voice was pitched high, as for a small theater. "Ah, Mme. Roche," she said, and held out a hand with two topaz rings on it. Then M. Roche. And then she saw Blackbird, who had not moved, standing with his feet set squarely apart and his head bowed forward slightly, watching her from under his brows.

"Ah, M. Blackbird," she said, "an unexpected pleasure. Are you also in the region?"

"I'm circulating," Blackbird said.

"Are you still dealing in the wines of the place?"

"It keeps me entertained."

"Excellent."

"I was just on my way," Blackbird said.

"Don't let me hurry you."

"It's unavoidable," Blackbird said. He turned to M. Roche. "I'll come by with the material later," he said. "It's not the moment." And he shook hands with them all and ducked out the door.

"How lucky to have seen you," Mme. Lesage said as he went, and then turned to M. and Mme. Roche, and he heard her ask, "You received my card?"

Albert and Micq had moved close to the foot of the steps, almost within earshot.

"Your colleague," Micq said.

"She travels in remarkable wines," Blackbird said, "one has to say." He considered suggesting to them that they must be thirsty, after their game, and must be ready for a bit of refreshment up in the café, but he thought better of it. Besides, they probably had a bottle leaning against a tree somewhere. He got into the truck. They stood watching him and he waved. They went on waving as he circled the *place* and left the way he had come. M. Gouli was still there astride his white Mobylette, at the intersection, watching the road. Blackbird drove along the ridge toward the hamlet of Nard, where the Irish painter and his Dutch wife lived, for whom Blackbird had brought the wine rack.

The double row of walnut trees stretched ahead of him with the gray lichened limestone wall linking them. A small field shaped like a half moon on his right had larger trees on the far side, along the route of the older road that was now a cow path with oak woods beyond it. Straight ahead between the trees he could see empty sky above the valley.

The hamlet lay like a fabric draped along the ridge and a little way down toward the river winding far below. All the houses and barns were of indeterminate age, in a place where the architecture had not changed essentially in the course of five hundred years, and they were set into turns and dips in the land so that they looked as though they had grown out of it, especially the barns, whose steep roofs swept down to eaves that at one end almost touched the ground.

It was close to noon. The cows were all in the barns in the heat of the day, and there was no one in the fields, no one in sight as Blackbird drove past the oak woods and corn fields. He turned in at the first gate, where a pair of stone barns faced the road, parked on the dry grass under a walnut tree, and walked on toward the house. Over the wall to his left he could see the garden, the yellowing leaves of cherry trees, a row of tall dry hollyhocks near the garden gate. He walked down the slope toward the house. The building on his right, with a collapsing stone ramp to a small upper door and a pigeon loft, enclosed the oven where the whole village had once baked its bread. Now, Blackbird knew, it was M. Riordan's studio. Its door faced the house, whose heavy wooden shutters were closed against the sun. There were stone troughs of petunias on either side of the faded blue front door, which opened as Blackbird approached, and Mme. Riordan came out.

She was a short, ample woman of fifty or so, in a none too clean brown-checked gingham dress which she had tucked up at all the hems in one way or another. It was a hot day. Her skirt was pinned up at the bottom, the shoulders were turned in, the neckline had been stuffed in on itself down to the top of her much-soiled blue apron. She was shielding her eyes from the glare of the sunlight and did not see Blackbird at first, and when she did she gave a start, said "Oh," and put her hand over her mouth. Then she peered forward, squinting, and fishing in her apron pocket.

"Who is it?" she asked, in French, and pulled out a pair of dark glasses with broad rims and put them on.

"Myself," Blackbird said.

"Blackbird!" she cried. He had forgotten what a loud voice she had. She laughed. "I didn't hear anyone. I was coming out to get something from the barn, and you surprised me."

"Where's your dog?" Blackbird asked.

"You remember old Pompom. He wasn't really ours. He adopted us. He came down from the village when he was too old and rheumatic to go with the cows anymore, and we took to feeding him, so he stayed."

"Right there," Blackbird said, pointing to the smooth stone in front of the door.

"He liked the sun. He was cold."

"He growled."

"He growled at everybody. The mailman was always sure Pompom was going to bite him. He'd get up and follow the mailman to the gate, growling at his heels. Everybody said, 'He growls, he's a terrible fighter, he bites.' They say he fought with all the dogs in the village when he was younger, and apparently he bit quite a few people. A bad character, poor Pompom. He had no teeth left. He looked like a pile of straw lying there. We miss him. Come in out of the heat. I saw you without my glasses and I thought it was somebody from the electric company."

She pushed open the door behind her, gave Blackbird a kiss on both cheeks, and went in ahead of him.

"You were expecting them?"

"They never come when I'm expecting them. Only when I'm not."

"What do they come for?" Blackbird asked, following her in.

"Nothing good. I'm very happy it was you."

Inside the closed shutters the casement windows were propped open to let the air into the large room, made of two rooms of the old farmhouse. It was dark and cool, and on the far side of the room a window, at the end of a stone arch, and a glass door stood open. Through them he could see the noon sky, the tops of plum and walnut trees, and the valley far away.

"I've thought of you," Blackbird said.

"I'm happy to hear it."

"I told you I'd come over."

"We didn't doubt it. Let me get you something. You must be thirsty."

"Don't go to any trouble," Blackbird said. "I won't be long."

"Blackbird wine? Or something cool?"

"A little Pernod," Blackbird said, to see whether she had it, "and water."

"Ah. I think there may be some."

"Or anything."

She opened the door of an old chest and rummaged through a crowd of bottles.

"M. Riordan is here?"

"Out in the oven. He's working. Ah, here it is." She brought out a dusty bottle of Pernod with approximately three inches left in it. Blackbird followed her to the kitchen. Everything in the house was old, like the things he had seen as a child: the long polished farmhouse table, the straw-bottomed armchairs, the cupboards, the jugs on the mantelpieces. And everything was a jumble. A table at the shuttered windows piled with papers, and in the kitchen a wall hung with hats and old clothes on hooks, racks of old dishes with pictures and writing on them, the sink jammed with unwashed dishes.

"I remembered your keg," Blackbird said. "It's in the truck. And I have something else for you."

As he took the glass from her he looked at her over the rim as though he were flirting.

"Your health, madame," he said.

"I'll call my husband," she said, and slipped out past him to the front door. "He'll want to see you right away."

Blackbird stood looking at the assembly of things in the long room. It was like an antique dealer's, he thought, except that the things in the house had not been fixed and polished the way they would be in a shop, but were just the way they would be in an old house, a bit dingy and dusty. He could not imagine what some of the things were. Wooden dishes in odd shapes. Mason's sieves overflowing with drying flower petals. China statues of cows. A curtain made of the hand-kerchiefs they used to issue in the army, with instructions for packing your kit, for pitching your tent, for assembling your rifle. He heard doors closing and their voices in a foreign language and the door opened again.

M. Riordan was taller than Blackbird, and had always looked young to him in a way, he decided, that northern people had of continuing to look young when you knew they must be older. M. Riordan was thin and his skin was dark from the sun. Blackbird knew that he worked in the garden. He talked with Gérard about the hotel garden when he came to Aylac. He was wearing very old, torn farm clothes covered with splashes of paint, and was wiping his hands on a rag as he came in, smelling of paint and turpentine, and greeting Blackbird with obvious pleasure.

"We're lucky, Blackbird. We've been talking of coming over to see you, to fetch the keg, and here you are. How have you been?"

They exchanged news. Madame had been to Amsterdam for a few weeks. M. Riordan had been working hard all summer.

"He has a show in Paris in the autumn," Mme. Riordan said, "and one in London in the spring."

"You'll stay and eat with us," M. Riordan said.

"No, no. I hesitated to come by so near to noon and disturb you at your meal."

"No disturbance."

"We do everything at barbaric hours," Mme. Riordan said. "Go to bed too late, get up too late, eat too late. I had not even begun the meal. I don't know whether you will like what we—"

"Don't trouble yourself," Blackbird said. "I was on my way over to have a trout at Mireille's place down on the river. I just thought I would stop on the way and drop off your things."

"It's all decided," M. Riordan said. "We don't get to see you very often, and we're always eating at your table and you never eat here. It's your turn."

Mme. Riordan said something to her husband in another language.

"Of course he'll eat what we do. It's French cooking, after all."

Mme. Riordan went into a speech about being embarrassed to serve French food to someone who was the proprietor of the kitchen at the Hotel Blackbird. Blackbird said tut to all that, and suggested that they unload the keg before they ate. Mme. Riordan had put a lot of Pernod in the glass. He asked for some more water to add to it and all three of them went into the kitchen, where M. Riordan filled Blackbird's glass at the faucet and filled another for himself.

"Still rainwater," he said. "They brought the public water to the village a year ago but we're keeping the cistern. We use the new water for the garden."

"Wise," Blackbird said. "The things they put into the water. Bleach. We've kept the cistern over at the hotel too, for drinking."

The sound of a distant train whistle floated up from the valley.

"It's twelve-thirty," Mme. Riordan said. "That's the train on the bridge at Gorse. When you hear it, the wind is from the north. Fair weather."

"Supposed to rain south of here," Blackbird said. "If you believe the radio."

M. Riordan and Blackbird went up to the truck and drove out onto the road to the lane between the house and the garden, and down to the lower gate that led to the cellar door. M. Riordan opened it with a big key and they worked the keg out of the truck and Blackbird rolled it down over the parched grass to the doorsill, and over it, and stood in the outer cellar admiring the place, as usual. The ceiling was at least fifteen feet above the beaten earth of the floor, and the center posts and the beams had not been sawn but trimmed with an adze. It was cool inside, and it seemed to Blackbird that the cellar should house something more noble than trunks and stacks of old furniture and doorless cupboards full of jars of preserves.

M. Riordan opened the door to the inner cellar, and they rolled the keg in. It was still cooler in there, and when they had stood facing each other over the keg, with their legs apart, and then bowed until the tops of their heads touched, and heaved it up together into one of the cradles on top of an old chest, Blackbird looked around. He disapproved of the electric pump for the water tank, in one corner, but on the other side of the cellar that wall of solid rock, a section of the ridge itself, always struck him as a remarkable gift. The one wine rack was fastened to the rock by pieces of iron and bolts cemented into clefts in the rock. The rack was almost full and there were boxes of wine stacked on the floor beside it—some of them, as he could see, from Mme. Lesage. Many of the bottles in the rack had been sealed with wax, and must have been filled, he knew, there in the cellar. Blackbird noted the decrepit corking machine with one cast-iron leg broken and splinted with wood, and the iron hedgehog with its tiers of empty bottles. Much of the wine that had been bottled there was wine he had brought.

"You need another rack," Blackbird said, as he had on each visit for the past few years.

"Do you still have the one you were going to sell?" M. Riordan asked.

"It's in the truck," Blackbird said, and he could see from M. Riordan's face how pleased he was with the news.

"We haven't said anything about money," M. Riordan said.

"We'll come to an agreement about that without any trouble," Blackbird said. "Let's bring it in."

So they left both cellar doors open and went out into the heat and wrestled the rack with its wrought-iron grapevine and its locking gates out into the lane. It was heavy for two of them and M. Riordan fetched pieces of firewood to use as rollers, and they sweated down the incline holding it upright, moving the rollers ahead of it one by one.

"It's a hot day for this," M. Riordan said. Blackbird grunted. They got to the cellar and over the sill and stopped for a breather.

"We should have done this last winter." M. Riordan laughed.

"In the mud?" Blackbird asked. "It's not far." As they started again they heard Mme. Riordan call, "Soup!"

"We'll need just a little longer," M. Riordan called up. "As soon as we can."

"We can leave it," Blackbird said.

"We're almost there," M. Riordan said. "You won't want to come back to this after you've eaten. And I could never move it by myself."

They rolled it the rest of the way, through the second door and across the inner cellar, and leaned it against the cliff-face wall, in its place next to the other rack.

"There," Blackbird said.

"It's perfect," M. Riordan said. "It's much more beautiful than the other one. I never saw it, you know. It was back there in the dark. And you didn't tell me."

"It's beautiful," Blackbird agreed.

M. Riordan admired the vines and the iron heart.

"It's just the beginning," Blackbird said. "You need more racks along this wall to the side, and the *tonnes* along there."

M. Riordan laughed. "There was one *tonne* in here when I bought the house," he said, "all those years ago. It was dried out, but the former owner said that it was the one thing in the house he wanted to keep."

"There are others to be found," Blackbird said.

"For the moment," M. Riordan said, "I don't need anything so ambitious. But now you must tell me what I owe you."

"For the wine," Blackbird said, "here is the bill, all made out." He brought his notebook out of the pocket in the bib of his overalls and drew a page out of it, which he handed over.

"I'll write you the check upstairs," M. Riordan said.

"As for the price of the rack—" Blackbird began.

"I'm sure you won't ask enough," M. Riordan said.

"I've decided that it's a present."

M. Riordan was clearly startled, and he protested, but Blackbird would not discuss the matter.

"We'll have something of yours to celebrate its arrival," M. Riordan said finally, and went to the full rack, where they decided on the appropriate vintage. M. Riordan drew out a dusty bottle, cradled it gently, and started for the door.

"You can take the truck on down the lane and around through the village, if you remember the way, and leave it in the shade up where you had it before. I'll go on up and open the bottle."

Blackbird had not moved. "You really have all the space you need," he said.

"It's true," M. Riordan said, "though one always manages to fill it up with this and that."

"I mean, when you take over Blackbird's wine business," Blackbird said.

"Me?" he said. "I couldn't do it."

"You'd do it very well."

"I'm a foreigner."

"I know about that. It's been done."

"And I'm a painter."

"That doesn't matter."

"And I don't know anything."

"You have the nose for it. You have the taste for it. It interests you. You know more than you say. And you will ride with Blackbird and learn the rest in no time."

"And I have no capital."

"We can talk about that."

"I'm honored that you would think of me—"

"Yes, yes," Blackbird interrupted him, thinking that he had heard that before.

There was a long pause. They were both still breathing heavily.

"Let's go up," M. Riordan said, starting for the door.

"Oh, how beautiful," Mme. Riordan said, appearing in the doorway. M. Riordan stopped.

"Isn't it?" he said. She went over to the rack and exclaimed over the iron vines and the heart.

"It's a present from Blackbird," M. Riordan said.

It was her turn to be surprised and she thanked Blackbird effusively.

M. Riordan said, "I'm on the way up to uncork the bottle," and they filed out into the daylight at the foot of the stone stairs, and M. Riordan locked the door as Blackbird, with his rocking gait, climbed to the truck in the lane.

He drove down to the foot of the village and the stone cross on the wall at the corner, and turned slowly in the narrow opening between the walls, feeling a weight pressing him down, the heat of noon, the silence of the village, the distance of the tangles of brambles and dead plum branches hanging over the lane. The truck echoed as he climbed to the road through the village, turned left toward Aubillac, and the Riordans' gate on the way, and stopped once more under the walnut tree. He walked down to the house, thinking of nothing at all, and knocked at the door.

When it opened he saw that Mme. Riordan had put on some makeup and straightened her clothes.

"Just in time," she said. *"A table."*

Blackbird removed his beret as he sat down, and put it on the bench beside him. Mme. Riordan had made good use of the time it had taken him to unload the wine and the rack. The fish soup must have been made earlier but she appeared to have been improving upon it, and then there was *pâté de lièvre truffé* and the wine brought up from the cellar. They talked about the truffle fair in Mujeac, Gérard and the garden, and Blackbird returned to his disappointment with his son-in-law, the drinker of milk.

"It ruined Mendès-France," he said. "You can't have a French head of state who's a milk drinker. It's not reasonable."

M. Riordan filled his glass.

"The rack, and its new home, and its future," Blackbird said, raising the wine before him and rolling the words as though he were tasting them. He allowed a long pause after they had joined in the toast, and fixed each of them for a moment with his flattened, smoky blue eyes, before he took a deep breath and said, *"Enfin,"* and let the conversation drift away to mutual friends, the wool merchant in Renat, the retired English general across the valley, and M. Riordan, watching Blackbird's glass, got up while continuing to talk and fetched another bottle from the cupboard by the kitchen door, and opened it. It was of the same vintage as the first, and as Blackbird set down his glass, after fairly savoring it and nodding, he said, "You will have that one to depend on."

"I'm glad to know that," Mme. Riordan said.

"You know how fond we are of this one," M. Riordan mumbled.

"I mean as a line, every year."

"How lucky for us," Mme. Riordan said.

How polite they were being, Blackbird noticed. And how foreign their politeness sounded to him as he drank the familiar wine and remembered the first taste of it, when it was still new.

"I have spoken to your husband," he said to Mme. Riordan over the edge of the glass after he had drunk more than half of it, "about the succession. I have told him that in view of the composition of my family, the ideas of my daughter and of my son-in-law, for example, I would be happy if your husband were to succeed me in the wine business. To follow Blackbird."

Again Mme. Riordan's hand flew to her mouth and she stared at him. Naturally she would be surprised, he thought.

"Yes," M. Riordan said, and his enthusiasm sounded like a cracked glass. "Blackbird just told me. It's a great surprise. I can't get used to the idea."

"One gets used to it quite easily," Blackbird said. "I never considered anything else." He finished his glass.

"That's how I am too," M. Riordan said, filling it, "but I'm a painter."

"You'll have time for your painting, most of the year. You'll be taken up in the autumn, for a while, at the time of the new wine. And again in the spring, transferring the wine to its respective lodgings. But much of the year you are free to conduct your affairs according to your own disposition. It's an aspect of the profession that I have always appreciated."

Blackbird was sampling the cheeses, and he allowed the subject to stray to a discussion of cheese in the southwest from Saint-Nectaire to Roquefort. He was an amateur of Roquefort and for years had made an annual pilgrimage to the region.

"They too understand about cellars," he said, with a knowing glance at M. Riordan. "And they have been concerned about continuity. The young are not there."

M. Riordan described what he had seen of the broad stone-paved catchment basins near Roquefort, where the sheep drank.

"At one time they did," Blackbird said. "Now I believe they have —conveniences." He took a deep breath. "We should go to the wine tasting again, this autumn, so that you can get to know your suppliers."

"I'll have to be in Paris at that very time," M. Riordan said.

"He has a show," Mme. Riordan said. "Of his paintings. He's working on the paintings now. He's been working very hard on them all this year."

"When do you have to go up there?" Blackbird asked M. Riordan.

"October," Mme. Riordan said.

"November," M. Riordan said. "Late October I have to go up, in fact, to get the show ready for November."

"We can pick you up when you come back."

"Blackbird," M. Riordan said, filling Blackbird's glass carefully, "I don't think it would be possible for me to do that. You must not count on me to take over from you." He raised his glass. "The house of Blackbird," he said, standing, and Mme. Riordan also stood, and repeated the toast. Blackbird got to his feet, and drank when they had finished. He looked up into the gray dust lying in the adze marks along the sooty beams, the cobwebs billowing slightly in a current he did not feel. He heard M. Riordan mumble something about a bottle and slip out the door behind him, and Mme. Riordan clattering plates together and departing to the kitchen, and the knocking of the old clock leaning against the wall.

"It's lucky I made these yesterday. I had to use up the cream," Mme. Riordan said, coming back in with plates of *crème caramel* and a bowl of wafers and another of walnuts. Blackbird was not listening. He felt, as he put it to himself, much older than he really was, standing there in the middle of the room. He had not always been so polite, he thought. Once he had been known for other things, and that was not so long ago either. As Mme. Riordan set down the plate of *crème caramel* in front of him he stared quite openly into the low-cut front of her dress and the deep fold displayed before him, and was seized with an impulse to reach out and thrust his fingers, indeed his whole hand, down between her breasts. Then he looked up and caught her eye, and the presence of the Bad Blackbird whom many remembered withered in a rush of heat like that of the day outside, as the door opened and M. Riordan came in, and he heard the sound of yet another bottle being opened, and became aware that his face was caught in an uncomfortable smile. He heard that nobody was saying anything.

"Did you get much hay over here?" he asked M. Riordan. He would have to go back over to Aubillac, he remembered, and deliver the barrel, and he thought of Mme. Lesage and felt tired.

"It wasn't as bad as we feared it would be," M. Riordan said. "Our neighbor keeps his cows in that first barn and their hay on the upper floor. They've got that about two-thirds full and that will be enough. But it doesn't look as though there will be much more hay this summer."

"Year for the wine, no year for the hay," Blackbird said, repeating the proverb in patois, as though he were speaking in a dream. The mention of the hay had made him aware that he longed for a nap.

"I must be going," he said.

"You'll stay for coffee, surely," Mme. Riordan said. "No need to rush off in the heat of the day."

Blackbird nodded and began to eat his *crème caramel* absentmindedly. "I have deliveries still to make," he said, addressing the far side of the room.

He saw Mme. Riordan go out again, and he smelled coffee, and talked with M. Riordan of the renovations at the hotel, the danger of storms at this time of year, and of hailstorms above all, and when Mme. Riordan brought in the coffee he had two cups and then stood up.

"Must you really leave in this heat?" M. Riordan asked. "Why not stay for a nap?"

"Thank you," Blackbird said, shaking his hand, trying not to think of the shade inside the barn, with a hen slipping through the sunbeam at the cat door. M. Riordan laid a check before him on the table and Blackbird put it into the notebook inside the pocket of his overalls and turned toward the door. They both walked up to the truck with him and said goodbye affectionately and Mme. Riordan kissed him on both cheeks.

On the way back to Aubillac he drove up the lane to the Peyres' sheep barn, into the shade out of sight of the road, and had a nap after all. The afternoon was well advanced and somewhat cooler by the time he got to the café in Aubillac to deliver his wine there.

M. Gouli had abandoned his post at the intersection, but as Blackbird drove into the square he saw the white motorbike leaning against a tree, and over near a wall Albert and Micq sitting on a stone bench, elbows on their knees, M. Gouli standing beyond them with arms folded, gazing toward the valley. They looked up as Blackbird parked the truck, but at once sank back to their meditations. Blackbird walked to the steps below the café and M. Roche came around the corner of the building below him.

"You've come back," he said.

"I'll bring the truck over," Blackbird said, and went back to do it, keeping as far as possible from the group on the bench. He and M. Roche unloaded the barrel on a ramp, rolled it into the cellar, and went up into the café to do the paperwork.

"The hunter has not returned, it seems," Blackbird said. M. Roche smiled.

"My wife won't serve them anything to drink," he said, "and Annette, in the store, won't sell them anything either. She says she won't have them walk out of the store with a bottle and start drinking it before they're out of sight. They are not feeling happy."

"No further news."

"They told me a little more about the plan. They have all been collecting advertisements for months. They have a number of them by heart, if you are interested."

"I must be going," Blackbird said. "It's late."

"You'll have one before you go."

"Another time," Blackbird said. At that point they heard a car drive into the square and stop.

"Frizat," M. Roche said. "The taxi." They both hurried to the door to look out, and as they did so Blackbird could see, in the next room, Mme. Roche looking out of the window. The car door opened and Nestor got out. He looked as though he had been rescued from drowning. His clothes hung on him like wilted leaves and he swayed on his feet. Micq and Albert had risen from their bench and they and Gouli were closing in on the taxi.

"That's it," M. Frizat said, with commercial cheerfulness, to the company in general. "Good evening, gentlemen." The taxi started forward. But Albert was blocking the way, looking straight into the car.

"Where is she?" Micq asked.

"Where is she?" Albert repeated.

"Exactly what I want to know," M. Gouli said, holding up his hand. "Not so fast."

"Gentlemen," M. Frizat said, "there is nothing of yours in my taxi."

"Where is she?" Micq asked again.

"As you see, I have no other passengers," M. Frizat said.

"What happened to her?" Albert asked, with desperation in his voice.

"Gentlemen, I agreed to take this gentleman to Mujeac for the day and return. That's all, and I have done what I agreed to do."

Albert began to drum on the car radiator with his fist and M. Frizat shouted, "Stop that. Get out of my way."

"Where is she?" Albert called, near tears.

"Where is she?" Micq asked Nestor, who was standing watching the scene as though he had just stumbled upon it.

"It rained," Nestor said. "It rained." He mimed the rain with his hands.

"It didn't rain," Micq said. "Not a drop."

"It rained," Nestor said.

"Where is she?" Albert asked, moving around the car. M. Frizat seized the moment and put his foot down on the accelerator, lurching across the square leaving marks in the gravel, and disappearing around the corner on the road to the valley.

"He must have got Nestor to pay him the whole thing in advance," M. Roche said to Blackbird. "They're lucky he waited at all."

"Look at me," Nestor said, gazing down at his swamp of clothes.

Micq seized him by the soaked corduroy lapels. "What did you do with her?" he asked.

"She wouldn't come," Nestor said.

"Why not?" M. Gouli asked.

"I tried," Nestor said.

"Which one?" M. Gouli asked.

"Not the first one."

"Not the first one," Albert said sadly.

"She wasn't there."

"And the others?" Micq asked.

"Come back later," one said. She was busy. "Come back later. But I found one—" Nestor smiled. "But I couldn't stay. And she—she couldn't come. She said her husband was coming back. It was raining then."

"It never rained."

"It rained," Nestor said. "I got lost. I don't know that place."

"Where is she?" Albert said again, drumming the air with his fist.

"She wouldn't come," Nestor said. "She said she couldn't come."

"What did you tell her?" Micq asked.

"I told her," Nestor said, "everything."

"The money?" M. Gouli asked.

"I told her."

"Where is she?" Albert called, louder, pounding his brother's shoulder.

"Why didn't you bring her?" Micq shouted, striking Nestor's other shoulder.

"There were too many of us," Nestor said.

"What did you do with the money?" M. Gouli said, and he pushed Nestor in the chest. Nestor reeled backward.

"What did you do?" Micq roared, hitting him again. Micq had a very loud voice when he shouted. Nestor fell against a tree and the three of them began to thump him with their fists, Albert bleating over and over, "Where is she?" Nestor fell down, covering his head, and Blackbird and M. Roche ran down the café steps together and across the *place*.

"Eh, enough," M. Roche said.

"Stop that," Blackbird said, and they hauled the angry assailants away from Nestor, who was curled up on the ground like a baby.

"It's a disgrace," M. Roche said. "Think of your parents."

"She wouldn't come," Albert cried.

"You'd better go home. All of you," M. Roche said. He pointed his finger at M. Gouli, who turned away, then turned back.

"The money, Nestor. We will have to talk about that. About many things, in fact." He lurched toward his white motorbike, straddled it, tried to start it, thought better of it, got off, and wheeled it across the *place* and around the corner.

"I'll take them home," Blackbird said to M. Roche, indicating the others with a motion of his head.

"To the crossroads. That would be a good thing."

"I'd better take them all the way. They're not in any state for parading."

"Come," M. Roche said, and herded Micq and the two others to the back of Blackbird's truck, into which they climbed meekly and collapsed.

"It's what the sign says on the truck," Blackbird said, as he got into the cab. "Wine transport." He said goodbye to M. Roche and they shook their heads and he drove out of the square, hearing the quarreling, grumbling, complaining voices rise and fall behind him. He drove to Nard and waited while the three of them eased themselves to the ground, and he went on as the quarreling boiled up again at the brothers' gate. At the crossroads he turned right and started back across the upland through the long shadows of the late-summer evening, dark bars lying on the gold of the dry grass and on the gray walls bathed in bronze and rust before sunset. He felt the lightness of the empty truck with a mixture of relief and sadness, something that he had known many times without heeding it, when he had finished a day of delivering wine. The road wound over the rolling country, passing walls and rocks and oak woods. He was heading south and west, and the hilltops as he approached them had lost their color. The first lights came on in some of the farms. The evening turned cool. Indeed, he said to himself, he could feel the autumn.

It was late twilight, almost dark all at once, as he drove into Renat. He could hear the roar of the fête loudspeakers before he came to the first houses along the road, and then he could see the bloom of bright light over the trees of the square, like the light over a night game in a stadium. As he got nearer to the square he could hear nothing but the fête. The road and the side streets were blocked. Two gendarmes were directing traffic in a detour to avoid the square, and Blackbird went where they pointed and found another gendarme pointing, and ended up in a back square that was being used as a parking lot. He was directed to an empty parking space, and decided to stop, after all, and walk around the fête.

The air was chill, and the familiar streets seemed like an alien place, jammed with cars and people and a steady rush of noise. In the main square they were wasting no time. All the booths were open, the barkers were shouting, the rifles were popping at the gallery, the crash of bottles breaking—a new thing that had come in with nonreturnable bottles—rose in waves, squeals and shrieks rang from the Dodgem cars and the Ferris wheel. Some of the acts had been going around the fêtes for years. "Zelda," the plump woman in a black bikini who sat on the ground in a cage with a large snake said to be a python, which she watched so closely that nobody ever saw her face. And her colleague "Oona," who did the same thing in a cage with vampire bats—except that someone from the colonies had told Blackbird that they were really fruit bats. "Atlas," the strong man, who could pick up one end of a car by a cable he held in his mouth. "Observe the strength of his neck and jaw," the barker shouted. There was the wooden silo into which a ring of spectators, warned constantly over the loudspeakers of the mortal danger of their position, peered while a motorcyclist down inside drove around and around on the wall, horizontal to the ground. And a pavilion where four massive men in tights challenged any four men in the audience to last one round wrestling with them. The crowd there was rapt and excited.

Just beyond that pavilion was a plywood structure striped like a tent, with a long porch in front on which four women in bathing suits and high heels stood looking bored and cold, while a fifth, older, stout, wrapped in a gabardine, bawled into a microphone, her syllables throttled by a heavy cold.

"These ravishig baidends," she roared, "these four exquisite dabsels! Who is bad edough to take his choice? This blod berbaid, this gorgeous brudette, this delicious fiery redhead"—the red wig was missing, and the third young woman glowered at the crowd from under close-cropped dark hair—"this raved-haired sultry charber! Choose, gentlbed! Choose!" "Any brave bad in the audiess" was to buy his ticket and retire with the woman of his choice, and if he could last four minutes with her without her undressing him completely he would receive his money back and a doll with the color of hair that he had chosen. One by one the nervous challengers climbed the steps, were cheered, posed as boastfully as they could, and disappeared into one of the curtained doorways, and one by one the women emerged a few minutes later waving a pair of underpants, which they flung to the cheering crowd, and the men slid out looking sheepish, to more applause than they wanted.

"*Te*, Blackbird." It was Berliot, the mason, and his helper André, two of Blackbird's friends from the soccer café in Renat. They tried to exchange news but the noise was overpowering and they could not hear each other. One made a gesture of having a drink but Blackbird shook his head. They stood watching the performance. When they had been shown four pairs of underpants André called Blackbird's and Berliot's attention to the fact that he was making sure of his own undergarments, and then pointed to his chest and to the "gorgeous brudette," to let them know that he was going up.

"I want to see how it's done," he shouted into Blackbird's ear, and they watched him go the same way as the others, and creep out in his turn, rumpled and barely dressed, as his underwear sailed over the heads of the spectators, who drew aside to let it fall. Berliot edged away to rejoin André, and Blackbird waved good night to him and moved off through the crowd. It was already, he thought, long past his dinnertime, and he considered staying to eat in Renat, but decided to drive home and eat when he got there. The thought of the late kitchen after the evening meal was finished in the hotel, everything put away, the high ceiling echoing, beckoned to him like his childhood as he pushed through the mass of people he did not know. How could there be so many strangers in a place he had known all his life?

Farther along the square the road that ran through it fanned out to the main intersection, and there the gendarmes had cleared a long stretch of the thoroughfare, not to allow traffic to pass but to prepare for one of the principal events of the evening. A drum was rolling like thunder on the amplifiers. Toward one end of the open area a wooden incline had been set up, rising a few feet off the ground like a ramp for loading barrels onto a truck.

"Ladies and gentlemen," a woman's voice cut through the roll of the drums like a buzz saw, and she announced another motorcycle act in defiance of death. Once again it would be "Bobo" the motorcyclist, whom they had been watching inside the silo on the Rampart of Death. This time they would watch him in a different act. "Do I have five brave young volunteers, five daring lads, five sporting types, ready for anything?" She coaxed until five shambling adolescents had been pushed or had peeled themselves out of the crowd. They were standing a few feet away from her but she continued to roar through the microphone and the loudspeakers.

"Now, my bold fellows—are you feeling brave? There's a tough one—" She pinched the biceps of the smallest one, a skinny, short boy with a fixed grin, obviously terrified. "Well, then, one by one, say your prayers first, if you want to—you can kneel right down here. And then you are to—lie down, there. Facing upward to heaven." She pointed to the road at the upper end of the ramp, and she took them one by one by the elbow and pushed them to their places.

"Who's first?" she asked, and seized the dullest-looking. "Right there, sir," she said, and he stretched out obediently on the road.

"And the next brave boy," she said, and seized another and pointed him to his place. She saved the little one for last.

"You're the toughest, so you get the most dangerous position. The end," she said. "There, sir. I admire you. I am glad I am not in your place. And now. The Flying Fool! Bobo will come up the road there on his motorcycle and go up the ramp and fly over these five young men, whose lives will depend on lying absolutely still."

The little one, number five, sat up and pretended to be about to dash for the safety of the crowd, but she roared at him, "My brave young man, are you going to turn coward before all your friends?" He stood up, grinning, and bowed to all the spectators, then lay down again, crossing his hands on his breast as though he were in his coffin.

"Are you ready?" she bellowed. "Ladies and gentlemen, the Flying Fool!" A trumpet rang out and the drumroll became deafening. Only those closest to the road could hear the passing motorcyclist, as Bobo, in an aviator's helmet and goggles, with long silk streamers whipping behind him, raced up the road on his big motorbike, and up the ramp, and through the air over the five recumbent bodies. There was a moment of silence and then a riffle of applause.

"Superb! Bravo!" she shouted into the loudspeaker. "None of them was even touched." The young men started to get up and be on their way. "Don't move, sirs," she said. "We have just begun. I want three more daredevils. Three more fearless young lads, three more sports." It took longer this time to wheedle them out of the crowd but she succeeded finally in shaming three more youths to step out, and then to lie down, clowning desperately, beside the first five. Once again she worked up her announcement of Bobo's imminent appearance and his death-defying intent, and the drum rolled and the trumpet sounded and he flashed up the road and the ramp and out over the eight bodies. The rear wheel came down only a couple of feet from the eighth, and the crowd's interest was obviously increasing.

"Ladies and gentlemen," she repeated. "He has cleared eight. Now we shall see how brave you all are. Can you bear to watch? I want two more dauntless volunteers. Two more brave men. Two more sports." And she got them at last and Bobo flew over the ten of them, coming down with his tail pipe a foot or so beyond the last one.

The drum did not stop rolling now. She sighed audibly. "What a relief," she said. "And now. One more. One more—" and on she went. Bobo cleared eleven. And after an interminable amount of wheedling and shaming and suspense, twelve. Then she started to elicit the thirteenth. "Unlucky thirteen," she said. "The bravest of them all."

Blackbird had completely forgotten himself, standing watching, and he laughed. He wondered what it would be like to walk out there and lie down and be number thirteen as the motorbike flashed up the ramp. People would recognize him as he walked out, they would wave to him, try to dissuade him, cheer him. Blackbird. The last. For an instant the urge to walk out there seized him like a spasm. Then he turned away, back toward the car.

"M. Blackbird!" a voice said from behind him as he reached the confectioner's store on the corner and was thinking of going in and getting something for Françoise. He looked around and saw Popeye, with Josette on his arm. They had just come out of the confectioner's shop and passed him.

"Good evening," he said, turning to shake hands but not stopping.

"I've been meaning to come up and see you," Popeye said. It was true, Blackbird noticed, what Françoise said of him. He did walk that way, and he did always seem to be on the point of suggesting some sneaking indecency. Blackbird went on past the shop without pausing.

"Ah," he said to Popeye, over his shoulder, and kept moving, though the crowd kept him from going very fast.

"I have been planning to become a customer of yours," Popeye said.

"Who knows?" Blackbird said. He realized that Josette, standing smiling behind Popeye, could not hear a word they were saying. She kept nodding, whatever was said.

"I have heard something amusing," Popeye said.

Blackbird waved as though he were leaving, but the crowd was too dense. A trio of fat people, one of them an old woman, blocked his way.

"I did not know that you and your priest were such good friends," Popeye said. Blackbird looked at him hard.

"Neighbors," Blackbird said.

"The old pigeon tower, by moonlight," Popeye said, with a smile.

"What about it?"

"Baylo." The smile stayed there.

Blackbird knew at once part of what Popeye meant. Baylo was a local figure of a certain age, generally considered to be at least half mad, who lived by himself in a collapsing vineyard cabin on a hill south of Aylac, appeared never to wash or to change his clothes, and eked out a living gathering dandelions in January, St. George mushrooms in March, wild strawberries in May, boletus in the autumn, and squabs from unguarded dovecotes all year round. He must have been hiding near the tower on the night when Blackbird showed it to the priest.

"What about him?" Blackbird said.

"We've spoken."

"Thirteen!" he heard the woman roar from the square behind him.

"Is that so?" Blackbird said.

The fat people moved out of the way and Blackbird smiled back at Popeye and waved good night. As he walked to the truck he was puzzled by the exchange. Then he began to smile again, at the thought that Popeye clearly imagined that the nocturnal visits to the spring were still a secret. He found pleasure once again in the image of the ducks turning into the priest and the priest's mother and himself. Blackbird, waddling and lurching down the road to the gate and over the wall and along the tangled path to the spring, in full daylight. He was already in the truck and driving too fast when the recollection of Popeye's smile with its sidelong innuendo returned to him, and this time he was taken by surprise by what Popeye evidently had been suggesting about Blackbird's friendship with the priest. His eyes opened wide, staring at the curves in the road, and then he shook his head, laughing under his breath, and returned to imagining what it would have been like to bow his way through the crowd in the square, at the fête, and to walk over to the ramp, waving, and lie down, face upward, to listen for the approaching motorcycle. You probably could not even hear it coming with the sound of the drum and the crowd.

He was tired and hungry and cold when he got back to the hotel and put the truck in the barn, and more than ever he felt that it was already autumn. Françoise and Gérard were still up in the kitchen, and he was glad to see them there.

"You're late," Françoise said. "Did you stop for dinner?"

"There's a fête at Renat," Blackbird said. "You can hardly get through. I saw Berliot."

"I don't like it when you're that late," Françoise said. "The way you drive."

"I take care of myself." It was an exchange that they repeated regularly.

"Mme. Guiselin died this afternoon."

"Who?" Blackbird said blankly, trying to remember who Mme. Guiselin had been. Françoise was setting a place for him at the table.

"The priest's mother," she said.

It was true, he said to himself. He had known the priest's name and he had forgotten it. He must have known it. Of course he must have known it. Everybody must have known it.

"He sent the widow Gaire around to tell us," Françoise said, "to be sure we knew."

He and Françoise and Gérard went over to the presbytery the next morning, dressed as though they were going to church, and walked in at the front door, propped open with a stone, to the main room, which clearly had not been used for years. It was empty except for a bin under one high window, a stack of wooden boxes in a corner, and a bench along the wall with a vase of dahlias on it. The marks of a broom in the deep dust on the floor. They were led into an adjoining bedroom to see Mme. Guiselin laid out in bed under a white sheet and bedspread, with a white napkin over her hair. Vases of flowers stood on the few pieces of furniture and Françoise added another vase of dahlias, which the widow Gaire arranged beyond the bed.

Mme. Guiselin's face looked like that of a drowned gray kitten, and her hands with the rosary twined around them appeared to have grown that way, like roots. The priest was sitting in a chair against the wall at the foot of the bed with his prayer book open on his lap, and a group of the neighbors filled the rest of the room, standing saying nothing, one of the women moving her lips and her rosary. Blackbird nudged Françoise and Gérard ahead of him into the faintly sweet stale smell, and one by one they filed up to the side of the bed, looked down at what remained of Mme. Guiselin, and after what seemed the proper interval turned to the small peeling bedside cupboard with its crocheted covering, its porcelain statue of the Virgin, and its glass of water with the sprig of box in it. They took the sprig from the glass and shook a few drops of the holy water over the body so that the drops fell to the points of the cross, and then they turned away and walked to the foot of the bed to bow their heads to the priest and mumble something. When it was Blackbird's turn he said distinctly, "I regret—" The priest looked up at him for a moment, nodded, and Blackbird turned away.

He went to the funeral of course, and sat with Gérard and Pierre while Françoise and Martine sat together across the aisle. As usual, he stood up and knelt and bowed his head when everyone else did, but did not join in the liturgy or the genuflections. His friend the priest was there in the chancel and said some of the prayers, but the service was conducted by two other priests who had come to assist him. One of them was from the nearby village with the "nightingales" school, and was referred to in Aylac as "the nightingale priest." The other was from the northern edge of the upland, the priest who was known to Blackbird for his love of soccer and old frescoes. He was a short, rapid, energetic man who conducted the ritual with vigor and precision. Blackbird studied his movements in the ceremony as he would have observed a soccer player, and concluded that the man was in good shape, none the worse for the years since the one time Blackbird had met him, at a soccer match between two local teams. He had noticed the priest several times since then, when he was in the priest's village and caught sight of him playing soccer with the village boys, once in his soutane.

The coffin was loaded into the baker's corrugated gray van, and Blackbird and his family followed it to the cemetery. As Blackbird walked he kept seeing the image of the ducks turning into the priest, the priest's mother, and himself, all of them climbing like ducks over the dilapidated wall. He found himself smiling, and he noticed that each time the sight of the three of them returned to him the priest's mother seemed steadier on her feet, more practiced at the wall. She was becoming positively nimble, and occasionally the priest walked on ahead and Blackbird remained behind making conversation with the old woman, whom he found interesting, rather elegant and flirtatious, on her way to her bath.

He was recalled to the funeral as the van stopped at the iron gate of the cemetery and the coffin was carried out, raised to the shoulders of the bearers, and borne through the lines of headstones to the open grave. As he followed, Blackbird wondered whether there were not many others present who had known her no better than he had. Mme. Guiselin, he said to himself, repeating her name as though he feared he might forget it and recall nothing about her at all except the glimpse of her huddled like a black pile of clothes on the bench in the fireplace, that face like a drowned gray kitten's between the napkin and the sheet, and her hands when they had finished with everything. He listened for the priests at the grave to say her name, her Christian name, because he was sure that he had never known that. He paid attention to the prayers as he had not done since his wife's funeral inside those same walls. There: Marie-Claude Estelle Guiselin. That had been her name all her life, which was over. He could not see her as Marie-Claude. A Marie-Claude had plump pink cheeks and so on. Estelle was in another room, not visible, a cobweb among cobwebs. The names were nothing. He filed past with the people he had known for his whole life, or for the whole of theirs, and tossed a lump of dry yellow limestone clay onto the boards at the bottom of the grave, and then turned as the others turned to stand by the graves of their own families. He walked with Françoise and Gérard, Pierre and Martine, to the graves of his parents, his grandparents, his wife, who had been buried there at the end of winter as the plum blossoms were beginning to open, in the rain. In the church he had wanted to speak to the visiting priest, the soccer player, but he had forgotten about that, and when he looked up from his wife's grave the priests had left and he was surprised to see that the light was bright and burnished and that it was still summer.

• • •

He kept thinking of the priest alone in the house, and a few days after the funeral he went over to see him, the back way. As he came in the gate he saw Mme. Gaire come out the back door to take the bedclothes off the terrace railing, and he turned and went back through the lane, deciding to leave it till later.

Françoise insisted that she was getting back to normal, but it seemed to Blackbird that there was something that was not recovering. It was not just the lack of energy and stamina, the way she faded out and had to go and lie down. That was to be expected. She was quieter. More muted, he said to himself. Some sharpness of hers that had not yet come back. Gérard said that the region of the operation was still giving her pain, and Blackbird went with Gérard to take her to Mujeac for the regular examinations, one of them a few days after the funeral. The doctor would say nothing positive. He said he saw no cause for alarm. It had been a complicated operation and it was not abnormal to recover slowly. He reeled off some averages, some figures which seemed, Blackbird thought, to have something to do with the horizon. They would have to wait and see, he kept telling himself.

He watched the way Gérard took care of Sylvie, the way he worked in the garden. He even went out into the garden to walk along the rows and praise the fattening leeks and the tomato vines sagging with ripening fruit. He went over again to see the priest and nobody answered the door. Wrong time, he said to himself, but felt that something had been accomplished just by making the visit, openly, as it occurred to him, even though no one had seen him. He thought of Popeye at the fête in Renat and he shrugged as he went out the gate.

Those run-down days at the end of summer he went most afternoons, after a nap in his bachelor quarters, to the café at the far end of the village behind the church, where his red-faced soccer friends from the neighborhood would heave through the doorway at unpredictable times and wheeze out bits of local news, and they would stare at the snowy television, barely audible, up in the corner, and perhaps play a game or two at the soccer table, or sit and talk about the prospects for the walnuts, the wool, and when the wine harvest was likely to begin, and of the opening of school and of the hunting season. Pierre also sometimes dropped by at the end of the afternoon, and he did so more often after Blackbird took to going there regularly.

The sun came through the frosted-glass windows and congealed on the surfaces of the modernized room, the Formica tables with chromium legs, the pale yellow textured walls with gray trim tacked around the windows, the green plastic door curtain pulled back and tied, the children's plastic fire engines and bulldozers, and the calendars on the wall with pictures of women in evening dress, gladioli, a running soccer player, a harbor full of motorboats. Besides the muffled voice of the television the radio was turned up when there was news or a sporting event. The noise seemed to Blackbird like being in town, where he was glad not to be, but when he looked out the door he saw the late-afternoon light on the unfenced common behind the church, an area bigger than the village itself, a place that had never been plowed and was full of stone outcroppings and clumps of brambles and sloes, the ruins of a round building that was said to have been a hut of the Gauls. The land sloped away to the line of oak woods down near the stream where the railroad ran between the rock walls of an artificial canyon, out of sight. At that time of year the pasture was the color of an old yellow dog losing his hair. A few sheep wandered among the sloe bushes, hens appeared and disappeared, the shadows reached farther each time he looked.

He was sitting there one afternoon with Pierre and several of his friends, while the children shrieked outside on the road, when the priest knocked and stepped through the door.

"*Te*," Blackbird said, and stood up to shake his hand.

"Your son-in-law said I might find you here," the priest said. "I have a friend who wants to meet you."

The priest turned back in the doorway and motioned to someone behind him, and the soccer-playing priest followed him into the café. Blackbird shook his hand.

"We've already met," he said, and reminded the visiting priest of the occasion.

"But I did not realize then who you were," the visitor said. "The author of 'Talking Foot.' I've been reading you since I was that high," and he put his hand down beside the table.

"Will you sit down?" Blackbird asked. "Will you have something?"

"I don't drink," the visitor said.

"Of course." Blackbird laughed. "An athlete." The priest smiled.

"Come back to the hotel," Blackbird said. "Stay to dinner. Both of you."

"That's all right, that's all right, thank you," the visitor said, in his energetic, hurried fashion. "I have to get home. But I appreciate your asking. I just wanted to get to meet you."

"You'll come by again soon and have dinner, I hope," Blackbird said, "with our friend here."

"I will."

"This is the priest from Dorgeac who plays soccer," Blackbird said, introducing the visitor to his friends in the café, who stepped up one by one and shook his hand and asked him questions about his playing and his parishes and his life. Blackbird's friend, the curate of Aylac, beamed, his long, gaunt, gray features looking more ungainly than ever in the harsh light. The woman who ran the café came out and Blackbird introduced her to the visitor and she insisted on bringing them two lemonades, assuring them that there was nothing wrong with the lemonade, it was what she made for the children. And Blackbird left with the priests and walked with them to the visitor's 2CV, parked outside the presbytery.

"Come back," Blackbird said. "My friend here needs someone to teach him to play soccer."

"It's true," the priest from Aylac said.

"It's possible," the priest from Dorgeac said. "And I would like a chance to hear some more of the author of 'Talking Foot,' " he said.

They watched him drive off.

"I came around to see you," Blackbird said, "but at the wrong times."

"I have been out," the priest said, "it's true. It makes a change, after all, to one's life. I have altered my hours of doing one thing and another, now that there is no one else in the house. I have even been down to the spring by myself."

He waited for Blackbird's surprised look.

"I thought, 'I know the way now,' and I went in the middle of the afternoon. I seem to have recovered, by the way, from my trouble. It may return, of course, but for the time being it seems to have released me. I went because I thought it was a good thing to do again, before the summer was over. A good thing to do, what can I say? Look," he said, and pulled up the sleeve of the raveled soutane to show Blackbird his bony white arm, and then lifted the hem of the skirt to show Blackbird, one after the other, his ivory shins above his high-buttoned shoes. He appeared to be demonstrating a peculiar dance step.

"Admirable," Blackbird said, quite aware that they were standing in the main square, across from the church.

"No one can say it was faith alone," the priest said, "as some say about other springs, you know. The book goes into that. But I had

no particular faith in the spring when I went. I simply thought I would
try it. So it has to be something in the spring."

"I'm not surprised at the result," Blackbird said. "It's well known,
that place. And now that we are face to face, perhaps you would like
to join me at the hotel for dinner."

The priest declined, saying that he had the evening service to prepare, and though Blackbird suggested dinner later in the evening the
priest said he thought he had better get home. Blackbird could see
that he was doubtful about the very idea of dining out.

"But I would like to learn something about soccer," the priest said.

"You could drop by the café sometimes in the afternoons. All the
soccer devotees turn up there."

"It's hardly appropriate for a priest, after all."

"It would be all right," Blackbird said. "Everyone knows you and
they could be informed that it was for your instruction, so that you
could make up a parish team for the good of the vicinity. We will all
swear that you are drinking nothing but lemonade."

They shook hands at the back gate of the presbytery.

The evenings were turning cool. It was too late in the season now,
Blackbird thought, to embark on anything like the alterations to the
hotel entrance, and the knowledge was a relief, but he was glad the
subject had not come up again. Perhaps by spring Françoise would
have forgotten it. One evening when he was in the kitchen with her
and Gérard he asked her, "Have you ever been down to the spring
in the old park?"

"When I was little." He saw a slight smile, a smile at some secret,
run across her face, and wondered what it was about.

"Have you ever bathed there?"

"Is it true," she asked, "that you showed Monsieur the priest the
pigeon tower down there one night?"

"We were conducting an investigation," Blackbird said, "for his
mother. To see whether the spring would do her any good."

"So you went down at night."

"We didn't want to make a public announcement."

"You make me laugh," she said.

"The waters are very efficacious," Blackbird said. "You would come
to no harm trying them yourself."

Françoise shook her head.

"Gérard could go with you."

"At night?"

"Why at night?"

"Not to make a public announcement."

"Don't wait too long," Blackbird said. "It will be too cold soon."
She smiled at him.

The priest visited the café a few days later and Blackbird introduced
him to several more of his friends from nearby villages who had been
over behind Aylac cutting firewood. Blackbird explained that the priest
was eager to learn about soccer, and the regulars set about teaching
him as though they were force-feeding a goose. It was not long before
the priest was practicing with the handles at the soccer table and had
graduated to crème de menthe.

One afternoon as Blackbird sat there he discovered that he had
decided to leave the wine business to Pierre, and when Pierre came
in he told him about it. The place was noisy enough so that they could
talk privately. Pierre nodded gravely at the news and shook Blackbird's
hand with evident emotion.

"Of course I will have to break you in," Blackbird said. "You have
a great deal to learn."

"I do," Pierre said.

"You will have to come with me to the wine harvest," Blackbird
said, "and meet my suppliers, the ones you don't already know."

"I will be happy to do that," Pierre said.

"It will stay in the family, that way," Blackbird said, "even though
your name is not Blackbird. And I think you will come to appreciate
the fine points in due course."

"I hope so," Pierre said. He was like a hat sitting square on a head,
Blackbird thought. But he was steady and responsible. They left the
café together and Blackbird said good evening to him at the corner
of the church.

The hotel would go to Françoise, of course, and Gérard and Sylvie.
The light before sunset glowed in the upper branches of the lime
trees in front of the hotel. This is the year, Blackbird thought, when
I decided on a successor for the wine business. It will never be written
on the labels of the bottles.

He found that he was looking forward once again to the grape
harvest and the rumors about what the new wine would be like. For
some years he had not bothered to go to the vineyards at the time of
the harvest. He had done it again the year the Belgian tried to buy
up a whole vineyard as soon as it was harvested. And this year, if the

grapes survived without hail, he would make the rounds again and the thought gave him pleasure. He would take Pierre with him on those mornings, as he had done once or twice before. Pierre was all right, after all. He did not talk too much. He was sensible. He seemed to know what he was doing, by the time he did it.

And then there would be the autumn, the foggy mornings with no breakfast, setting out in the cold to compare the new wines. It had always seemed to him one of the crowning moments of the year, he thought, as he turned in at the hotel entrance, under the iron trellis with its wisteria vine. Pierre would be with him this year, and Pierre would learn all right. Pierre kept his head. He would continue the business in a perfectly reasonable way. Blackbird resolved to teach him everything that could be taught, and he was sure that Pierre would learn everything that could be learned. There was just something, Blackbird thought, that did not seem to be there. A twist, an oddity, something out of the ordinary. He had never seen it in Pierre. Something, Blackbird said to himself, that would allow him to believe, when they went out on those cold autumn mornings to sample the summer's wine, that Pierre really knew what he was tasting.

A Note About the Author

W. S. Merwin was born in New York City in 1927 and grew up in Union City, New Jersey, and in Scranton, Pennsylvania. From 1949 to 1951 he worked as a tutor in France, Portugal, and Majorca. After that, for several years he made the greater part of his living by translating from French, Spanish, Latin, and Portuguese. In addition to poetry, he has written articles, chiefly for *The Nation*, and radio scripts for the BBC. He has lived in Spain, England, France, Mexico, and Hawaii, as well as New York City. His books of poetry are *A Mask for Janus* (1952), *The Dancing Bears* (1954), *Green with Beasts* (1956), *The Drunk in the Furnace* (1960), *The Moving Target* (1963), *The Lice* (1967), *The Carrier of Ladders* (1970), for which he was awarded the Pulitzer Prize, *Writings to an Unfinished Accompaniment* (1973), *The Compass Flower* (1977), *Opening the Hand* (1983), and *The Rain in the Trees* (1988). His translations include *The Poem of the Cid* (1959), *Spanish Ballads* (1961), *The Satires of Persius* (1960), *Lazarillo de Tormes* (1962), *The Song of Roland* (1963), *Selected Translations 1948–1968* (1968), for which he won the PEN Translation Prize for 1968, *Transparence of the World* (1969), a translation of his selection of poems by Jean Follain (1969), *Osip Mandelstam, Selected Poems* (with Clarence Brown) (1974), *Selected Translations 1968–1978*, *Iphigenia at Aulis* of Euripides, with George Dimock, Jr. (1978), *Vertical Poetry*, a selection of poems by Roberto Juarroz (1988), and *Sun at Midnight*, a selection of poems by Musō Soseki, translated with Sōiku Shigematsu (1989). He has also published three books of prose in addition to the present volume, *The Miner's Pale Children* (1970), *Houses and Travellers* (1977), and *Unframed Originals* (1982). He has been a recipient of several fellowships, including Rockefeller, Guggenheim, Rabinowitz, NEA, Chapelbrook grants, and awards including the Bollingen, the Harriet Monroe, Shelley, Maurice English, Oscar Williams and Gene Derwood, and Aiken-Taylor prizes for poetry. In 1974 he was awarded the Fellowship of the Academy of American Poets. In 1987 he received the Governor's Award for Literature of the state of Hawaii.

A Note on the Type

The text and display of this book were set in a typeface called Ehrhardt, named for Wolfgang Dietrich Ehrhardt. The original types on which this version is based were in the Ehrhardt type foundry in Leipzig in the early eighteenth century, but were cut in the second half of the seventeenth century, probably by Nicholas Kis, a Hungarian who soon returned to his native country to set up as typefounder and printer. This revival of the face was first issued by the Monotype Corporation in 1938.

Composed by Crane Typesetting Service, Inc.,
West Barnstable, Massachusetts

Printed and bound by Fairfield Graphics,
Fairfield, Pennsylvania

Designed by Harry Ford